A BIBLIOGRAPHY OF YEATS CRITICISM
1887–1965

A BIBLIOGRAPHY OF YEATS CRITICISM 1887–1965

by

K. G. W. CROSS and R. T. DUNLOP

With a foreword by
A. NORMAN JEFFARES

The Macmillan Company, New York, New York

THE MACMILLAN COMPANY
866 Third Avenue, New York, N.Y. 10022

Library of Congress Catalog Card Number: 75-179961

First American Edition

Printed in Great Britain

Contents

Foreword

This most useful account of the vast amount of writing on W. B. Yeats has been compiled over many years by the late Professor K. G. W. Cross of the University of Newcastle, New South Wales, and by his friend and sometime colleague at the University of Sydney, Mr R. T. Dunlop. In writing this foreword to introduce their work it seemed to me that I should say something of Professor Cross, whose early death cut short a most promising academic career and deprived his many friends of the friendship of an unusually lively and gifted man.

Kenneth Gustav Walter Cross grew up in Norfolk, and was educated at Diss Grammar School. After three years in the Royal Army Educational Corps he read English and French at Trinity College, Dublin. This was at a period when the English School was run by Professor H. O. White, benign and only apparently absent-minded; his colleagues were Dr Fitzroy Pyle and Mr R. B. D. French. All three blended – as did Dr Sheehy Skeffington of the School of French – the imparting of knowledge with a sociable informality. It was a civilised atmosphere to which Gus Cross responded with delight. After winning his First Class Moderatorship he became Lefroy Stein Research Fellow in Trinity College and began work on John Marston under Fitzroy Pyle's supervision. This resulted in a thesis crammed with exhaustive work: indeed it could have been sent to the printer on its completion. But this was one of the many things Gus Cross might have done one day – he was fastidious in assessing his own work, and so we can read only a dozen articles (and two dozen notes on Marston's vocabulary) on such diverse matters as dating the plays and a general assessment of Marston.

Out of his deep interest in sixteenth- and seventeenth-century drama came Cross's knowledge of bibliography and the minutiae of scholarship. He thought the state of most of the texts of seventeenth-century drama left much to be desired. One of the last evenings I spent with him, in Leeds in 1963, was devoted to drawing up a scheme for old spelling texts. This resulted in the Fountainwell Drama Texts, a series which Robin Lorimer the publisher and I had had in mind for some years, to the planning of which Cross brought his own special brand of missionary zeal. Cross himself was engaged in editing two Shakespeare texts for this series in his last two years – the standard of his editorial work can be seen in his edition of *Titus Andronicus* (a Pelican Shakespeare, 1965). He had much imagination in suggesting texts and editors for them, and, as befitted an honorary Dubliner, his conversational comments were flippant, witty and gay, a foil to the common sense of his serious arguments.

Cross, however, was a man of inclusive tastes in his scholarship. His education at Trinity had encouraged this, and he had a passionate interest in the Anglo-Irish literary revival – in Synge and Yeats especially – while he could recite long passages from all of Joyce's writings with gusto and delight. His reading in French literature ran far beyond anything expected of a first-class graduate and his collection of French books was large. But his whole appetite for literature was enormous. Twentieth-century American literature he knew very well indeed, and his 'Writers and Critics' study of F. Scott Fitzgerald reveals his appreciative attitude to writers whose work he admired. When he left Dublin he taught for a time at Rhodes University, Grahamstown, where he disliked the current attitudes to black Africans. Once he moved to Australia (he held university posts, first in Adelaide, then in Sydney and finally in Newcastle) he indulged his hydropic thirst for knowledge by plunging into the reading of Australian literature. To this he brought a critical view particularly sympathetic: used to making comparisons, he believed in the importance – and the immediacy – of writing in rapidly developing countries. He came to Leeds to teach Australian Literature as our Visiting Fellow in Commonwealth Literature in 1963, and during his time in Yorkshire we began to edit a volume of essays to commemorate the centenary of Yeats's birth, *In Excited Reverie*. As he toured the United States in the autumn of 1963 Gus hurled letter after letter at me, filled with pleasure and excitement as the book took shape and as he met many of the scholars whose work he admired. Although by now he knew his days were numbered, his temperament did not allow him any self-commiseration or any world-weary air. In the Jacobeans and perhaps in Joyce he found pessimism enough to satisfy him; but he weighed up his own life in such a way that delight overcame despair. This balancing often led him to an endearing self-mockery – he had acquired in Dublin an Irish capacity to tell a story against himself. Yet he was drawn to the positive and the creative: in American, in Australian, and especially in Anglo-Irish writers. His interest in Yeats was deep, and in his 1963 visit to Europe and America he added new items to his already profound knowledge of what had been written on Yeats, and indeed on the work of his critics.

This amalgam of scholar in seventeenth-century drama and savant in modern writing and criticism was a man whose eyes could dance with excited enthusiasm or amusement: his laugh was bound to emerge at some stage in any conversation. He was indeed an excellent conversationalist with a sense of dramatic intensity as well as a relish for the absurd. He was kind, generous – even careless – with his money when he had any, and he never had, nor ever would have had enough, because he used it fully as a means to other ends: hospitality mainly, the buying of books incessantly. All his life was lived as though in some subconscious extra awareness of its brevity. And so he crammed it full with work and enjoyment. Yet, paradoxically, he seemed to be born unlucky. Things happened to him in an endless succession of misfortunes, small and large. He always shook these troubles off, after brief moments of intense private melancholia and perhaps after a quick worried harangue of one of his many friends, something bound to end in his firm changing of the subject with an invitation to a drink, a meal, or the contemplation of some ironic absurdity of life or literature or both.

Always he was a kind and lovable person, for he had an instinctive friendliness and was baffled by the malice or mischief-making propensities of others, even at times by their dullness. His sense of pleasure in varied experience was conveyed to others with gay generosity, an unselfconscious disregard for the conventions, and an enthusiasm which overflowed into so many different directions: he liked art, and so he painted well; he liked speed and so he drove cars, both large and small, with dash and a certain amount of abandon; he liked parties and talk and so he liked people; and this is the quality which gave his Renaissance-like multiplicity of character its integrity of purpose. He was in the right place as a professor: he was a scholar rather than an administrator; he conveyed encouragement as well as giving help to others; and he was a teacher, not an indoctrinator. This is perhaps why he sought to provide – as in this bibliography – the materials upon which others would form their own opinions and judgements. His ambition from his undergraduate days had been to be a professor whose work would be known and lasting. He worked extremely hard. Yet there was not time enough, not nearly enough, in his thirty-nine years to match his intellectual appetency and the scholarly achievement he desired. It will be some small solace to his friends and family that Mr Dunlop has completed the work on this bibliography which in its account of Yeatsian scholarship and criticism should prove an invaluable work of reference.

Lédenon, France, 1970   A. NORMAN JEFFARES

Introduction

Katharine Tynan published her review of *Mosada* in 1887, taking up publicly and with relish the task that Gerard Manley Hopkins evaded privately when John Butler Yeats showed him his son's poems. Between Miss Tynan's approving observations and the encouraging comments of critics like Fr Matthew Russell, editor of the *Irish Monthly*, on the one hand, and on the other the close of 1965, the year in which the centenary of Yeats's birth was celebrated 'from China to Peru' as a *Times Literary Supplement* reviewer put it in 1966, a daunting amount has been written about Yeats, visible measure of the growth of his reputation as a poet (laudatory to the extent that the occasional dissidence of F. Hugh O'Donnell, the *Daily Nation*, the *Catholic Bulletin*, or more recently of Yvor Winters is a refreshing reminder that disagreement about the greatness of even a great poet is still possible). Writings on Yeats now exceed those on any of his contemporaries writing in English or, one suspects, in any other language. Much of the material, however, especially that written before 1900, appeared in newspapers and journals that are now forgotten by most Yeats readers, and is preserved only in the files of the older libraries of the English-speaking world. If, to the geographical scatter of this material, is added the increasing frequency with which Yeats finds his way into books that one would not automatically take up in the search for information about him, then the point of George Brandon Saul's reference to the 'labyrinth' of Yeats criticism becomes very clear.

The need to record the steadily increasing flow of periodical literature in general was recognised before the end of the century, and Yeats studies have found their place in listings of it since his work first began to appear. Publications like *Poole's Index to Periodical Literature* and *The Nineteenth Century Reader's Guide to Periodical Literature* provided a valuable account of early criticism. The successors to these, together with the British Library Association's *Subject Index to Periodicals*, continued the service to scholars. *The Annual Bibliography of English Literature* and the annual bibliographical supplements in the *Publications of the Modern Language Association of America*, now the two most comprehensive listings of writings on literature in English, have greatly increased the available resources. *The Year's Work in English Studies* has regularly included Yeats criticism in its annual commentary, and one or two specialist journals now issue annual lists in which Yeats material may be found. In all, then, the various bibliographical collections have provided a generous coverage of the growing literature on Yeats. It may well be that the expansion of computer services to the field will write *finis* to the conventional check-list. However that may be, the accessibility of current criticism has increased enormously over the past twenty-five years, and there seems to be no reason why, whatever the means, it should not continue to do so.

Bibliographies devoted exclusively to Yeats are of two kinds: descriptive bibliographies of his own writings and bibliographies of writings about him and his work. Both began to make their appearances early in the present century. The late Allan Wade devoted a lifetime to the task of arranging and describing Yeats's published work (adding to it the equally exacting one of collecting the Yeats Letters). As early as 1908 he published his first *Bibliography*, reprinted as part of Vol. VIII of the *Collected Edition of the Works* in the same year. A. J. A. Symons issued his *Bibliography* in 1924; and in 1951 Wade's definitive *Bibliography of the Writings of W. B. Yeats* appeared. At the time of his death he was working on the second edition, which was completed by his publisher, Rupert Hart-Davis, and issued in 1958. Ten years later the third edition was published, revised and edited by Russell K. Alspach, who fully maintained the standard of scholarship set in the earlier editions, and who had already contributed his 'Additions to Allan Wade's *Bibliography of W. B. Yeats*' to the *Irish Book* in 1963. More, of course, remains to be done. John P. Frayne's edition of the *Uncollected Prose*, to be published by Macmillan & Co. Ltd (Vol. I has appeared already), will no doubt provide material for additions to the Wade *Bibliography*. But the foundations are secure.

Even before the descriptive bibliographies, lists of Yeats criticism began to appear. F. Sidgwick appended a short one to his study of Yeats in the *English Illustrated Magazine* in 1903. A carefully compiled reading list, prepared by Alice Thurston McGirr, was printed in the Boston *Bulletin of Bibliography* in 1913. Between such early lists and the 1940s, the task of recording Yeats material – primary and secondary – was shared by the Indexes and Bibliographies already referred to. After Yeats's death in 1939, writings about him began to increase rapidly, an increase heralded by the memorial volume, *Scattering Branches*, edited by Stephen Gwynn (1940) and Joseph M. Hone's biography, *W. B. Yeats 1865–1939* (1943). The number and quality of the reviews accorded to the second of these books was a pointer to the way in which the scholarly interest in Yeats was to develop. Also in 1940, *The Cambridge Bibliography* included a classified list of books and articles about Yeats, compiled by Seán O'Faoláin, supplemented in the fifth volume (1957) by T. R. Henn's revision of Peter Allt's 'William Butler Yeats'. Meanwhile, A. Norman Jeffares had published surveys of Yeats criticism in *Hermathena* (1948) and *Levende Talen* (1949). In 1950 there appeared a collection of critical essays of the sort that has had much currency in recent years, *The Permanence of Yeats: Selected Criticism*, edited by James Hall and Martin Steinmann. Still one of the most distinguished anthologies of its kind, it contains one of the fullest lists of books and articles compiled up to that time – almost fifty closely-printed pages in the original edition. All three editions of Wade's *Bibliography* included a select list of books about Yeats, the most comprehensive of them being in Russell K. Alspach's third edition which contains many of the important 1965 items together with a number of Japanese contributions. George Brandon Saul's select bibliographies, first printed in the *Bulletin of the New York Public Library*, appeared later in his *Stephens, Yeats, and Other Irish Concerns*. Two of his later books, *Prolegomena to the Study of Yeats's Poems* (1957) and *Prolegomena to the Study of Yeats's Plays* (1958), contain much material of general bibliographical interest. Of the bibliographies that appear from time to time in general studies of Yeats, one of the most helpful is that printed in *W. B. Yeats 1865–1965*, a collection of essays edited by D. E. S. Maxwell and S. B. Bushrui, which lists unpublished theses and a selection of works on Yeats in languages other than English. Finally, there are three specialised listings of considerable interest. *Poetry Explication*, by Joseph M. Kuntz (revised edition, 1962), includes a section on Yeats in which the locations of explications of individual poems are set out poem by poem. One of the most notable of the books to appear in 1965, Shotaro Oshima's *William Butler Yeats in Japan*, includes with much other valuable material two chapters that have special relevance here: 'Bibliography of Yeats in Japan' (a description of Japanese editions) and 'Books and Periodicals on Yeats in Japan' (a list of critical writings). Since Professor Oshima's book is available to scholars interested in this area of Yeats studies, we have not sought to reproduce his material, though a small number of Japanese items that we have found independently are included. The last of the three is K. P. S. Jochum's *W. B. Yeats's Plays: An Annotated Checklist of Criticism*, published in 1966, the first book given over exclusively to the systematic listing of Yeats criticism.

With so much done, the appearance of yet another list of books and articles about Yeats may seem unnecessary. But contemplating a quite different Yeats project in the early sixties, we soon realised that there was still no indexed account of Yeats criticism as a whole. We decided to provide ourselves with one, and this bibliography, with short-comings of which no one is more aware than its remaining compiler, is the result. In shaping it to our needs we were presumptuous enough to believe that they might be the needs of others.

Quite early, we realised that some of the most illuminating Yeats criticism was to be found in reviews of his own work and in those of books about him. *The Wanderings of Oisin*, for example, attracted the attention of Oscar Wilde, Katharine Tynan, Francis Thompson and W. E. Henley (William Morris was preoccupied with his other com-mitments); much of Edmund Wilson's writing on Yeats is to be found in his reviews for the *New Republic;* and George Orwell's observation on Yeats's fascist tendencies was made in one of his reviews of V. K. N. Menon's study of Yeats. On the other hand, most reviews call for no more than formal listing. From the outset, then, there seemed to be a need for some classification of our material, and as our work progressed the book began to settle into its sections more or less of its own accord. Despite the disparity of their length, each of them seemed to have its own identity, a special emphasis which we wished to preserve. One luxury, perhaps, was the separate section for special or commemora-tive issues of journals. But most of these have literary or historical significance that seemed to distinguish them from the pamphlets listed in Part III or the workaday journals in which the great body of periodical criticism is to be found. The Yeats issue of the *Southern Review*, for example, proved to be one of the most influential contri-butions to Yeats studies, as the extensive reprinting of many of its articles suggests; the special issue of the *Massachusetts Review* was first designed as a memorial to John F. Kennedy. And the section generally is rich evidence of the international standing that has been accorded to Yeats. While preserving the identity of the various sections, however, we tried by liberal cross-reference between sections and to Wade's *Bibliography* to draw attention to the wider implications of individ-ual entries and to give more unity to the book as a whole.

The division of the book into sections made some duplication inevitable. One of the main reasons for this is that many books have their origin in published articles, and the authors of such books find their way into two, even three, sections of the bibliography. We tried to reduce duplication of this sort by excluding from Part III general critical anthologies in which an article about Yeats, already published in a periodical, is collected with other material. Books of this sort (Morton Dauwen Zabel's *Literary Opinion in America*, for example) are fully described in the original article entry in Part V. On the other hand, some reviews are duplicated, appearing under the appropriate entries in Parts I, II, III or IV, and as articles in Part V. Only in this way could we ensure that reviews of the kind mentioned earlier were fully described. Also included in Part V are reviews taking in more than one book, which would otherwise appear only fragmentarily under the various book entries; in this way, some important items would have been lost.

In general, poems about Yeats have been omitted, though those appearing in special issues of journals have been noted in Part IV. The determining question here, arbitrarily resolved, was whether a poem constitutes a critical comment. Rightly or wrongly, we decided that it does not. On the other hand, we included the *Index to Pound's Cantos* by J. H. Edwards and W. W. Vasse on the grounds (perhaps sophistical) that it was a book about Pound in which attention was drawn to a Pound–Yeats link. We did not consider including T. S. Eliot's *Little Gidding*, but regretted that we were unable to see and list the letter in which Eliot acknowledges Yeats's presence in the poem.

As the material for the book accumulated, problems of consistency of presentation began to arise. In an attempt to resolve these, we adopted certain rules of procedure which are here set out formally to assist those using the bibliography:

1. Except in titles, the house style of Macmillan & Co. Ltd has been adopted.
2. Typographical errors in titles have not been reproduced.
3. The cataloguing procedures of the British Museum have been adopted for German and Scandinavian words with umlaut, namely:

   In German index words, *ä*, *ö* and *ü* are printed as *ae*, *oe* and *ue* and so indexed. In non-index words the umlaut is preserved.
   In all Scandinavian words the umlaut is preserved and the letters indexed as *a*, *o* or *u*.
4. References to Wade are to Allan Wade's *Bibliography of the Writings of W. B. Yeats*, third edition revised by Russell K. Alspach (London: Hart-Davis, 1968). Reference is to the item numbering or, where there is none, to the page.
5. Because the original edition of *The Permanence of Yeats*, ed. James Hall and Martin Steinmann, which is frequently cited, is not

readily available, page references to the paperback edition (Collier Books, 1960) are given in brackets.

6. The place of publication of journals is omitted from the text, but is given in the list of newspapers and periodicals, where the few abbreviations used are also shown.

7. Items not seen by Gustav Cross (as far as I can ascertain) or by myself are marked with a dagger (†).

The items referred to in (7) above call for brief comment. In the final revision of the manuscript, I have not been able to see every item listed. Many, of course, were collected by Gustav Cross (although we worked in close collaboration, we naturally made an initial division of labours). Information about others, however, has come from scholars aware of and sympathetic with what we were trying to do, from published bibliographical sources and from books about Yeats and his times. We managed to locate most references, but a few have remained elusive. Some (those written in Arabic, for example) have proved inaccessible to me even when they have been found. Four periodicals, too, are as yet unidentified. But all these items are entered in the hope that some scholar will have the answers that have so far escaped us.

The division of labour and a change of method in the citation of journals led to a number of inconsistencies in the early drafts of the bibliography. Despite checking and re-checking, it is possible that some still remain. If so, I accept full responsibility, though I believe that in all cases, except occasionally in items marked (†), sufficient information is given to locate the entry. What appear to be inconsistencies are sometimes unavoidable. Editors of some journals complicate the work of a bibliographer by varying not only titles but also the volume numbering and other information included on the title page and even the method of page numbering. In the case of some book reviews, the information is limited to that noted on the author's or publisher's file of cuttings; this is usually adequate for identification, if not perhaps as full as might be desired for speedy reference or for consistency of our entries.

For the limits of the book (1887–1965) I make no apology. The *terminus ad quem* was agreed on before Gustav Cross's last illness and I have departed from it in only four instances. References to Wade are to the third edition (1968); it is therefore included in Part I. Before our manuscript was completed, we were aware of three books in preparation, which are listed: *The Variorum Edition of the Plays*, edited by Russell K. Alspach, Dr Jochum's *Annotated Checklist* of the plays, and

Poetry: Reading and Understanding by K. G. W. Cross and D. R. C. Marsh. I have also noted the completion of the Dolmen Press Centenary Papers, a series of which the first five were published in 1965. Many important additions to Yeats scholarship have been made since the Yeats centenary year and it is clearly desirable that these should ultimately be included with the earlier criticism in a single volume. In the meantime, the large quantity of new material to be found in books and periodicals has been scrupulously recorded in the exhaustive bibliographies available to the modern scholar.

As we worked on this book, particularly during the time we were able to spend overseas, we became increasingly aware of the generosity of fellow workers in Yeats studies. Much of the information given to us was unasked, and to questions we did ask answers were invariably full and willingly given. Much help came from scholars with whom Gustav Cross was personally acquainted, and one of my regrets is that his death anticipated the compilation of a list of those to whom we are indebted but whom I am unable to name without fear of discourteous omissions. Under the circumstances, I trust that all those who have shared their time and knowledge with us will accept this general acknowledgement of their help and my very sincere thanks. It is no diminution of gratitude to them that I make a small number of specific acknowledgements. Gustav Cross spoke often of his indebtedness to Russell K. Alspach for material that he made available to him. Similarly, I recall the help of Dr Oliver Edwards of Queen's College, Belfast, remembering especially his unannounced arrival in the Reading Room of the British Museum in 1962 with a suitcase containing papers that he thought I should see before my return to Australia. My debt to Professor Jeffares, who gave us access to many items that we might not have seen otherwise, is increased by his graceful tribute to my late colleague. I should like to record my thanks to Dr Jochum, who put his research findings and his home at my disposal during a rewarding stay in Illinois; and to the Rev. Mgr F. J. Lally of *The Pilot* (Boston) who personally searched the early files of his journal to provide the answer to an urgent question. My thanks are due, too, to the Public Libraries of Boston, Chicago and New York for information carefully put together and forwarded at short notice; to the Berg Collection of the New York Public Library for permission to examine material, particularly from the library of Lady Gregory which it has now acquired; to F. W. Faxon Co. Inc. of Boston for a photocopy of copyright material; to the Macmillan Press Ltd for their patience and in particular to Mr T. M. Farmiloe of the Press who has been generous not only with his time but also with his considerable knowledge of Yeatsiana; to Mr Alan Hunt, also of the Press, for his editorial help and patience; and finally to the University of Sydney without whose initial financial grant and generous leave conditions this book might never have materialised.

R.T.D.

London,
1970

William Butler Yeats, 1865–1939
A Chronology of the Works

This list includes works edited or with an introduction by Yeats, and books to which he made a significant contribution. The date and publication details are those of the first edition; subsequent editions are unnoticed unless they embody substantial revisions of the text, or are included in collections made by Yeats.

1886   *Mosada: A Dramatic Poem. Dublin University Review.*

1888   *Poems and Ballads of Young Ireland.* Contributions by W. B. Yeats. Dublin: M. H. Gill & Son.
Fairy and Folk Tales of the Irish Peasantry. Edited and with an Introduction and contributions by W. B. Yeats. London: Walter Scott.

1889   *The Wanderings of Oisin and Other Poems.* London: Kegan Paul Trench & Co.
Stories from Carleton. Introduction by W. B. Yeats. London: Walter Scott.

1891   *Representative Irish Tales.* Edited and with an Introduction and Notes by W. B. Yeats. London: G. P. Putnam's Sons.
John Sherman and Dhoya. London: T. Fisher Unwin.

1892   *The Book of the Rhymers' Club.* Contributions by W. B. Yeats. London: Elkin Mathews.
Irish Fairy Tales. Edited and with an Introduction by W. B. Yeats. London: T. Fisher Unwin.
The Countess Kathleen and Various Legends and Lyrics. London: T. Fisher Unwin.

1893   *The Works of William Blake, Poetic, Symbolic, and Critical.* Edited by E. J. Ellis and W. B. Yeats. London: Bernard Quaritch.
The Poems of William Blake. Edited and with an Introduction and Notes by W. B. Yeats. London: Lawrence & Bullen; New York: Charles Scribner's Sons.
The Celtic Twilight. London: Lawrence & Bullen.

1894   *The Land of Heart's Desire.* London: T. Fisher Unwin.
The Second Book of the Rhymers' Club. Contributions by W. B. Yeats. London: Elkin Mathews & John Lane; New York: Dodd Mead & Co.

1895   *A Book of Irish Verse*. Edited and with an Introduction and Notes by W. B. Yeats. London: Methuen.
Poems. London: T. Fisher Unwin.

1897   *The Secret Rose*. London: Lawrence & Bullen.
The Tables of the Law: The Adoration of the Magi. London: privately printed.

1898   *A Book of Images* by W. T. Horton. Introduction by W. B. Yeats. London: Unicorn Press.

1899   *The Wind Among the Reeds*. London: Elkin Mathews.
Literary Ideals in Ireland by John Eglinton, W. B. Yeats, A. E., and W. Larminie. London: T. Fisher Unwin; Dublin: Daily Express Office.

1899–1900   *Beltaine: The Organ of the Irish Literary Theatre* (i–iii), Edited by W. B. Yeats. London: Unicorn Press.

1900   *The Shadowy Waters*. London: Hodder & Stoughton.

1901   *Ideals in Ireland*, edited by Lady Gregory. Contributions by W. B. Yeats. London: Unicorn Press.
Is the Order of R.R. and A.C. to Remain a Magical Order? Privately printed and circulated.
A Postscript to Essay Called 'Is the Order of R.R. and A.C. to Remain a Magical Order? Privately printed and circulated.

1901–8   *Samhain* (i–vii). Edited for the Irish Literary Theatre by W. B. Yeats. Nos. i–iv, vii, London: T. Fisher Unwin; nos. v, vi, Dublin: Maunsel.

1902   *Cuchulain of Muirthemne* by Lady Gregory. Preface by W. B. Yeats. London: John Murray.
Irish Fairy and Folk Tales. New York: A. L. Burt Co.
The Celtic Twilight. Revised edition. London: Bullen.
Cathleen ni Houlihan. London: Bullen.
Where There is Nothing. Supplement to *The United Irishman*, 1 Nov.

1903   *Ideas of Good and Evil*. London: Bullen.
In the Seven Woods. Dundrum: Dun Emer Press.
The Hour-Glass. London: Heinemann.

1904   *The Hour-Glass and Other Plays*. (Includes *The Pot of Broth*.) New York: Macmillan; London: Bullen.
Gods and Fighting Men by Lady Gregory. Preface by W. B. Yeats. London: John Murray.
The King's Threshold and On Baile's Strand. London: Bullen.
The Love Songs of Connacht, edited by Douglas Hyde. Preface by W. B. Yeats. Dundrum: Dun Emer Press.

1905   *Twenty One Poems* by Lionel Johnson. Selected by W. B. Yeats. Dundrum: Dun Emer Press.
Stories of Red Hanrahan. Dundrum: Dun Emer Press.
Sixteen Poems by William Allingham. Selected by W. B. Yeats. Dundrum: Dun Emer Press.

1906   *The Well of the Saints* by J. M. Synge. Introduction by W. B. Yeats. London: Bullen. (*English Catalogue* gives Dec 1905.)
Poems, 1899–1905. London: Bullen; Dublin: Maunsel.
Poems of Spenser. Selected and with an Introduction by W. B. Yeats. Edinburgh: T. C. and E. C. Jack.
The Poetical Works. I. Lyrical Poems. New York and London: Macmillan.

1906–7   *The Arrow* (i–v). Edited by W. B. Yeats. Dublin: Abbey Theatre.

1907   *The Poetical Works. II. Dramatical Poems*. New York and London: Macmillan.
Twenty One Poems by Katharine Tynan. Selected by W. B. Yeats. Dundrum: Dun Emer Press.
Deirdre. London: Bullen; Dublin: Maunsel.
Discoveries. Dundrum: Dun Emer Press.

1908   *The Unicorn from the Stars and Other Plays* by W. B. Yeats and Lady Gregory. New York: Macmillan.
The Golden Helmet. New York: John Quinn.
The Collected Works in Verse and Prose, 8 vols. Stratford-upon-Avon: Shakespeare Head Press.
Poetry and Ireland by W. B. Yeats and Lionel Johnson. Churchtown, Dundrum: Cuala Press.

1909   *Poems and Translations* by J. M. Synge. Introduction by W. B. Yeats. Churchtown, Dundrum: Cuala Press.

1910 *Poems: Second Series*, London and Stratford-upon-Avon: Bullen. (Title page gives 1909.)
Deirdre of the Sorrows by J. M. Synge. Preface by W. B. Yeats. Churchtown, Dundrum: Cuala Press.
The Green Helmet and Other Poems. Churchtown, Dundrum: Cuala Press.

1911 *Synge and the Ireland of His Time*. Churchtown, Dundrum: Cuala Press.
Plays for an Irish Theatre. London and Stratford-upon-Avon: Bullen.

1912 *Poems*. Sixth edition, revised. London: T. Fisher Unwin. *The Green Helmet and Other Poems*. London and New York: Macmillan.
Selections from the Writings of Lord Dunsany. Selected and with an Introduction by W. B. Yeats. Churchtown, Dundrum: Cuala Press.
The Cutting of an Agate. New York: Macmillan.
Gitanjali by Rabindranath Tagore. Introduction by W. B. Yeats. London: Chiswick Press.

1913 *Stories of Red Hanrahan: The Secret Rose: Rosa Alchemica*. London and Stratford-upon-Avon: Bullen.
Poems Written in Discouragement. Churchtown, Dundrum: Cuala Press.

1914 *Responsibilities: Poems and a Play*. Churchtown, Dundrum: Cuala Press.
The Post Office by Rabindranath Tagore. Preface by W. B. Yeats. Churchtown, Dundrum: Cuala Press.

1915 *Reveries over Childhood and Youth*. Churchtown, Dundrum: Cuala Press.

1916 *Eight Poems*. London: Morland Press.
Certain Noble Plays of Japan, chosen by Ezra Pound. Introduction by W. B. Yeats. Churchtown, Dundrum: Cuala Press.
Easter, 1916. London: privately printed and circulated.
Responsibilities and Other Poems. London: Macmillan.

1917 *The Wild Swans at Coole, Other Verses and a Play in Verse*. Churchtown, Dundrum: Cuala Press

1918   *Per Amica Silentia Lunae*. London: Macmillan.
       Nine Poems. London: privately printed and circulated.

1919   *Two Plays for Dancers*. Churchtown, Dundrum: Cuala Press.
       The Wild Swans at Coole. London: Macmillan.

1920   *Visions and Beliefs in the West of Ireland* by Lady Gregory. Contributions by W. B. Yeats. New York and London: G. P. Putnam's Sons.

1921   *Michael Robartes and the Dancer*. Churchtown, Dundrum: Cuala Press. (Title page gives 1920.)
       Four Plays for Dancers. London: Macmillan.
       Four Years. Churchtown, Dundrum: Cuala Press.

1922   *Seven Poems and a Fragment*. Churchtown, Dundrum: Cuala Press.
       The Trembling of the Veil. London: privately printed by Werner Laurie.
       Later Poems. London: Macmillan.
       Plays in Prose and Verse. (Includes *The Player Queen*.) London: Macmillan.

1923   *The Complete Works of Oscar Wilde*, vol. III. Introduction by W. B. Yeats. New York: Doubleday, Page.
       Early Memories by J. B. Yeats. Preface by W. B. Yeats. Churchtown, Dundrum: Cuala Press.
       Plays and Controversies. London: Macmillan.

1924   *An Offering of Swans* by Oliver Gogarty. Preface by W. B. Yeats. Dublin: Cuala Press. (Title page gives 1923.)
       Essays. London: Macmillan.
       The Cat and the Moon and Certain Poems. Dublin: Cuala Press.

1925   *Axël* by Villiers de l'Isle-Adam. Preface by W. B. Yeats. London: Jarrolds.
       The Bounty of Sweden: A Meditation and a Lecture Delivered before the Royal Swedish Academy. Dublin: Cuala Press.
       Early Poems and Stories. London: Macmillan.

1926   *A Vision: An Explanation of Life Founded upon the Writings of Giraldus and upon Certain Doctrines Attributed to Kusta Ben Luka*. London: privately printed by Werner Laurie. (Title page gives

1926 1925. Issued to subscribers Jan 1926).
cont. *Estrangement: Being some Fifty Thoughts from a Diary Kept by William Butler Yeats in the Year Nineteen Hundred and Nine.* Dublin: Cuala Press.
  The Midnight Court by Percy Arland Ussher. Introduction by W. B. Yeats. London: Jonathan Cape.
  Autobiographies: Reveries over Childhood and Youth and The Trembling of the Veil. London: Macmillan.

1927 *Poems.* New revised edition. London: T. Fisher Unwin.
  October Blast. Dublin: Cuala Press.

1928 *The Tower.* London: Macmillan.
  Sophocles' King Oedipus. London: Macmillan.
  The Death of Synge and Other Passages from an Old Diary. Dublin: Cuala Press.
  Coinage of Saorstát Eireánn. Contribution by W. B. Yeats. Dublin: The Stationery Office.

1929 *A Packet for Ezra Pound.* Dublin: Cuala Press.
  The Winding Stair. New York: The Fountain Press.
  Three Things. London: Faber & Faber.

1930 *Wild Apples* by Oliver Gogarty. Preface by W. B. Yeats. Dublin: Cuala Press.

1931 *Stories of Michael Robartes and His Friends: An Extract from a Record Made by His Pupils: And a Play in Prose.* (Includes *The Resurrection.*) Dublin: Cuala Press.
  Bishop Berkeley: His Life, His Writings and Philosophy by J. M. Hone and M. M. Rossi. Introduction by W. B. Yeats. London: Faber & Faber.

1932 *An Indian Monk* by Shri Purohit Swami. Introduction by W. B. Yeats. London: Macmillan.
  Words for Music Perhaps and Other Poems. Dublin: Cuala Press.

1933 *The Winding Stair and Other Poems.* London: Macmillan.
  The Collected Poems of W. B. Yeats. New York and London: Macmillan.

1934 *Letters to the New Island.* Cambridge, Mass.: Harvard University Press.
  The Words upon the Window Pane. Dublin: Cuala Press.

The Holy Mountain by Shagwan Shri Hamsa. Introduction by W. B. Yeats. London: Faber & Faber.
Wheels and Butterflies. London: Macmillan.
The Collected Plays of W. B. Yeats. London: Macmillan.
The King of the Great Clock Tower, Commentaries and Poems. Dublin: Cuala Press.

1935 *A Full Moon in March.* London: Macmillan.
Dramatis Personae. Dublin: Cuala Press.

1936 *Selections from the Poems of Dorothy Wellesley.* Introduction by W. B. Yeats. London: Macmillan.
The Oxford Book of Modern Verse, 1892–1935. Chosen and with an Introduction by W. B. Yeats. Oxford: Clarendon Press.
Modern Poetry. London: British Broadcasting Commission.

1937 *The Ten Principal Upanishads.* Translated by Shri Purohit Swami and W. B. Yeats and with an Introduction by W. B. Yeats. London: Faber & Faber.
The Lemon Tree by Margaret Ruddock. Introduction by W. B. Yeats. London: J. M. Dent.
A Vision. London: Macmillan.
A Speech and Two Poems. Dublin: At the Sign of the Three Candles.
Essays: 1931–1936. Dublin: Cuala Press.

1938 *The Herne's Egg and Other Plays.* London: Macmillan.
New Poems. Dublin: Cuala Press.
Aphorisms of Yoga by Bhagwan Shree Patanjali. Introduction by W. B. Yeats. London: Faber & Faber.
The Autobiography. New York: Macmillan.

1939 *Last Poems and Two Plays.* Dublin: Cuala Press.
On the Boiler. Dublin: Cuala Press.

1940 *Last Poems and Plays.* London: Macmillan.
Letters on Poetry to Lady Dorothy Wellesley. London: Oxford University Press.
If I Were Four and Twenty. Dublin: Cuala Press.

1941 *Florence Farr, Bernard Shaw and W. B. Yeats.* Dublin: Cuala Press.

1944 *Pages from a Diary Written in Nineteen Hundred and Thirty.* Dublin: Cuala Press.

1947   *Tribute to Thomas Davis*. Cork: Cork University Press; Oxford: Blackwell.

1949   *The Poems of W. B. Yeats*, 2 vols. London: Macmillan.

1950   *The Collected Poems of W. B. Yeats*. London: Macmillan.

1951   *Diarmuid and Grania* by George Moore and W. B. Yeats. *Dublin Magazine*, Apr–June.

1952   *The Collected Plays of W. B. Yeats*. London: Macmillan.

1953   *Some Letters from W. B. Yeats to John O'Leary and His Sister*. New York: New York Public Library.
        Letters to Katharine Tynan. Dublin: Clonmore & Reynolds; London: Burns Oates & Washbourne.
        W. B. Yeats and T. Sturge Moore: Their Correspondence, 1901–1937. London: Routledge & Kegan Paul; New York: Oxford University Press.

1954   *The Letters of W. B. Yeats*. London: Rupert Hart-Davis.

1955   *Autobiographies*. London: Macmillan.

1956   *A Vision*. With the author's final revisions. New York: Macmillan.

1957   *The Variorum Edition of the Poems of W. B. Yeats*. New York: Macmillan.

1959   *Mythologies*. London: Macmillan.

1960   *The Senate Speeches of W. B. Yeats*. Bloomington: Indiana University Press.

1961   *Essays and Introductions*. London: Macmillan.

1962   *Explorations*. London: Macmillan.

1966   *The Variorum Edition of the Plays of W. B. Yeats*. London: Macmillan.

Part I

BIBLIOGRAPHIES, CONCORDANCES AND DESCRIPTIONS OF YEATSIANA

ADAMS, HAZARD, 'The William Butler Yeats Collection at Texas', *Library Chronicle of the University of Texas*, VI (1957) 33–8 (description of the Roth Collection, with list of desiderata).

'Yeats Scholarship and Criticism: A Review of Research', *Texas Studies in Literature and Language*, III 4 (winter 1962) 439–51.

ALLT, PETER. *See* O'FAOLÁIN, SEÁN.

ALSPACH, RUSSELL K., 'Additions to Allan Wade's *Bibliography of W. B. Yeats*', *Irish Book*, Special Yeats Issue, II 3–4 (autumn 1963) 91–114.

ALTICK, RICHARD D., and MATTHEWS, WILLIAM R., *Guide to Doctoral Dissertations in Victorian Literature 1886–1958* (Urbana: University of Illinois Press, 1960) 95–6, Items 2058–2104. Also Items 110, 789, 1475, 1505, 1698, 1699, 1700.

ANON., *Irish Book Lover*, VIII 5–6 (Dec 1916–Jan 1917) 62 (sale of an autograph letter written by Yeats to Arthur Symons).

Irish Book Lover, XII 1–2 (Aug–Sep 1920) 16 (sale of first edition of *Eight Poems*, Wade 114).

'Bibliographies of Modern Authors: William Butler Yeats', *London Mercury*, II 8 (June 1920) 220–1.

ARMS, GEORGE W., and KUNTZ, JOSEPH M., *Poetry Explication: A Checklist of Interpretation since 1925 of British and American Poems, Past and Present* (New York: Morrow, 1950; second edition by Joseph M. Kuntz, Denver, Colorado: Alan Swallow, 1962) 298–316 (lists locations for individual poems).

BAKER, BLANCH M., *Theatre and Allied Arts: A Guide to Books Dealing with the History, Criticism, and Technic of the Drama and Theatre and Related Arts and Crafts* (New York: Wilson, 1952) 118–20.

BANGS, FRANCIS R., 'Julia Ellsworth Ford: An Appreciation', *Yale University Gazette*, XXVI (1952) 153–92 (lists books and letters by the Yeats family in Yale University Library).

BIBLIOGRAPHIES AND ABSTRACTS. Yeats material is included in the following annual and periodical publications:
Abstracts of English Studies (*see* List of Periodicals)
Annual Bibliography of English Literature (Cambridge)
Book Review Digest (New York: Wilson)

3

Dissertation Abstracts (Ann Arbor, Michigan)

Essay and General Literature Index (New York: Wilson)

International Index to Periodicals (New York: Wilson)

Modern Philology (*see* List of Periodicals)

Poole's Index to Periodical Literature (Boston: Osgood, London: Trübner)

PMLA Annual Bibliography (*see* List of Periodicals)

Reader's Guide to Periodical Literature (New York: Wilson)

Subject Index to Periodicals (London: Library Association)

Twentieth Century Literature Annual Bibliography (*see* List of Periodicals)

Victorian Studies Annual Bibliography (*see* List of Periodicals)

The Year's Work in English Studies (London: John Murray)

BLACK, HESTER M., *William Butler Yeats: A Catalog of an Exhibition from the P. S. O'Hegarty Collection in the University of Kansas Library* (Lawrence: University of Kansas Library, 1958) pp. 42. Wade 347.
Reviewed by *TLS*, 2976 (13 Mar 1959) 152.

BROWN, STEPHEN J., S. J., *A Guide to Books on Ireland. Part I: Prose Literature, Poetry, Music and Plays* (Dublin: Hodges, Figgis; London and New York: Longmans, Green, 1912) *passim*.

Ireland in Fiction: A Guide to Irish Novels, Tales, Romances and Folk Lore (Dublin and London: Maunsel, 1916) 257–8.

CAMBRIDGE BIBLIOGRAPHY OF ENGLISH LITERATURE. *See* O'FAOLÁIN, SEÁN.

CLARK, ALEXANDER P., 'The Manuscript Collections of the Princeton University Library', *Princeton University Library Chronicle*, XIX (1958) 159–90.

COURTNEY, Sr MARIE-THÉRÈSE. *See* Part III.

CROSS, K. G. W., 'The Fascination of What's Difficult: A Survey of Yeats Criticism and Research', in *In Excited Reverie*, ed. A. Norman Jeffares and K. G. W. Cross, 315–37.

CUTLER, B. D., and STYLES, VILLA, 'William Butler Yeats 1865–', in *Modern British Authors: Their First Editions* (London: Allen & Unwin, 1930) 164–7.

DOUGAN, R. O. *See* TRINITY COLLEGE DUBLIN.

DURKAN, MICHAEL J. *See* WESLEYAN UNIVERSITY.

EXHIBITIONS. *See* BLACK, HESTER M. (Kansas); GORDAN, JOHN D. (Berg Collection); HODGES, FIGGIS; MANCHESTER; NATIONAL GALLERY OF IRELAND; NEWCASTLE UPON TYNE; READING; ROTH, WILLIAM M. (Yale); TRINITY COLLEGE DUBLIN; UNIVERSITY OF VICTORIA; YEATS AT THE MUNICIPAL GALLERY (Irish Georgian Society, Dublin) (all Part I).

GERSTENBERGER, DONNA, 'Yeats and the Theater: A Selected Bibliography', *Modern Drama*, VI 1 (May 1963) 65–71.

GORDAN, JOHN D., 'New in the Berg Collection: 1952–1958', *Bulletin of the New York Public Library*, LXI 7 (July 1957) 353–63; 'New in the Berg Collection: 1957–1958', ibid., LXIII 4 (Apr 1959) 205–15.

'An Anniversary Exhibition. The Henry W. and Albert A. Berg Collection; 1940–1965', *Bulletin of the New York Public Library*, LXIX 9 (Nov 1965) 605 (description of the holograph of *The Wild Swans at Coole*, 1919).

HALL, JAMES, and STEINMANN, MARTIN, 'A Select Bibliography of Articles and Books, in Whole or in Part, on Yeats', in *The Permanence of Yeats*, ed. James Hall and Martin Steinmann, 365–414 (349–71).

HODGES, FIGGIS & CO. LTD, *William Butler Yeats 1865–1939* (Dublin: Designed and Printed for Hodges, Figgis by the Dolmen Press, June 1965) pp. viii (descriptive catalogue of the Hodges, Figgis Centenary Exhibition, Dublin, 1965).

[HONE, JOSEPH], 'W. B. Yeats – A Bio-Bibliography: A Succinct Table of Events and Works', *Irish Library Bulletin*, IX (Oct 1948) 167–72.

JAPANESE BIBLIOGRAPHY. *See* OSHIMA, SHOTARO.

JEFFARES, A. NORMAN, 'An Account of Recent Yeatsiana', *Hermathena*, LXXII (Nov 1948) 21–43.

'The Last Twelve Years' Yeatsiana', *Levende Talen*, CXLIX (1949) 109–13.

'Bibliography', in *Poems of W. B. Yeats*, selected with an Introduction and Notes by A. Norman Jeffares (London: Macmillan, 1962) 260–1.

JOCHUM, K. P. S., *W. B. Yeats's Plays: An Annotated Checklist of Criticism* (Saarbrücken: Anglistisches Institut der Universität des Saarlandes, 1966) pp. 180.

JUCHHOFF, RUDOLF (compiler), *Sammelkatalog der bibliographischen und literarkritischen Werke zu englischen Schrifstellern des 19. und 20. Jahrhunderts (1830–1958): Verzeichnis der Bestände in deutschen Bibliotheken* (Krefeld: Scherpe Verlag, [1959]) 267–72.

LEARY, LEWIS (ed.), *Contemporary Literary Scholarship: A Critical Review* (New York: Appleton-Century-Crofts, 1958) 197–8, 332 *et passim*.

LINATI, CARLO. *See* Part III.

McGIRR, ALICE THURSTON, 'Reading List on William Butler Yeats', *Bulletin of Bibliography*, VII 4 (Jan 1913) 82–3.

MANCHESTER EXHIBITION, 1961. *W. B. Yeats: Images of a Poet*, Catalogue of the Exhibition held at the Whitworth Art Gallery, University of Manchester, from 3 May to 3 June 1961, at The Building Centre, Dublin, from 17 June to 1 July, and at the National Book League, London, 17–22 July (Wilmslow, Cheshire: Richmond Press, 1961) pp. 151. An expansion of the Reading Exhibition (q.v.). Contains descriptive essays by D. J. Gordon, Ian Fletcher, Frank Kermode and Robin Skelton. The Catalogue was republished as a book by Manchester University Press. *See* GORDON, D. J. (Part III).
Exhibitions and Catalogue reviewed by W. L. Webb, *Guardian*, 3 May 1961, 7; *Irish Times*, 3 May and 22 June 1961; G. S. Fraser, *New Statesman*, LXI (12 May 1961) 763; Richard Ellmann, ibid., LXII (8 Dec 1961) 887–8; Robert Armstrong, *Poetry Review*, LIII (Jan–Mar 1962) 44 (briefly); *TLS*, 3089 (12 May 1961) 293; correspondence by Frank Kermode, ibid., 3090 (19 May) 305, 309; ibid., 3108 (22 Sep) 631.

MARRINER, ERNEST C., 'Fifty Years of the Cuala Press', *Colby Library Quarterly*, III (Aug 1953) 171–83 (abbreviated from an address on the occasion of the Jubilee Exhibition of Cuala Press books and prints, 1 May 1953, with photographic reproductions of a rough draft of 'Politics' and comment by W. B. Yeats in James A. Healey's copy of *Twenty-One Poems* by Lionel Johnson).

MAXWELL, D. E. S., and BUSHRUI, S. B., 'A Select Bibliography', in *W. B. Yeats 1865–1965*, ed. D. E. S. Maxwell and S. B. Bushrui, 227–42 (includes list of unpublished theses on Yeats and of a selection of works on Yeats in languages other than English).

MAXWELL, WILLIAM, *The Dun Emer Press: Churchtown, Dundrum, July 1903–September 1907. The Cuala Press: Churchtown, Dundrum, October 1908–July 1923. Merrion Square, Dublin, October 1923– October 1924. Lower Baggot Street, Dublin, from May 1925. A Complete List of the Books, Pamphlets and Broadsides Printed by Miss Yeats with Some Notes by the Compiler* (Edinburgh: Privately Printed, 1932) pp. 68.

MILLER, LIAM, 'The Dun Emer and the Cuala Press', in *The World of W. B. Yeats*, ed. Robin Skelton and Ann Saddlemyer, 141–51.

MILLET, FRED. B., *Contemporary British Literature* (New York: Harcourt, Brace, third edition revised and enlarged by John M. Manly and Edith Rickert, 1948) 518–22.

NATIONAL GALLERY OF IRELAND (Gailearai Náisúnta na hÉireann), *W. B. Yeats: A Centenary Exhibition* (Dublin: Dolmen Press for the National Gallery of Ireland, 1965) pp. 104.

NELICK, FRANK C., 'Yeats, Bullen, and the Irish Drama', *Modern Drama*, I 3 (Dec 1958) 196–202 (on the acquisition of the P. S. O'Hegarty collection by the Watson Library, University of Kansas).

NEWCASTLE UPON TYNE EXHIBITION, 1965. *William Butler Yeats, 1865–1939*, Catalogue of an Exhibition, 13–22 May 1965, at the University of Newcastle upon Tyne, opened by T. R. Henn.

NILAND, NORA, 'The Yeats Memorial Museum, Sligo', *Irish Book*, II 3–4 (1963) 122–6.

O'FAOLÁIN, SEÁN, 'William Butler Yeats', in *The Cambridge Bibliography of English Literature*, ed. F. W. Bateson (Cambridge University Press, 1940) vol. III, 1059–62. Supplemented by Peter Allt, 'William Butler Yeats', revised by T. R. Henn, ibid., vol. V (Supplement), ed. George Watson (Cambridge University Press, 1957) 700–4.

Ó hAODHA, MICHEÁL, 'Bibliographical Notes: Unrecorded Yeats Contributions to Periodicals', *Irish Book*, Special Yeats Issue, II 3–4 (autumn 1963) 129.

O'HEGARTY, P. S., 'Notes on the Bibliography of W. B. Yeats: I. Notes on, and Supplemental to, the existing Bibliographies by Mr Allan Wade and Mr A. J. A. Symons, 1886–1922. II. A Handlist, 1922–1939, to complete Symons. III. Varia', *Dublin Magazine*, XIV (Oct–Dec 1939) 61–5; XV (Jan–Mar 1940) 37–42.

'The Abbey Theatre (Wolfhound) Series of Plays', *Dublin Magazine*, XXII (Apr–June 1947) 41–2 (bibliographical note on the series of which vols IV–VI contain plays by Yeats (Wade 54, 57–8)).

OSHIMA, SHOTARO, 'Bibliography of Yeats in Japan', in *William Butler Yeats and Japan*, 149–89 (a comprehensive listing of books, periodicals and articles published in Japan in Japanese and English); 'Books and Periodicals on Yeats in Japan', ibid., 137–45 (a general survey of Yeats scholarship in Japan).

PARRISH, STEPHEN MAXFIELD (ed.), *A Concordance to the Poems of W. B. Yeats*, programmed by James Allan Painter (Ithaca, New York: Cornell University Press, 1963) pp. xxxvii + 967. Wade 211 AA.

Reviewed by Robert B. Davis, *Modern Philology*, LXIII 1 (Aug 1965) 87–8; Peter Ure, *Review of English Studies*, n.s., XVI 62 (Apr 1965) 221–2; *TLS*, 3230 (23 Jan 1964) 69; correspondence by D. J. Foskett, ibid., 3231 (30 Jan) 87; Josephine Miles, *Victorian Studies*, VIII 3 (Mar 1965) 290–2.

QUINN LIBRARY, THE JOHN, 'William Butler Yeats', in *Complete Catalogue of the Library of John Quinn* (New York: Anderson Galleries, 2 vols, 1924) vol. II, 1128–60, 1204–5 (with printed prices).

QUINN, Sr M. BERNETTA, 'Bibliography', in *The Metamorphic Tradition in Modern Poetry*, 260–3.

RANSOM, H. H., 'The Hanley Library', *Library Chronicle of the University of Texas*, VI 1959) 33–5.

READING EXHIBITION, 1957. D. J. Gordon and Ian Fletcher, *I, the Poet William Yeats: A Descriptive Guide to the Photographic Exhibition Illustrating the Life and Works of W. B. Yeats*, University of Reading, 1957 (mimeographed, Reading, 1957) pp. ii + 32. *See also* MANCHESTER EXHIBITION *above*.

Reviewed by G. S. Fraser, *New Statesman*, LIII (1 June 1957) 706; *TLS*, 2884 (7 June 1957) 349.

ROTH, WILLIAM M., *A Catalogue of English and American First Editions of William Butler Yeats by William M. Roth, Prepared for an Exhibition of his Works held in the Yale University Library beginning May 18, 1939* (New Haven, Connecticut: Yale University Press, 1939) pp. 104.

SADDLEMYER, ANN, 'Bibliographical Notes: On Paragraphs from *Samhain* and Some Additional Yeats Letters', *Irish Book*, Special Yeats Issue, II 3–4 (autumn 1963) 127–8.
See also SKELTON, ROBIN.

SAUL, GEORGE BRANDON, 'Thread to a Labyrinth: A Selective Bibliography in Yeats', *Bulletin of the New York Public Library*, VIII 7 (July 1954) 344–7; 'Introductory Bibliography in Anglo–Irish Literature', *ibid.*, 429–35. Reprinted in his *Stephens, Yeats, and Other Irish Concerns*, 13–18, 19–22.

Prolegomena to the Study of Yeats's Poems (Philadelphia: Pennsylvania University Press, 1957; Minneapolis: Minnesota University Press; London: Oxford University Press, 1958) pp. 196.

Reviewed by F. L. Gwynn, *College English*, XX 1 (Oct 1958) 58; George Freedley, *Library Journal*, LXXXIV (15 May 1959) 1621 (briefly); T. J. P. Spencer, *Modern Language Review*, LIII 4 (Oct 1958) 626–7; Peter Ure, *Review of English Studies*, n.s., XI 41 (Feb 1960) 113–14; Thomas Parkinson, *Sewanee Review*, LXVIII 1 (Jan–Mar 1960) 143–9; *TLS*, 2933 (16 May 1958) 270.

Prolegomena to the Study of Yeats's Plays (Philadelphia: Pennsylvania University Press, 1958) pp. 106.

Reviewed by Sarah Youngblood, *Books Abroad*, XXXIII 2 (spring 1959) 219–20; William C. Burto, *Educational Theatre Journal*, XII (1959) 233–4; Thomas Parkinson, *Sewanee Review*, LXVIII 1 (Jan–Mar 1960) 143–9; *TLS*, 2982 (24 Apr 1959) 239.

'W. B. Yeats: Corrigenda', *Notes and Queries*, CCV, n.s. VII (Aug 1960) 302–3 (two corrections to items in *Prolegomena to the Study of Yeats's Poems*, . . . *Plays*).

SCHWARTZ, JACOB, *1100 Obscure Points: The Bibliographies of 25 English and 21 American Authors* (Bristol: Chatford House Press, 1931) 41–2 (description of first editions).

SIDGWICK, F. *See* Part V.

SIDNELL, M. J., 'Manuscript Versions of Yeats's *The Countess Cathleen*', *Papers of the Bibliographical Society of America*, LVI 1 (first quarter, 1962) 79–103 (describes the nine folders of *Countess Cathleen* MSS. in the National Library of Ireland, and establishes chronological sequence of the notebooks).

SKELTON, ROBIN, 'Images of a Poet: W. B. Yeats: A Note on the Exhibition held at the Whitworth Art Gallery, Manchester, 3 May to 3 June 1961, and in the Building Centre, Dublin, 19 June to 1 July 1961', *Irish Book*, I 4 (spring 1962) 89–97 (supplements his contribution to *W. B. Yeats: Images of a Poet*, ed. D. J. Gordon and Ian Fletcher).

and SADDLEMYER, ANN, 'Catalogue: Books and Manuscripts', in *The World of W. B. Yeats*, ed. Robin Skelton and Ann Saddlemyer, 70–9, 177–89, 266–77; 'Catalogue: Photographs, Paintings and Graphics', ibid., 80–3, 190–2, 278. *See* Part III.

STEWART, J. I. M., 'Bibliographical Notes: Yeats', *Eight Modern Writers* (Oxford: Clarendon Press; New York: Oxford University Press, 1965) 671–9.

SYMONS, A. J. A., 'Book Collectors' Notes', a series of six articles contributed to *Spectator* in 1924, with special reference to the work of the First Editions Club. The following are wholly or partly about books by Yeats: '. . . I', *Spectator*, CXXXII 4997 (5 Apr 1924) 540 (announcing an exhibition of Yeats first editions); '. . . II', ibid., 5001 (3 May) 708 (postponement of Yeats exhibition); '. . . V', ibid., CXXXIII 5015 (9 Aug) 191 (quoted in *Irish Book Lover*, LIV 9–10 (Sep–Oct 1924) 128).

A Bibliography of the First Editions of Books by William Butler Yeats (London: First Editions Club, 1924) pp. 54.

Reviewed by R. J., *Dublin Magazine*, II (Oct 1924) 211; *Irish Book Lover*, XV 3 (July 1925) 47; *TLS*, 1180 (28 Aug 1924) 526.

TAYLOR, ROBERT H., 'The J. Harlin O'Connell Collection', *Princeton University Library Chronicle*, XIX 3–4 (spring–summer 1958) 149–52.

TRINITY COLLEGE DUBLIN EXHIBITION, 1956 (held by the Friends of the Library of Trinity College Dublin to mark the seventieth anniversary of the publication of *Mosada*). *W. B. Yeats: Manuscripts and Printed Books Exhibited in the Library of Trinity College, Dublin, 1956,* compiled by R. O. Dougan (Dublin: Printed for the Friends of the Library by C. O Lochlainn, At the Sign of the Three Candles, 1956) pp. 50. Wade 346.

Reviewed by *TLS*, 2827 (4 May 1956) 276.

ULLRICH, KURT, *Who Wrote About Whom: A Bibliography of Books on Contemporary British Authors* (Berlin: Arthur Collignon, 1932) *passim* (an alphabetical list, indexed). (Of the books listed, I have been unable to trace BATES, KATHERINE LEE, *The New Drama: Yeats, Synge, Lady Gregory and Others* (Chicago, 1911) pp. 12. K. P. S. Jochum has established that another, *W. B. Yeats* by Viola Garvin (*née* Taylor) (London: Shaylor, 1939) was projected but not published. – R.D.)

UNIVERSITY OF VICTORIA EXHIBITION, 1965. *See* SKELTON, ROBIN, and SADDLEMYER, ANN (eds), *The World of W. B. Yeats* (Part III).

WADE, ALLAN, *A Bibliography of the Writings of William Butler Yeats* (Stratford-upon-Avon: Shakespeare Head Press, 1908) pp. 96. Also in *The Collected Works in Verse and Prose*, vol. VIII (Wade 82) 197–287. Wade 303.

Reviewed by D. J. O'D., *Irish Book Lover*, II 10 (May 1911) 162.

A Bibliography of the Writings of W. B. Yeats (London: Hart-Davis, 1951; second edition, revised and completed by Rupert Hart-Davis, London: Hart-Davis; Fair Lawn, New Jersey: Essential Books, 1958; third edition, revised and edited by Russell K. Alspach, London: Hart-Davis, 1968) pp. 449 (third edition, pp. 514).

Reviewed by *Book Collector*, 1 1 (spring 1952) 62–3; Horace Reynolds, *Christian Science Monitor*, 12 June 1952, 7; W. P. M., *Dublin Magazine*, XXVII (Apr–June 1952) 38–40; Donagh Mac-Donagh, *Irish Press*, 8 Jan 1952; John Hayward, *Library*, VII 1 (Mar 1952) 66–8; T. R. Henn, *New Statesman*, XLIII (12 Jan 1952) 43; Gerald D. McDonald, *Papers of the Bibliographical Society of America*, LII (fourth quarter, 1958) 332–6; *TLS*, 2608 (25 Jan 1952) 84; correspondence by Marion Witt (*see below*); ibid., 2923 (7 Mar 1958) 126.

WELLESLEY COLLEGE LIBRARY. *William Butler Yeats at Wellesley: Bulletin of the Friends of Wellesley College Library*, no. 10 (July 1952) 1–19 (an account of Yeats material in Wellesley College Library, and of the poet's association with the college).

WESLEYAN UNIVERSITY. *William Butler Yeats, 1865–1965. A Catalogue of his Works and Associated Items in Olin Library, Wesleyan University, together with an Essay by David R. Clark. Catalogue by Michael J. Durkan* (Middletown, Connecticut: Olin Memorial Library; Dublin: Dolmen Press, 1965) pp. 92.

WING, DONALD G., and GALLUP, DONALD, 'The Blum Library: From A'Beckett to Zangwill', *Yale University Library Gazette*, XXXIII (1958) 4143 (Yeats material in the Blum Library).

WITT, MARION, 'W. B. Yeats', correspondence, *TLS*, 2619 (11 Apr 1952) 251 (on two items not in Wade's *Bibliography*).

YALE EXHIBITION, 1939. *See* ROTH, WILLIAM M.

YEATS AT THE MUNICIPAL GALLERY, with an Introduction by Arland Ussher and reproductions of the pictures (Dublin: Charlemont House, 1959) pp. 12. Catalogue of an exhibition of paintings organised by the Irish Georgian Society in Dublin, June–Aug 1959, together with a printing of 'The Municipal Gallery Revisited'.

Part II

REVIEWS OF WRITINGS
BY W. B. YEATS

Note: Reviews are arranged in alphabetical order of periodicals. The reference after each title is to Allan Wade, *A Bibliography of the Writings of W. B. Yeats*, 3rd edn.

AUTOBIOGRAPHIES: REVERIES OVER CHILDHOOD AND YOUTH AND THE TREMBLING OF THE VEIL (1926) Wade 151–2

Booklist, XXIII (June 1927) 382;
Francis Bickley, *Bookman*, LXXI (Feb 1927) 272–3;
Richard Church, *Calendar of Modern Letters*, III (Jan 1927) 316–19;
Catholic World, CXXV (July 1927) 566;
Thomas Walsh, *Commonweal*, V (27 Apr 1927) 696–7;
Hamish Miles, *Criterion*, V 3 (June 1927) 353–6;
John Eglinton (W. K. Magee), *Dial*, LXXXIII 2 (Aug 1927) 94–7;
T. G. K., *Dublin Magazine*, n.s., II (Apr–June 1927) 20;
A. E., *Irish Statesman*, VI (Dec 1926) 302–3;
Babette Deutsch, *Library Review*, 7 May 1927, 5;
Mark van Doren, *Nation*, CXXIV (16 Mar 1927) 291;
Edmund Wilson, *New Republic*, L (23 Feb 1927) 22–3;
Elinor Wylie, *NYHTB*, 13 Feb 1927, 1;
H. J. Forman, *NYTB*, 15 May 1927, 13;
Outlook, CXLV (23 Mar 1927) 376;
Marie Luhrs, *Poetry* (Chicago), XXX 5 (Aug 1927) 279–83;
Quarterly Review, CCXLVIII 492 (Apr 1927) 427;
Charles M. Garnier, *Revue Anglo-Américaine*, VII 3 (Feb 1930) 270–1;
L. W. Payne, Jr, *Southwest Review*, XIII (Oct 1927) 123–35;
Richard Church, *Spectator*, CXXXVII 5134 (20 Nov 1926) Supplement, 912.

AUTOBIOGRAPHIES (1955) Wade 211L

J. H., *Belfast Telegraph*, 18 June 1955;
Thomas Bodkin, *Birmingham Post*, 22 Mar 1955;
Gabriel Fallon, *Books of the Month*, LXX (May 1955) 15, 24;
Neville Braybrooke, *Catholic Herald*, 5 Aug 1955;
Bernard Donoughue, *Cherwell*, 14 June 1955;
Church Times, 29 Apr 1955;
Guy Ramsay, *Daily Telegraph*, 18 Mar 1955;
Donald Davie, *Dublin Magazine*, XXXI (Oct–Dec 1955) 17–18;
Economist, CLXXV (30 Apr 1955) Spring Book Supplement, 9;
Gerard Fay, *Guardian*, 25 Mar 1955;
Irish Book Lover, XXXII 5 (July 1956) 117;
Austin Clarke, *Irish Times*, 2 Apr 1955;
S. J. White, *Irish Writing*, no. 31 (summer 1955) 7–8;
Anthony Bailey, *Isis*, 27 Apr 1955, 24;

Lennox Robinson, *Library Review* (autumn 1955) 162, 164;

Kathleen Raine, *Listener*, LIII (24 Mar 1955) 540;
correspondence, Henry Lamb, ibid. (31 Mar) 577;

L. A. G. Strong, *London Magazine*, II 6 (June 1955) 83–6;

A. N. Jeffares, *Meanjin*, XIV 4 (summer 1955) 565–8;

Louis Johnson, *Numbers*, I 4 (Oct 1955) 38–40;

Philip Toynbee, *Observer*, 24 Apr 1955;

Anthony Powell, *Punch*, CCXXVIII (18 May 1955) 620;

Quarterly Review, CCXCII 606 (Oct 1955) 558–9;

L. S., *Rand Daily Mail*, 16 Apr 1955;

William Kean Seymour, *St Martin's Review*, no. 770 (May 1955) 174;

Scotsman, 31 Mar 1955;

Harold Elliott, *Sheffield Telegraph*, 18 Mar 1955;

Vincent Buckley, *Sydney Morning Herald*, 11 June 1955;

Allan Wade, *Time and Tide*, XXXVI 13 (26 Mar 1955) 402–3;

The Times, 17 Mar 1955, 9;

TLS 2774 (29 Apr 1955) 201; correspondence by R. F. Rattray, ibid., 2795 (23 Sep) 557 (Yeats and Vacher Burch);

David Paul, *Twentieth Century*, CLVIII (July 1955) 66–75;

Western Mail, 30 Mar 1955;

Denis Botterill, *Yorkshire Post*, 30 Mar 1955.

THE AUTOBIOGRAPHY OF   Wade 198, 211 G, 211 O
W. B. YEATS (1938, etc.)

Alex Jackinson, *American Poetry Magazine*, no. 4 (1953);

Booklist, XXXV (15 Sep 1938) 29;

John Holmes, *Boston Evening Transcript*, 17 Sep 1938;

Don A. Keister, *Cleveland Plain Dealer*, 7 Feb 1954;

Frederick Wellman, *Durham Morning Herald*, 8 Nov 1953;

M. M. Colum, *Forum*, C (Nov 1938) 226;

Kate Trimble Sharber, *Nashville Tennessean*, 1 Nov 1953;

Horace Gregory, *Nation*, CXLVIII 6 (4 Feb 1939) 155–6;

M. Cowley, *New Republic*, XCVI (21 Sep 1938) 191–2; correspondence, Delmore Schwartz, ibid., XCVI (12 Oct 1938) 272; James P. O'Donnell, ibid., XCVII (7 Dec 1938) 133–4;

G. F. Whicher, *NYHTB*, 11 Apr 1954, 10;

Murray Kempton, *New York Post*, 15 Nov 1953;

Charles Poore, *New York Times*, 12 Dec 1953;

E. L. Tinker, *NYTB*, 4 Sep 1938, 12;

Harvey Breit, *NYTB*, 14 Mar 1954, 18; Delmore Schwartz, ibid.,
   13 June 1954, 2;
New Yorker, XIV (3 Sep 1938) 64;
Peg O'Connor, *News Sentinel*, 20 Feb 1954;
Richard Armour, *Pasadena Star News*, 29 Nov 1953;
Horace Gregory, *Poetry* (Chicago), LXXXIV 3 (June 1954) 153–7;
Edward C. McAleer, *Richmond News Leader*, 2 June 1954;
Alvin R. Rolfs, *St Louis Post-Dispatch*, 29 Dec 1953;
Sign, XVIII (Oct 1938) 187–8;
Helen Bevington, *South Atlantic Quarterly*, LIII 2 (Apr 1954) 300–1;
Catherine Perrine, *Southwest Review*, XXXIX (winter 1954) 96;
R. J. C., *Springfield Republican*, 18 Sep 1938, 7;
Fred S. Holley, *Virginian Pilot*, 7 Feb 1954;
Hazard Adams, *Western Review*, XIX 2 (winter 1955) 232–3.

A BOOK OF IRISH VERSE (1895)   Wade 225

Elsa d'Esterre Keeling, *Academy*, XLVII 1199 (27 Apr 1895) 349–50;
Francis Thompson, *Academy*, LVIII 1454 (17 Mar 1900) 235–6;
Athenaeum, 3519 (6 Apr 1895) 434;
Dublin Review, CXVII (July 1895) 241 (briefly);
Spectator, LXXIV (13 Apr 1895) 502.

THE BOOK OF THE RHYMERS' CLUB (1892) Wade 291

H. W., *Irish Monthly*, XX 225 (Mar 1892) 212–16.

THE BOUNTY OF SWEDEN (Cuala Press, 1924)   Wade 146

S. L. M., *Irish Statesman*, IV (1 Aug 1925) 658;
Edmund Gosse, *Sunday Times*, 26 July 1925, 6; replies in *Irish Statesman*, IV (1 Aug 1925) 645, and *Catholic Bulletin*, XIV (Jan 1924) 5–7.

BROADSIDES (1935)   Wade 249

Dublin Magazine, X (Apr–June 1935) 83–4.

CATHLEEN NI HOULIHAN (1902)   Wade 40

E. K. Chambers, *Academy*, LXIV 1618 (9 May 1903) 465–6;
H. W. Boynton, *Atlantic Monthly*, XCIII (May 1904) 712–13;
Stephen Gwynn, *Fortnightly Review*, LXXVIII (1 Dec 1902) 1051–4;
New York Drama, LXVI (6 Dec 1911) 6.

THE CELTIC TWILIGHT (1893)   Wade 8–9

Ernest Rhys, *Academy*, XLV 1142 (24 Mar 1894) 244;
Athenaeum, 3459 (10 Feb 1894) 173–4;
G-Y, *Bookman*, V (8 Feb 1894) 157–8;
Catholic World, LIX (July 1894) 573;
Critic, XXII (8 Sep 1894) 154;
Dial, XVII (1 Aug 1894) 69–70;
Dora M. Jones, *London Quarterly Review*, XCIV, n.s., IV (July 1900)
    61–70;
Saturday Review, LXXVII (6 Jan 1894) 27.

THE CELTIC TWILIGHT   Wade 35–8
(Reprinted with additions, 1902)

H. W. Boynton, *Atlantic Monthly*, XCII (Oct 1903) 565–9;
Weekly Review, 13 Sep 1902.

CERTAIN NOBLE PLAYS OF JAPAN   Wade 269
(ed. W. B. Yeats, 1916)

Nation (London), XX (14 Oct 1916) 87.

COLLECTED EDITION OF   Wade 134–7, 139–42, 147–8
THE WORKS (1922–6)

See under individual volumes, viz.:
    I. *Later Poems* (1922)   Wade 134–5
   II. *Plays in Prose and Verse*   Wade 136–7
      (1922, 1924)
  III. *Plays and Controversies* (1923–4)   Wade 139–40
  IV. *Essays* (1924)   Wade 141–2
   V. *Early Poems and Stories* (1925)   Wade 147–8

COLLECTED PLAYS (1934)   Wade 177–8

H. Brown, *Book-of-the-Month Club News* (Sep 1935) 12;
Booklist, XXXII (Sept 1935) 11;
Edmund Blunden, *Book Society News* (Dec 1934);
Christian Science Monitor, 28 Aug 1935, 11;
John Garrett, *Criterion*, XIV 56 (Apr 1935) 488–91;
Dublin Magazine, XI (Jan–Mar 1936) 71–2;
Arthur Ball, *Fortnightly Review*, CXXXVII (Apr 1935) 380–1;
Mary Colum, *Forum*, XCIV (Nov 1935) 278–9;

Glasgow Herald, 27 Dec 1934;

Padraic Colum, *Irish Book Lover*, XXIII 2 (Mar–Apr 1935) 54;

Irish Times, 5 Jan 1935;

L. A. G. Strong, *John O'London's Weekly*, XXXII (5 Jan 1935) 550;

Life and Letters, XI 61 (Jan 1935) 483–6;

Listener, XIII (30 Jan 1935) 209;

Austin Clarke, *London Mercury*, XXXI 184 (Feb 1935) 391–2;

Horace Gregory, *New Republic*, LXXXIV (18 Sep 1935) 164–5;

Babette Deutsch, *NYHTB*, 1 Sep 1935, 2;

Horace Reynolds, *NYTB*, 1 Sep 1935, 2, 8;

Oxford Magazine, 2 May 1935, 536;

Morton Dauwen Zabel, *Poetry* (Chicago), XLV 3 (Dec 1934) 152–6;

Horace Gregory, *Poetry* (Chicago), XLVIII 4 (July 1936) 226–7;

Scotsman, 17 Dec 1934;

Springfield Republican, 15 Dec 1935, 7;

TLS, 1721 (24 Jan 1935) 37–8;

A. T. G. Edwards, *Western Mail*, 13 Dec 1934;

Wisconsin Library Bulletin, XXXI (Nov 1935) 100.

COLLECTED PLAYS (1952–3) Wade 211 D–E

Val Mulkerns, *Bell*, XVIII (Dec 1952) 444–5;

Booklist, XLIX (July 1953) 378;

Elinor Hughes, *Boston Sunday Herald*, 14 June 1953;

Peggy de Morinni, *Buffalo Courier Express*, 28 June 1953;

Delos Avery, *Chicago Sunday Tribune*, 5 July 1953;

Horace Reynolds, *Christian Science Monitor*, 30 July 1953, 9;

Church Times, 12 Dec 1952;

Michael Habart, *Critique*, X (Sep 1954) 739–53;

C. Buddingh, *Critisch Bulletin*, XX 3 (Mar 1953) 135–8;

L. N. Morgan, *Daily Oklahoman*, 31 May 1953;

Ann Ridler, *Drama* (summer 1955) 37–8;

Frederick Wellman, *Durham Morning Herald*, 31 May 1953;

Ada Richards, *Globe and Mail*, 20 Dec 1952;

Leo Salingar, *Highway* (Mar 1953) 222–5;

Donagh MacDonagh, *Irish Press*, 18 Nov 1952;

Austin Clarke, *Irish Times*, 18 Oct 1952;

Library Journal, LXXVIII (15 June 1953) 1156;

Listener, XLIX (5 Mar 1953) 397–8;

K. T. S[harber]., *Nashville Tennessean*, 21 June 1953;

Nation, CLXXVII (4 July 1953) 16;

Joseph T. Shipley, *New Leader*, 9 Nov 1953, 19;
Frank O'Connor, *NYTB*, 31 May 1953, 1, 16;
W. P. Eaton, *NYTB*, 14 June 1953, 6;
New Yorker, XXIX (12 Sep 1953) 148;
Louis Johnson, *Numbers*, I 4 (Oct 1955) 38–40;
Louis MacNeice, *Observer*, 2 Nov 1952;
B. R. McElderry, *Personalist*, XXXV 4 (autumn 1954) 427–8;
Edward C. McAleer, *Richmond News Leader*, 22 Jan 1953;
L. F., *San Francisco Chronicle*, 13 Sep 1953, 16;
W. R. Davies, *Saturday Night*, LXVIII (31 Jan 1953) 22;
Scotsman, 7 Nov 1952;
Mary A. Updike White, *South Atlantic Quarterly*, LIII 1 (Jan 1953)
    153–4;
M. P. Worcester, *Sunday Telegraph*, 9 Aug 1953;
Anthony Bertram, *Tablet*, CC 5875 (27 Dec 1952) 530–1;
TLS, 2651 (21 Nov 1952) 760;
Virginian Pilot, 6 Sep 1953.

COLLECTED POEMS (1933)   Wade 171–2

R. P. Blackmur, *American Mercury*, XXXI (Feb 1934) 244–6;
Annual Register, 1933, Part II, 29–30 (*see* Part III);
V., *Belfast News-Letter*, 1 Feb 1934;
W. R. Benét, *Book-of-the-Month-Club News* (Jan 1934) 7;
Booklist, XXX (Jan 1934) 156;
Boston Evening Transcript, 6 Jan 1934, 1;
J. Bronowski, *Cambridge Review*, LIV (8 June 1933) 475–6;
Catholic World, CXL (Nov 1934) 241;
Christian Century, LI (3 Jan 1934) 27;
Herbert Read, *Criterion*, XIII 52 (Apr 1934) 468–72;
Bernt von Heiseler, *Deutsche Zeitschrift*, XLVII 11–12 (Aug–Sep 1934)
    579–80;
Dublin Magazine, IX (July–Sep 1934) 63–6;
C. P., *Guardian*, 5 Feb 1934;
C. E., *Irish News*, 23 Dec 1933;
D. M., *Irish Press*, 1 Jan 1934;
Edward Shanks, *John O'London's Weekly*, XXX (10 Feb 1934) 721;
Listener, XI (31 Jan 1934) 213;
Eda Lou Walton, *Nation*, CXXXVII (13 Dec 1933) 684–6;
Desmond Hawkins, *New English Weekly*, IV (22 Feb 1934) 448;

Horace Gregory, *New Republic*, LXXVII (13 Dec 1933) 134–5;

New Statesman and Nation, VII (3 Feb 1934) 160, 162;

Isabel Paterson, *NYHTB*, 3 Dec 1933, 9;

Percy Hutchison, *NYTB*, 24 Dec 1933, 2;

R. Ellis Roberts, *News Chronicle*, 24 Jan 1934;

Northern Whig, 10 Jan 1934;

Arthur W. Fox, *Papers of the Manchester Literary Club*, LXI (1936) 62–88;

Morton Dauwen Zabel, *Poetry* (Chicago), XLIII 4 (Jan 1934) 279–87;

Punch, CLXXXIX (20 Dec 1933) 698 (briefly);

C. E. Lawrence, *Quarterly Review*, CCLXII 520 (Apr 1934) 311–14;

W. R. Benét, *Saturday Review of Literature*, X (16 Dec 1933) 349–50;

Frederick T. Wood, *Sheffield Daily Telegraph*, 4 Jan 1934;

Stephen Spender, *Spectator*, CLII 5513 (23 Feb 1934) 284;

Desmond MacCarthy, *Sunday Times*, 4 Feb 1934, 8;

E. J. Scovell, *Time and Tide*, XV (10 Mar 1934) 322–3;

TLS, 1675 (8 Mar 1934) 167 (briefly);

Babette Deutsch, *Virginia Quarterly Review*, X 2 (Apr 1934) 298–300;

Martin Armstrong, *Weekend Review*, 6 June 1934;

F. O. Matthiessen, *Yale Review*, XXIII 3 (Mar 1934) 615–17;

COLLECTED POEMS (1950; New York, 1951) Wade 211–11A

Adelphi, XXVII 1 (Nov 1950) 80–1;

W. Y. Tindall, *American Scholar*, XX 4 (autumn 1951) 482–6;

Peter Viereck, *Atlantic Monthly*, CLXXXIX 1 (Jan 1952) 83;

Booklist, XLVII (15 May 1951) 331;

Bookmark, X (July 1951) 231;

A. E. J., *Boston Sunday Herald*, 1 June 1951;

Buffalo Courier Express, 8 July 1951;

Charles A. Brady, *Buffalo Evening News*, 9 Jan 1951;

I. P. W., *Cambridge Review*, LXXII (Oct 1950) 82;

M. Avison, *Canadian Forum*, XXX (Feb 1951) 261;

Katherine Brégy, *Catholic World*, CLXXIII (July 1951) 316;

William Risen, *Cincinnati Daily Enquirer*, 13 May 1951;

Cleveland Plain Dealer, 1 July 1951;

Vernon Watkins, *Critique*, IX (Nov 1953) 915–30;

Kester Svensden, *Daily Oklahoman*, 24 Jan 1951;

Earl F. Guy, *Dalhousie Review*, XXX 4 (Jan 1951) 428–30;

Ann F. Wolfe, *Dispatch*, 17 June 1951;

A. Rivoallan, *Études Anglaises*, V 2 (May 1952) 173;

Sr M. Camillus, *The Globe*, 7 June 1956;

Guardian, 29 Aug 1950, 4;

Richard Ellmann, *Kenyon Review*, XIII 3 (summer 1951) 512–19;

József Reményi, *Látóhatár*, V 5 (1954) 305–7;

G. D. McDonald, *Library Journal*, LXXXVI (15 June 1951) 1029;

T. R. Henn, *Listener*, XLIV (21 Dec 1950) 790–2;

Kate Trimble Sharber, *Nashville Tennessean*, 8 July 1951;

M. L. Rosenthal, *Nation*, CLXXXII (23 June 1956) 533–5;

Eric Gillett, *National and English Review*, CXXXV (Sep 1950) 292–4;

Louise Bogan, *New Republic*, CXXV (17 Sep 1951) 19–20;

Rex Warner, *New Statesman and Nation*, XLII (23 Sep 1951) 300–1;

D. A. Stauffer, *NYHTB*, 6 May 1951, 3;

Charles Poore, *New York Times*, 18 July 1951;

Harvey Breit, *NYTB*, 3 June 1951, 23;

Jessica Nelson North, *New York World Telegram*, 10 July 1951;

New Yorker, XXVII (20 Oct 1951) 152 (briefly);

Newsweek, XLVII (9 Apr 1956) 120–2;

Louis Johnson, *Numbers*, I 4 (Oct 1955) 38–40;

Louis MacNeice, *Observer*, 27 Aug 1950, 7;

B. R. McE[lderry]., *Personalist*, XXXVIII (July 1957) 314–15;

Alice Very, *Poet Lore*, LVI (1951) 277–82;

Leonard Unger, *Poetry* (Chicago), LXXX 1 (Apr 1952) 43–51;

Oliver Edwards, *Rann*, no. 9 (summer 1950) 1–3;

Edward C. McAleer, *Richmond News Leader*, 15 June 1956;

Lawrence Ferling, *San Francisco Chronicle*, 25 Nov 1951, 15;

Norman K. Dorn, *San Francisco Chronicle*, 1 May 1959;

B. R. Redman, *Saturday Review of Literature*, XXXIV (21 July 1951) 33 (briefly);

Lucy McIntire, *Savannah Morning News*, 6 May 1956;

Scotsman, 18 Aug 1950;

Richard Murphy, *Spectator*, CLXXXV 6372 (11 Aug 1950) 183;

James Gallagher, *Spirit* (July 1951);

Desmond MacCarthy, *Sunday Times*, 6 Aug 1952;

Time, LVII (21 May 1951) 50, 52;

John Bryson, *Time and Tide*, XXXI (7 Oct 1950) 998–9;

TLS, 2534 (25 Aug 1950) 525–6; *see also* correspondence by R. Auty and others, Part V;

Thomas Cole, *Voices*, CXLVI (Sep–Dec 1951) 48–50;

August Derleth, *Voices*, CLI (Sep–Dec 1956) 44–5;

L. G., *Washington Post*, 8 July 1951.

COLLECTED WORKS IN   Wade 75–82
EIGHT VOLUMES (1908)

Walter de la Mare, *Bookman*, XXXV (Jan 1909) 191–2;
Daily Chronicle, 6 Mar 1909;
Edward Garnett, *English Review*, II 1 (Apr 1909) 148–52;
E. M. D[owden]., *Fortnightly Review*, n.s., LXXXV (1 Feb 1909) 253–70;
A. O'L., *Freeman's Journal*, 2 Jan 1909, 5;
Charles Tennyson, *Quarterly Review*, CCXV 428 (July 1911) 219–43;
E. M. D[owden]., *Saturday Review*, CVI (7 Nov 1908) 577–8 (vols I and II); ibid., CVII (27 Feb 1909) 107, 280 (vols III–VIII);
Lytton Strachey, *Spectator*, CI 4190 (17 Oct 1908) 588–9 (vols I and II).

THE COUNTESS KATHLEEN (1912)   Wade 93

Athenaeum, 4421 (20 July 1912) 71–2;
Illustrated London News, CXLI (20 July 1912) 88.

THE COUNTESS KATHLEEN AND   Wade 6–7
VARIOUS LEGENDS AND LYRICS (1892)

Lionel Johnson, *Academy*, XLII 1065 (1 Oct 1892) 278–9;
Athenaeum, 3402 (7 Jan 1893) 14–16;
Lionel Johnson, *Beltaine*, 1 (May 1899) 10–11;
C. W., *Bookman*, III (Oct 1892) 25–6;
Critic, XXI (9 June 1894) 387 (very briefly);
F. Hugh O'Donnell, *Freeman's Journal*, 1 Apr 1899, 6;
Irish Monthly, XX (1892) 557–8;
Literature, VIII (25 May 1901) 439–41;
George O'Neill, S. J., *New Ireland Review*, XI 4 (June 1899) 246–52;
Outlook, III (22 July 1899) 810–11;
Arthur Symons, *Saturday Review*, LXXXVII (6 May 1899) 553–4;
Max Beerbohm, *Saturday Review*, LXXXVII (13 May 1899) 586–8.

THE CUTTING OF AN AGATE (1919)   Wade 126

T. S. E[liot]., *Athenaeum*, 4653 (4 July 1919) 552–3;
Francis Bickley, *Bookman*, LVI (Aug 1919) 174;
Nation (London), XXV (28 June 1919) 395–6;
Nation and Athenaeum, XXXVII (13 June 1925) 345–6;
TLS, 902 (1 May 1919) 235.

THE DEATH OF SYNGE AND OTHER   Wade 162
PASSAGES FROM AN OLD DIARY (1928)

    Seán O'Faoláin, *Irish Statesman*, XI (Sep 1928) 71–2.

DEIRDRE (Plays for an Irish Theatre, vol. V, 1907)   Wade 69

    Athenaeum, 4171 (5 Oct 1907) 415–16; ibid., 4232 (5 Dec 1908)
       729–30; ibid., 4261 (26 June 1909) 767–8;
    E[dward]. T[homas]., *Bookman*, XXXIII 193 (Oct 1907) 47;
    Daily Chronicle, 28 Sep 1907;
    Francis Bickley, *Irish Review*, II 17 (July 1912) 252–4;
    Henri Ruyssen, *Revue Germanique*, V 1 (Jan–Feb 1909) 123–5.
    See also GWYNN, STEPHEN (Part V).

DISCOVERIES (1907)   Wade 72

    Academy, LXXIV 1873 (28 Mar 1908) 621;
    Athenaeum, 4185 (11 Jan 1908) 41;
    Bookman, XXXIII (Feb 1908) 216–17;
    Daily Chronicle, 18 May 1908.

DRAMATIS PERSONAE (Cuala Press, 1935)   Wade 183

    Dublin Magazine, XI (Apr–June 1936) 67–8;
    Richard Church, *New Statesman and Nation*, XI (14 Mar 1936) 398;
    Old Castle Garden (Mar 1936)
    Spectator, CLVI 5631 (29 May 1936) 998.

DRAMATIS PERSONAE 1896–1902:   Wade 186–7
ESTRANGEMENT, THE DEATH OF
SYNGE, THE BOUNTY OF SWEDEN (1936)

    R., *Belfast News-Letter*, 9 July 1936;
    Booklist, XXXII (July 1936) 319;
    Buffalo Evening News, 29 May 1936;
    Iris Conlay, *Catholic Herald*, 7 Aug 1936;
    C. M., *Catholic World*, CXLIII (Aug 1936) 626–7;
    Christian Century, LIII (15 July 1936) 990;
    V. S. Pritchett, *Christian Science Monitor*, 1 July 1936, Weekly
      Magazine, 11;
    Church of England Newspaper, 5 June 1936;
    Isabel Ackerman, *Cincinnati Enquirer*, 1 May 1936;
    Commonweal, XXIV (24 July 1936) 332;

Cork Examiner, 3 June 1936;
Louis MacNeice, *Criterion*, XVI 62 (Oct 1936) 120–2;
Hugh N. Comfort, *Daily Oklahoman*, 27 Sep 1936;
J. W. Rogers, *Dallas Times Herald*, 12 July 1936;
Clyde Beck, *Detroit News*, 31 May 1936;
Dublin Evening Mail, 22 May and 5 June 1936;
Esquire, VI 2 (Aug 1936) 184–5;
Jonathan Schnell, *Forum*, XCV (June 1936) v;
Glasgow Herald, 18 June 1936;
G. W., *Granta*, XLV (June 1936) 437–8;
B. Ifor Evans, *Guardian*, 19 June 1936;
Hartford Daily Courant, 2 June 1936;
Bess W. Scott, *Houston Post*, 24 May 1936;
Illustrated London News, 20 June 1936;
Donagh MacDonagh, *Ireland Today*, I 2 (July 1936) 75–6;
Walter Starkie, *Irish Independent*, 14 July 1936;
C., *Irish News*, 17 June 1936;
M. J. McM[anus]., *Irish Press*, 2 June 1936;
Osbert Burdett, *John O'London's Weekly*, XXXV (20 June 1936) 421;
Babette Deutsch, *Kansas City Post*, 24 May 1936;
Kansas City Star, 13 May 1936;
Sherard Vines, *Listener*, XVI (1 July 1936) 43;
A., *Liverpool Daily Post*, 29 July 1936;
Austin Clarke, *London Mercury*, XXXIV 200 (June 1936) 169–70;
Los Angeles Times, 17 May 1936;
Geoffrey Grigson, *Morning Post*, 26 May 1936;
Kate Trimble Sharber, *Nashville Banner*, 31 May 1936;
William Troy, *Nation*, CXLII (17 June 1936) 780–1;
Raymond Mortimer, *New Statesman and Nation*, XI (30 May 1936) 861;
Lewis Gannett, *New York Herald Tribune*, 12 May 1936;
Babette Deutsch, *NYHTB*, 17 May 1936, 6;
Kimball Flaccus, *New York Sun*, 15 June 1936;
Horace Reynolds, *NYTB*, 17 May 1936, 1;
Northern Whig, 13 June 1936;
Humbert Wolfe, *Observer*, 14 June 1936;
Una Jeffers, *Pacific Weekly*, 20 July 1936;
Helen E. Haines, *Pasadena Star News*, 6 June 1936;
Morton Dauwen Zabel, *Poetry* (Chicago), XLVIII 5 (Feb 1936) 268–77;

Poetry Review, XXVII 4 (Aug 1936) 317–19;

B. K. H., *Providence Sunday Journal*, 17 May 1936;

Punch, CXC (3 June 1936) 642 (briefly);

Quarterly Review, CCLXVII 529 (July 1936) 185;

Mark Lutz, *Richmond News Leader*, 1 July 1936;

C. McP., *St Louis Post-Dispatch*, 14 June 1936;

Ben Hamilton, *San Francisco Chronicle*, 21 June 1936;

Padraic Colum, *Saturday Review of Literature*, XIV (16 May 1936) 7;

Edwin Muir, *Scotsman*, 28 May 1936;

H. A. Mason, *Scrutiny*, V 3 (Dec 1936) 330–2;

Lawrence J. Zillman, *Seattle Post Intelligencer*, 18 Feb 1937;

Frederick T. Wood, *Sheffield Telegraph*, 25 June 1936;

L. A. G. Strong, *Spectator*, CLVI 5631 (29 May 1936) 998;

E. N. Jenckes, *Springfield Republican*, 16 May 1936;

G. M. Young, *Sunday Times*, 31 May 1936;

Time, 18 May 1936, 83;

Theodora Bosanquet, *Time and Tide*, XVII (13 June 1936) 849;

The Times, 22 May 1936, 19;

TLS, 1790 (23 May 1936) 434;

J. F. Carroll, *Worcester Sunday Telegram*, 17 May 1936;

Kerker Quinn, *Yale Review*, XXVI 1 (Sep 1936) 208–10.

EARLY POEMS AND STORIES   Wade 147–8
(1925; vol. v of the Collected Edition of the Works, 1922–6)

W. P. Ryan, *Bookman*, LXIX (Mar 1926) 323–4;

B. H., *Calendar of Modern Letters*, II (Nov 1925) 210–11;

A. E. (George Russell), *Irish Statesman*, V (Oct 1925) 176–7; correspondence by Neal Gilbayne, Frank O'Connor and Geoffrey Phibbs, ibid. (Nov) 238, 269–70; Frank O'Connor, ibid. (Dec) 429; Seán O'Faoláin (Jan 1926) 558–9; The Editor (George Russell), ibid., 559;

A. E., *Living Age*, 28 Nov 1925, 464–6;

Nation and Athenaeum, XXXVIII 4 (24 Oct 1925) 156;

Edmund Wilson, *New Republic*, XLII (15 Apr 1925) Spring Books Section, 8;

Quarterly Review, CCXLVI 487 (Jan 1926) 217–18;

Charles M. Garnier, *Revue Anglo-Américaine*, III 5 (June 1926) 454–6;

J. B. Priestley, *Saturday Review*, CXL (31 Oct 1925) 374;

E. W. Jones, *Sewanee Review*, XXXIV 4 (Oct–Dec 1926) 492–4;

TLS, 1238 (8 Oct 1925) 652.

ESSAYS (1924; vol. IV of the Collected   Wade 141–2
Edition of the Works, 1922–6)

George Sampson, *Bookman*, LXVI (July 1924) 201–2;
J. Hoops, *Englische Studien*, LVIII 3 (1924) 454–5;
Irish Book Lover, XIV 6 (June 1924) 89;
A. E. (George Russell), *Irish Statesman*, II (June 1924) 397–8;
Nation and Athenaeum, XXXV 13 (28 June 1924) 416;
Edmund Wilson, *New Republic*, XLII (15 Apr 1925) Spring Books
    Section, 8;
New Statesman, XXIII (12 Feb 1924) 414;
Charles M. Garnier, *Revue Anglo-Américaine*, II 5 (June 1925) 448–51;
E. W. Jones, *Sewanee Review*, XXXIV 4 (Oct–Dec 1926) 492–4;
Hugh l'A. Fausset, *Spectator*, CXXXII 5004 (24 May 1924) 844–5;
TLS, 1166 (22 May 1924) 318; correspondence by Henry Festing
    Jones, ibid., 1167 (29 May) 340.

ESSAYS (1931–6; Cuala Press, 1937)   Wade 194

Seán O'Faoláin, *London Mercury*, XXXVII 220 (Feb 1938) 454–5;
Morton Dauwen Zabel, *Southern Review*, V 3 (winter 1939–40) 605–
    8;
TLS, 1877 (22 Jan 1938) 56.

ESSAYS AND INTRODUCTIONS (1961)   Wade 211 T–U

Robert Langbaum, *American Scholar*, XXXI 3 (summer 1962) 454–60;
Patrick J. McCarthy, *Arizona Quarterly*, XIX (autumn 1963) 277–9;
J. M. Richardson, *Birmingham Post*, 14 Mar 1961;
Booklist, LVIII (2 Oct 1961) 88;
Valentin Iremonger, *Catholic Herald*, 30 June 1961;
W. J. Igoe, *Chicago Sunday Tribune*, 9 July 1961, 2;
Horace Reynolds, *Christian Science Monitor*, 22 June 1961, 7;
Church Times, 21 Apr 1961;
Daily Telegraph, 17 Feb 1961;
David Daiches, *Encounter*, XIX 3 (Sep 1962) 71–4;
Evening Herald, 31 Mar 1961;
Donald Davie, *Guardian*, 17 Feb 1961;
Diana Hobby, *Houston Post*, 25 June 1961;
F. J. K., *Irish Independent*, 22 Apr 1961;
Cahir Healy, *Irish News*, 8 Apr 1961;
Austin Clarke, *Irish Times*, 25 Feb 1961;

Richard Church, *John O'London's Weekly*, LXXXIV (16 Feb 1961) 176;

Hugh Kenner, *Jubilee*, IX 10 (Feb 1962) 39–43;

Roger McHugh, *Kilkenny Magazine*, IV (summer 1961) 24–30;

Lloyd W. Griffin, *Library Journal*, LXXXVI (1 Oct 1961) 3285;

Herbert Read, *Listener*, LXV (9 Mar 1961) 459;

Ronald Gaskell, *London Magazine*, n.s., I 3 (June 1961) 89–93;

Richard M. Kain, *Louisville Times*, 6 June 1961;

John Unterecker, *Modern Drama*, IV 3 (Dec 1961) 249–50;

Anne Sweeney, *Nashville Banner*, 30 Jan 1961;

R. F. Brissenden, *Nation* (Sydney), 17 June 1961, 22;

Richard Ellmann, *New Statesman*, LXI (23 June 1961) 1011–12;

Babette Deutsch, *NYHTB*, 6 Aug 1961, 4;

Frank O'Connor, *NYTB*, 2 July 1961, 4;

John Wain, *Observer*, 5 May 1961, 31;

George Watson, *Oxford Magazine*, 4 May 1961, 324;

Charles Tomlinson, *Poetry* (Chicago), XCVIII 4 (July 1961) 263–6;

Peter Dickinson, *Punch*, CCXL (26 Apr 1961) 663 (briefly);

Quadrant, V (autumn 1961) 95;

R. Crinkley, *Richmond News Leader*, 13 Dec 1961;

Alexander M. Buchan, *St Louis Post-Dispatch*, 20 Aug 1961;

Richard W. Lid, *San Francisco Chronicle*, 23 July 1961;

Scotsman, 25 Feb 1961;

Frank Kermode, *Spectator*, CCVI 6927 (31 Mar 1961) 448–9;

A. Norman Jeffares, *Stand*, V 2 (1961) 55–7;

J. I. M. Stewart, *Sunday Telegraph*, 5 Mar 1961;

Raymond Mortimer, *Sunday Times*, 19 Feb 1961, 26;

J. B. Morton, *Tablet*, 8 Apr 1961;

Time, 16 June 1961, 88–90;

John Broadbent, *Time and Tide*, XLII 9 (2 Mar 1961) 335;

TLS, 3077 (17 Feb 1961) 97–8;

H. R. MacCallum, *University of Toronto Quarterly*, XXXII 3 (Apr 1963) 307–13.

ESTRANGEMENT: BEING SOME FIFTY   Wade 150
THOUGHTS FROM A DIARY KEPT BY
WILLIAM BUTLER YEATS IN THE YEAR
NINETEEN HUNDRED AND NINE (1926)

A. E. (George Russell), *Irish Statesman*, VI (Sep 1926) 713–14.

EXPLORATIONS (1962)   Wade 211 Y–Z

Morse Allen, *Daily Courant*, 9 Jan 1963;

Frank Kermode, *New Statesman*, LXIV (21 Sep 1962) 366;

New York Sunday Times, 26 Aug 1962;

Richard Murphy, *Observer*, 7 Oct 1962, 29;

Micheál MacLiammóir, *Spectator*, CCIX 7004 (21 Sep 1962) 403–4;

Studies, LII (spring 1963) 112;

Cyril Connolly, *Sunday Times*, 26 Aug 1962, 21;

Gustav Cross, *Sydney Morning Herald*, 17 Nov 1962;

TLS, 3162 (5 Oct 1962) 778;

H. R. MacCallum, *University of Toronto Quarterly*, XXXII 3 (Apr 1963) 307–13.

FAIRY AND FOLK TALES OF THE   Wade 212
IRISH PEASANTRY (1888)

Athenaeum, 3198 (9 Feb 1889) 174–5;

Irish Monthly, XVI (Nov 1888) 687–8;

Spectator, LXII 3158 (5 Jan 1889) 25 (briefly);

[Oscar Wilde], *The Woman's World* (Feb 1889) 221–2.

FLORENCE FARR, BERNARD SHAW   Wade 327–9
AND W. B. YEATS (1941–6)

Bell, XIII (Oct 1946) 80;

Horace Reynolds, *Christian Science Monitor*, 2 May 1942, Weekly Review, 12;

Gwen John, *Dublin Magazine*, XVIII (Apr–June 1942) 53–4;

Lorna Reynolds, *Dublin Magazine*, XXI (Jan–Mar 1947) 52–3;

B. Ifor Evans, *Guardian*, 3 Feb 1942;

New Statesman and Nation, XXIII (17 Jan 1942) 47;

NYTB, 1 Mar 1942, 9;

Richard Ellmann, *Sewanee Review*, LXIV 1 (winter 1946) 145–51;

Spectator, CLXVIII 5935 (27 Mar 1942) 312 (briefly);

TLS, 2092 (7 Mar 1942) 118.

FOUR PLAYS FOR DANCERS (1921)   Wade 129–30

Booklist, XVIII (Apr 1922) 230;

W. L. R., *Bookman*, LXI (Dec 1921) Supplement, 38, 40;

Padraic Colum, *Dial*, LXXII 3 (Mar 1922) 302–4;

Edmund Wilson, *Freeman*, V (29 Mar 1922) 68;

John Peale Bishop, *Literary Review*, 4 Mar 1922, 465;

Nation, CXIV (10 May 1922) 573;

Nation and Athenaeum, XXX (11 Feb 1922) 730–1; correspondence by Robert N. D. Wilson, ibid. (25 Feb) 793;

S[tark]. Y[oung]., *New Republic*, XXX (15 Mar 1922) 84;

NYTB, 20 Jan 1922, 11;

Outlook, CXXX (19 Apr 1922) 656;

Cloyd Head, *Poetry* (Chicago), XIX 5 (Feb 1922) 288–92;

Saturday Review, CXXXII (3 Dec 1921) 643;

Springfield Republican, 8 Mar 1922, 12;

Theatre Arts Monthly, V 1 (Jan 1922) 79;

TLS, 1039 (15 Dec 1921) 840;

O. W. Firkins, *Yale Review*, XII 1 (Oct 1922) 193–4.

A FULL MOON IN MARCH (1935)   Wade 182

Janet Adam Smith, *Criterion*, XV 60 (Apr 1936) 521–2;

Dublin Magazine, XI (Jan–Mar 1936) 74–5;

Ruth M. D. Wainewright, *English*, I 3 (autumn 1936) 259–60;

Glasgow Herald, 2 Jan 1936;

G. W., *Granta*, XLV (Feb 1936) 237;

Guardian, 30 Dec. 1935;

Irish Independent, 28 Jan 1936;

D. M., *Irish Press*, 10 Dec 1935;

Irish Times, 14 Dec 1935;

John O'London's Weekly, XXXIV 872 (28 Dec 1935) 530 (briefly);

Listener, XV (1 Jan 1936) 41;

Austin Clarke, *London Mercury*, XXXIII 195 (Jan 1936) 341–2;

Geoffrey Grigson, *Morning Post*, 18 Feb 1936;

Northern Whig, 18 Dec 1935;

C. E. Lawrence, *Quarterly Review*, CCLXVI 528 (Apr 1936) 300 (briefly);

M.-L. Cazamian, *Revue Anglo-Américaine*, III 3 (June 1936) 445–6;

Scotsman, 23 Dec 1935;

Michael Roberts, *Spectator*, CLV 5609 (27 Dec 1935) 1078–9;

Time and Tide, XVII (4 Jan 1936) 21 (briefly);

TLS, 1766 (7 Dec 1935) 833;

Hugh l'A. Fausset, *Yorkshire Post*, 19 Feb 1936.

THE GREEN HELMET AND OTHER POEMS (1910–11)	Wade 84–5

Academy, LXXX 2035 (6 May 1911) 547;
Athenaeum, 4347 (18 Feb 1911) 186;
Independent, LXXIII (21 Nov 1912) 1184;
Literary Digest, XLV (23 Nov 1912) 966;
Spectator, CVI 4327 (3 June 1911) 851 (briefly).

THE HERNE'S EGG (1938)	Wade 195

Catholic Bulletin, XXVIII (Mar 1938) 185–6;
Janet Adam Smith, *Criterion*, XVII 68 (Apr 1938) 520–2;
W. R. C., *Dublin Review*, CCII 405 (Apr–June 1938) 387;
M.-L. C[azamian]., *Études Anglaises*, III 1 (Jan–Mar 1939) 66–7;
Charles Powell, *Guardian*, 1 Mar 1938, 7; ibid., 24 Mar;
Seán Ó Meádhra, *Ireland Today*, III 2 (Feb 1938) 183;
George Barker, *Life and Letters To-Day*, XVIII 11 (spring 1938) 173;
Listener, XIX (23 Feb 1938) 431;
Austin Clarke, *London Mercury*, XXXVII 221 (Mar 1938) 551–2;
Austin Clarke, *New Statesman and Nation*, XV (Jan 1938) 178;
Northern Whig, 24 Mar 1938;
H. T. Hunt Grubb, *Poetry Review*, XXIX (July–Aug 1938) 327–30;
C. E. Lawrence, *Quarterly Review*, CCLXXI 537 (July 1938) 163–4;
Scotsman, 28 Feb 1938;
L. A. G. Strong, *Spectator*, CLX 5722 (25 Feb 1938) 330;
Helen Fletcher, *Time and Tide*, XIX (12 Mar 1938) 355;
TLS, 1877 (22 Jan 1938) 56; 1886 (26 Mar) 217.

THE HERNE'S EGG AND OTHER PLAYS (1938)	Wade 196

E. V. Wyatt, *Commonweal*, XXVIII (3 June 1938) 164;
E. L. Walton, *Nation*, CXLVII (9 July 1938) 51–2;
Edmund Wilson, *New Republic*, XCV (29 June 1938) 226;
Babette Deutsch, *NYHTB*, 29 May 1938, 9;
Horace Reynolds, *NYTB*, 29 May 1938, 8;
Paul Dottin, *Revue de France*, yr 19, vol. IV (15 July 1939) 236–49;
Kerker Quinn, *Yale Review*, XXVII 5 (summer 1938) 834–6.

THE HOUR GLASS AND OTHER PLAYS   Wade 52–3
(Plays for an Irish Theatre, vol. II, 1904)

> *Academy*, LXVI 1665 (2 Apr 1904) 383–4;
> *Athenaeum*, 3995 (21 May 1904) 665–6;
> H. W. Boynton, *Atlantic Monthly*, XCIII (May 1904) 712–13;
> *Daily Chronicle*, 8 June 1904;
> *Nation*, LXXIX (18 Aug 1904) 144;
> *Spectator*, XCII 3965 (25 June 1904) 989;
> *Standard*, 13 Apr 1904.

IDEAS OF GOOD AND EVIL (1903)   Wade 46–7

> *Academy*, LXIV 1619 (16 May 1903) 475 (briefly); ibid., 1623 (13 June)
>   589–90; correspondence by A. Clutton-Brock, ibid., 1624 (20
>   June) 617–19;
> *Athenaeum*, 3948 (27 June 1903) 807–8;
> H. W. Boynton, *Atlantic Monthly*, XCII (Oct 1903) 565–9;
> *British Weekly*, 21 May 1903;
> *Guardian*, 19 May 1903;
> *Nation*, LXXVII (16 July 1903) 52;
> *New Ireland*, July 1903;
> *New York Times*, 17 Jan 1903;
> Elizabeth Luther Cary, *New York Times*, 11 July 1908;
> *The Pilot*, 24 Aug 1903;
> *Saturday Review*, XCVI (12 Sep 1903) 334;
> *The Speaker*, VIII 191 (30 May 1903) 213;
> C. K. Shorter, *The Sphere*, 6 June 1903.

IF I WERE FOUR AND TWENTY (1940)   Wade 205

> *Bell*, 1 (Nov 1940) 91, 93;
> A. C., *Dublin Magazine*, XVI (Jan–Mar 1941) 64;
> *TLS*, 2024 (16 Nov 1930) 580.

IRISH FAIRY TALES (1892)   Wade 216

> T. W. Rolleston, *Library Review* (Aug 1892) 342–5.

JOHN SHERMAN AND DHOYA (1891)   Wade 4–5

> *Athenaeum*, 3348 (26 Dec 1891) 859.

THE KING OF THE GREAT CLOCK TOWER (1934–5)
Wade 179–9A

Booklist, XXXI (July 1935) 371;

Boston Evening Transcript, 8 June 1935, 4;

T. M., *Catholic World*, CXLII (Nov 1935) 254;

Horace Reynolds, *Christian Science Monitor*, 17 July 1935, Weekly Magazine, 11;

Dublin Magazine, XI (Jan–Mar 1936) 70–2;

Irish Times, 5 Jan 1935;

Nation, CXLI (7 Aug 1935) 167 (briefly);

Horace Gregory, *New Republic*, LXXXIV (18 Sep 1935) 164–5;

Babette Deutsch, *NYHTB*, 11 Aug 1935, 6;

C. G. P., *NYTB*, 2 June 1935, 2;

Robert Lynd, *News Chronicle*, 1 Feb 1935;

M. D. Z[abel]., *Poetry* (Chicago), XLVI 2 (May 1935) 104–8;

W. R. Benét, *Saturday Review of Literature*, XII (18 May 1935) 20;

I. M. Parsons, *Spectator*, CLIV 5559 (11 Jan 1935) 57;

TLS, 1721 (24 Jan 1935) 37–8.

THE KING'S THRESHOLD AND ON BAILE'S STRAND
Wade 56

(Plays for an Irish Theatre, vol. III, 1904)

Academy, LXVI 1665 (2 Apr 1904) 383–4;

Athenaeum, 3995 (21 May 1904) 665–6;

Daily Chronicle, 8 June 1904;

Monthly Review, XVII (Nov 1904) 157–60;

Nation, LXXIX (18 Aug 1904) 144;

Max Beerbohm, *Saturday Review*, XCVII (9 Apr 1904) 455–7;

Spectator, XCII 3965 (25 June 1904) 989;

Standard, 13 Apr 1904;

See also GWYNN, STEPHEN (Part V).

LAND OF HEART'S DESIRE
Wade 10 etc., 94

(1894, 1903, 1912)

G. Y., *Bookman*, VI (June 1894) 87;

Critic, XXII (7 July 1894) 4 (briefly);

Margaret F. Sullivan, *Dial*, XXX (16 June 1901) 391–2;

Irish Book Lover, III (July 1912) 210;

Lawrence Gilman, *The Lamp*, XXVII (1903) 231–4;

G. K. Chesterton, *Living Age*, CCLXXIV (3 Aug 1912) 317–19;

Frank Fay, *United Irishman* (July 1901);

William Archer, *World*, no. 1031 (4 Apr 1894) 27 (a performance of the play).

LAST POEMS AND PLAYS (1940)   Wade 203–4

Coleman Rosenberger, *Accent*, I 1 (autumn 1934) 56–7;

Atlantic Monthly, CLXVI (Aug 1940) Bookshelf;

Booklist, XXVI (15 June 1940) 396;

Bookmark, II (Jan 1941) 7;

Edmund Blunden, *Book Society News* (Mar 1940) 19;

John Holmes, *Boston Evening Transcript*, 24 June 1940, 11;

The Bulletin, 10 July 1930;

Amos N. Wilder, *Christian Century*, LVII (10 July 1940) 878;

Eric Forbes-Boyd, *Christian Science Monitor*, 13 Apr 1940, Weekly Magazine, 13;

W. B. Ruggles, *Dallas Morning News*, 19 May 1940;

Dublin Evening Mail, 18 Feb 1940;

M. M. Colum, *Forum*, CIII (June 1940) 323;

Indianapolis News, 14 May 1940;

Irish Book Lover, XXVII 4 (July 1940) 238–9;

Francis MacManus, *Irish Press*, 5 Mar 1940;

Irish Times, 9 Mar 1940;

Edward Shanks, *John O'London's Weekly*, XLIII (5 Apr 1940) 14;

John Crowe Ransom, *Kenyon Review*, II 3 (summer 1940) 345–7;

Listener, XXIII (21 Mar 1940) 593–4;

Liverpool Daily Post, 8 Mar 1940;

Alfred Kreymborg, *Living Age*, CCCLVIII (June 1940) 394;

Milton Merlin, *Los Angeles Times*, 7 July 1940;

M. D. Zabel, *Nation*, CLI (12 Oct 1940) 333–5;

Louis MacNeice, *New Republic*, CII (24 June 1940) 862–3;

Babette Deutsch, *NYHTB*, 2 June 1940; 4;

F. W. Dupee, *New York Sun*, 30 May 1940;

J. V. Healy, *NYTB*, 19 May 1940, 1, 16;

Louise Bogan, *New Yorker*, XVI (1 June 1940) 81–2;

L. Aaronson, *Nineteenth Century and After*, CXXVII 759 (May 1940) 634–7;

Observer, 25 Feb 1940;

Pasadena Star News, 22 June 1940;

H. T. Hunt Grubb, *Poetry Review*, XXXI 3 (May–June 1940) 217–26;

Allen Curnow, *Press*, 15 June 1940;

Richard Donovan, *San Francisco Chronicle*, 30 June 1940;
W. H. Auden, *Saturday Review of Literature*, XXII (8 June 1940) 14;
Savannah Morning News, 2 June 1940;
Scotsman, 29 Feb 1940;
F. R. Leavis, *Scrutiny*, VIII 4 (Mar 1940) 437–40;
Seattle Post Intelligencer, 21 July 1940;
F. W. R., *Sewanee Review*, XLIX 3 (Oct–Dec 1941) 568–9;
Andrews Wanning, *Southern Review*, VI 4 (spring 1941) 798–800;
J. J. H[ogan]., *Studies*, XXIX 116 (Dec 1940) 650–3;
Desmond MacCarthy, *Sunday Times*, 16 June 1940, 4;
TCD: A College Miscellany, 15 Feb 1940;
Theatre Arts, XXIV 8 (Aug 1940) 613;
Time, XXXV (3 June 1940) 76, 78–9;
L. A. G. Strong, *Time and Tide*, 9 Mar 1940;
TLS, 1993 (13 Apr 1940) 182, 186;
Times of India, 18 May 1940;
Lawrence Lee, *Virginia Quarterly Review*, XVI 3 (summer 1940) 481–2;
M. M. Colum, *Yale Review*, XXIX 4 (summer 1940) 806–8.

LAST POEMS AND TWO PLAYS (1939)   Wade 200

Stephen Gwynn, *Fortnightly Review*, CXLVI (Oct 1939) 457–8;
Listener, XXII (24 Aug 1939) 394–5;
Frederic Prokosch, *Poetry* (Chicago), LIV 6 (Sep 1939) 338–42;
Morton Dauwen Zabel, *Southern Review*, V 3 (winter 1939–40) 605–8;
Frederic Prokosch, *Spectator*, CLXIII 5797 (4 Aug 1939) 190;
Desmond MacCarthy, *Sunday Times*, 13 Aug 1939;
TLS, 1955 (22 July 1939) 438.

LATER POEMS (1922; vol. II of the   Wade 134–5
Collected Edition of the Works, 1922–6)

Joseph Auslander, *Atlantic Monthly*, CXXXIV (Aug 1924) Bookshelf;
Laurence Binyon, *Bookman*, LXIII (Jan 1923) 196–9;
N. J. O'Conor, *Bookman* (New York), LX (Sep 1924) 91;
Boston Evening Transcript, 17 May 1924, 3;
Willem van Doorn, *English Studies*, V 6 (Dec 1923) 202–5;
J. C. Squire, *London Mercury*, VII 40 (Feb 1923) 431–40;
Nation and Athenaeum, XXXII 4834 (30 Dec 1922) 520–2;

Edmund Wilson, *New Republic*, XLII (15 Apr 1925) Spring Book
Section, 8–10;

J. C. Squire, *Observer*, 26 Nov 1922, 4;

Outlook (New York), CXXXVII (6 Aug 1924) 549;

Saturday Review, LXXXV (20 Jan 1923) 82;

E. W. Jones, *Sewanee Review*, XXXIV 4 (Oct–Dec 1926) 492–4;

TLS, 1093 (28 Dec 1922) 871;

Padraic Colum, *Yale Review*, XIV 2 (Jan 1925) 381–5.

THE LETTERS OF W. B. YEATS (1954–5)   Wade 211 J–K

Hazard Adams, *Accent*, XV 4 (autumn 1955) 234–7;

William Burford, *Baltimore Evening Sun*, 15 Mar 1955;

Booklist, LI (1 Apr 1955) 315;

Harry T. Moore, *Boston Sunday Herald*, 27 Feb 1955;

Buffalo Evening News, 11 June 1955;

Horace Reynolds, *Christian Science Monitor*, 24 Feb 1955, 7;

Mary Lapsley, *Cincinnati Enquirer*, 6 Mar 1955;

Don A. Keister, *Cleveland Plain Dealer*, 27 Mar 1955;

College English, XVI 7 (Apr 1955) 466;

Vivian Mercier, *Commonweal*, LXI (25 Mar 1955) 660–1;

Morse Allen, *Daily Courant*, 27 Feb 1955;

J. P. Pritchard, *Daily Oklahoman*, 27 Mar 1955;

Catherine Perrine, *Dallas Times Herald*, 24 Apr 1955;

Ann F. Wolfe, *Dispatch*, 6 Mar 1955;

W. P. M., *Dublin Magazine*, XXXI (Jan–Mar 1955) 52–3;

Durham Morning Herald, 13 Mar 1955;

H. W. Häusermann, *English Studies*, XXXVI 5 (Oct 1955) 284–6;

Madeleine-L. Cazamian, *Études Anglaises*, VIII 1 (Jan–Mar 1955)
50–60;

Maurice Dolbier, *Harper's Magazine*, CCX (Apr 1955) 98;

Hugh Kenner, *Hudson Review*, VIII 4 (winter 1956) 609–17;

P. P., *Irish Independent*, 2 Oct 1954;

T[erence]. S[mith]., *Irish Writing*, no 28 (Sep 1954) 67–8;

Natalie H. Calderwood, *Kansas City Star*, 28 Mar 1955;

Robert Phelps, *Kenyon Review*, XVII 4 (summer 1955) 495–500;

Kirkus, XXII (Dec 1954) 833;

M. H. Ziprids, *Library Journal*, LXXX (15 Feb 1955) 451;

Herbert Read, *Listener*, LII (7 Oct 1954) 582, 585;

A. N. Jeffares, *Meanjin*, XVI 4 (summer 1955) 565–8;

Kate Trimble Sharber, *Nashville Tennessean*, 6 Mar 1955;

Nation, CLXXXI (9 July 1955) 29;

Seon Manley, *New Leader*, (16 May 1955) 21–2;

Leon Edel, *New Republic*, CXXXII (14 Mar 1955) 21–2;

Louis MacNeice, *New Statesman and Nation*, XLVIII (2 Oct 1954) 398;

Babette Deutsch, *NYHTB*, 6 Mar 1955, 3;

Murray Kempton, *New York Post*, 8 May 1955;

Mary Colum, *NYTB*, 20 Feb 1955, 7;

W. H. Auden, *New Yorker*, XXXI (19 Mar 1955) 142–50;

Peg O'Connor, *News Sentinel*, 5 Mar 1955;

Louis Johnson, *Numbers*, I 4 (Oct 1955) 38–40;

W. R. Rodgers, *Observer*, 6 Feb 1955, 9;

F. W. Dupee, *Partisan Review*, XXIII 1 (winter 1955) 108–11;

Anthony Powell, *Punch*, CCXXVIII (18 May 1955) 620;

H. Marshall McLuhan, *Renascence*, XI 3 (spring 1959) 166;

Edward C. McAleer, *Richmond News Leader*, 12 Aug 1955;

Lewis Vogler, *San Francisco Chronicle*, 10 Apr 1955, 21;

DeLancey Ferguson, *Saturday Review of Literature*, XXVIII (14 May 1955) 12;

Lucy B. McIntire, *Savannah Morning News*, 20 Feb 1955;

Richard Ellmann, *Sewanee Review*, LXIV 1 (winter 1956) 145–51;

Iain Hamilton, *Spectator*, CXCIII 6588 (1 Oct 1954) 416, 418; Sir Compton Mackenzie, ibid., 395;

Cyril Connolly, *Sunday Times*, 9 Jan 1955, 5;

Illtud Evans, *Tablet*, 19 Mar 1955, 279–80;

Michael J. O'Neill, *Thought*, XXX (winter 1955) 618–19;

TLS, 2750 (15 Oct 1954) 656; correspondence by Eileen Souffrin-le-Breton, ibid., 2756 (26 Nov) 759 (Yeats and Mallarmé);

Curtis S. Bradford, *Virginia Quarterly Review*, XXXII 1 (winter 1956) 157–60;

G. C. D., *Washington Post*, 22 May 1955;

John L. Bradley, *Worcester Sunday Telegram*, 20 Feb 1955;

M. Cooke, *Yale Literary Magazine* (May 1955);

Cleanth Brooks, *Yale Review*, n.s., XLIV 4 (June 1955) 618–20.

LETTERS ON POETRY FROM W. B. YEATS TO DOROTHY WELLESLEY (1940)   Wade 325–5A

Winfield Townley Scott, *Accent*, I 4 (summer 1941) 247–50;

Atlantic Monthly, CLXVI (Dec 1940) Bookshelf;

Booklist, XXXVII (1 Dec 1940) 136;

John Holmes, *Boston Evening Transcript*, 11 Nov 1940, 9;

Christian Science Monitor, 2 Nov 1940, 12;

Commonweal, XXXII (18 Oct 1940) 532–3;

Dublin Magazine, XVI (Jan–Mar 1941) 65–6;

E. H. W. Meyerstein, *English*, III 15 (autumn 1940) 136–8;

Basil de Selincourt, *Guardian*, 24 June 1940, 7;

Cleanth Brooks, *Modern Language Notes*, LVII 4 (Apr 1942) 312–13;

M. D. Zabel, *Nation*, CLI (12 Oct 1940) 333;

Allen Tate, *New Republic*, CIII (25 Nov 1940) 730, 732;

Babette Deutsch, *NYHTB*, 13 Oct 1940, 20;

P. M. Jack, *NYTB*, 1 Dec 1940, 20;

Louise Bogan, *New Yorker*, XVI (19 Oct 1940) 107;

Saturday Night, no. 56 (18 Jan 1941) 20;

Dudley Fitts, *Saturday Review of Literature*, XXIII (21 Dec 1940) 20;

W. H. Mellers, *Scrutiny*, IX 2 (Sep 1940) 197–9;

Richard Ellmann, *Sewanee Review*, LXIV 1 (winter 1956) 145–51;

E. N. Jenckes, *Springfield Republican*, 21 Sep 1940, 6;

Desmond MacCarthy, *Sunday Times*, 16 June 1940, 4;

TLS, 2001 (8 June 1940) 272, 282;

Louis Untermeyer, *Yale Review*, XXX 3 (Dec 1941) 378–80.

LETTERS TO THE NEW ISLAND (1934)   Wade 173

Booklist, XXX (Apr 1934) 249;

Boston Evening Transcript, 17 Mar 1934, 1;

R. P., *Christian Science Monitor*, 27 June 1934, Weekly Magazine, 10;

Dublin Magazine, IX (July–Sep 1934) 66–8;

Irish Times, 23 June 1934;

F. W. C. Hersey, *Modern Language Notes*, L 6 (June 1935) 411–12;

Nation, CXXXVIII (14 Mar 1934) 309;

H[orace]. G[regory]., *New Republic*, LXXIX (13 June 1934) 136 (briefly);

Richard Church, *New Statesman*, VIII (4 Aug 1934) 157–8;

E. L. Walton, *NYTB*, 8 Apr 1934, 4;

Padraic Colum, *Saturday Review of Literature*, X (2 June 1934) 722–3;

Springfield Republican, 3 Feb 1934, 8;

Desmond MacCarthy, *Sunday Times*, 17 June 1934;

TLS, 1680 (12 Apr 1934) 259;

Wisconsin Library Bulletin, XXX (June 1934) 136;

Kerker Quinn, *Yale Review*, XXVI 1 (Sep 1936) 208–10.

LITERARY IDEALS IN IRELAND (1899)   Wade 297

[Francis Thompson], *Academy*, LVII 1417 (1 July 1899) 8–10;
Fiona Macleod (William Sharp), *Bookman*, XVI (Aug 1899) 136–7;
Daily Chronicle, 29 July 1899;
Literature, V 90 (8 July 1899) 9.

MOSADA (1886)   Wade 1

K[atharine]. T[ynan]., *Irish Monthly*, XV (Mar 1887) 166–7.

MYTHOLOGIES (1959)   Wade 211 P–Q

G. B. Saul, *Arizona Quarterly*, XVI (spring 1960) 90–2;
Gilbert Thomas, *Birmingham Post*, 24 Mar 1959;
Herbert Kenney, *Boston Sunday Globe*, 26 July 1959;
Edward Wagerknecht, *Boston Sunday Herald*, 2 Aug 1959;
James Reaney, *Canadian Forum*, XXXIX (June 1959) 64;
Cape Times, 7 May 1959;
Richard Ellmann, *Chicago Sunday Tribune*, 2 Aug 1959, 2;
William B. Ready, *Critic*, XVIII (Oct–Nov 1959) 50;
Anthony Powell, *Daily Telegraph*, 17 Apr 1959;
Jay McCormick, *Detroit News*, 16 Aug 1959;
René Fréchet, *Études Anglaises*, XIV 1 (Jan–Mar 1961) 36–7;
Herbert Kenney, *Indianapolis News*, 22 Aug 1959;
Austin Clarke, *Irish Times*, 28 Mar 1959;
Cahir Healy, *Irish Times*, 29 Aug 1959;
Kirkus, XXVII (1 May 1959) 338;
Burton A. Robie, *Library Journal*, LXXXIV (15 June 1959) 2065;
R. C. B., *Nashville Tennessean*, 6 Sep 1959;
Eric Gillett, *National and English Review*, CLII (June 1959) 234;
T. R. Henn, *New Statesman*, LVII (11 Apr 1959) 518–19;
Babette Deutsch, *NYHTB*, 23 Aug 1959, 8;
Vivian Mercier, *NYTB*, 2 Aug 1959, 4;
Leslie Hansom, *New York World Telegram*, 10 Aug 1959;
New Yorker, XXXV (31 Oct 1959) 207 (briefly);
Rayner Heppenstall, *Observer*, 15 Mar 1959, 22;
B. R. McE[lderry]., *Personalist*, XLI 3 (July 1960) 402 (briefly);
Vincent Buckley, *Quadrant*, IV (winter 1960) 90–1;
William Hogan, *San Francisco Chronicle*, 30 July 1959, 33;
Padraic Colum, *Saturday Review*, XLII (1 Aug 1959) 16–17;
Malcolm Bell, *Savannah Morning News*, 20 Sep 1959;

Scotsman, 25 Apr 1959;
Donat O'Donnell, *Spectator*, CCII 6829 (22 May 1959) 736;
James McAuley, *Sydney Morning Herald*, 30 May 1959;
James Reeves, *Time and Tide*, XL 18 (2 May 1959) 508.

NEW POEMS (Cuala Press, 1938)   Wade 197

Winfield Townley Scott, *Poetry* (Chicago), LIII 2 (Nov 1938) 84–8;
Morton Dauwen Zabel, *Southern Review*, V 3 (winter 1939–40) 605–8.

NINE ONE-ACT PLAYS (1937)   Wade 190

Madeleine-L. Cazamian, *Études Anglaises*, II 1 (Jan–Mar 1938) 65–6;
T. C. M[urray]., *Irish Press*, 13 July 1937.

OCTOBER BLAST (Cuala Press, 1927)   Wade 156

A. E. (George Russell), *Irish Statesman*, VIII (Aug 1927) 597–8;
Padraic Colum, *Saturday Review of Literature*, IV (Oct 1927) 206.

ON THE BOILER (Cuala Press, 1939)   Wade 201–2

Stephen Spender, *New Statesman*, XVIII (11 Nov 1939) 686–7;
TLS, 1968 (21 Oct 1939) 612.

THE OXFORD BOOK OF   Wade 250–1
MODERN VERSE (1936)

R. Hillyer, *Atlantic Monthly*, CLIX (Mar 1937) Bookshelf;
Booklist, XXXIII (Jan 1937) 150;
John Holmes, *Boston Evening Transcript*, 26 Dec 1936, 2;
J. J. R., *Catholic World*, CXLV (Apr 1937) 113–14;
Frank Swinnerton, *Chicago Daily Tribune*, 19 Dec 1936, 16;
Horace Reynolds, *Christian Science Monitor*, 10 Feb 1936, Weekly
    Magazine, 6;
P. Crowley, *Commonweal*, XXV (4 Dec 1936) 163–4;
Karl Arns, *Englische Studien*, LXXII 1 (Oct 1937) 136–8;
Laurence Binyon, *English*, I 4 (summer 1937) 339–40;
Frederick T. Wood, *English Studies*, XIX 4 (Aug 1937) 187–8;
Stephen Gwynn, *Fortnightly Review*, CXLI (Feb 1937) 237–9;
Basil de Selincourt, *Guardian*, 27 Nov 1936, 7;
M. J. McM[anus]., *Irish Press*, 1 Dec 1936;
G. M. Young, *London Mercury*, XXXV 206 (Dec 1936) 112–22; corre-
    spondence by A. C. Boyd, ibid., 207 (Jan 1937) 314;

R. Hillyer, *Modern Language Notes*, LII 12 (Dec 1937) 618–19;
Eda Lou Walton, *Nation*, CLXIII (5 Dec 1936) 663, 665;
National Review, CVIII (Feb 1937) 261–2;
Malcolm Cowley, *New Republic*, LXXXIX (16 Dec 1936) 221–2;
G. W. Stonier, *New Statesman and Nation*, XII (5 Dec 1936) 940, 942;
Babette Deutsch, *NYHTB*, 13 Dec 1936, 9;
Margaret Widdemer, *NYTB*, 13 Dec 1936, 2;
Notes and Queries, CLXXII (2 Jan 1937) 16;
Basil de Selincourt, *Observer*, 22 Nov 1936, 5;
Morton Dauwen Zabel, *Poetry* (Chicago), XLIX 5 (Feb 1937) 273–8;
Joseph Hone, *Poetry* (Chicago), XLIX 6 (Mar 1937) 332–6;
W. R. Benét, *Saturday Review of Literature*, XV (21 Nov 1936) 22;
H. A. Mason, *Scrutiny*, V 4 (Mar 1937) 449–51;
F. O. Matthiessen, *Southern Review*, II 4 (spring 1937) 815–27;
John Hayward, *Spectator*, CLVII 5656 (20 Nov 1936) Supplement, 3; correspondence by W. J. Turner, ibid., 5657 (27 Nov) 950; W. B. Yeats and I. M. Parsons, ibid., 5658 (4 Dec) 995;
Springfield Republican, 18 Oct 1936, 7; ibid., 17 Jan 1937, 7;
TLS, 1816 (21 Nov 1936) 957.

A PACKET FOR EZRA POUND (1929)   Wade 163

Commonweal, X (1929) 512–23;
A. E. (George Russell), *Irish Statesman*, XIII (Sep 1929) 11–12;
Living Age, 1 Oct 1929, 186–8;
Seán O'Faoláin, *Nation*, CXXIX (4 Dec 1929) 681–2.

PER AMICA SILENTIA LUNAE (1918)   Wade 120–1

American Review of Reviews, LVII (May 1918) 555;
Athenaeum, 4628 (Apr 1918) 196–7;
Bookman, LIV (May 1918) 74;
Edward Shanks, *Dial*, LXIV (28 Mar 1918) 286–7;
[T. S. Eliot], *Egoist*, V 6 (June–July 1918) 87 (briefly);
Nation, CVI (21 Mar 1918) 326;
NYTB, 19 May 1918, 236;
Outlook, CXVIII (20 Mar 1918) 456;
Springfield Republican, 2 June 1918, 15;
Katharine Tynan, *Studies*, VII (Mar 1918) 188–9;
TLS, 838 (7 Feb 1918) 66.

PLAYS AND CONTROVERSIES (1923–4)   Wade 139–40

W. P. Ryan, *Bookman*, LXV (Mar 1924) 310;

AE (G. W. Russell), *Irish Statesman* I 17 (5 Jan 1924) 534;

Edmund Wilson, *New Republic*, XLII (15 Apr 1925) Spring Book
    Section, 8;

F. L. Lucas, *New Statesman*, XXII (8 Mar 1924) 634;

E. W. Jones, *Sewanee Review*, XXXIV 4 (Oct–Dec 1926) 492–4;

TLS, 1147 (10 Jan 1924) 20.

PLAYS FOR AN   Wade 44–5, 52–3, 56, 69, 262
IRISH THEATRE (1903–7)
See under individual volumes, viz.:

    I. *Where There Is Nothing* (1903)
   II. *The Hour Glass and Other Plays* (1904)
       (*The Hour Glass, Cathleen ni Houlihan, The Pot of Broth*)
  III. *The King's Threshold and On Baile's Strand*
[IV. J. M. Synge, *The Well of Saints*]
   V. *Deirdre* (1907).

PLAYS FOR AN IRISH THEATRE (1911)   Wade 92

(*The Green Helmet, On Baile's Strand, The King's Threshold, The
Shadowy Waters, The Hour Glass, Cathleen ni Houlihan*)
Athenaeum, 4394 (13 Jan 1912) 51–2;

Darrell Figgis, *Bookman*, XLI (Mar 1912) 304–5;

C[harles]. T[ennyson]., *Contemporary Review*, CI 558 (June 1912)
    902–3;

English Review, XI 3 (May 1912) 330–1;

New York Drama, no. 66 (6 Dec 1911) 6;

TLS, 520 (28 Dec 1911) 540.

PLAYS IN PROSE AND VERSE (1922–4;   Wade 136–7
vol. II of the Collected Edition of the Works, 1922–6)

Laurence Binyon, *Bookman*, LXIII (Jan 1923) 196–9;

Willem van Doorn, *English Studies*, V 6 (Dec 1923) 202–5;

Nation and Athenaeum, XXXII (30 Dec 1922) 520–2;

Edmund Wilson, *New Republic*, XLII (15 Apr 1925) Spring Book
    Section, 8, 10;

H. O. Meredith, *New Statesman*, XX (27 Jan 1923) 481–3;

J. C. Squire, *Observer*, 26 Nov 1922, 4;

Saturday Review, CXXXV (20 Jan 1923) 82;
E. W. Jones, *Sewanee Review*, XXXIV 4 (Oct–Dec 1926) 492–4;
TLS, 1093 (28 Dec 1922) 871;
Padraic Colum, *Yale Review*, XIV 2 (Jan 1925) 381–5.

POEMS (1895)   Wade 15–16

   Ernest Rhys, *Academy*, XLIX 1242 (22 Feb 1896) 151–2;
Blackwood's Magazine, CLIX 967 (May 1896) 719–20;
A. M., *Bookman*, IX (Dec 1895) 94–5;
Bookman (New York), II (Jan 1896) 423–4;
Catholic World, LXII (Jan 1896) 565;
Critic, XXIV (Nov 1895) 284; ibid. (Dec) 426;
Dial, XX (1 Apr 1896) 207;
Spectator, LXXVI 3526 (25 Jan 1896) 136–7;
The Times, 25 Oct 1895, 14.

POEMS (1899)   Wade 17

   [Francis Thompson], *Academy*, LVI 1409 (6 May 1899) 501–2;
Athenaeum, 3738 (17 June 1899) 747–8;
[Francis Thompson], *Daily Chronicle*, 26 May 1899 (with a cartoon on
   the Celtic Movement, entitled 'Celtades Ambo: Mr Yeats and
   Mr Martyn', by Max Beerbohm);
Literature, IV 85 (3 June 1899) 565–6;
Dora M. Jones, *London Quarterly Review*, XCIV, n.s. iv (July 1900) 61–
   70;
Outlook (London), III (22 July 1899) 810–11;
[Arthur Symons], *Saturday Review*, LXXXVII (6 May 1899) 553–4.

POEMS (1901)   Wade 18

   Academy, LX 1514 (11 May 1901) 409–10;
Athenaeum, 3880 (8 Mar 1902) 298–300;
Current Literature, XXXI (Aug 1901) 244–5;
Literature, VIII 188 (25 May 1901) 439–41;
Quarterly Review, CXCV 390 (Apr 1902) 444–9;
Spectator, LXXXVI 3804 (25 May 1901) 773–4.

POEMS (1904)   Wade 19

   Geraldine E. Hodgson, *Contemporary Review*, XCVIII (Sep 1910)
   332–8;

Charles Johnston, *North American Review*, CLXXXVII (Apr 1908) 614–18.

POEMS 1899–1905 (1906) Wade 64

Athenaeum, 4129 (15 Dec 1906) 770;
H. C. Beeching, *Bookman*, XXXI (Nov 1906) 74–5;
E. T., *Daily Chronicle*, 1 Jan 1907;
Edinburgh Review, CCIX 427 (Jan 1909) 94–118;
Saturday Review, CIII (16 Feb 1907) 206;
Spectator, XCVII 4093 (8 Dec 1906) 931;
TLS, 257 (14 Dec 1906) 414;
T.P.'s Weekly, VIII (2 Nov 1906) 556.

POEMS (1908) Wade 20

Edinburgh Review, CCIX 427 (Jan 1909) 94–118;
T.P.'s Weekly, XII (10 July 1908) 40.

POEMS (1912) Wade 99

Academy, LXXXIV 2122 (4 Jan 1913) 6–7;
Edward Thomas, *Poetry and Drama*, 1 1 (Mar 1913) 53–6.

POEMS (1927) Wade 153

New Statesman, XXIX (16 Apr 1927) 17.

THE POETICAL WORKS Wade 65, 71
IN TWO VOLUMES (vol. I, 1906; vol. II, 1907)

Ferris Greenslet, *Atlantic Monthly*, C (Dec 1907) 850;
Independent, LXXIII (10 Oct 1912) 854;
Nation, LXXXIV (10 Jan 1907) 34 (vol. I);
Nation, XCV (17 Oct 1912) 365;
Bliss Carman, *New York Times*, 2 Feb 1907, 68;
Louise Collier Willcox, *North American Review*, CLXXXVI 622 (Sep 1907) 92–4; Charles Johnston, ibid., CLXXXVII 629 (Apr 1908) 614–18;
Outlook, LXXXV (26 Jan 1907) 238; ibid., LXXXVII (9 Nov 1907) 544;
Jessie B. Rittenhouse, *Putnam's Monthly*, II (Apr 1907) 118; ibid., III (Dec 1907) 363–4.

REPRESENTATIVE IRISH TALES (1891) Wade 215

T. W. Rolleston, *Academy*, XL 1014 (10 Oct 1891) 306–7;
Irish Monthly, XIX (July 1891) 378–9.

RESPONSIBILITIES (Cuala Press, 1914)   Wade 110

   Ezra Pound, *Poetry* (Chicago), IV 2 (May 1914) 64–9.

RESPONSIBILITIES (1916)   Wade 115–16

   American Review of Reviews, LIV (Dec 1916) 675;
   Athenaeum, 4611 (Nov 1916) 529;
   W. S. B., *Boston Evening Transcript*, 6 Dec 1916, 4;
   Irish Book Lover, VIII (Dec 1916–Jan 1917) 60–1;
   Nation (London), XX 4 (28 Oct 1916) 150, 152;
   E[zra]. P[ound]., *Poetry* (Chicago), IX 3 (Dec 1916) 150–1;
   Saturday Review, CXXII 11 (Nov 1916) 460–1;
   C[athoir]. O' B[aonain]., *Studies*, VI (Mar 1917) 154–6;
   TLS, 770 (19 Oct 1916) 499.

REVERIES OVER CHILDHOOD   Wade 111–13
AND YOUTH (1915–16)

   American Review of Reviews, LIII (June 1916) 764;
   Athenaeum, 4611 (Nov 1916) 529;
   Dial, LXI (15 July 1916) 68;
   Independent, LXXXVII (24 July 1916) 130;
   Irish Book Lover, VIII 5–6 (Dec 1916–Jan 1917) 59–60;
   Literary Digest, LIII (9 Sep 1916) 621;
   Nation (London), XX 4 (28 Oct 1916) 150, 152;
   New Republic, VII (24 June 1916) 202;
   NYTB, 20 Aug 1916, 328;
   Poetry (Chicago), XII 1 (April 1918) 51;
   Poetry Review, I (July 1916) 45;
   Saturday Review, CXXII (4 Nov 1916) Supplement, 5;
   Spectator, CXVII 4615 (9 Dec 1916) 738;
   TLS, 770 (19 Oct 1916) 499;
   Barton Blake, *Yale Review*, n.s., VI (Jan 1917) 410–12.

SAMHAIN (1901–4)   Wade 227–30

   Academy, LXIII 1595 (29 Nov 1902) 566;
   Quarterly Review, CXCV 390 (Apr 1902) 444–9;
   TLS, 156 (6 Jan 1905) 5.

THE SECRET ROSE (1897)   Wade 21–2

   [Francis Thompson], *Academy*, LI 1304 (1 May 1897) 467; ibid., 1311
      (19 June) 638;

Athenaeum, 3630 (22 May 1897) 671;

A. M., *Bookman*, XII (May 1897) 36–7;

Bookman (New York), VI (Oct 1897) 152–4;

Critic, n.s., XXVIII (27 Nov 1897) 320;

George Moore, *Daily Chronicle*, 24 Apr 1897;

Dial, XXIV (16 Apr 1898) 266–7;

New Ireland Review, VII (May 1897) 182–3;

Saturday Review, LXXXIII (10 Apr 1897) Supplement, 365;

Speaker, 8 May 1897; reply by Yeats, ibid., 18 May (reprinted in *Letters of W. B. Yeats*, ed. Allan Wade, p. 285);

Spectator, LXXIX 3603 (17 July 1897) 82–3.

SELECTED POEMS (1921)   Wade 128

Padraic Colum, *Dial*, LXXI 4 (Oct 1922) 464–8;

North American Review, CCXV (Mar 1922) 426–7;

Herbert Gorman, *Outlook*, CXXX (19 Apr 1922) 655–6.

SELECTED POEMS (1929)   Wade 165

Wilfrid Gibson, *Bookman*, LXXVII (Jan 1930) 227–8;

Y. O., *Irish Statesman*, XIII (Nov 1929) 191–2;

Seán O'Faoláin, *New Criterion*, IX 36 (Apr 1930) 523–8;

A. Brulé, *Revue Anglo-Américaine*, VIII 3 (Feb 1931) 256–66.

A SELECTION FROM THE LOVE POETRY   Wade 106
OF W. B. YEATS (1913)

Athenaeum, 4476 (9 Aug 1913) 131 (briefly).

SENATE SPEECHES OF   Wade 211 R–S
W. B. YEATS (1960–1)

Sarah Youngblood, *Books Abroad*, XXXV (summer 1961) 292;

Christian Science Monitor, 12 Jan 1961, 7;

Donald Davie, *Guardian*, 22 Dec 1961, 8;

A. T., *Irish Independent*, 3 Feb 1962;

Lloyd W. Griffin, *Library Journal*, LXXXV (1 Nov 1960) 3988;

T. R. Henn, *Listener*, LXVI (21 Dec 1961) 1084;

Vivian Mercier, *Nation*, CXCI (10 Dec 1960) 460–1;

Richard Ellmann, *New Statesman*, LXII (8 Dec 1961) 887–8; correspondence by William Empson, ibid. (29 Dec) 989; E. McLysaght and Richard Ellmann, ibid., LXIII (19 Jan 1962) 85;

A. Norman Jeffares, *Poetry* (Chicago), XCVIII 4 (July 1961) 253–6;

Joseph O'Rourke, *Quarterly Journal of Speech*, XLVII 3 (Oct 1961) 318;
Frank O'Connor, *Reporter*, XXIII (Dec 1960) 44;
W. B. Stanford, *Review of English Literature*, IV 3 (July 1963) 71–80;
K. R. E. Dobbs, *Saturday Night*, 17 Mar 1962, 35–6;
Robert Speaight, *Tablet*, LXI (9 Dec 1961) 1176;
TLS, 3121 (22 Dec 1961) 916.

THE SHADOWY WATERS   Wade p. 359

(*North American Review*, May 1900)
Francis Thompson, *Academy*, LVIII 1464 (26 May 1900) 439–40.

THE SHADOWY WATERS (1900–1)   Wade 30–2

Academy, LX 1499 (26 Jan 1901) 81–2;
Athenaeum, 3820 (19 Jan 1901) 39;
Bookman, XIX (Mar 1901) 196;
Dial, XXXI (1 Oct 1901) 329;
Independent, LIII (22 Aug 1901) 1988–90;
Literature, VIII 169 (12 Jan 1901) 34 (briefly);
Nation, LXXIII (22 Aug 1901) 152–3;
Saturday Review, XC (29 Dec 1900) 824–5;
William Norman Guthrie, *Sewanee Review*, IX 3 (July 1901) 328–31;
Standard, 13 Aug 1901.

SOPHOCLES' KING OEDIPUS (1928)   Wade 160–1

Contemporary Review, CXXXIII (May 1928) 673–5;
TLS, 1399 (22 Nov 1928) 876.

STORIES OF MICHAEL ROBARTES   Wade 167
AND HIS FRIENDS (1931)

TLS, 1573 (24 Mar 1932) 214.

STORIES OF RED HANRAHAN (1904)   Wade 59

Academy, LXIX 1733 (22 July 1905) 759;
Athenaeum, 4101 (2 June 1906) 667 (briefly).

STORIES OF RED HANRAHAN AND   Wade 157
THE SECRET ROSE (1927)

Y. O., *Irish Statesman*, IX 15 (17 Dec 1927) 354;
TLS, 1349 (8 Dec 1927) 929.

STORIES OF RED HANRAHAN,   Wade 104–5
THE SECRET ROSE, ROSA ALCHEMICA
(1913–14)

   American Review of Reviews, L (July 1914) 121;
   Athenaeum, 4453 (5 Apr 1913) 382 (briefly);
   Dial, LVII (16 Aug 1914) 110;
   Independent, LXXIX (6 July 1914) 29;
   Nation, XCVIII (30 Apr 1914) 501.

SYNGE AND THE IRELAND   Wade 88
OF HIS TIME (1911)

   Academy, LXXXI 2058 (14 Oct 1911) 485–6; correspondence by M. P.,
     ibid., 2059 (21 Oct) 522–3;
   Athenaeum, 4374 (26 Aug 1911) 240–1;
   NYTB, 17 Sep 1911, 556.

THE TABLES OF THE LAW   Wade 25
AND THE ADORATION OF THE MAGI (1904)

   Daily Chronicle, 15 Aug 1904.

THE TEN PRINCIPAL UPANISHADS (1937)   Wade 252

   M. D., *Irish Independent,* 2 Apr 1937;
   Morton Dauwen Zabel, *New Republic,* XCIII (22 Dec 1937) 206;
   Horace Reynolds, *NYTB,* 30 Jan 1938, 3, 20;
   Stanley J. Kunitz, *Poetry* (Chicago), LI 4 (Jan 1938) 216–18;
   TLS, 1842 (22 May 1937) 393.

THREE THINGS (1929)   Wade 166

   Y. O., *Irish Statesman,* XIII (Nov 1929) 191–2;
   TLS, 1456 (26 Dec 1929) 1095.

THE TOWER (1928)   Wade 158–9

   Annual Register, 1928, Part II, 30 (*see* Part III);
   Booklist, XXV (Oct 1928) 22;
   R. Ellis Roberts, *Bookman,* LXXIV (Apr 1928) 42–3;
   Boston Evening Transcript, 11 Aug 1928, 3;
   Seán O'Faoláin, *Commonweal,* IX (1928) 751;
   John Gould Fletcher, *Criterion,* VIII 30 (Sep 1928) 131–2;

John Eglinton (W. K. Magee), *Dial*, LXXXVI 1 (Jan 1929) 62–5;
Stephen Gwynn, *Fortnightly Review*, CXXIII 736 (Apr 1928) 561–3;
F. R. H., *Irish Statesman*, X (Apr 1928) 112–13;
Living Age, CCCIV (15 Apr 1928) 747;
E. G. Pritchett, *London Mercury*, XVIII 106 (Aug 1928) 433–4;
Theodore Spencer, *Nation and Athenaeum*, XLIII (21 Apr 1928) 81;
Robert Hillyer, *New Adelphi*, n.s., III 1 (Sep–Nov 1929) 78–80;
New Statesman, XXX (7 Apr 1928) 829;
Theodore Spencer, *New Republic*, LVI (10 Oct 1928) 219–20;
J. D. Tasker, *Outlook*, CL (19 Sep 1928) 831;
Horace Gregory, *Poetry* (Chicago), XXXIII 1 (Oct 1928) 41–4;
Quarterly Review, CCL 406 (Apr 1928) 424 (briefly);
A. Brulé, *Revue Anglo-Américaine*, V 6 (Aug 1928) 570–1;
Humbert Wolfe, *Saturday Review*, CXLVII (25 Feb 1929) 225;
Richard Church, *Spectator*, CXL 5201 (3 Mar 1928) 324;
Naomi Royde-Smith, *Time and Tide*, IX (22 June 1928) 609–10 (briefly);
TLS, 1361 (1 Mar 1928) 146;
G. R. Stewart, *University of California Chronicle*, XXX (Oct 1928) 484–5.

THE TREMBLING OF THE VEIL — Wade 133
(Privately Printed, 1922)

Laurence Binyon, *Bookman*, LXIII (Jan 1923) 196–9;
S. M. Ellis, *Fortnightly Review*, CXIII 676 (1 Apr 1923) 690–5; correspondence, ibid., CXIV 679 (2 July) 163;
Nation and Athenaeum, XXXII (30 Dec 1922) 520–2;
TLS, 1088 (23 Nov 1922) 761.

TRIBUTE TO THOMAS DAVIS (1947) — Wade 208

Dublin Magazine, XXII (Oct–Dec 1947) 68.

TWO PLAYS FOR DANCERS (Cuala Press, 1919) Wade 123

Ernest A. Boyd, *Dial*, LXVII 2 (26 July 1919) 53–5;
A. C., *Irish Statesman*, I (Oct 1919) 438–9 (*The Dreaming of the Bones*);
Nation, CVIII (Apr 1919) 20–1.

THE UNICORN FROM THE STARS AND OTHER PLAYS (1908)   Wade 73

Dial, XLV (16 Oct 1908) 255–6;

Nation, LXXXVI (11 June 1908) 540;

New York Times, 11 Apr 1908, 217.

THE VARIORUM EDITION OF THE POEMS (1957)   Wade 211 N

George Brandon Saul, Arizona Quarterly, XIII (1957) 373;

Marion Witt, Assembly, XVII 2 (summer 1958) 23;

Horace Reynolds, Christian Science Monitor, 31 Oct 1957, 11;

College English, XIX (Mar 1958) 273;

Frank Kermode, Encounter, X 6 (June 1958) 76–8;

Peter Ure, English Studies, XLI 4 (Aug 1960) 281–3;

W. J. Harvey, Essays in Criticism, IX 3 (July 1959) 287–99;

Thomas Parkinson, Kenyon Review, XX 1 (winter 1958) 154–9;

Louis MacNeice, London Magazine, V 12 (Dec 1958) 69–75;

M. L. Rosenthal, Nation, CLXXXVI (5 Apr 1958) 298–9;

F. A. C. Wilson, New Statesman, LV (1 Mar 1958) 273; NYHTB, 17 Dec 1957, 12;

Horace Gregory, NYTB, 22 Dec 1957, 5, 18; correspondence, ibid., 26 Jan 1958, 24;

Edwin Muir, Observer, 30 Mar 1958, 16;

Andrew G. Hoover, Quarterly Journal of Speech, XLIV 1 (Feb 1958) 90–1;

Winfield Townley Scott, Saturday Review of Literature, XL (7 Dec 1957) 47–50;

Curtis Bradford, Sewanee Review, LXVI 4 (autumn 1958) 668–78;

R. Schoeck, Spirit, XXV (May 1958) 56–8;

George Johnston, Theatre Arts Monthly Review, no. 11 (1959) 97–102;

TLS, 2923 (7 Mar 1958) 126; correspondence by R. W. Chapman, ibid., 2926 (28 Mar) 169; J. C. Bryce, 2929 (18 Apr) 209; Katherine Haynes Gatch, 2934 (23 May) 283;

James Reaney, University of Toronto Quarterly, XVIII 2 (Jan 1959) 203–4;

Iain Fletcher, Victorian Studies, II 1 (Sep 1958) 72–5;

F. D. Reeve, Voices, no. 166 (May–Aug 1958) 35–7.

A VISION (1926) Wade 149

Catholic Bulletin, XVI (Mar 1926) 242–52 *passim* (reply to following
    article);
A. E. (George Russell), *Irish Statesman*, V (Feb 1926) 714–16;
Edmund Wilson, *New Republic*, LVII (16 Jan 1929) 249–51;
TLS, 1266 (22 Apr 1926) 296.

A VISION (1937) Wade 191–2

John Holmes, *Boston Evening Transcript*, 23 Apr 1938, 2;
J. Bronowski, *Cambridge Review*, LIX 1440 (19 Nov 1937) 113;
Catholic Herald, 13 Dec 1937;
Christian Century, LV (23 Feb 1938) 242;
Church of Ireland Gazette, 4 Feb 1938;
Michael Williams, *Commonweal*, XXVII (25 Mar 1938) 611;
Stephen Spender, *Criterion*, XVII 68 (Apr 1938) 356–7;
M.-L. Cazamian, *Études Anglaises*, II 3 (July–Sep 1938) 315;
M. M. Colum, *Forum*, XCIX (Apr 1938) 213–15;
Illustrated London News, 22 Jan 1938;
R[oibeárd]. Ó F[aracháin]., *Irish Independent*, 2 Nov 1937;
C. E., *Irish News*, 8 Nov 1937;
Thomas Good, *Life and Letters Today*, XVII 10 (winter 1937) 168–9
    (briefly);
Listener, XVIII (8 Dec 1937) 1281;
O[liver]. E[dwards]., *Liverpool Daily Post*, 9 Nov 1937;
Seán O'Faoláin, *London Mercury*, XXXVII 217 (Nov 1937) 69–70;
Eda Lou Walton, *Nation*, CLXVII 2 (9 July 1928) 51–2;
New English Weekly, 20 Jan 1938, 291–2;
Edmund Wilson, *New Republic*, XCIV (20 Apr 1938) 339;
New Statesman and Nation, XV (22 Jan 1938) 140;
Babette Deutsch, *NYHTB*, 8 May 1938, 16;
Horace Reynolds, *NYTB*, 13 Mar 1938, 2;
R. C. Bald, *Philosophical Review*, XLVIII (Mar 1939) 239;
H. T. Hunt Grubb, *Poetry Review*, XXIX 2 (Mar–Apr 1938) 123–40;
Quarterly Review, CCLXX 535 (Jan 1938) 183 (briefly);
R. W. Benét, *Saturday Review of Literature*, XVII (12 Mar 1938) 19;
Edwin Muir, *Scotsman*, 18 Oct 1937;
Sheffield Daily Telegraph, 16 Dec 1937;
Michael Roberts, *Spectator*, CLIX 5708 (19 Nov 1937) Supplement, 14;
Charles Williams, *Time and Tide*, XVIII (4 Dec 1937) 1675–6;
Kerker Quinn, *Yale Review*, XXVII 4 (summer 1938) 834–6.

A VISION (1956–62) Wade 211 M

Arthur M. Sampley, *Dallas Morning News*, 21 Oct 1956;

Sr M. Camillus, *The Globe*, 7 June 1956;

Denis Donoghue, *Guardian*, 11 Jan 1963, 5;

Kate Trimble Sharber, *Nashville Tennessean*, 10 June 1956;

M. L. Rosenthal, *Nation*, CLXXXII (23 June 1956) 533–5;

Newsweek, XLVII 15 (9 Apr 1956) 120–2;

William H. Davenport, *Personalist*, XXXVIII 3 (July 1957) 315;

Norman K. Dorn, *San Francisco Chronicle*, 10 May 1959;

Lucy B. McIntire, *Savannah Morning News*, 27 May 1956;

James Gallagher, *Spirit*, XXIII (Nov 1956) 154–5.

THE WANDERINGS OF OISIN (1889) Wade 2

J. Todhunter, *Academy*, XXXV 882 (30 Mar 1889) 216–17;

Atalanta, II 8 (May 1889) 552;

Dublin Evening Mail, 13 Feb 1889 [4];

Freeman's Journal, 1 Feb 1889, 2;

Fr Matthew Russell, *Irish Monthly*, XVII 188 (Feb 1889) 109–10. *See also* Rosa Mulholland, *below*.

Irish Times, 4 Mar 1889, 6;

Carter Blake, *Lucifer*, IV (15 Mar 1889) 84–6;

Katharine Tynan, *Magazine of Poetry*, I 4 (Oct 1889) 454;

†*Manchester Chronicle* [Jan 1889 (?)];

Manchester Guardian, 28 Jan 1889, 6;

Rosa Mulholland, *Melbourne Advocate*, 9 Mar 1889; reprinted in *Irish Monthly*, XVII (May 1889) 365–71;

[Oscar Wilde], *Pall Mall Gazette*, 12 July 1889, 3

St James Budget, XVIII 451 (16 Feb 1889) 15;

Saturday Review, LXVII 1741 (9 Mar 1889) 293;

W. E. Henley, *Scots Observer*, no. 16 (9 Mar 1889) 446–7;

Spectator, LXIII 3187 (27 July 1889) 122;

Francis Thompson, *Weekly Register*, LXXXII 2127 (27 Sep 1890) 407–8;

[Oscar Wilde], *The Woman's World* (Mar 1889) 278.

WHEELS AND BUTTERFLIES (1934–5) Wade 175–6

Booklist, XXXI (Apr 1935) 261;

E. V. W., *Catholic World*, CXLI (Sep 1935) 755;

John Garrett, *Criterion*, XIV 56 (Apr 1935) 488–91;

Douglas Goldring, *Daily Post*, 15 Jan 1935;
Dublin Evening Mail, 22 Nov 1934;
Dublin Magazine, XI (Jan–Mar 1936) 70–2;
Glasgow Herald, 27 Dec 1934;
F. C., *Granta*, XLIV (23 Jan 1935) 198;
Great Thoughts (Jan 1935);
C. P., *Guardian*, 20 Dec 1934;
Irish Independent, 4 Dec 1934;
D. M., *Irish Press*, 18 Dec 1934;
Irish Times, 5 Jan 1935;
Life and Letters, XI 61 (Jan 1935) 483–6;
Listener, XIII (30 Jan 1935) 209;
Austin Clarke, *London Mercury*, XXXI 184 (Feb 1935) 391–2;
P. B. Rice, *Nation*, CXL (3 Apr 1935) 397–8;
Horace Gregory, *New Republic*, LXXXIV (18 Sep 1935) 164–5;
Genevieve Taggard, *NYHTB*, 12 May 1935, 2;
C. G. Poore, *NYTB*, 24 Feb 1935, 3, 15;
Robert Lynd, *News Chronicle*, 1 Feb 1935;
Humbert Wolfe, *Observer*, 2 Dec 1934, 19;
Oxford Magazine, (2 May 1935) 536;
Louise Bogan, *Poetry* (Chicago), XLVI 2 (May 1935) 100–4;
M.-L. Cazamian, *Revue Anglo-Américaine*, XII 5 (June 1935) 450–1;
Horace Reynolds, *Saturday Review of Literature*, XI (9 Mar 1935) 535;
Scotsman, 17 Dec 1934;
John Gould Fletcher, *Southern Review*, I 1 (summer 1935) 199–203;
Denis Johnston, *Spectator*, CLIII 5553 (30 Nov 1934) 843;
Desmond MacCarthy, *Sunday Times*, 13 Jan 1935;
Theatre Arts, XIX (Aug 1935) 657;
TLS, 1721 (24 Jan 1935) 37–8.

WHERE THERE IS NOTHING   Wade 41–5
(Samhain, 1902; *Plays for an Irish Theatre*, vol. I, 1903)

Academy, LXIII 1597 (13 Dec 1902) 661–2;
Academy, LXV 1626 (4 July 1903) 10;
H. W. Boynton, *Atlantic Monthly*, XCII (Oct 1903) 565–9;
Life, XLII (13 Aug 1903) 152;
C. F. G. Masterman, *Living Age*, CCXLIV (28 Jan 1905) 193–208;
Nation, LXXVII (16 July 1903) 52–3;

Poet-Lore, xv (spring 1904) 146;
A. B. Walkley, *TLS*, 76 (26 June 1903) 210–12.

THE WILD SWANS AT COOLE   Wade 118, 124–5
(1917, 1919)

American Review of Reviews, LIX (May 1919) 556;
[J. Middleton Murry], *Athenaeum*, 4640 (4 Apr 1919) 136–7;
Katharine Tynan, *Bookman*, LVI (May 1919) 78–9;
C. H. Towne, *Bookman* (New York), XLIX (July 1919) 617;
W. S. B., *Boston Evening Transcript*, 12 Apr 1919, 9;
Dial, LXVII (26 July 1919) 72;
Living Age, CCCI (10 May 1919) 342–5;
Nation, CVIII (7 June 1919) 917;
Nation (London), XXV (5 Apr 1919) 20–1;
NYTB, 21 Sep 1919, 477;
Marianne Moore, *Poetry* (Chicago), XIII 1 (Oct 1918) 42–4;
O. W. Firkins, *Review*, I 7 (28 June 1919) 151–3;
Saturday Review, CXXVII (12 Apr 1919) 353;
Spectator, CXXIII 4752 (26 July 1919) 119 (very briefly);
Springfield Republican, 6 May 1919, 8;
TLS, 896 (20 Mar 1919) 149.

W. B. YEATS AND T. STURGE MOORE: Wade 340–1
THEIR CORRESPONDENCE (1953)

Melvin W. Askew, *Books Abroad*, XXVIII (1954) 357;
F. O'Donoghue, *Dublin Review*, CCXXVIII 463 (Jan 1954) 102–4;
Laurence Haward, *Guardian*, 9 Oct 1953, 4;
Stephen Spender, *Listener*, L (8 Oct 1953) 608;
T. Jones, *Month*, XI (Mar 1954) 187;
Nation, CLXXVII (5 Dec 1953) 472–3 (briefly);
T. R. Henn, *New Statesman and Nation*, XLVI (3 Oct 1953) 386, 388;
Babette Deutsch, *NYHTB*, 13 Dec 1953, 8;
Horace Reynolds, *NYTB*, 27 Dec 1953, 4;
Hugh Kenner, *Poetry* (Chicago), LXXXIII 6 (Mar 1954) 357–61;
Richard Ellmann, *Sewanee Review*, LXIV 1 (winter 1956) 145–61;
Clifford Collins, *Spectator*, CXCI 6543 (20 Nov 1953) 598;
T. White, *Studies*, XLII (winter 1953) 474;
TLS, 2699 (23 Oct 1953) 681;
Hazard Adams, *Western Review*, XIX 2 (winter 1955) 229–32.

W. B. YEATS: Wade 211 H–J
LETTERS TO KATHARINE TYNAN (1953–4)

Katherine Brégy, *Catholic World*, CLXXVIII (Oct 1953) 76;

L. H., *Dublin Magazine*, XXX (Jan–Mar 1954) 48–9;

F. O'Donoghue, *Dublin Review*, CCXXVIII 463 (Jan 1954) 102–4;

Gerard Fay, *Guardian*, 19 June 1953, 4;

T. O'H., *Irish Independent*, 15 Aug 1953;

Benedict Kiely, *Irish Press*, 20 June 1953;

Austin Clarke, *Irish Times*, 11 July 1953;

Listener, L (20 Aug 1953) 312;

Month, XI (Feb 1954) 126;

W. R. Rodgers, *New Statesman and Nation*, XLVI (18 July 1953) 78, 80;

Babette Deutsch, *NYHTB*, 13 Dec 1953, 8;

Horace Reynolds, *NYTB*, 27 Dec 1953, 4;

New Yorker, XXIX (17 Oct 1953) 169 (briefly);

Louis MacNeice, *Observer*, 12 July 1953, 7;

T. Connolly, *Renascence*, VIII (spring 1956) 156;

San Francisco Chronicle, 23 Aug 1953, 15;

Richard Ellmann, *Sewanee Review*, LXIV 1 (winter 1956) 145–51;

Rex Warner, *Spectator*, CXCI 6526 (24 July 1953) 108;

T. White, *Studies*, XLII (winter 1953) 474;

Sunday Independent, 3 Jan 1954; correspondence by Pamela Hinkson, ibid., 7 Feb;

D. Berrigan, *Thought*, XXIX (spring 1954) 144;

TLS, 2685 (17 July 1953) 462.

See also M. DOMINICA LEGGE (Part V).

THE WIND AMONG THE REEDS (1919) Wade 27–9

[Francis Thompson], *Academy*, LVI 1409 (6 May 1899) 501–2;

A. B. W[alkley]., *Academy*, LVIII 1446 (20 Jan 1900) 63;

Athenaeum, 3738 (15 July 1899) 88;

A. M., *Bookman*, XVI (May 1899) 45–6;

Bookman (New York), IX (Aug 1899) 555;

Geraldine E. Hodgson, *Contemporary Review*, XCVIII (Sep 1910) 326–8;

Literature, IV 80 (29 Apr 1899) 439;

Dora M. Jones, *London Quarterly Review*, XCIV, n.s., IV (July 1900) 61–70;

Henry D. Davray, *Mercure de France*, XXXIII (July 1899) 267–8;

Arthur Symons, *Saturday Review*, LXXXVII (6 May 1899) 553–4;
Spectator, LXXXIII 3706 (8 July 1899) 54.

THE WINDING STAIR (1929)   Wade 164

A. E. (George Russell), *Irish Statesman*, XIII (Feb 1930) 436–7;
TLS, 1501 (6 Nov 1930) 910.

THE WINDING STAIR   Wade 169–70
AND OTHER POEMS (1933)

C. Henry Warren, *Bookman* (New York), LXXXV (Dec 1933) Christmas Supplement, 230–2;
Richard Church, *Christian Science Monitor*, 23 Dec 1933, 9;
Church of Ireland Gazette, 10 Nov 1933;
Church Times, 29 Sep 1933;
Hugh Gordon Porteus, *Criterion*, XIII 51 (Jan 1934) 313–15;
James Douglas, *Daily Express*, 30 Sep 1933;
Padraic Fallon, *Dublin Magazine*, IX (Apr–June 1934) 58–65;
Karl Arns, *Englische Studien*, LXIX 1 (July 1934) 145;
Richard Church, *Fortnightly Review*, CXXXIV (Nov 1933) 629–30;
Glasgow Herald, 28 Sep 1933;
B., *Granta*, XLIII (15 Nov 1933) 118;
Great Thoughts (Feb 1933);
C. P., *Guardian*, 2 Oct 1933;
P. C. T., *Irish Book Lover*, XXII 3 (May–June 1934) 72–3;
Irish News, 23 Sep 1933;
Francis Stuart, *Irish Press*, 30 Oct 1933;
Irish Times, 14 Oct 1933;
Stephen Spender, *Listener*, X (11 Oct 1933) Supplement, xi;
E., *Liverpool Post*, 4 Oct 1933;
Wynyard Browne, *London Mercury*, XXVIII 168 (Oct 1933) 549–50;
Geoffrey Grigson, *Morning Post*, 15 Sep 1933;
Eda Lou Walton, *Nation*, CXXXVII (13 Dec 1933) 684–6;
K. Boenninger, *Neue Zürcher Zeitung*, no. 663 (1934);
Edwin Muir, *New Britain*, 4 Oct 1934;
Horace Gregory, *New Republic*, LXXVII (13 Dec 1933) 134–5;
Richard Church, *New Statesman and Nation*, VI (14 Oct 1933) Supplement, vi, vii;
Percy Hutchinson, *NYTB*, 24 Oct 1933, 2;
L. A. G. Strong, *Nineteenth Century and After*, CXIV 682 (Dec 1933) Literary Supplement, iii–iv (briefly;

Humbert Wolfe, *Observer*, 1 Oct 1933, 5;
Marianne Moore, *Poetry* (Chicago), XLII 1 (Apr 1933) 40–4;
Morton Dauwen Zabel, *Poetry* (Chicago), XLIII 4 (Jan 1934) 279–87;
A. Brulé, *Revue Anglo-Américaine*, XI 4 (Apr 1934) 360–1;
W. R. Benét, *Saturday Review of Literature*, X (16 Dec 1933) 349–50;
Scotsman, 28 Sep 1933;
F. R. Leavis, *Scrutiny*, II 3 (Dec 1933) 293–5;
F. T. W., *Sheffield Daily Telegraph*, 5 Oct 1933;
I. M. Parsons, *Spectator*, CLI 5492 (6 Oct 1933) 10;
Richard Sunne, *Time and Tide*, XIV (30 Sep 1933) 1151–2;
TLS, 1653 (5 Oct 1933) 666;
J. M. Hone, *Weekend Review*, 21 Oct 1933;
F. O. Matthiessen, *Yale Review*, XXIII 3 (Mar 1933) 615–17;
Hugh l'A. Fausset, *Yorkshire Post*, 25 Oct 1933.

WORDS FOR MUSIC PERHAPS AND OTHER POEMS (1932)

Wade 168

Theodore Spencer, *Hound and Horn*, VII (1933–4) 164–74;
Marianne Moore, *Poetry* (Chicago), XLII 1 (Apr 1933) 40–4;
Muriel C. Bradbrook, *Scrutiny*, II 1 (June 1933) 77–8;
Padraic Colum, *Spectator*, CL 5476 (9 June 1933) 841.

Part III

BOOKS AND PAMPHLETS
WHOLLY OR PARTLY ABOUT
W. B. YEATS

ABBOT, CLAUDE COLLEER (ed.), *Further Letters of Gerard Manley Hopkins Including his Correspondence with Coventry Patmore* (London: Oxford University Press, 1938; second edition, revised and enlarged, 1956) 373–4 (Hopkins comments on *Mosada* in a letter to Patmore, dated 7 Nov 1886).

ADAMS, HAZARD, *Blake and Yeats: The Contrary Vision* (Ithaca, New York: Cornell University Press, 1955; London: Cumberlege, 1956) pp. xi + 328. Wade 345.

Reviewed by C. D. Linton, *Anglistisches Seminar*, XXV (1957) 378; John P. Hughes, *Books Abroad*, XXXI 1 (winter 1957) 80; T. R. Henn, *Modern Language Review*, LII 2 (Apr 1957) 263–5; Thomas Parkinson, *Modern Philology*, LIV 4 (May 1957) 281–4; Sven Armens, *Western Review*, XXI 1 (autumn 1956) 69–76.

The Contexts of Poetry (New York: Little, Brown, 1963; London: Methuen, 1965) 72–4 ('Leda and the Swan'), 159–62 ('The Wild Swans at Coole') *et passim*.

'Some Yeatsian Versions of Comedy', in *In Excited Reverie*, ed. A. Norman Jeffares and K. G. W. Cross, 152–70 (on the comic in *Autobiographies* and *A Vision*).

Æ, AE, A. E. *See* RUSSELL, GEORGE WILLIAM.

ALCALAY, ESTHER. *See* CAPAIN, JEAN.

ALDINGTON, RICHARD, 'W. B. Yeats', in *A. E. Housman and W. B. Yeats: Two Lectures* (Hurst, Berkshire: The Peacocks Press, 1955) 20–35 (one of a series of lectures delivered in New York about 1938).

ALLT, PETER, and ALSPACH, RUSSELL K. (eds), *The Variorum Edition of the Poems of W. B. Yeats* (New York: Macmillan, 1957) pp. xxxvi + 884. For reviews, *see* Part II.

ALSPACH, RUSSELL K., *A Consideration of the Poets of the Literary Revival in Ireland 1899–1929* (Philadelphia: College Offset Press, 1942) *passim* (the substance of his University of Pennsylvania dissertation, 1932).

Irish Poetry from the English Invasion to 1798 (Philadelphia: University of Pennsylvania Press, 1943; second edition, revised, 1959) 23–4 ('I am of Ireland') *et passim*.

Yeats and Innisfree, Being No. III of the Dolmen Press Yeats Centenary Papers MCMLXV (Dublin: Dolmen Press, 1965) pp. 16 (numbered [69]–[84]). *See* MILLER, LIAM (Part III).

'The Variorum Edition of Yeats's Plays', in *In Excited Reverie*, ed. A. Norman Jeffares and K. G. W. Cross, 194–206.
See also ALLT, PETER, and Addenda, p. 158 below.

ALVAREZ, A., 'Eliot and Yeats: Orthodoxy and Tradition', in *The Shaping Spirit: Studies in Modern English and American Poets* (London: Chatto & Windus; as *Stewards of Excellence*, New York: Scribner's, 1958) 11–47. *See* Part V.

ANNUAL REGISTER, THE: *A Review of Public Events at Home and Abroad for the Year 1923* (London: Longmans, Green, 1924) Part II, 16 (notes Yeats's Nobel Prize award); 1928, Part II, 30 (*The Tower*); 1933, Part II, 29–30 (*Collected Poems*); 1939, 425 (obituary).

ANON., *Some Critical Appreciations of William Butler Yeats as Poet, Orator and Dramatist* (n.d., *c.* 1903) pp. 23 (excerpts from criticisms and reviews of Yeats by G. K. Chesterton, Richard Ashe King, William Sharp (Fiona MacLeod), Clement K. Shorter and others). (Copy in the Douglas Library, Queen's University, Kingston, Ontario.)

'William Butler Yeats', in *Le théâtre d'hier et d'aujourd'hui*, ed. Jean-Jacques Bernard and others (Paris: Pavois, 1945) 136–42 (includes translations into French of extracts from *The Pot of Broth* and *The Land of Heart's Desire*).

ARCHER, WILLIAM, 'William Butler Yeats', in *Poets of the Younger Generation* (London: Lane, 1902) 531–57 (*Poems*, 1895; *The Land of Heart's Desire; The Countess Cathleen* – reprinted from *The World; The Shadowy Waters* – Yeats and Maeterlinck compared).

The Old Drama and the New: An Essay in Re-Valuation (London: Heinemann; Boston: Small, Maynard, 1923) 369–74 (on Yeats as dramatist).

ARMSTRONG, WILLIAM A. (ed.), *Classic Irish Drama* (Harmondsworth: Penguin Books, 1964) 7–15 ('Introduction: The Irish Dramatic Movement'), 17–18 ('*The Countess Cathleen*').

ARNS, KARL, 'Alte und Junge Anglo-Iren', in *Literatur und Leben im heutigen England* (Leipzig: Rohmkopf, 1933) 111–20 *passim* (brief historical sketch of modern Irish writing).

AUSUBEL, HERMAN, *In Hard Times: Reformers among the Late Victorians* (New York: Columbia University Press, 1960) *passim*.

BACHCHAN, HARBANS RAI (Raya Haravaṃśa), *W. B. Yeats and Occultism: A Study of his Work in Relation to Indian Lore, the Cabbala, Swedenborg, Boehme and Theosophy*, foreword by T. R. Henn (Delhi, Varanasi, Patna: Motilal Banarsidass, 1965) pp. xxii + 296. Wade 360.

BAILEY, RUTH, *A Dialogue of Modern Poetry* (London: Oxford University Press, 1939) *passim* (general comments on Yeats's poetry).

BAIRD, JAMES, *Ishmael: A Study of the Symbolic Mode in Primitivism* (Baltimore: Johns Hopkins Press, 1956; New York: Harper, 1960) 70–1, 173, 394, 423 (on Yeats's use of symbolism).

BAKER, GEORGE PIERCE, 'Speech in the Drama', in *Academy Papers: Addresses on the Evangeline Wilbour Blashfield Foundation of the American Academy of Arts and Letters* (New York, 1951) vol. II, 34–5 (on Yeats's dramatic dialogue).

BARING, MAURICE, 'Mr Yeats's Poems', in *Punch and Judy and Other Essays* (London: Heinemann; New York: Doubleday, Page, 1924) 228–32.

BARLEY, JOSEPH WAYNE, *The Morality Motive in Contemporary English Drama* (Mexico, Mo.: Missouri Printing and Publishing Co., 1912) 22–5 (*The Hour Glass*), 36–7 (*Where There Is Nothing*). University of Pennsylvania doctoral dissertation 1911.

BARNET, SYLVAN, BERMAN, MORTON, and BURTO, WILLIAM (eds), *Eight Great Tragedies* (New York: New American Library, 1957) 324–7 (Introduction to *On Baile's Strand*).

(eds), *The Genius of the Irish Theatre* (New York: New American Library, 1960) 194–7 (Introduction to *The Words upon the Window-Pane*).

BARTLETT, PHYLLIS, *Poems in Process* (New York: Oxford University Press, 1951) 119–20 ('Upon a House Shaken by the Land Agitation'), 193–5 ('The Sorrow of Love'), 196–7 ('To Dorothy Wellesley').

BATESON, F. W., *English Poetry: A Critical Introduction* (London: Longmans, Green, 1950) 28, 124–5, 213.

BAX, Sir ARNOLD, *Farewell My Youth* (London: Longmans, Green, [1943]) 41–8 (on Bax's indebtedness to *The Wanderings of Oisin*).

BAX, CLIFFORD, *Inland Far: A Book of Thoughts and Impressions* (London: Heinemann, 1925) 36–8 (on meeting Yeats at Woburn).

'Prefatory Note', in *Florence Farr, Bernard Shaw and W. B. Yeats*, ed. Clifford Bax (Dublin: Cuala Press; as *Florence Farr, Bernard Shaw, W. B. Yeats Letters*, New York: Dodd, Mead, 1942; London: Home & Van Thal, 1946) ix–xi. Wade 327–9.

'W. B. Yeats: Chameleon of Genius', in *Some I Knew Well* (London: Phoenix House, 1951) 97–103; ibid., *passim*.

BAYLEY, JOHN, *The Romantic Survival: A Study in Poetic Evolution* (London: Constable; Fair Lawn, New Jersey: Essential Books, 1957) *passim*.

BEACH, JOSEPH WARREN, 'Yeats and AE', in *The Concept of Nature in Nineteenth Century English Poetry* (London and New York: Macmillan, 1936) 522–46 *passim*.

'William Butler Yeats: "The Celtic Mythos"', in *A History of English Literature*, ed. Hardin Craig and others (New York: Oxford University Press, 1950; Collier Books, 1962) 592–5, 599–600. Reprinted in *The Permanence of Yeats*, ed. James Hall and Martin Steinmann, 217–22 (195–9).

Obsessive Images: Symbolism in Poetry of the 1930's and 1940's, ed. William Van O'Connor (Minneapolis: University of Minnesota Press, 1960) 3–12 (Yeats and 'ceremony') *et passim*.

BEACH, SYLVIA, *Shakespeare and Company* (London: Faber & Faber, 1960) *passim* (gossipy references to Yeats and Joyce.)

BEARDSLEY, AUBREY. *See* WALKER, A. R.

BEERBOHM, Sir MAX, 'Some Irish Plays and Players', in *Around Theaters* (New York: British Book Centre; London: Hart-Davis, 1953; New York: Simon & Schuster, 1954) 314–19 (*The King's Threshold*). *See* Part V.

'First Meetings with W. B. Yeats', in *Mainly on the Air* (London: Heinemann, enlarged edition, 1957) 95–101.

BEHAN, BRENDAN, *Brendan Behan's Island: An Irish Sketchbook* (London: Hutchinson; New York: Geis, 1962) 26 (Yeats, food and drink).

Confessions of an Irish Rebel (London: Hutchinson, 1965) 223, 239 (anecdotes – Yeats and the Nobel Prize).

BENTLEY, ERIC, *The Playwright as Thinker: A Study of Drama in Modern Times* (New York: Reynal & Hitchcock, 1946; Meridian Books, 1955) 187–9.

The Modern Theatre: A Study of Dramatists and the Drama (London: Hale, 1948, 1950) 159–61.

'A Note on *A Full Moon in March* (1936)', in *From the Modern Repertoire: Series One*, ed. Eric Bentley (Bloomington: Indiana University Press, 1949, 1958) 404–6.

'Yeats's Plays', in *In Search of Theater* (New York: Knopf; Toronto: McClelland, 1953; London: Dennis Dobson, 1954) 315–26 (*see* Part V); 'Heroic Wantonness', ibid., 332–41 (the Abbey Theatre).

'On Staging Yeats's Plays', in *The Dramatic Event: An American Chronicle* (New York: Horizon Press, 1954; London: Dennis Dobson, 1956; Boston: Beacon Press, 1957) 132–5. See Part V.

BENZIGER, JAMES, *Images of Eternity: Studies in the Poetry of Religious Vision from Wordsworth to T. S. Eliot* (Carbondale: Southern Illinois University Press, 1962) 226–35.

BERGHOLZ, HARRY VON. *See* VON BERGHOLZ, HARRY.

BERRY, FRANCIS, *Poetry and the Physical Voice* (London: Routledge & Kegan Paul, 1962) 180–2 (Yeats reading poetry).

BERTI, LUIGI, 'Memoria per Yeats', in *Boccaporto* (Florence: Parenti, 1940) 87–95.

BICKLEY, FRANCIS, 'Yeats and the Movement', in *J. M. Synge and the Irish Dramatic Movement* (London: Constable, 1912) 49–66; 'The Irish Theatre', ibid., 67–85.

BIENS, FRIEDRICH, *'A.E.' George William Russell: Sein Leben und Werk im Lichte seiner theosophischen Weltanschauung* (Greifswald: Greifswald University dissertation, 1934) *passim*.

BITHELL, JETHRO, *W. B. Yeats*, translated by Franz Hellens (Brussels: H. Lamertin, 1912; Paris: Librairie générale des sciences, arts et lettres: Éditions du Masque, 1913) pp. 49.

Reviewed by *Academy*, LXXXIII 2106 (14 Sep 1912) 340.

BJERSBY, BIRGIT, *The Interpretation of the Cuchulain Legend in the Works of W. B. Yeats*, Uppsala Irish Studies I (Uppsala: Lundequistska Bokhandeln; Copenhagen: Munksgaard; Cambridge, Mass.: Harvard University Press; Dublin: Hodges, Figgis, 1950) pp. 190. *See also* BRAMSBÄCK, BIRGIT.

Reviewed by Horace Reynolds, *Christian Science Monitor*, 12 June 1952, 7; William Becker, *Dublin Magazine*, XXVII (Jan–Mar 1952) 46–7; A. Koszul, *Études Anglaises*, V 3 (Aug 1952) 263–4; Peter Allt, *English Studies*, XXXV 1 (Feb 1954) 31–3; Austin Clarke, *Irish Times*, 7 Apr 1951; William Becker, *Poetry* (Chicago), LXXXI 5 (Feb 1953) 331–4; A. Norman Jeffares, *Review of English Studies*, LV 1 (Jan 1953) 86–8; F. Biens, *Studia Neophilologica*, XXIV (1951–2) 155–7; Roger McHugh, *Studies*, XLI 163–4 (Sep–Dec 1952) 334–5; *TLS*, 2574 (1 June 1952) 339.

BLACAM, AODH DE. *See* DE BLACAM, AODH.

BLACKBURN, THOMAS, 'W. B. Yeats and the Contemporary Dream', in *The Price of an Eye* (London: Longmans, Green; New York: Morrow, 1961) 30–49. *See* Part V.

BLACKMUR, R. P., 'The Later Poetry of W. B. Yeats', in *The Expense of Greatness* (New York: Arrow Editions, 1940) 74–106. *See* Part V.

'The Later Poetry of W. B. Yeats', in *Language as Gesture: Essays in Poetry* (New York: Harcourt, Brace, 1952; London: Allen & Unwin, 1954) 80–104 (reprinted from *The Expense of Greatness*); 'Between Myth and Philosophy: Fragments of W. B. Yeats', ibid., 105–23. *See* Part V.

Form and Value in Modern Poetry (New York: Doubleday, Anchor Books, 1956) *passim*.

BLAIR, ERIC. *See* ORWELL, GEORGE.

BLOOM, EDWARD A., PHILBRICK, CHARLES H., and BLISTEIN, ELMER M., *The Order of Poetry: An Introduction* (New York: Odyssey Press, 1961) 43–52 ('The Second Coming').

BLOOM, HAROLD, *Shelley's Mythmaking* (New Haven, Connecticut: Yale University Press, 1959) *passim* (on the relation of Blake and Shelley to Yeats).

BLUNT, WILFRID SCAWEN, *My Diaries 1884–1914*, with a Preface by Lady Gregory (London: Secker, 1922) *passim*.

BODKIN, MAUDE, *Studies of Type-Images in Poetry, Religion and Philosophy* (London and New York: Oxford University Press, 1951) *passim* (contains analyses of 'Sailing to Byzantium' and 'The Second Coming').

BOGAN, LOUISE, '*The Oxford Book of Modern Verse*', in *Selected Criticism* (New York: Noonday Press, 1955; London: Peter Owen, 1958) 52–4; 'William Butler Yeats', ibid., 86–104; 'On the Death of William Butler Yeats', ibid., 133–7; 'The Later Poetry of William Butler Yeats', ibid., 202–6; ibid., *passim. See* Part V.

BORSA, MARIO, 'Il Teatro Nazionale Irlandese', in *Il Teatro Inglese Contemporaneo* (Milan: Fratelli Treves, 1906) 257–84. Translated and edited with a prefatory note by Selwyn Brinton as 'The Irish National Theatre' in his *The English Stage of To-Day* (London and New York: Lane, 1908) 286–314.

BOSE, ABINASH CHANDRA, 'William Butler Yeats', in *Three Mystic Poets: A Study of W. B. Yeats, AE and Rabindranath Tagore*, with an Introduction by J. H. Cousins (Kolhapur: School and College Bookstall, 1945) 1–46.

BOTTOMLEY, GORDON, *Scenes and Plays* (London: Constable, 1929) 120–3 (Yeats and the Noh).

A Stage for Poetry: My Purposes with My Plays (Kendal: Privately printed for the author by Titus Wilson and Son, 1948) 20–4 (Yeats and the Noh).

BOURGEOIS, MAURICE, *John Millington Synge and the Irish Theatre* (London: Constable, 1913) *passim*.

BOURNIQUEL, CAMILLE, 'Abbey Street', in *Irlande* (Paris: Éditions du Seuil, 1955) 156–63. Translated by John Fisher as *Ireland* (London: Vista Books; New York: Viking Press, 1960) 157–76.

BOWRA, Sir C. M., 'William Butler Yeats', in *The Heritage of Symbolism* (London and Toronto: Macmillan, 1943, 1951) 180–218; ibid., *passim*.

Inspiration and Poetry (London: Macmillan; New York: St Martin's Press, 1955) 15 ff.

BOYD, ERNEST AUGUSTUS, 'William Butler Yeats: The Poems', in *Ireland's Literary Renaissance* (London and Dublin: Maunsel; New York: Lane, 1916; revised edition, New York: Knopf, 1922; London: Grant Richards, 1923) 122–44; '. . . The Plays', ibid., 145–65; '. . . Prose Writings', ibid., 166–87; ibid., *passim*.

'William Butler Yeats', in *The Contemporary Drama of Ireland* (Boston: Little, Brown, 1917, 1924; Dublin: Talbot Press; London: Fisher, Unwin, 1918) 47–87; ibid., *passim*.

'William Butler Yeats', in *Portraits: Real and Imaginary* (New York: Doran, 1924) 236–45.

BRADBROOK, MURIEL C., 'Yeats and the Revival', in *English Dramatic Form: A History of Its Development* (London: Chatto & Windus, 1965) 123–42.

BRADFORD, CURTIS, *Yeats at Work* (Carbondale: Southern Illinois University Press, 1965) pp. ix +407.

Reviewed by Harry T. Moore, *Saturday Review*, XLVIII (11 Dec 1965) 81.

BRAMSBÄCK, BIRGIT, *James Stephens: A Literary and Bibliographical Study*, Uppsala Irish Studies IV (Uppsala: Lundequistska Bokhandeln; Copenhagen: Munksgaard; Cambridge, Massachusetts: Harvard University Press; Dublin: Hodges, Figgis, 1959) *passim*. *See also* BJERSBY, BIRGIT.

BRAWLEY, BENJAMIN, 'William Butler Yeats', in *A Short History of the English Drama* (New York: Harcourt, Brace, 1921; London: Harrap, 1922) 232–3.

BRENNAN, CHRISTOPHER, 'Vision, Imagination and Reality' [1901], in *The Prose of Christopher Brennan*, ed. A. R. Chisholm and J. J. Quinn (Sydney: Angus & Robertson, 1962) 19–39 *passim*.

BRENNER, RICA, 'William Butler Yeats', in *Poets of Our Time* (New York: Harcourt, Brace, 1941) 355–411.

BRIDGE, URSULA, 'Introduction', in *W. B. Yeats and T. Sturge Moore: Their Correspondence*, ed. Ursula Bridge (London: Routledge & Kegan Paul, 1953) ix–xix. *See* Part II.

BRINTON, SELWYN. *See* BORSA, MARIO.

BROADBENT, J. B., *Poetic Love* (London: Chatto & Windus, 1964) *passim*.

BRONOWSKI, J., 'William Butler Yeats', in *The Poet's Defence* (Cambridge: Cambridge University Press, 1939) 229–52.

BROOKE-ROSE, CHRISTINE, *A Grammar of Metaphor* (London: Secker & Warburg, 1958) 315–17 *et passim* (Yeats's grammar).

BROOKS, CLEANTH, JR, 'Symbolist Poetry and the Ivory Tower', in *Modern Poetry and the Tradition* (Chapel Hill: University of North Carolina Press, 1939; London: Editions Poetry, 1948) 62–74 *passim*; ibid., 171–98 ('Yeats: The Poet as Myth-Maker' – *see* Part V).

'Yeat's Great Rooted Blossomer', in *The Well-Wrought Urn: Studies in the Structure of Poetry* (New York: Reynal & Hitchcock, 1947; London: Dennis Dobson, 1949) 163–75 ('Among School Children').

'W. B. Yeats: Search for a New Myth', in *The Hidden God: Studies in Hemingway, Faulkner, Yeats, Eliot and Warren* (New Haven, Connecticut, and London: Yale University Press, 1963) 44–67.

and WARREN, ROBERT PENN, *Understanding Poetry* (New York: Holt, 1938, 1950; third edition, revised, 1961) 160–4 ('A Deep-Sworn Vow'), 164–6 ('After Long Silence'), 403–9 ('Two Songs from a Play').

PURSER, JOHN THIBAUT, and WARREN, ROBERT PENN, *An Approach to Literature* (New York: Crofts, revised edition, 1942) 456–7 ('The Wild Swans at Coole'), 469–71 (on Yeats's symbols).

BROOKS, VAN WYCK, *Opinions of Oliver Allston* (New York: Dutton, 1941) *passim*.

BROWER, REUBEN ARTHUR, 'William Butler Yeats', in *Major British Writers*, ed. G. B. Harrison (New York: Harcourt, Brace, 1954) vol. II, 619–30.

The Fields of Light: An Experiment in Critical Reading (New York: Oxford University Press, 1951; Galaxy Books, 1962) 83–8 ('Two Songs from a Play'); ibid., *passim*.

BROWN, MALCOLM, *George Moore: A Reconsideration* (Seattle: University of Washington Press, 1955) *passim*.

BRUGSMA, REBECCA PAULINE CHRISTINE, 'W. B. Yeats and the Irish Revival', in *The Beginnings of the Irish Revival* (Gröningen: P. Noordhoff, 1933) 48–73; 'W. B. Yeats and the Irish Dramatic Movement', ibid., 74–98. Amsterdam doctoral dissertation, 1933.

BRUNIUS, AUGUST, 'Yeats och Moore', in *Vår Tid Årsbok av Samfundet De Nio 1923* (Stockholm: Wahlström & Widstrand, 1923) 75–95.

Modern Engelsk Litteratur (Stockholm: Natur och Kultur, 1923) *passim*.

BUCKLEY, JEROME HAMILTON, *William Ernest Henley: A Study in the 'Counter-Decadence' of the 'Nineties'* (Princeton, New Jersey: Princeton University Press, 1945) *passim*.

BUCKLEY, VINCENT, *Essays on Poetry: Mainly Australian* (Melbourne: Melbourne University Press, 1957) *passim* (refers briefly to Yeats in relation to some contemporary Australian and English poets).

Poetry and Morality: Studies on the Criticism of Matthew Arnold, T. S. Eliot and F. R. Leavis (London: Chatto & Windus, 1959) *passim*.

BULFIN, WILLIAM, *Rambles in Eirinn* (Dublin: Gill, 1935) 296–8 (a tinker's view of *Where There Is Nothing*).

BULLOUGH, GEOFFREY, 'W. B. Yeats and Walter de la Mare', in *The Trend of Modern Poetry* (Edinburgh: Oliver & Boyd, 1934) 27–43.

Mirror of Minds: Changing Psychological Beliefs in English Poetry (London: University of London, Athlone Press, 1962) 242–4 *et passim*.

BURKE, KENNETH, 'The Problem of the Intrinsic', in *A Grammar of Motives* (New York: Prentice-Hall, 1945) 465–84 (a reply in part to Elder Olson, q.v., Part V). Reprinted in *A Grammar of Motives and a Rhetoric of Motives* (New York: World Publishing Company, 1962) 465–84.

'Yeats: "Byzantium" and the Last Poems', in *A Rhetoric of Motives* (New York: Prentice-Hall, 1950; George Braziller, 1955) 316–17 (on Yeats's images). Reprinted in *A Grammar of Motives and a Rhetoric of Motives* (*see* preceding item) 840–1.

BURLINGHAM, RUSSELL, *Forrest Reid: A Portrait and a Study*, Introduction by Walter de la Mare (London: Faber & Faber, 1953) 196–202 (Reid's *W. B. Yeats* considered) *et passim*.

BUSH, DOUGLAS, *Mythology and the Romantic Tradition in English Poetry* (Cambridge, Massachusetts: Harvard University Press, 1937; New York: Pageant Book Company, 1957) 162–6, 461–3 *et passim* (on Yeats's use of classical mythology).

English Poetry: The Main Currents from Chaucer to the Present Day (London: Methuen, 1952; University Paperback, 1965) 199–202 *et passim*.

BUSHRUI, S. B., *Yeats's Verse Plays: The Revisions 1900–1910* (London: Oxford University Press, 1964) pp. 258.

'Yeats's Arabic Interests', in *In Excited Reverie*, ed. A. Norman Jeffares and K. G. W. Cross, 280–314.

'The Hour Glass: Yeats's Revisions, 1903–1922', in *W. B. Yeats, 1865–1965*, ed. D. E. S. Maxwell and S. B. Bushrui, 189–216.

See also MAXWELL, D. E. S.

BYRNE, DAWSON, *The Story of Ireland's National Theatre: The Abbey Theatre, Dublin* (Dublin: Talbot Press, 1929) *passim*.

CAMBON, GLAUCO, 'Yeats e la Lotta con Proteo', in *La Lotta con Proteo* (Milan: Bompiani, 1963) 71–111. *See* Part V.

CAMPBELL, Mrs PATRICK (Beatrice Stella Cornwallis-West), *My Life and Some Letters* (London: Hutchinson; New York: Dodd, Mead, 1922) *passim*. Wade 314.

CANFIELD, CURTIS, 'Plays based on Ancient Gaelic Legend and Mythology', in *Plays of the Irish Literary Renaissance 1880–1930*, ed. with an introduction and notes by Curtis Canfield (New York: Washburn, 1929) 15–26 (*On Baile's Strand* and *The Only Jealousy of Emer*).

'Notes on *The Words upon the Window-Pane*', in *Plays of Changing Ireland*, ed. with an introduction and notes by Curtis Canfield (New York: Macmillan, 1936) 4–7; 'William Butler Yeats', ibid., Appendix A, 473–4 (brief biographical and bibliographical note).

CAPAIN, JEAN, and ALCALAY, ESTHER, 'Ce théâtre au milieu d'un peuple', in *Le théâtre irlandais*. Cahiers de la Compagnie Madeleine Renaud–Jean-Louis Barrault, XXXVII (1962) 42–51.

CATTAUI, GEORGES, 'William Butler Yeats et le Réveil Celtique', in *Trois Poètes: Hopkins, Yeats, Eliot* (Paris: Egloff, 1947) 45–63.

CAZAMIAN, LOUIS, *A History of English Literature: Modern Times 1660–1950* (London and New York: Dent, 1929; revised edition, issued in a single volume with Émile Legouis's *A History of English Literature: The Middle Ages and the Renaissance*, 1954, 1957) 1285–6 *et passim*.

Symbolisme et Poésie: L'Exemple Anglais (Neuchâtel: Éditions de la Baconnière, 1947) 217–20 (*The Wanderings of Oisin*), 224–7, 228.

CAZAMIAN, MADELEINE L., 'W. B. Yeats: Formation esthétique et mystique', in *Le Roman et les Idées en Angleterre*, tome II: *L'Anti-intellectualisme et l'esthétisme 1880–1900* (Paris: Belles-Lettres, 1936) 327–32; 'W. B. Yeats, théoricien', ibid., 333–5; 'W. B. Yeats: Le culte de la Rose', ibid., 335–45; ibid., *passim*.

CHAMBERS CYCLOPAEDIA OF ENGLISH LITERATURE. 'W. B. Yeats', in *Chambers Cyclopaedia of English Literature*, ed. David Patrick (London and Edinburgh, 1903) vol. III, 700 (claims that Yeats's art is 'not characteristically Celtic').

CHANDLER, FRANK WADLEIGH, *Aspects of Modern Drama* (New York: Macmillan, 1914) 238–47 *et passim*.

CHASE, RICHARD, 'Myth as Literature', in *English Institute Essays 1947* (New York: Columbia University Press, 1948) 18–20 ('Among School Children').

Quest for Myth (Baton Rouge: Louisiana State University Press, 1949) 120–1 ('Among School Children').

CHATTERJEE, BHABATOSH, *The Poetry of W. B. Yeats* (Calcutta: Orient Longmans, 1962) pp. 163.

Reviewed by A. Bose, *Indian Journal of English Studies*, III 1 (1962) 163–6; F. A. C. Wilson, *Modern Language Review*, LVIII (3 July 1963) 468–9; Peter Ure, *Notes and Queries*, CCVIII n.s., X 10 (Oct 1963) 400; H. R. MacCallum, *University of Toronto Quarterly*, XXXII 3 (Apr 1963) 307–13.

CHESTERTON, GILBERT KEITH, *Autobiography* (New York: Sheed & Ward; London: Hutchinson, 1937) 139–42, 146–50, 293–4.

'Some Literary Celebrities I Have Known', in *Saturday Review Gallery*, selected by Jerome Beatty, Jr, and others, introduction by John T. Winterich (New York: Simon & Schuster, 1959) 156–61.

CHETTUR, G. K., 'Oxford Poets', in *The Last Enchantment: Recollections of Oxford* (Mangalore: B. M. Bookshop, 1934) 30–2; 'W. B. Yeats', ibid., 33–45.

CHEW, SAMUEL C., 'The Nineteenth Century and After (1789–1939)', in *A Literary History of England*, ed. Albert C. Baugh (New York: Appleton-Century-Crofts; London: Routledge & Kegan Paul, 1948) book IV, 1508–12 ('W. B. Yeats').

CHIARI, JOSEPH, *Landmarks of Contemporary Drama* (London: Herbert Jenkins, 1965) 81–5 *et passim* (on Yeats's verse plays).

CHILD, HAROLD, 'The Mystery of Yeats', in *Essays and Reflections*, ed. with a memoir by S. C. Roberts (Cambridge: Cambridge University Press, 1948) 12–19 (Louis MacNeice, *The Poetry of W. B. Yeats*).

CHISLETT, WILLIAM, 'On the Influence of Lady Gregory on William Butler Yeats', in *Moderns and Near-Moderns: Essays on Henry James, Stockton, Shaw and Others* (New York: Grafton Press, 1928) 165–7.

CHURCH, RICHARD. 'The Later Yeats', in *Eight for Immortality* (London: J. M. Dent, 1941) 41–5. *See* Part V.

'W. B. Yeats', in *British Authors: A Twentieth Century Portrait Gallery* (London: Longmans, Green, 1943, 1948) 40–2.

CLARK, BARRETT H., 'William Butler Yeats', in *The British and American Drama of Today: Outlines for Further Study* (Cincinnati, Ohio: Stewart & Kidd, 1921) 181–4; '*The Countess Cathleen*', ibid., 185–7.

'William Butler Yeats', in *A Study of the Modern Drama: A Handbook for the Study and Appreciation of the Best Plays, European, English, and American, of the Last Half-Century* (New York and London: Appleton-Century-Crofts, 1925) 331–6 (*The Countess Cathleen*).

See also FREEDLEY, GEORGE.

CLARK, DAVID R., *W. B. Yeats and the Theatre of Desolate Reality* (Dublin: Dolmen Press; London: Oxford University Press; Chester Springs, Pennsylvania: Dufour, 1965) pp. 125. *See also* Part V.

Reviewed by John Unterecker, *Massachusetts Review*, VI 2 (winter–spring 1965) 433–4; *TLS*, 3395 (1 July 1965) 552.

' "Metaphors for Poetry": W. B. Yeats and the Occult', in *The World of Yeats*, ed. Robin Skelton and Ann Saddlemyer, 54–66.

'Vision and Revision: Yeats's *The Countess Cathleen*', in *The World of Yeats*, ed. Robin Skelton and Ann Saddlemyer, 158–76.

'Key Attitudes in Yeats', in *William Butler Yeats 1865–1965: A Catalogue of his Works and Associated Items in Olin Library, Wesleyan University*, comp. Michael J. Durkan, 11–21. *See* Part I.

CLARKE, AUSTIN, 'My First Visit to the Abbey Theatre', in *First Visit to England and Other Memories* (Dublin: Bridge Press; London: Williams & Norgate, 1945) 37–40; 'The Seven Woods', ibid., 49–53.

Poetry in Modern Ireland (Dublin: At the Sign of the Three Candles, for the Cultural Relations Committee of Ireland, Irish Life and Culture No. 2, 1951; second edition, 1961) *passim*.

Reminiscences of Yeats in *The Yeats We Knew*, ed. Francis Mac-Manus, 78–94 (the Thomas Davis Lectures).

CLINTON-BADDELEY, V. C., 'W. B. Yeats and the Art of Song', in *Words for Music* (Cambridge: Cambridge University Press; New York: Macmillan, 1941) 149–64; ibid., *passim*.

COFFMAN, STANLEY K., JR, *Imagism: A Chapter for the History of Modern Poetry* (Norman: Oklahoma University Press, 1951) *passim*.

COHEN, J. M., *Poetry of This Age, 1908–1958* (London: Arrow Books, 1959; Hutchinson, 1960; Philadelphia: Dufour Editions, 1962) 29–31, 71–82.

COLDWELL, JOAN, ' "The Art of Happy Desire": Yeats and the Little Magazine', in *The World of Yeats*, ed. Robin Skelton and Ann Saddlemyer, 40–53.

' "Images That Yet Fresh Images Beget": A Note on Book-Covers', in *The World of Yeats*, ed. Robin Skelton and Ann Saddlemyer, 152–7 (on the cover designs of Yeats's books).

COLUM, MARY M., *From These Roots: The Ideas That Have Made Modern Literature* (London: Cape, 1938; New York: Columbia University Press, 1944) *passim*.

'The Yeats I Knew', in *Life and the Dream: Memories of a Literary Life in Europe and America* (New York: Doubleday; London: Macmillan, 1947; Dublin: Dolmen Press, 1964) 127–45; ibid., *passim*.

COLUM, PADRAIC, 'Dublin Through the Abbey Theatre', in *The Road Round Ireland* (New York: Macmillan, 1926) 260–338.

Arthur Griffith (Dublin: Browne & Nolan; as *Ourselves Alone! The Story of Arthur Griffith as the Origin of the Irish Free State*, New York: Crown Publisher, 1959) *passim*.

Reminiscences of Yeats in *The Yeats We Knew*, ed. Francis Mac-Manus, II 24 (the Thomas Davis Lectures).

CONNELY, WILLART, *Adventures in Biography: A Chronicle of Encounters and Findings* (London: Werner Laurie, 1956) 41–9.

CONNOR, GEORGE. *See* DREW, ELIZABETH.

COOKE, JOHN D., and STEVENSON, LIONEL, 'William Butler Yeats (1865–1939)', in *English Literature of the Victorian Period* (New York: Appleton-Century-Crofts, 1949) 211–14; ibid., 124–5.

COOMBES, H., *Literature and Criticism* (London: Chatto & Windus, 1953) 86–8 (a reading of 'Death').

COOPER, CHARLES WILLIAM, and HOLMES, JOHN, *Preface to Poetry* (New York: Harcourt, Brace, 1946) 124–6 ('The Lake Isle of Innisfree').

CORKERY, DANIEL, *Synge and Anglo-Irish Literature: A Study* (Cork: Cork University Press; London and New York: Longmans, Green, 1931) *passim*.

CORNWELL, ETHEL F., 'Yeats and his System', in *The 'Still Point': Theme and Variations in the Writings of T. S. Eliot, Coleridge, Yeats, Henry James, Virginia Woolf and D. H. Lawrence* (New Brunswick, New Jersey: Rutgers University Press, 1962) 89–125. *See* Part VI.

COURTNEY, Sr MARIE-THÉRÈSE, *Edward Martyn and the Irish Theatre* (New York: Vantage Press, 1956) *passim* (the substance of her University of Fribourg dissertation, 1952); ibid., 172–88 (bibliography).

COUSINS, JAMES HENRY, 'Poet and Occultist: W. B. Yeats', in *New Ways in English Literature* (Madras: Ganesh, 1920) 32–41.

'Poets of the Irish Literary Revival', in *Modern English Poetry: Its Characteristics and Tendencies*, Keiogijuku University, Tokyo, *Public Lectures in Literature, Autumn 1919* (Madras: Ganesh, [1921]) 99–102; ibid., *passim*.

and COUSINS, MARGARET, *We Two Together* (Madras: Ganesh, 1950) *passim*.

COWASJEE, SAROS, *Sean O'Casey: The Man Behind the Plays* (Edinburgh and London: Oliver & Boyd, 1963) *passim*.

COX, C. B., and DYSON, A. E., 'W. B. Yeats: "Easter 1916"', in *Modern Poetry: Studies in Practical Criticism* (London: Edward Arnold, 1963) 57–65 (a reading of the poem).

COXHEAD, ELIZABETH, *Lady Gregory: A Literary Portrait* (London: Macmillan; New York: Harcourt, Brace & World, 1961) *passim*.

J. M. Synge and Lady Gregory (London: Longmans, Green, for British Book News: Supplements on Writers and Their Works, no. 149, 1962) *passim*.

Daughters of Erin: Five Women of the Irish Renaissance (London: Secker & Warburg, 1965) *passim*.

CRAIG, EDWARD GORDON, *Index to the Story of My Days: Some Memoirs of Edward Gordon Craig, 1872–1907* (London: Hulton, 1957) *passim*.

CROSLAND, T. W. H., 'W. B. Yeats', in *The Wild Irishman* (London: Werner Laurie, 1905) 112–22.

CROSS, K. G. W., and MARSH, D. R. C., 'Long-Legged Fly', in *Poetry: Reading and Understanding* (Melbourne: F. W. Cheshire, 1966) 170–5 (a reading).

See also JEFFARES, A. NORMAN, and CROSS, K. G. W.

CRUMP, GEOFFREY, *Speaking Poetry* (London: Methuen, 1953) *passim* (on Yeats and verse-speaking).

CUMBERLAND, GERALD. *See* KENYON, CHARLES F.

CUNLIFFE, JOHN W., 'The Irish Movement', in *English Literature During the Last Half Century* (New York and London: Macmillan, 1919) 223–43.

'The Irish Drama and J. M. Synge', in *Modern English Playwrights: A Short History of the English Drama from 1825* (London and New York: Harper, 1927) 131–41 *passim;* ibid., 245–56 (*Manchester Guardian* report of the opening night of O'Casey's *The Plough and the Stars*).

'William Butler Yeats', in *English Literature in the Twentieth Century* (New York: Macmillan, 1933) 101–5.

'William Butler Yeats', in *Leaders of the Victorian Revolution* (New York: Appleton-Century-Crofts, 1934) 305–11.

DAICHES, DAVID, *The Place of Meaning in Poetry* (London and Edinburgh: Oliver & Boyd, 1935) 42–4 ('The White Birds' and 'Symbols').

'W. B. Yeats – I', in *Poetry and the Modern World: A Study of Poetry in England between 1900 and 1939* (Chicago: Chicago University Press, 1940) 128–55. Reprinted in *The Permanence of Yeats*, ed. James Hall and Martin Steinmann, 118–39 (106–24). 'W. B. Yeats – II', in *Poetry and the Modern World*, 156–89.

'Religion, Poetry and the Dilemma of the Modern Writer', in *Literary Essays* (London and Edinburgh: Oliver & Boyd, 1956) 217–20.

Critical Approaches to Literature (London: Longmans, Green; Englewood Cliffs, New Jersey: Prentice-Hall, 1956) *passim.*

The Present Age: After 1920 (London: Cresset Press, 1958) 154–6.

The Present Age in British Literature (Bloomington: Indiana University Press, 1958) 30–9, 176–9 *et passim.*

A Critical History of English Literature (London: Secker & Warburg; New York: Ronald Press, 2 vols, 1960) II 1117–20 *et passim.*

'The Earlier Poems: Some Themes and Patterns', in *In Excited Reverie*, ed. A. Norman Jeffares and K. G. W. Cross, 48–67.

and CHARVAT, WILLIAM (eds), *Poems in English, 1530–1940: Edited with Critical and Historical Notes and Essays* (New York: Ronald Press, 1950) 733–7 (readings of 'Byzantium' and 'Long-Legged Fly').

DALGARD, OLAV, *Teatret i det 20 hundreåret* (Oslo: Norske Samlaget, 1955) *passim.*

DALY, JAMES J., 'The Paganism of Mr Yeats', in *A Cheerful Ascetic and Other Essays* (New York: Bruce, *c.* 1931) 87–102. *See* Part V.

DAUTHENDEY, MAX, *Gesammelte Werke* (Munich: Langen, 1925) vol. I, 584–6 (cf. *Autobiographies* (1955) 347–8).

DAVIDSON, DONALD, 'Yeats and the Centaur', in *Still Rebels, Still Yankees and Other Essays* (Baton Rouge: Louisiana State University Press, 1957) 23–30. *See* Part V.

DAVIE, DONALD, *Purity of Diction in English Verse* (London: Chatto & Windus, 1952) *passim.*

'Berkeley and Yeats: Syntax and Metre', in *Articulate Energy: An Inquiry into the Syntax of English Poetry* (London: Routledge & Kegan Paul, 1955; New York: Harcourt, Brace, 1958) 123–5; ibid., *passim.*

'The Young Yeats', in *The Shaping of Modern Ireland*, ed. Conor Cruise O'Brien (Toronto: Toronto University Press; London: Routledge & Kegan Paul, 1960) 140–51.

'Yeats, the Master of a Trade', in *The Integrity of Yeats*, ed. Denis Donoghue, 59–70.

Ezra Pound: Poet as Sculptor (London: Routledge & Kegan Paul; New York: Oxford University Press, 1964) *passim.*

'Michael Robartes and the Dancer', in *An Honoured Guest*, ed. Denis Donoghue and J. R. Mulryne, 73–87.

DAVIS, E., *Yeats's Early Contacts with French Literature* (Pretoria: Communications of the University of South Africa, 1961) pp. 63. Reviewed by Peter Ure, *Notes and Queries*, CCVIII, n.s., X 10 (Oct 1963) 400.

DAVISON, EDWARD L., 'Three Irish Poets: AE, W. B. Yeats and James Stephens', in *Some Modern Poets and Other Critical Essays* (New York: Harper, 1928) 173–96.

DE BLACAM, AODH S., *A First Book of Irish Literature: Hiberno-Latin, Gaelic, Anglo-Irish, from the Earliest Times to the Present Day* (Dublin and Cork: Talbot Press, 1934) 213–16.

DE BLAGHD, EARNÁN, Reminiscences of Yeats in *The Yeats We Knew*, ed. Francis MacManus, 59–75 (the Thomas Davis Lectures).

DE MAN, PAUL, 'Symbolic Language in Wordsworth and Yeats', in *In Defence of Reading: A Reader's Approach to Literary Criticism*, ed. Reuben A. Brower and Richard Poirier (New York: Dutton, 1962, 1963) 22–37 (a reading of 'Coole Park and Ballylee, 1931').

DEMETILLO, RICAREDO, 'Leda and the Swan', in *The Authentic Voice of Poetry* (Diliman, Quezon City: University of the Philippines, 1962) 7–9; 'Byzantium', ibid., 10–11.

DE NAGY, N. CHRISTOPH, *The Poetry of Ezra Pound: The Pre-Imagist Stage* (Berne: Francke-Verlag, 1960) *passim* (Pound's influence on Yeats).

DENSON, ALAN (ed.), *Letters from AE*, selected and edited by Alan Denson with a foreword by Dr Monk Gibbon (London, New York, Toronto; Abelard-Schuman, 1961) *passim*.

DEUTSCH, BABETTE, *This Modern Poetry* (New York: Norton, 1935; London: Faber & Faber, 1936) 31–2, 115–19, 181–4, 214–24 *et passim*.

Poetry in Our Time: A Critical Survey of Poetry in the English-Speaking World, 1900–1960 (New York: Henry Holt, 1952; Columbia University Press, 1956, 1958; second edition, revised and enlarged, Doubleday Anchor Books, 1963) 287–312 *et passim*.

DICKINSON, PAGE LAWRENCE, *The Dublin of Yesterday* (London: Methuen, 1929) 49–55 (Yeats at the Arts Club), 82–98 (the Abbey Theatre) *et passim*.

[DICKINSON, PAGE LAWRENCE and HONE, J. M.], *The Abbey Row NOT edited by W. B. Yeats* (Dublin: Maunsel, *c.* 1904; British Museum copy dated 8 Feb 1907) pp. 12. (Details of authorship as entered in Dublin National Library copy, on information supplied by J. M. Hone. According to the catalogue of the Houghton Library, Harvard University, Susan L. Mitchell also contributed.)

DICKINSON, PATRICK, *The Good Minute: An Autobiographical Study* (London: Gollancz, 1965) *passim*.

DIETRICH, MARGRET, *Das moderne Drama: Strömungen, Gestaltungen, Motive* (Stuttgart: Kröner, 1961) *passim*.

DOBRÉE, BONAMY, *The Broken Cistern: The Clark Lectures 1952–1953* (London: Cohen & West, 1954) *passim*.

DODDS, E. R., *Journal and Letters of Stephen MacKenna* (London: Constable; New York: Morrow, 1936) *passim*.

DOLMEN PRESS CENTENARY PAPERS MCMLXV. *See* MILLER, LIAM.

DONOGHUE, DENIS, 'Yeats and the Clean Outline', in *The Third Voice: Modern British and American Verse Drama* (Princeton, New Jersey: Princeton University Press, 1959) 32–61; ibid., *passim*.

'Yeats and Modern Poetry: An Introduction', in *The Integrity of Yeats*, ed. Denis Donoghue, 9–20.

'On *The Winding Stair*', in *An Honoured Guest*, ed. Denis Donoghue and J. R. Mulryne, 106–23 (an examination of the leading terms of the book).

(ed.), *The Integrity of Yeats* (Cork: Mercier Press, for Radio Eireann, 1964) pp. 70. Contributions by Donald Davie, Denis Donoghue, T. R. Henn, A. Norman Jeffares and Frank Kermode (q.v.) (the Thomas Davis Lectures, Radio Eireann).

Reviewed by *Quarterly Review*, CCCIII 646 (Oct 1965) 465.

and MULRYNE, J. R. (eds), *An Honoured Guest: New Essays on W. B. Yeats* (London: Edward Arnold, 1965) pp. viii +196. Contributions by Donald Davie, Denis Donoghue, Ian Fletcher, Northrop Frye, T. R. Henn, John Holloway, Graham Martin, J. R. Mulryne, Charles Tomlinson and Peter Ure (q.v.).

DOREN, CARL VAN, and DOREN, MARK VAN. *See* VAN DOREN.

DOUGLAS, Lord ALFRED, *Without Apology* (London: Secker; New York: Ryerson, 1938) 21–3, 46, 117, 136.

The Principles of Poetry. An Address Delivered by Lord Alfred Douglas before the Royal Society of Literature on 2 Sep 1943 (London: The Richards Press, 1943) 6, 22 ('Anti-formal' tendencies in Yeats).

DOUGLAS, WALLACE, LAMSON, RAY, and SMITH, HALLETT, *The Critical Reader* (New York: Norton, 1949) 115–18 (a reading of 'Sailing to Byzantium').

DOWNER, ALAN S., *The British Drama: A Handbook and Brief Chronicle* (New York: Appleton-Century-Crofts, 1950) 326–8.

DOWNES, GWLADYS V., 'W. B. Yeats and the Tarot', in *The World of Yeats*, ed. Robin Skelton and Ann Saddlemyer, 67–9.

DREW, ELIZABETH, *Discovering Poetry* (Oxford: Oxford University Press; London: Milford; New York: Norton, 1933; New York: Norton, 1961) *passim*.

Poetry: A Modern Guide to its Understanding and Enjoyment (New York: Norton, 1959) *passim*.

and CONNOR, GEORGE, 'Mystic Vision', in *Discovering Modern Poetry* (New York: Holt, Rinehart & Winston, 1961) 129–41 ('The Second Coming', 'The Tower', 'Crazy Jane Talks with the Bishop').

and SWEENEY, JOHN L., 'W. B. Yeats', in *Directions in Modern Poetry* (New York: Norton, 1940) 148–71 *et passim*.

DRINKWATER, JOHN (ed.), 'W. B. Yeats', in *The Outline of Literature* (London: Newnes, fifth edition revised by Horace Shipp, 1957) 725–6.

DUFFY, Sir CHARLES GAVIN, 'Books for the Irish People', in *The Revival of Irish Literature* (London: Fisher Unwin, 1894) 35–60.

DULAC, EDMUND, 'Without the Twilight', in *Scattering Branches*, ed. Stephen Gwynn, 135–44.

DUNCAN, G. A., *The Abbey Theatre in Pictures* (Dublin: National Press Service of Ireland, 1963).

DUNCAN, JOSEPH E., *The Revival of Metaphysical Poetry: The History of a Style, 1800 to the Present* (Minneapolis: University of Minnesota Press, 1959) 130–42.

DURRELL, LAWRENCE, *A Key to Modern British Poetry* (Norman: University of Oklahoma Press; London: Peter Nevill; Toronto: Copp Clark, 1952) 104–9.

DURYEE, MARY BALLARD, *Words Alone Are Certain Good: William Butler Yeats: Himself, The Poet, His Ghost* (Dublin: Dolmen Press, 1961) pp. 52 (poems with author's comment).

Reviewed by *TLS*, 3201 (5 July 1963) 498.

DYBOSKI, ROMAN, *Sto lat literatury angielskiej* (Warsaw: Pax, 1957) 803–50 ('Wkt Irlandii'), 812–24 (W. B. Yeats and George William Russell (AE)).

EBBUTT, MAUDE I., 'The Countess Cathleen', in *Hero Myths and Legends of the British Race* (London: Harrap, 1910) 156–83 (a prose version of Yeats's play with quotations from it).

EDGAR, PELHAM, 'The Enigma of Yeats', in *Across My Path*, ed. Northrop Frye (Toronto: Ryerson Press, 1952) 145–53. *See* Part V.

EDWARDS, HILTON, *The Mantle of Harlequin* (Dublin: Progress House, 1958) 1–6, 16–17, 80–1 (Yeats and the Irish theatre).

EDWARDS, JOHN HAMILTON, and VASSE, WILLIAM W., *Annotated Index to the Cantos of Ezra Pound. Cantos I–LXXXIV* (Berkeley and Los Angeles: University of California Press, 1957; second printing, with additions and corrections, 1959) 249 (lists references to Yeats in Pound's *Cantos*).

EGK, WERNER, *Irische Legende: Text zu einer Oper. Mit 5 Originallithographien von Oskar Kokoschka* (Freiburg: Klemm – Erich Seemann, British Museum Catalogue date, [1956]). Based on the story 'Countess Cathleen O'Shea' from *Irish Fairy and Folk Tales*, and *The Countess Cathleen*.

EGLINTON, JOHN. *See* MAGEE, WILLIAM KIRKPATRICK.

ELIOT, T. S., *The Use of Poetry and the Use of Criticism* (London: Faber & Faber, 1933) 140.
After Strange Gods (London: Faber & Faber, 1934) 43–7 (on Yeats's search for a 'universal philosophy').
The Music of Poetry (Glasgow: Jackson, 1942), 7.
'Yeats', in *On Poetry and Poets* (London: Faber & Faber; New York: Farrar, Strauss & Cudahy, 1957) 252–62. *See* Part V.
(ed.), *The Literary Essays of Ezra Pound. See* POUND, EZRA.

ELLIS, STEWART M., 'W. B. Yeats', in *Mainly Victorian* (London: Hutchinson, 1925) 280–6. *See* Part V.

ELLIS-FERMOR, UNA, 'Ideals in the Workshop', in *The Irish Dramatic Movement* (London: Methuen, 1939; second edition, 1954) 59–90; 'W. B. Yeats', ibid., 91–116.
'William Butler Yeats', in *The Oxford Companion to the Theatre*, ed. Phyllis Hartnoll (London: Oxford University Press, 1951) 850–1.

ELLMANN, RICHARD, *Yeats: The Man and the Masks* (London and New York: Macmillan, 1948; New York: Dutton, 1958; London: Faber & Faber paperback, 1961) pp. viii +331. Chap. viii, 'Reality', reprinted in *Yeats: A Collection of Critical Essays*, ed. John Unterecker, 163–74. Wade 334–5.

Reviewed by Leo Kennedy, *Chicago Sun*, 19 Nov 1948, 56; Horace Reynolds, *Christian Science Monitor*, 16 Dec 1948, 15; *College English*, x 3 (Dec 1948) 232–3; John Cournos, *Commonweal*, XLIX (31 Dec 1948) 308; Lorna Reynolds, *Dublin Magazine*, XXVI (Oct–Dec 1951) 58–60; Margaret Willy, *English*, VIII 43 (spring 1950) 37–8; A. Rivoallan, *Études Anglaises*, V 1 (Feb 1952) 80–1; Charles Weir, Jr, *Furioso*, IV (spring 1949) 61–3; M. A. R., *Irish Independent*, 31 Dec 1949; ibid., 22 Apr 1961; C. ff. Salkeld, *Irish Writing*, no. 10 (Jan 1950) 72–4; A. W. J. Becker, *Isis*, 19 May 1949; D. A. Stauffer, *Kenyon Review*, XI 2 (spring 1949) 330–6; *Kirkus*, XVI (15 Aug 1948) 430; *Library Journal*, LXXIII (15 Sep 1948) 1269; *Listener*, XLIII (19 Jan 1950) 124; David Daiches, *Modern Language Notes*, LXV 3 (Mar 1950) 267–9; Elizabeth Schneider, *Nation*, CLXXI (29 July 1950) 112–13; Babette Deutsch, *New Republic*, CXX (21 Mar 1949) 22–3; Kathleen Raine, *New Statesman*, XXXVIII (10 Dec 1949) 700, 702; Horace Gregory, *NYHTB*, 14 Nov 1948, 5; J. Sweeney, *NYTB*, 19 Dec 1948, 5; Edmund Wilson, *New Yorker*, XXIV (18 Dec 1948) 91–3; William Troy, *Partisan Review*, XVI 2 (spring 1949) 196–8; H. C., *Poetry* (Chicago), LXXIV 4 (July 1949) 244–5; Hermann Peschmann, *Poetry Quarterly* (May 1959) 26–8; Horace Reynolds, *Saturday Review of Literature*, XXXI (13 Nov 1948) 11–12; Brian Inglis, *Spectator*, CCVI 6940 (30 June 1961) 956; *Time and Tide*, XXXI (3 June 1950) 560; *TLS*, 2492 (4 Nov 1949) 716; J. Hall, *Virginia Quarterly Review*, XXV 3 (summer 1949) 456–8; J. V. Healy, *Western Review*, XIII (1949) 182–4; G. Whalley, *Yale Review*, XXXIX 1 (Sep 1949) 165–7.

The Identity of Yeats (London: Macmillan; New York: Oxford University Press, 1954; London: Faber & Faber paperback, 1965) pp. ix +343. pp. 219–22 reprinted in *Introduction to Literature*, ed. Louis G. Locke, William M. Gibson and George Arms (New York: Rinehart, 1957) 168–70. Wade 343.

Reviewed by Hazard Adams, *Accent*, XV (1955) 234–7; V. Mercier, *Commonweal*, LXI (21 Jan 1955) 435–6; J. A. Dowling, *Dublin Magazine*, XXX (Oct–Dec 1954) 56–8; *Guardian*, 24 Apr 1954, 4;

Hugh Kenner, *Hudson Review*, VIII 4 (winter 1956) 109–17; G. T., *Irish Independent*, 20 Nov 1954; T[erence]. S[mith]., *Irish Writing*, no. 28 (Sep 1954) 67–8; Herbert Read, *Listener*, LII (7 Oct 1954) 582, 585; T. R. Henn, *New Statesman*, XLVIII (9 Oct 1954) 447–8; *New Yorker*, XXX (18 Dec 1954) 156 (briefly); *Quarterly Review*, CCCIII 644 (Apr 1965) 233 (briefly); Iain Hamilton, *Spectator*, CXCIII 6580 (6 Aug 1954) 176–7; Raymond Mortimer, *Sunday Times*, 15 Aug 1954, 3; Sally Appleton, *Thought*, XXX (1955) 319–20; *TLS*, 2744 (3 Sep 1954) 554; correspondence by J. M. Hone, ibid., 2754 (10 Sep) 573 (Yeats and Leibniz); Reuben A. Brower, *Yale Review*, XLIV 2 (Dec 1954) 290–2.

James Joyce (New York: Oxford University Press, 1959) *passim*.

ELTON, OLIVER, 'Living Irish Literature', in *Modern Studies* (London: Edward Arnold, 1907) 299–307.

ELVIN, LIONEL, *Introduction to the Study of Literature*, vol I: *Poetry* (London: Sylvan Press, 1949) 211–17 (a reading of 'Byzantium').

EMPSON, WILLIAM, *Seven Types of Ambiguity* (London: Chatto & Windus, 1930; revised edition, 1947; Harmondsworth: Penguin Books, 1961) 187–90 (a reading of 'Who Goes with Fergus?').

'The Variants for the Byzantium Poems', in *Essays Presented to Amy G. Stock, Professor of English, Rajasthan University, 1961–1965*, ed. R. K. Kaul (Jaipur: Rajasthan University Press, 1965) 111–36. Reprinted in *Phoenix*, no. 10, Yeats Centenary Number, 1–26.

EMSLIE, MACDONALD, 'Gestures in Scorn of an Audience', in *W. B. Yeats, 1865–1965*, ed. D. E. S. Maxwell and S. B. Bushrui, 102–26 (on Yeats's rhetorical gestures).

ENCYCLOPEDIAS. Yeats entries are to be found in the following encyclopedias:
Aschehougs Konversasjons Leksikon (Oslo)
Bonniers Konversations Lexikon (Stockholm)
Catholic Encyclopedia
Chambers Encyclopaedia. See also Part III above.
Collier's Encyclopedia (New York)
Diccionario Enciclopedico U.T.E.H.A. (Mexico)
Dictionary of National Biography. See HONE, J. M. (Part III).
Enciclopedia Italiana
Enciclopedia Universal Ilustrada Europea Americana (Madrid)

Encyclopaedia Britannica
Encyclopedia Americana
Encyclopédie Française Grand Larousse
Grande Enciclopédia Portuguesa e Brasileira
Das Grosse Brockhaus (Wiesbaden, Germany)
Gydendals Store Konversasjons Leksikon (Norway)
Masarykův Slovník Naučný (Czechoslovakia)
Otovan Iso Tietosanakirja (*Encyclopaedia Fennica*) (Helsinki)
Salmonsens Konversations Leksikon (Copenhagen)
Svensk Uppslagsbok (Malmö, Sweden)
Winkler Prins Encyclopaedie (Amsterdam and Brussels)

ENGELBERG, EDWARD, *The Vast Design: Patterns in W. B. Yeats's Aesthetic* (Toronto: University of Toronto Press, 1964; London: Oxford University Press, 1965) pp. xxxi +224. *See also* Part V.
Reviewed by George T. Wright, *Journal of Aesthetics and Art Criticism*, XIII 3 (spring 1965) 392–3; Hazard Adams, *Journal of English and Germanic Philology*, LXIX 3 (July 1965) 596–8; Thomas Parkinson, *Michigan Quarterly Review*, IV 2 (Apr 1965) 146–7; James L. Allen, Jr, *Modern Philology*, LXII 4 (May 1965) 369–70; Anthony Burgess, *Spectator*, CCXIV 7125 (15 Jan 1965) 73; *TLS*, 3304 (24 June 1965) 529–30.

' "He Too Was in Arcadia": Yeats and the Paradox of the Fortunate Fall', in *In Excited Reverie*, ed. A Norman Jeffares and K. G. W. Cross, 69–92 (*The Island of Statues*).

'The New Generation and the Acceptance of Yeats', in *W. B. Yeats, 1865–1965*, ed. D. E. S. Maxwell and S. B. Bushrui, 88–101.

ERSKINE, JOHN, 'Modern Irish Poetry', in *The Delight of Great Books* (New York: Columbia University Press, 1916; London: Nash & Grayson, 1928; New York: Bobbs–Merrill, 1928, 1935) 293–312.

ERVINE, ST JOHN, *Bernard Shaw: His Life, Work and Friends* (London: Constable; New York: William Morrow, 1956) *passim*.

'William Butler Yeats', in *Some Impressions of My Elders* (New York: Macmillan, 1922; London: Allen & Unwin, 1923) 264–86. *See* Part V.

EVANS, B. IFOR (Lord Evans), 'W. B. Yeats and the Continuance of Tradition', in *Tradition and Romanticism: Studies in English Poetry from Chaucer to W. B. Yeats* (London: Methuen, 1940) 201–8.

'W. B. Yeats', in *English Literature Between the Two Wars* (London: Methuen, 1948) 83–90.

A Short History of English Literature (Harmondsworth: Penguin Books, 1948; second revised library edition, London: MacGibbon & Kee, 1965) 179–81.

FAIRCHILD, HOXIE NEALE, *Religious Trends in English Poetry*, vol. V: *1880–1920. Gods of a Changing Poetry* (New York: Columbia University Press, 1962) 44–5, 169–70, 181–91, 539–50, 615–16.

FALLON, GABRIEL, *Sean O'Casey: The Man I Knew* (London: Routledge & Kegan Paul, 1965) *passim*.

FARAG, F. F., 'Oriental and Celtic Elements in the Poetry of W. B. Yeats', in *W. B. Yeats, 1865–1965*, ed. D. E. S. Maxwell and S. B. Bushrui, 33–53.

FARMER, ALBERT J., *Le Mouvement esthétique et 'décadent' en Angleterre (1873–1900)*, (Paris: Librairie Ancienne Honoré Champion, 1931) *passim*.

FARREN, ROBERT (Roibeárd Ó Faracháin), *The Course of Irish Verse in English* (New York: Sheed & Ward, 1947; London, 1948) 64–78; ibid., *passim*.

FARRINGTON, BRIAN, *Malachi Stilt-Jack: A Study of W. B. Yeats* (Dublin: Connolly Publications, 1965) pp. 12.

FAULKNER, PETER, *William Morris and W. B. Yeats* (Dublin: Dolmen Press, 1962) pp. 36.

Reviewed by Denis Donoghue, *Guardian*, 11 Jan 1963; Ian Fletcher, *Modern Language Review*, LVIII 4 (Oct 1963) 623.

Yeats and the Irish Eighteenth Century, Being No. V of the Dolmen Press Yeats Centenary Papers MCMLXV (Dublin: Dolmen Press, 1965) pp. 16 (numbered 109–24). *See* MILLER, LIAM (Part III).

FAY, GERARD, *The Abbey Theatre: Cradle of Genius* (Dublin: Clonmore & Reynolds; London: Hollis & Carter; New York: Macmillan, 1958) *passim*.

'Dublin of the Books', in *Passenger to London* (London: Hutchinson, 1960) *passim*.

FAY, WILLIAM GEORGE, 'The Poet and the Actor', in *Scattering Branches*, ed. Stephen Gwynn, 115–34.

and CARSWELL, CATHERINE, *The Fays of the Abbey Theatre: An Autobiographical Record* (London: Rich & Cowan; New York: Harcourt, Brace, 1935) *passim*.

FECHTER, PAUL, *Das europäische Drama: Geist und Kultur im Spiegel des Theaters* (Mannheim: Bibliographisches Institut, 1957) vol. II, 169–78.

FEHR, BERNHARD, 'W. B. Yeats: Sein Symbolismus', in *Die englische Literatur des 19. u. 20. Jahrhunderts: Mit einer Einführung in die englische Frühromantik* (Potsdam: Akademie Verlagsges. Athenaion, 1923; Leipzig, 1932) 454–7; 'Yeats als Dramatiker', ibid., 500–3.

FIGGIS, DARRELL, 'Mr W. B. Yeats's Poetry', in *Studies and Appreciations* (London: Dent, 1912) 119–37. *See* Part V.

AE (George W. Russell): A Study of a Man and a Nation (Dublin and London: Maunsel, 1916) 26–9, 135–8.

FLANAGAN, THOMAS, *The Irish Novelists 1800–1850* (New York: Columbia University Press, 1959) *passim* (notes Yeats's views on Gerald Griffin and William Carlton).

FLETCHER, IAN, 'Rhythm and Pattern in *Autobiographies*', in *An Honoured Guest*, ed. Denis Donoghue and J. R. Mulryne, 165–89.

'Yeats and Lissadell', in *W. B. Yeats, 1865–1965*, ed. D. E. S. Maxwell and S. B. Bushrui, 62–78.

See also GORDON, D. J., and FLETCHER, IAN.

FOAKES, R. A., *The Romantic Assertion: A Study in the Language of Nineteenth Century Poetry* (London: Methuen, 1958) *passim*.

FOX, R. M., *Green Banners: The Story of the Irish Struggle* (London: Secker & Warburg, 1938) *passim*.

FRANKENBERG, LLOYD, 'For Seumas', in *James, Seumas and Jacques: Unpublished Writings of James Stephens*, chosen and edited with an Introduction by Lloyd Frankenberg (London: Macmillan, 1964) ix–xxxii *passim*. *See also* STEPHENS, JAMES.

FRASER, G. S., *The Modern Writer and His World* (London: Verschoyle; New York: British Book Centre, 1953; revised edition, London: Deutsch; Harmondsworth: Penguin Books, 1964) 215–21 *et passim*.

W. B. Yeats (London, New York, Toronto: Longmans, Green, for the British Book Council and the National Book League, 1954, revised edition, 1960) pp. 40 (Bibliographical Series of Supplements to British Book News on Writers and Their Work, No. 50).

Reviewed by A. Chapey, *Letterature Moderne*, XLVII (1954) 93; Kathleen Raine, *New Statesman*, XLVII (12 June 1954) 764–5; Louis Johnson, *Numbers*, I 4 (Oct 1955) 38–40; *TLS*, 2739 (30 July 1954) 490 (briefly).

'Prologo: W. B. Yeats', in *William Butler Yeats: Teatro Completo y Otras Obras: Teatro, Poesia, Ensayo*, Traducción de Amando Cázaro Ros (Madrid: Aguilar, 1956) xv–lvi.

'W. B. Yeats and T. S. Eliot', in *T. S. Eliot: A Symposium for His Seventieth Birthday*, ed. Neville Braybrooke (London: Hart-Davis; New York: Farrer, Strauss & Cudahy, 1958) 196–216.

'W. B. Yeats', in *Vision and Rhetoric: Studies in Modern Poetry* (London: Faber & Faber, 1959; New York: Barnes & Noble, 1960) 39–64 (reprinted from his *W. B. Yeats*); 'Yeats and "The New Criticism"', ibid., 65–83 (on the criticism of Yeats by Walter E. Houghton and Delmore Schwartz in *The Permanence of Yeats*, ed. James Hall and Martin Steinmann (*see* Part V); ibid., *passim*.

Ezra Pound (Edinburgh and London: Oliver & Boyd, 1960) 93–6 (Yeats on Pound).

FRÉCHET, RENÉ, 'Yeats and the English Poets: I. Yeats's "Sailing to Byzantium" and Keats's "Ode to a Nightingale" ', in *W. B. Yeats, 1865–1965*, ed. D. E. S. Maxwell and S. B. Bushrui, 217–19.

FREEDLEY, GEORGE, 'Irish Drama', in *A History of Modern Drama*, ed. Barrett H. Clark and George Freedley (New York: Appleton-Century, 1947) 216–33.

and REEVES, JOHN A., 'The Irish National Theatre (1899–1940)', in *A History of the Theatre* (revised with a supplementary section, New York: Crown, 1955) 481–94.

FREEMAN, JOHN, *A Portrait of George Moore in a Study of His Work* (London: Werner Laurie, 1922) 140–5 (on *Diarmuid and Grania*).

FRENCH, CECIL (ed.), *Modern Woodcutters: No. 3: T. Sturge Moore* (London: Little Art Rooms, 1921) (contains a reproduction of the woodcut 'Leda and the Swan' made for A. G. B. Russell).

See GULLANS, CHARLES B. (Part V).

FREYER, GRATTAN, 'The Irish Contribution', in *The Pelican Guide to English Literature*, vol. VII: *The Modern Age*, ed. Boris Ford (Harmondsworth: Penguin Books, 1961) 196–208.

FRIAR, KIMON, and BRINNIN, JOHN MALCOLM, (eds), 'William Butler Yeats', in *Modern Poetry: American and British* (New York: Appleton-Century-Crofts, 1951) 431–2, 546–60 (comments on *A Vision* and a number of Yeats's poems).

FRICKER, ROBERT, *Das historische Drama in England von der Romantik bis zur Gegenwart* (Berne: Francke, 1940) 288–96, 311–15.

'William Butler Yeats', in *Das moderne englische Drama* (Göttingen: Vandenhoeck & Ruprecht, 1964) 32–45.

FRYE, NORTHROP, *Anatomy of Criticism: Four Essays* (Princeton, New Jersey: Princeton University Press, 1957) *passim*.

'Yeats and the Language of Symbolism', in *Fables of Identity: Studies in Poetic Mythology* (New York: Harcourt, Brace & World, 1963) 218–37. *See* Part V.

'The Rising of the Moon: A Study of *A Vision*', in *An Honoured Guest*, ed. Denis Donoghue and J. B. Mulryne, 8–33.

FULLER, ROY, 'Poetry: Tradition and Belief', in *The Craft of Letters in England: A Symposium*, ed. John Lehmann (London: Cresset Press, 1956) 80–3, 92.

[GALE, NORMAN ROWLAND], *All Expenses Paid* (London: Constable, 1895) pp. viii + 116 (a skit on a group of minor poets, including Yeats, on a trip to Parnassus).

GALLAGHER, PATRICK. *See* KIRBY, SHEELAH.

GARDNER, CHARLES, 'W. B. Yeats', in *Vision and Vesture: A Study of William Blake in Modern Thought* (London: Dent; New York: Dutton, 1916) 156–65 (on Yeats and Blake).

GASSNER, JOHN W., 'John Millington Synge and the Irish Muse', in *Masters of the Drama* (New York: Random House, 1940; revised and enlarged edition, New York: Dover; London: Mayflower, 1954) 542–53.

The Theatre in Our Times: A Survey of the Men, Materials and Movements in the Modern Theatre (New York: Crown Publishers, 1954; second printing, 1955) 226–33 *et passim*.

Form and Idea in Modern Theatre (New York: Dryden Press, 1956) *passim*.

GERSTENBERGER, DONNA, *John Millington Synge* (New York: Twayne, 1964) *passim*.

'Yeats and Synge: A Young Man's Ghost', in *W. B. Yeats, 1865–1965*, ed. D. E. S. Maxwell and S. B. Bushrui, 79–87.

GHOSH, PRABODH CHANDRA, 'Yeats and the Noh', in *Poetry and Religion as Drama* (Calcutta: World Press, 1965) 124–43.

GIBBON, MONK, *The Masterpiece and the Man: Yeats as I Knew Him* (London: Hart-Davis, 1959) pp. 226. Wade 349.

Reviewed by *Booklist*, LVI (15 Mar 1960) 442; Richard Ellmann, *Chicago Sunday Tribune*, 13 Mar 1960, 2; Eric Forbes-Boyd, *Christian Science Monitor*, 23 July 1959, 5; René Fréchet, *Études Anglaises*, XIV 1 (Jan–Mar 1961) 37–41; W. L. Webb, *Guardian*, 22 May 1959, 4; P. P., *Irish Independent*, 16 May 1959, 8; Lloyd W. Griffin, *Library Journal*, LXXXV (1 Apr 1960) 1422; Louis MacNeice, *London Magazine*, VII (Aug 1960) 72–3; Jacques Vallette, *Mercure de France*, CCCXXXVIII (Apr 1960) 738–9; Frank O'Connor, *Nation*, CXC (27 Feb 1960) 190–1; Eric Gillett, *National and English Review*, CLII 916 (June 1959) 234; Donald Davie, *New Statesman*, LVII (16 May 1959) 695; DeLancey Ferguson, *NYHTB*, 4 Sep 1960, 6; Charles Poore, *New York Times*, 23 Feb 1960; John Unterecker, *NYTB*, 17 Apr 1960, 20; A[erol]. A[rnold]., *Personalist*, XLII 2 (Apr 1961) 254–5; Vivienne Koch, *Poetry* (Chicago), XCVIII 1 (Apr 1961) 61–2; N. K. D., *San Francisco Chronicle*, 10 Apr 1960, 32; Donat O'Donnell, *Spectator*, CCII 6829 (22 May 1959) 736; Ulick O'Connor, *Sunday Independent*, 5 July 1959; *TLS*, 2984 (8 May 1959) 274; *see also* G. S. Fraser, 'Yeats and the New Criticism' (Part V).

Reminiscences of Yeats in *The Yeats We Knew*, ed. Francis Macmanus, 41–57.

GILBERT, KATHERINE, *Aesthetic Studies: Architecture and Poetry* (Durham, North Carolina: Duke University Press, 1952) 58–9 (Yeats and symbols), 72–3 (the poet's place in the world), 92–4 ('spatial configuration' in Yeats).

GILBERT, SANDRA M., *The Poetry of William Butler Yeats* (New York: Monarch Press, 1965) pp. 133 (notes and study guide).

GILBERT, STUART (ed.), *Letters of James Joyce* (London: Faber & Faber, 1957) 71–2, 83–4, 94–5, 325 (prints letters from Joyce to Yeats), 98–9 (the Irish Literary Theatre).

GILKES, MARTIN, 'William Butler Yeats', in *A Key to Modern English Poetry* (London and Glasgow: Blackie, 1937) 153–65.

GIROUX, ROGER, 'William Butler Yeats (1865–1939)', in *Le théâtre irlandais*, Cahiers de la Compagnie Madeleine Renaud–Jean-Louis Barrault, XXXVII (1962) 69–70.

GLASHEEN, ADALINE, *A Second Census of Finnegans Wake: An Index of Characters and their Roles* (Evanston, Illinois: Northwestern University Press, 1956; London: Faber & Faber, 1957) 283–4 (index of references).

GLENAVY, Lady BEATRICE, *Today We Will Only Gossip* (London: Constable, 1964) *passim* (personal reminiscences of Yeats and others).

GOGARTY, OLIVER ST JOHN, *As I Was Going Down Sackville Street: A Phantasy in Fact* (London: Rich & Cowan; New York: Reynal & Hitchcock, 1937; Harmondsworth: Penguin Books, 1954) *passim* (personal reminiscences of Yeats).

   'Reminiscences of Yeats', in *Mourning Became Mrs Spendlove and Other Portraits Grave and Gay* (New York: Creative Age Press, 1948) 209–24.

   Rolling Down the Lea (London: Constable, 1950) 108–11, 163, 219–21 (reminiscences of Yeats).

   'The Hawk's Well', in *It Isn't This Time of Year At All! An Unpremeditated Autobiography* (London: MacGibbon & Kee, 1954) 202–6 (on a performance of *At the Hawk's Well* held at Gogarty's house, and on Yeats's introductory speech).

   William Butler Yeats: A Memoir. With a Preface by Myles Dillon (Dolmen Press, 1963) pp. 27. Wade 353.

   Reviewed by *TLS*, 3247 (21 May 1964) 442 (briefly).

GOLDRING, DOUGLAS, *South Lodge: Reminiscences of Violet Hunt, Ford Madox Ford and 'The English Review' Circle* (London: Constable, 1943) 48–9 (Yeats, Pound and Ford at Woburn).

'Irish Influences', in *The Nineteen Twenties: A General Survey and Some Personal Memories* (London: Nicholson & Watson, 1945) 115–35 *passim*.

GONNE, MAUD. *See* MACBRIDE, MAUD GONNE.

GORDON, D. J. (ed.), *W. B. Yeats: Images of a Poet* (Manchester: Manchester University Press; New York: Barnes & Noble, 1961) pp. ii +151. For list of contributors and reviews, *see* MAN-CHESTER EXHIBITION (Part I).

and FLETCHER, IAN, 'The Image of a Poet', in *W. B. Yeats: Images of a Poet*, ed. D. J. Gordon, 7–14

'Persons and Places', in *W. B. Yeats: Images of a Poet*, ed. D. J. Gordon, 25–44 (Thoor Ballylee, Coole Park and Lady Gregory, Major Robert Gregory, Lionel Johnson, J. M. Synge, George Pollexfen, Maud Gonne, John O'Leary, John Butler Yeats, Lissadell, Sligo).

'The Poet and the Theatre', in *W. B. Yeats: Images of a Poet*, ed. D. J. Gordon, 56–65.

'Byzantium', in *W. B. Yeats: Images of a Poet*, ed. D. J. Gordon, 81–9. Reprinted in *Yeats: A Collection of Critical Essays*, ed. John Unterecker, 131–8.

'Symbolic Art and Visionary Landscape', in *W. B. Yeats: Images of a Poet*, ed. D. J. Gordon, 91–107 (on Yeats and painting).

GOWDA, HENNUR HANUPAPPA ANNIAH, 'The influence of the Noh on Verse Drama', in *The Revival of English Poetic Drama (In the Edwardian and Georgian Periods)* (Bangalore: Government Press, 1963) 221–55; 'Yeats's Verse Plays', ibid., 283–309.

GRAVES, ROBERT, 'The Perfect Modern Lyric', in *The Common Asphodel: Collected Essays on Poetry 1922–1949* (London: Hamish Hamilton, 1949) 185–95 (attacks 'The Lake Isle of Innisfree').

'These Be Your Gods', in *The Crowning Privilege: The Clark Lectures 1954–1955. Also Various Essays on Poetry and Sixteen New Poems* (London: Cassell, 1955; New York: Doubleday, 1956) 112–35. *See* Part V.

GREEN, H. M., *The Poetry of W. B. Yeats* (Sydney: Australian English Association, 1931) pp. 6.

GREENE, D. H., and STEPHENS, E. M., *J. M. Synge, 1871–1909* (New York: MacMillan, 1959; Collier Books, 1961) *passim*.

GREGORY, Lady AUGUSTA, *Our Irish Theatre: A Chapter of Autobiography* (London: Putnam, 1913; New York: Putnam, 1914) *passim*. Wade 307.

Hugh Lane's Life and Achievement, with Some Account of the Dublin Galleries (London: Murray, 1921) *passim* (includes comment on Yeats and Hugh Lane). Wade 313.

Case for the Return of Sir Hugh Lane's Pictures to Dublin (Dublin: Talbot Press, 1926) pp. 48. (Appendix I contains quotations from W. B. Yeats's speech in the Senate on 14 July 1926.)

Coole (Dublin: Cuala Press, 1931) *passim* ('Coole Park, 1929' is printed on pp. vii–viii. *See* Wade 168).

(ed.), *Ideals in Ireland* (London: At the Unicorn, 1901) pp. 108. Contributions by AE, George Moore, D. P. Moran, Douglas Hyde, Standish O'Grady and W. B. Yeats. Wade 300.

See also ROBINSON, LENNOX.

GREGORY, HORACE, 'W. B. Yeats and the Mask of Jonathan Swift', in *The Shield of Achilles: Essays on Belief in Poetry* (New York: Harcourt, Brace, 1944) 136–55. *See* Part V.

GRIERSON, Sir HERBERT J. C., *Lyrical Poetry from Blake to Hardy* (London: Hogarth Press, 1928) 148–52.

and SMITH, J. C., *A Critical History of English Poetry* (London: Chatto & Windus, 1944; revised edition, 1947) 512–32.

GRIFFIN, GERALD, 'William Butler Yeats', in *The Wild Geese* (London: Jarrolds, 1938) 151–63.

GROSS, HARVEY, 'Modern Poetry and the Metrical Tradition. 2: William Butler Yeats', in *Sound and Form in Modern Poetry* (East Lansing: University of Michigan Press, 1964) 48–55.

GRUBB, FREDERICK, 'Tragic Joy: W. B. Yeats', in *A Vision of Reality: A Study of Liberalism in Twentieth-Century Verse* (London: Chatto & Windus, 1965) 25–45; ibid., *passim*.

GUERRERO ZAMORA, JUAN, 'William Butler Yeats', in *Historia de teatro contemporáneo* (Barcelona: Flors, 1961) vol. II, 243–55.

GURD, PATTY, *The Early Poetry of William Butler Yeats* (Lancaster, Pennsylvania: New Era Printing Co., 1916) pp. iii +100 (doctoral dissertation, Zürich, 1916)

GWYNN, DENIS, 'The Irish Literary Theatre', in *Edward Martyn and the Irish Revival* (London: Cape, 1930) 109-70 *et passim.*

GWYNN, FREDERICK L., *Sturge Moore and the Life of Art* (Lawrence: Kansas University Press, 1951) *passim* (on Yeats and Sturge Moore).

GWYNN, STEPHEN L., 'The Gaelic Revival in Literature', in *Today and Tomorrow in Ireland: Essays on Irish Subjects* (Dublin: Hodges Figgis; London: Macmillan, 1903) 1-37; 'The Gaelic League and the Irish Theatre', ibid., 87-104 *passim.*

'The Irish Drama', in *Irish Literature*, vol. 10, ed. Justin McCarthy (Chicago: De Bower Elliott, 1904) xiii-xxv (on Yeats and the Irish Theatre Movement).

Experiences of a Literary Man (London: Thornton Butterworth, 1926) *passim.*

'The Ageing of a Poet', in *Garden Wisdom, or From One Generation to Another* (Dublin: Talbot Press; London: Fisher Unwin, 1921; New York: Macmillan, 1922) 1-19.

Irish Literature and Drama in the English Language: A Short History (London: Nelson, 1936) 152-64 *et passim.*

'Scattering Branches', in *Scattering Branches*, ed. Stephen L. Gwynn, 1-14.

(ed.), *Scattering Branches: Tributes to the Memory of W. B. Yeats* (London and New York: Macmillan, 1940; reprinted as *William Butler Yeats: Essays in Tribute* (Port Washington, New York: Kennikat Press, 1965) pp. viii +228. Contributions by Edmund Dulac, W. G. Fay, Maud Gonne, Stephen L. Gwynn, F. R. Higgins, C. Day Lewis, Lennox Robinson, Sir William Rothenstein and L. A. G. Strong (q.v.).

Reviewed by Winfield Townley Scott, *Accent*, I (1941) 247-50: E. Forbes-Boyd, *Christian Science Monitor*, 31 Aug 1940, Weekly Review, 11; J. Burnham, *Commonweal*, XXXIV (16 May 1941) 88-9; G. M. Brady, *Dublin Magazine*, XVI (Oct-Dec 1941) 64-5; Stephen Spender, *New Statesman and Nation*, XX (31 Aug 1940) 214-15; Babette Deutsch, *NYHTB*, 11 May 1941, 2; *NYTB*, 18 May 1941, 2; James Stephens, *Spectator*, CLXV 5846 (12 Jan

1940) 40; J. J. Hogan, *Studies*, XXIX 116 (Dec 1940) 650–3; *TLS*, 2009 (3 Aug 1940) 376.

HACKETT, F., 'William Butler Yeats', in *Invisible Censor* (New York: Huebsch, 1921) 114–18.

HAEUSERMANN, H. W., 'W. B. Yeats's Idea of Shelley', in *The Mint: A Miscellany of Literature, Art and Criticism*, ed. Geoffrey Grigson (London: Routledge, 1946) 170–94 ('The Philosophy of Shelley's Poetry' (1900); *Reveries over Childhood and Youth* (1914); *A Vision* (1925)).

HALL, JAMES and STEINMANN, MARTIN (eds), *The Permanence of Yeats: Selected Criticism* (New York: Macmillan, 1950; Collier Books, 1961) pp. vi +414 (Collier edition, x +371). Contributions by W. H. Auden, Joseph Warren Beach, Eric Bentley, R. P. Blackmur, Cleanth Brooks, Kenneth Burke, David Daiches, Donald Davidson, T. S. Eliot, James Hall and Martin Steinmann, Walter E. Houghton, A. Norman Jeffares, F. R. Leavis, Arthur Mizener, J. Middleton Murry, Elder Olson, J. C. Ransom, D. S. Savage, Delmore Schwartz, Stephen Spender, Allen Tate, W. Y. Tindall, Austin Warren, Edmund Wilson, Morton Dauwen Zabel (q.v.). *See also* Part I. (*Note*: In citations of this book, page references to the 1961 edition are given in brackets.)

Reviewed by *Chicago Sun*, 30 May 1950, 3; J. M. Flynn, *Chicago Sunday Tribune*, 5 Mar 1950, 10; *Christian Century*, LXVII (22 Mar 1950) 371; *Churchman*, CLXIV (1 Mar 1950) 18; Vivian Mercier, *Commonweal*, LII (2 June 1950) 204–5; *Current History*, XVIII (June 1950) 355; *Kirkus*, XVII (15 Nov 1949) 642; *Library Journal*, XXXIV (1 Dec 1949) 1817; T. Riggs, Jr, *Modern Language Notes*, LXVI 4 (Apr 1951) 280–1; Malcolm Brown, *Modern Language Quarterly*, XIII 4 (Dec 1952) 413–15; M. C. Bradbrook, *Modern Language Review*, XLVI 3–4 (July–Oct 1951) 498–9; D. A. Stauffer, *New Republic*, CXXII (20 Mar 1950) 20; Babette Deutsch, *NYHTB*, 5 Feb 1950, 3; Dudley Fitts, *NYTB*, 5 Feb 1950, 5; *New Yorker*, XXV (11 Feb 1950) 100; W. D. Templeman, *Personalist*, XXXII 2 (Apr 1951) 214; Isabel Gamble, *Poetry* (Chicago), LXXVI 4 (July 1950) 227–9; *San Francisco Chronicle*, 23 Apr 1950, 27; Richard Ellmann, *Saturday Review of Literature*, XXXIII (14 Apr 1950) 49; Robin Mayhead, *Scrutiny*, XIX 1 (Oct 1952) 69–71; J. Gallagher, *Spirit*, XVII (May 1950) 51–5; *TLS*, 2534 (25 Aug 1950) 525–6.

'The Seven Sacred Trances', in *The Permanence of Yeats*, ed. James Hall and Martin Steinmann, 1–9 (1–8).

HAMILTON, CLAYTON, 'The Irish National Theatre', in *Studies in Stagecraft* (London: Richards, 1914) 123–44.

HANLEY, MARY. *See* MILLER, LIAM.

HARDY, J. E., 'Yeats' "A Prayer for My Daughter", The Dimension of the Nursery', in *The Curious Frame: Seven Poems in Text and Context* (South Bend, Indiana: University of Notre Dame Press, 1962) 116–50 (a reading of the poem).

HARPER, GEORGE MILLS, 'The Reconciliation of Paganism and Christianity in Yeats' *Unicorn from the Stars*', in *Essays in Honor of C. A. Robertson: All These to Teach*, ed. Robert A. Bryan and others (Gainsville: University of Florida Press, 1965) 224–36.

HART, CLIVE, *Structure and Motif in Finnegans Wake* (London: Faber & Faber, 1962) 91–2 (on Joyce's use of *A Vision*).

HASSALL, CHRISTOPHER, *Notes on the Verse Drama* (London: Curtain Press, 1948) 14 (on the inadequacies of Yeats's verse plays).

Edward Marsh, Patron of the Arts: A Biography (London: Longmans, 1959) 95–6 *et passim*.

HEADLAM, MAURICE, *Irish Reminiscences* (London: Hale, 1947) *passim*.

HEATH-STUBBS, JOHN, *The Darkling Plain: A Study of the Later Fortunes of Romanticism in English Poetry from George Darley to W. B. Yeats* (London: Eyre & Spottiswoode, 1950) 203–11.

HEISELER, BERNT VON. *See* VON HEISELER, BERNT.

HENDERSON, PHILIP, 'Politics and W. B. Yeats', in *The Poet and Society* (London: Secker & Warburg, 1939) 132–53.

HENN, T. R., *The Lonely Tower: Studies in the Poetry of W. B. Yeats* (London: Methuen, 1950; New York: Pellegrini & Cudahy, 1952; second edition, revised, London: Methuen; New York: Barnes & Noble, 1965) pp. xx + 362.

Reviewed by *Bell*, XVI 5 (Feb 1951) 69–70; Peter Ure, *Cambridge Journal*, IV 12 (Sep 1951) 762–6; J. F. Nims, *Chicago Sunday Tribune*, 17 Feb 1952, 8; Horace Reynolds, *Christian Science Monitor*,

12 June 1952, 7; M.-L. Cazamian, *Études Anglaises*, V 1 (Feb 1952) 50–4; K. F., *Irish Book Lover*, XXXI (Nov 1951) 143; Austin Clarke, *Irish Times*, 27 Jan 1951; Roy McFadden, *Irish Writing*, no. 14 (Mar 1951) 63–5; *Listener*, LXV (25 Jan 1951) 152–3; W. R. Rodgers, ibid., LXXIV (25 Nov 1965) 867–8; Kimon Friar, *New Republic*, CXXVI (28 Apr 1952) 17; W. R. Rodgers, *New Statesman and Nation*, XLI (6 Jan 1951) 18; Babette Deutsch, *NYHTB*, 10 Feb 1952, 4; Mary Colum, *NYTB*, 10 Feb 1952, 1; Edwin Muir, *Observer*, 10 Dec 1950, 7; W. D. T., *Personalist*, XXXIV 2 (Apr 1952) 205–6; R. T. Dunlop, *Poetry Australia*, 1 6 (Oct 1965) 36–9; Laurence Ferling, *San Francisco Chronicle*, 23 Mar 1952, 27; Harry T. Moore, *Saturday Review*, XLVIII (11 Dec 1965) 39; Richard Ellmann, *Sewanee Review*, LXI 1 (Jan–Mar 1953) 149–56; Richard Murphy, *Spectator*, CLXXXV 6405 (23 Mar 1951) 390, 392; *TLS*, 2534 (16 Feb 1951) 104; Richard Eberhart, *Virginia Quarterly Review*, XXVIII 4 (autumn 1952) 618–21.

'Two Poems by Yeats: "The Stare's Nest by my Window" and "Before the World was Made"', in *The Apple and the Spectroscope, being Lectures on Poetry Designed (in the main) for Science Students* (London: Methuen, 1951) 49–56; ibid., *passim*.

'The Irish Tragedy', in *The Harvest of Tragedy* (London: Methuen, 1956; reprinted 1961) 197–216.

Address on the Occasion of the Gift of Dooras House Kinvara to An Óige, Irish Youth Hostel Association, Kinvara, 20 August 1961 (Dublin: Irish Times, 1961) pp. 4.

'Synge and Yeats', in *The Plays and Poems of J. M. Synge*, ed. T. R. Henn (London: Methuen, 1963) 308–11.

'Yeats's Symbolism', in *The Integrity of Yeats*, ed. Denis Donoghue, 33–46.

'The Rhetoric of Yeats', in *In Excited Reverie*, ed. A. Norman Jeffares and K. G. W. Cross, 102–22.

'*The Green Helmet* and *Responsibilities*', in *An Honoured Guest*, ed. Denis Donoghue and J. R. Mulryne, 34–53.

HENRY, MARJORIE LOUISE, *Stuart Merrill* (Paris: Librairie Ancienne Honoré Champion, 1927) *passim*.

HERING, GERHARD F., 'William Butler Yeats, *Das Einhorn von den Sternen*', in *Der Ruf zur Leidenschaft: Improvisationen über das Theater* (Cologne, Berlin: Kiepenheuer & Witsch, 1959) 165–71.

HERTS, B. RUSSELL, 'The Shadowy Mr Yeats', in *Depreciations* (New York: Boni, 1914) 33–9. *See* Part V.

HICKS, GRANVILLE, *Figures of Transition* (New York: Macmillan, 1939) *passim.*

HIGGINS, F. R., 'Yeats as an Irish Poet', in *Scattering Branches*, ed. Stephen Gwynn, 145–56.

'Yeats and Poetic Drama in Ireland', in *The Irish Theatre*, ed. Lennox Robinson (London: Macmillan, 1939) 65–88.

†HIGHET, GILBERT, *Clerk of Oxenford: Essays on Literature and Life* (New York: Oxford University Press, 1954).

'Yeats: The Old Wizard', in *The Powers of Poetry* (New York: Oxford University Press, 1960) 122–8.

HIND, C. LEWIS, 'W. B. Yeats', in *Authors and I* (New York: Lane, 1921) 318–24.

HINKSON, Mrs H. A. *See* TYNAN, KATHARINE.

HOARE, DOROTHY M., *The Works of Morris and Yeats in Relation to Early Saga Literature* (Cambridge: Cambridge University Press; Toronto: Macmillan, 1939) pp. vii + 179.

Reviewed by I. K., *Contemporary Review*, CLII (Oct 1937) 508–9; A. C., *Dublin Magazine*, XII (Oct–Dec 1937) 64–5; M.-L. Cazamian, *Études Anglaises*, II 1 (Jan–Mar 1938) 58; A[odh]. de B[lacam]., *Irish Press*, 8 June 1937, 8; J. A. Smith, *Medium Aevum*, VIII 3 (Oct 1939) 240–1; Edith C. Batho, *Modern Language Review*, XXXIII 2 (Apr 1938) 289–90; Margaret Schlauch, *Modern Philology*, XXXV 4 (May 1938) 469–70; *Notes and Queries*, CLXXIII (24 July 1937) 72; *TLS*, 1843 (29 May 1937) 409.

HODGINS, JAMES COBOURG, 'William Butler Yeats', in *The World's Best Literature*, ed. John W. Cunliffe and Ashley M. Thorndike (New York: Warner Library, 1917) vol. XXVI, 16260 a–h.

HOFFMAN, FREDERICK J., ALLEN, CHARLES, and ULRICH, CAROLYN F., *The Little Magazine: A History and A Bibliography* (Princeton, New Jersey: Princeton University Press, 1946) *passim* (on Yeats and the little magazine).

HOGAN, ROBERT GOODE, *The Experiments of Sean O'Casey* (New York: St Martin's Press, 1960) *passim*.

HOLLOWAY, JOHN, 'Style and World in *The Tower*', in *An Honoured Guest*, ed. Denis Donoghue and J. R. Mulryne, 88–105.

HOLM, INGVAR, 'Irlandskt', in *Från Baudelaire till första världskriget* (Stockholm: Bonniers Allmanna Literaturhistoria 6.7, 1964) 126–36 (on Yeats 131–6).

HOLROYD, STUART, 'W. B. Yeats: The Divided Man', *Emergence from Chaos* (London: Gollancz; Boston: Houghton, Mifflin, 1957) 113–37.

HONE, JOSEPH M., *William Butler Yeats: The Poet in Contemporary Ireland* (London and Dublin: Maunsel & Roberts [1915]) pp. 134. Reviewed by *Athenaeum*, 4601 (Jan 1916) 24; Robinson Ellis, *Bookman*, L 299 (Aug 1916) 139–40; *Irish Book Lover*, VII (Apr–May 1916) 160; *Spectator*, CXV 4565 (25 Dec 1915) 921–2; *TLS*, 730 (13 Jan 1916) 17.

The Life of George Moore (London: Gollancz; New York: Macmillan, 1936) 217–24, 238–41 (*Diarmuid and Grania*) et passim.

W. B. Yeats 1865–1939 (London and New York: Macmillan, 1942 (actually published Feb 1943); New York: Macmillan, 1947; second edition, revised, London: Macmillan; New York: St Martin's Press, 1962; paperback edition, 1965) pp. viii + 535 (revised edition pp. x + 504). Wade 331–1A.

Reviewed by *American Mercury*, LVI (May 1943) 630 (briefly); Howell Daniels, *Anglo-Welsh Review*, XIII 31 (1962) 94–6; Theodore Spencer, *Atlantic Monthly*, CLXXI 3 (Mar 1943) 148; R. H. M., *Belfast News-Letter*, 25 Feb 1943; Geoffrey Taylor, *Bell*, VI I (Apr 1943) 59–62; Thomas Bodkin, *Birmingham Post*, 16 Feb 1943; Sylvia Lynd, *Book Society News* (Mar 1943) 7–8; *Booklist*, XXXIX (15 Mar 1943) 291; *Bulletin*, 25 Aug 1943; Iris Conlay, *Catholic Herald*, 5 Mar 1943; James Meagher, *Catholic World*, CLVII (Apr 1943) 99–100; S. C. Chew, *Christian Science Monitor*, 6 Mar 1943, Weekly Magazine, 11; James Milne, *Church of England Newspaper*, 26 Feb 1943; W. L. C., *Churchman*, CLVII (1 May 1943) 16; E. V. Wyatt, *Commonweal*, XXXVIII (16 Apr 1943) 637–40; T. McAlindon, *Critical Quarterly*, V 2 (summer 1963) 183–5; Edward Shanks, *Daily Despatch*, 13 Feb 1943; Paul Vincent Carroll, *Daily Record and Mail*, 8 Mar 1943; Sydney

W. Carroll, *Daily Sketch*, 11 Feb 1943; M. D., *Dublin Magazine*, XVIII (Apr–June 1943) 60–3; Una Pope-Hennessy, *Dublin Review*, CCXIII 427 (Oct 1943) 180–2; *Durham University Journal*, IV (June 1943) 102–4; *Economist*, CCIII 6198 (9 June 1962) 992; E. Meyerstein, *English*, IV 23 (summer 1943) 161–2; Richard Church, *Fortnightly Review*, CLIX, n.s., cliii (Apr 1943) 258–62; *Glasgow Herald*, 3 Mar 1943; H[ugh]. l'A F[aussett]., *Guardian*, 17 Mar 1943; John Montague, ibid., 22 June 1962; correspondence by Lovatt Dickson (2 and 17 July), John Montague and Geoffrey Parmiter (6 July), R. T. Dunlop (13 July); D. H. I. P., *Herald of Wales*, 24 Apr 1943; Sir John Squire, *Illustrated London News*, 6 Mar 1943, 258; F. J. K., *Irish Independent*, 29 Mar 1943; Aodh de Blacam, *Irish Monthly*, LXXI (May 1943) 209–17; M. J. Mac[Manus]., *Irish Press*, 9 Mar 1943; Benedict Kiely, ibid., 27 Feb 1943; L. A. G. Strong, *John O'London's Weekly*, XLVIII (26 Mar 1943) 241–2; Myles Dillon, *Journal of English and Germanic Philology*, XLII 4 (Oct 1943) 610–14; E. C. G., *The Lady*, 18 Feb 1943, 84; M. Zipprich, *Library Journal*, LXVIII (1 Feb 1943) 127; Kate O'Brien, *Life and Letters*, XXXIX (Oct 1943) 59–60, 62; *Listener*, XXIX (15 Apr 1943) 457; W. Bardsley Brash, *London Quarterly* (July 1943) 273–4; Oliver St John Gogarty, *Montreal Gazette*, 24 Apr 1943; M. D. Zabel, *Nation*, CLVI (6 Mar 1943) 348; H. Peschmann, *New English Weekly*, XXIII (20 May 1943) 41–3; Malcolm Cowley, *New Republic*, CVIII (8 Feb 1943) 185–6; Raymond Mortimer, *New Statesman*, XXV (13 Feb 1943) 111–12; Babette Deutsch, *NYHTB*, 7 Feb 1943, 1; Mary Colum, *NYTB*, 7 Feb 1943, 1; Clinton Fadiman, *New Yorker*, XVIII (6 Feb 1943) 61; R. Jennings, *Nineteenth Century and After*, CXXXIII 744 (Apr 1943) 180–1; Cyril Connolly, *Observer*, 14 Feb 1943, 3; Louise Bogan, *Partisan Review*, X (1943) 223–8; J. V. Healy, *Poetry* (Chicago), LXII 4 (July 1943) 223–8; *Poetry Review*, XXXIV (Mar–Apr 1943) 126–8; H. K., *Punch*, CCIV (17 Feb 1943) 144; *Rand Daily Mail*, 5 June 1943; Joan Bennett, *Review of English Studies*, XX 77 (Jan 1944) 90–1; C. Roberts, *Saturday Review of Literature*, XXVI (13 Feb 1943) 5; reply by Mary Colum, ibid. (20 Feb) 15; *Scotsman*, 18 Feb 1943; L. Leary, *South Atlantic Quarterly*, XLII 8 (July 1943) 303–4; W. J. Turner, *Spectator*, CLXX 5982 (19 Feb 1943) 176; Lee Varley, *Springfield Republican*, 21 Feb 1943, 7; Anders Osterling, *Stockholms-Tidnimgen*, 8 Feb 1943; Frederick Book, ibid., 7 June;

P. Gannon, *Studies*, XXXII 125 (Mar 1943) 130–1; Joseph P. Hackett, ibid., 127 (Sep) 369–73; Desmond MacCarthy, *Sunday Times*, 14 Feb 1943, 3; G. B., *Sydney Morning Herald*, 19 June 1943; Gustav Cross, ibid., 17 Nov 1962; Robert Speaight, *Tablet*, 17 Apr 1943; Elizabeth Bowen, *Tatler and Bystander*, 24 Feb 1943, 246–8; *Time*, XLI (8 Feb 1943) 88; Naomi Royde Smith, *Time and Tide*, XXIV (13 Mar 1943) 201–2; *TLS*, 2141 (13 Feb 1943) 78; H. R. MacCallum, *University of Toronto Quarterly*, XXXII 3 (Apr 1963) 307–13; Charlotte Kohler, *Virginia Quarterly Review*, XXIX 3 (summer 1943) 472–4; Walter Shewring, *Weekly Review*, 11 Mar 1943; *Western Mail*, 16 June 1962; Horace Gregory, *Yale Review*, n.s., XXXII 3 (Mar 1943) 599–602.

'William Butler Yeats', in *Dictionary of National Biography 1931–1940* (London: Oxford University Press, 1949) 928–32.

(ed.), *J. B. Yeats: Letters to his Son W. B. Yeats and Others, 1869–1922*. Edited with a Memoir by Joseph Hone and Preface by Oliver Elton (London: Faber & Faber, 1944; New York: Dutton, 1946) pp. 296. Wade 332–3.

Reviewed by Robert Hillyer, *Atlantic Monthly*, CLXXVIII (Dec 1946) 182; *Bell*, VIII 1 (Apr 1944) 77–80; K. Rockwell, *Book Week*, 20 Oct 1946, 3; Helen Landreth, *Catholic World*, CLXIV (Dec 1946) 276–7; Jacob Bean, *Commonweal*, XLV (8 Nov 1946) 96; E. C., *Connoisseur*, CXIII (June 1944) 131–2; *Kirkus*, XIV (1 Sep 1946) 442; K. T. Willis, *Library Journal*, LXXI (1 Oct 1946) 1330; A. F. W., *New Quarterly of Poetry*, no. 1 (winter 1947) 17; T. C. Worsley, *New Statesman*, XXVII (1 Apr 1944) 229–30; Padraic Colum, *NYHTB*, 13 Oct 1946, 3; Horace Reynolds, *NYTB*, 18 June 1944, 25; Oliver St John Gogarty, ibid., 20 Oct 1946, 34; *New Yorker*, XXII (19 Oct 1946) 134; *Notes and Queries*, CLXXXIX (1 Dec 1945) 221–2; Babette Deutsch, *Poetry* (Chicago), LXIX 5 (Feb 1947) 291–5; M. Lindsay, *Poetry Review*, XXXV (July–Sep 1944) 246; *San Francisco Chronicle*, 10 Nov 1946, 22; Mary Colum, *Saturday Review of Literature*, XXIX (9 Nov 1946) 16–17; *TLS*, 2199 (25 Mar 1944) 152; *Wisconsin Library Bulletin*, XLII (Dec 1946) 167.

See also DICKINSON, P. L., and HONE, J. M.

HOPKINS, GERARD MANLEY. *See* ABBOTT, CLAUDE COLLEER.

HORTMANN, WILHELM, 'William Butler Yeats und die irische Renaissance', in *Englische Literatur im 20. Jahrhundert* (Berne: Francke, 1965) 27–35.

HOUGH, GRAHAM, 'Yeats', in *The Last Romantics* (London: Duckworth, 1949; New York: Barnes & Noble, 1962) 216–62; ibid., *passim* (*see* review by Austin Clarke, *Irish Times*, 12 Nov 1949).

Reflections on a Literary Revolution (New York: Catholic University Press, 1949; as *Image and Experience: Studies in a Literary Revolution*, London: Duckworth, 1960) *passim*.

HOWARTH, HERBERT, 'A Myth and a Movement', in *The Irish Writers 1880–1940: Literature under Parnell's Star* (London: Rockliff, 1958; New York: Hill & Wang, 1959) 1–31; 'William Butler Yeats 1865–1939', ibid., 110–64. *See* FRÉCHET, RENÉ (Part V).

'Whitman and the Irish Writers', in *Comparative Literature: Proceedings of the Second Congress of the International Comparative Literature Association of the University of North Carolina, September 8–12, 1958*, ed. Werner P. Friedrich (Chapel Hill: University of North Carolina Press, 2 vols, 1959) vol. II, 479–88.

Notes on Some Figures Behind T. S. Eliot (London: Chatto & Windus, 1965) *passim*.

HUDSON, LYNTON, 'The Irish Movement', in *Twentieth-Century Drama* (London: Harrap, 1946, 1949) 37–44.

HUETTEMAN, GERTA, *Wesen der Dichtung und Aufgabe des Dichters bei William Butler Yeats* (Bonn: Leopold, 1929) pp. 88 (the substance of her Bonn doctoral dissertation, 1929, on the shortcomings of Yeats's dramas).

Reviewed by H. Richter, *Beiblatt zur Anglia*, XLII 2 (Feb 1931) 52–4; Karl Arns, *Neueren Sprachen*, XL 7 (Oct 1932) 441; Charles M. Garnier, *Revue Anglo-Américaine*, VII 3 (Feb 1930) 271–2.

HUGHES, GLENN, *Imagism and the Imagists* (Stanford, California: Stanford University Press, 1931; revised edition, London: Bowes & Bowes, 1960) *passim*.

HUMAYUN, KABIR, 'William Butler Yeats', in *Poetry, Monads and Society* (Calcutta: University of Calcutta Press, 1941) 169–93 (Sir George Stanley Lectures, 1941).

HUNEKER, JAMES, 'A Poet of Visions', in *The Pathos of Distance: A Book of a Thousand and One Moments* (New York: Scribner's; London: Laurie, 1913) 235–44 (*The Collected Works*).

HUNGERLAND, ISABEL, *Poetic Discourse* (Berkeley and Los Angeles: University of California Publications in Philosophy XXXIII, 1958) 13–43 ('Her Praise').

HUTCHINS, PATRICIA, *Ezra Pound's Kensington: An Exploration 1885–1913* (London: Faber & Faber, 1965) *passim* (on Yeats and Pound in London).

HYMAN, STANLEY E., *The Armed Vision: A Study in the Methods of Modern Literary Criticism* (New York: Knopf, 1948; revised edition, Vintage Books, 1955) *passim*.

JABLONSKI, W. M., 'Bemerkenswertes aus dem Leben und der Gedankenwelt des irischen Dichters William Butler Yeats', in *Robert Boehringer: Eine Freundesgabe*, ed. Erich Boehringer and Wilhelm Hoffmann (Tübingen: Mohr, 1957) 325–9.

JACKSON, HOLBROOK, 'The Discovery of the Celt', in *The Eighteen Nineties: A Review of Art and Ideas at the Close of the Nineteenth Century* (London: Grant Richards, 1913, 1922; Cape, 1927, 1931; New York: Kennerley, 1914; Knopf, 1922; Harmondsworth: Penguin Books, 1939) 147–50 (Penguin Books: 132–40); ibid., *passim*.

Dreamers of Dreams: The Rise and Fall of Nineteenth Century Idealism (London: Faber & Faber, 1948) 283.

JACKSON, ROBERT WYSE (Bishop of Limerick), *A Memorial Sermon Preached at Drumcliffe on the Occasion of the Centenary of the Birth of William Butler Yeats: 13 June 1965* (Dublin: Dolmen Press, 1965) pp. 4.

JAECKLE, ERWIN, 'Yeats', in *Burgen des Menschlichen* (Zürich: Atlantis, 1945) 31–54.

JALOUX, EDMOND, 'Préface', *in Poèmes de W. B. Yeats*, traduits par Alliette Audra (Paris: La Colombe, 1956) 9–13. Wade p. 462.

JAMESON, STORM, *Modern Drama in Europe* (London: Collins, 1920) 207–10 (adversely criticises Yeats's *Cathleen ni Houlihan* and *The Land of Heart's Desire*).

JEFFARES, A. NORMAN, *A Poet and a Theatre* (Groningen: Walters, 1946) pp. 20 (Inaugural Lecture, University of Groningen, 21 May 1946).

Reviewed by R. Stamm, *English Studies*, XXVII (1946) 128.

W. B. Yeats: Man and Poet (London: Routledge & Kegan Paul; New Haven, Connecticut: Yale University Press, 1949; second edition, with corrections, Routledge & Kegan Paul, Routledge Paperback, 1962) pp. viii +365. Wade 336.

Reviewed by B. P. Howell, *Aryan Path*, xx 10 (Oct 1949) 462–3; C. G. M., *Auckland Weekly News*, 21 Sep 1949; Thomas Bodkin, *Birmingham Post*, 17 May 1949; Rex Warner, *Books of the Month* (Aug 1949); Russell MacFall, *Chicago Tribune*, 30 Oct 1949; Horace Reynolds, *Christian Science Monitor*, 29 Dec 1949, 9; Vivian Mercier, *Commonweal*, LI 2 (21 Oct 1949) 48–9; *Dublin Magazine*, xxv (Jan–Mar 1950) 54–6; J. Auchmuty, *Egyptian Gazette*, 17 Oct 1949; H. W. Häusermann, *English Studies*, xxx 5 (Oct 1949) 278–9; A. Rivoallan, *Études Anglaises*, v 1 (Feb 1952) 80–1; Lawrence Haward, *Guardian*, 3 June 1949, 4; O. H. W., *Hermathena*, LXXIV (Nov 1949) 76–7; M. J. Mac[Manus]., *Irish Press*, 7 July 1949; Austin Clarke, *Irish Times*, 14 May 1949; Cecil ffrench Salkeld, *Irish Writing*, no. 9 (Oct 1949) 68–9; A. W. J. Becker, *Isis*, 19 May 1949; M. M. W., *Johannesburg Sunday Times*, 22 May 1949; *John O'London's Weekly*, LVIII (24 June 1949) 375; Edith Shackleton, *Lady*, CXXIX (19 May 1949) 454; Jacques Vallette, *Mercure de France*, CCX (1 Nov 1950) 566–8; Richard Ellmann, *Modern Language Notes*, LXVI 5 (May 1951) 335–6; Elizabeth Schneider, *Nation*, CLXXI (29 July 1950) 112–13; Mario Rossi, *Nazione*, 18 Mar 1950; R. G. G. Price, *New English Review*, III, n. s., 2 (Aug 1949) 142–3; *New Republic*, CXXI (7 Nov 1949) 20 (briefly); George N. Schuster, *NYHTB*, 4 Dec 1949, 36; Horace Gregory, *NYTB*, 25 Dec 1949, 4, 14; J. B. Leishman, *Review of English Studies*, I, n.s., 4 (Oct 1950) 375–7; *San Francisco Chronicle*, 8 Jan 1950, 25; Mary Colum, *Saturday Review of Literature*, XXXIII (28 Jan 1950) 14–16; *Scotsman*, 27 June 1949; Patrick Kavanagh, *Spectator*, CLXXXII 6307 (13 May 1949) 650; Hermann Peschmann, *Student*, XLVII 5 (18 June 1951) 241–3; J. B. Morton, *Tablet*, 11 June 1949; John Lehmann, *Time and Tide*, xxx (2 July 1949) 679–80; *TLS*, 2470 (3 June 1949) 363.

The Poetry of W. B. Yeats (London: Arnold; Great Neck, New York: Barron's Educational Series, Studies in English Literature, No. 4, 1961) pp. 64.

Reviewed by Ruth Draper, *Critical Quarterly*, III 3 (autumn 1961) 276; F. N. Lees, *Durham University Journal*, LV, n.s., xxiv 2

(Mar 1963) 81; L. C. Bonnerot, *Études Anglaises*, xv 3 (July–Sep 1962) 296; Birgit Bramsbäck, *Studia Neophilologica*, xxxiv 1 (1962) 171–2.

'Introduction', in *Poems of W. B. Yeats*, selected with an Introduction and Notes by A. Norman Jeffares (London: Macmillan, 1962) xiii–xxii; 'Notes', ibid., 193–259; 'Bibliography', ibid., 260–1.

'Introduction', in *W. B. Yeats: Selected Poetry*, edited with an Introduction and Notes by A. Norman Jeffares (London: Macmillan, St Martin's Library, 1963) xiii–xxi; 'Notes', ibid., 209–20.

Wade 211X.

'Introduction', in *W. B. Yeats: Selected Plays*, edited with an Introduction and Notes by A. Norman Jeffares (London: Macmillan, St Martin's Library, 1964) 1–15; 'Notes', ibid., 257–76.

Wade 211BB.

'Introduction', in *W. B. Yeats: Selected Prose*, edited with an Introduction and Notes by A. Norman Jeffares (London: Macmillan, St Martin's Library, 1964) 9–18; 'Notes', ibid., 263–86.

Wade 211CC.

'Introduction', in *W. B. Yeats: Selected Criticism*, edited with an Introduction and Notes by A. Norman Jeffares (London: Macmillan, St Martin's Library, 1964) 7–16; 'Notes', ibid., 273–92.

Wade 211DD.

'Yeats the Public Man', in *The Integrity of Yeats*, ed. Denis Donoghue, 21–3.

'John Butler Yeats', in *In Excited Reverie*, ed. A. Norman Jeffares and K. G. W. Cross, 24–47.

and CROSS, K. G. W. (eds), *In Excited Reverie: A Centenary Tribute to William Butler Yeats 1865–1939* (London: Macmillan; New York: St Martin's Press, 1965) pp. viii + 360. Articles by Hazard Adams, Russell K. Alspach, S. B. Bushrui, K. G. W. Cross, David Daiches, Edward Engelberg, T. R. Henn, A. Norman Jeffares, Conor Cruise O'Brien, W. R. Rodgers, Lennox Robinson, Jon Stallworthy, A. G. Stock and Donald Torchiana (q.v.). Poems by A. D. Hope, Brendan Kennelly, Hugh MacDiarmid and Randolph Stow.

Reviewed by Katherine Hickey, *Belfast Telegraph*, 12 June 1965; Gareth Lloyd Evans, *Birmingham Post*, 5 June 1965; Leonie Kramer,

Bulletin, 23 Oct 1965; A. Lennox Short, *Cape Times,* 10 Nov 1965; R. O'D., *Cork Examiner,* 2 July 1965; *Economist,* CCXV (5 June 1965) 1179; M[argaret]. W[illy]., *English,* XV 89 (summer 1965) 185–6; *Evening Herald,* 18 June 1965; J. W. R. Purser, *Glasgow Herald,* 19 June 1965; Donald Davie, *Guardian,* 12 June 1965; Sir Charles Petrie, *Illustrated London News,* CCXLI (12 June 1965) 24; Denis Donoghue, *Irish Times,* 5 June 1965; W. R. Rodgers, *Listener,* LXXIV (25 Nov 1965) 867–8; William Empson, *New Statesman,* LXX (23 July 1965) 123–4; correspondence by Conor Cruise O'Brien (27 Aug) 284–5; reply by William Empson (10 Sep) 354; John Wain, *Observer,* 15 June 1965, 26; Ronald Dunlop, *Poetry Australia,* 1 6 (Oct 1965) 36–9; Patric Dickinson, *Punch,* CCXLIX 6521 (1 Sep 1965) 327 (briefly); *Quarterly Review,* CCCIII 646 (Oct 1965) 464–5; Harry T. Moore, *Saturday Review,* XLVIII (11 Sep 1965) 39; Charles Graves, *Scotsman,* 12 June 1965; Martin Seymour-Smith, *Spectator,* CCXIV 7046 (11 June 1965) 760; Michael P. Gallagher, *Studies,* LIV 214–15 (summer–autumn 1965) 284–8; Frank O'Connor, *Sunday Independent,* 13 June 1965; Francis MacManus, *Sunday Press,* 13 June 1965; *Sunday Telegraph,* 6 June 1965; Cyril Connolly, *Sunday Times,* 13 June 1965; Keith Mitchell, *Tablet,* 16 Oct 1965; *TLS,* 3304 (24 June 1965) 528–30.

JOHN, AUGUSTUS, *Chiaroscuro: Fragments of an Autobiography* (London: Jonathan Cape, 1952) 100, 101 (on painting Yeats's portrait).

JOHNSON, MAURICE, 'Eliot, Hardy, Joyce, Yeats and the Ghost of Swift', in *The Sin of Wit: Jonathan Swift as a Poet* (Syracuse, New York: Syracuse University Press, 1950) 130–5 (*The Words upon the Window-Pane*).

JONES, LLEWELLYN, 'The Later Poetry of Mr W. B. Yeats', in *First Impressions: Essays in Poetry, Criticism and Prosody* (New York: Knopf, 1925) 137–48. *See* Part V.

JORDAN, JOHN, 'The Irish National Theatre: Retrospect and Premonition', in *Contemporary Theatre,* ed. John Russell Brown and Bernard Harris (London: Edward Arnold, Stratford-upon-Avon Studies 4, 1962) 165–83 *passim.*

JOYCE, JAMES, 'The Day of Rabblement', in *Two Essays,* by F. J. C. Skeffington and James Joyce (Dublin: published by the authors, 1901; reprinted Minneapolis: McCosh's Book Store, 1957) 15–18 (criticises the Irish Literary Theatre for its parochialism). Also in

The Critical Writings of James Joyce, ed. Ellsworth Mason and Richard Ellmann, 68–71.

A Portrait of the Artist as a Young Man (New York: Huebsch, 1916; London: Egoist, 1917) 265–6 (Stephen Dedalus recalls the uproar on the opening night of *The Countess Cathleen*).

Chamber Music. See TINDALL, WILLIAM YORK.

The Critical Writings. See MASON, ELLSWORTH, and ELLMANN, RICHARD.

Finnegans Wake. See GLASHEEN, ADALINE.

Letters. See GILBERT, STUART.

Ulysses. See SULTAN, STANLEY.

JOYCE, STANISLAUS, *My Brother's Keeper*, edited with an Introduction and Notes by Richard Ellmann (London: Faber & Faber, 1957; New York: Viking Press, 1958) 182–6 (on James Joyce's first meeting with Yeats), 206–9 (prints a letter from Joyce to Yeats, dated 18 Dec 1902); ibid., *passim*.

KAIN, RICHARD M., *Dublin in the Age of William Butler Yeats and James Joyce* (Norman: University of Oklahoma Press, 1962) xii +216.

'Yeats and Irish Nationalism', in *W. B. Yeats, 1865–1965*, ed. D. E. S. Maxwell and S. B. Bushrui, 54–61.

KAPOOR, A. N., ' William Butler Yeats', in *Modern English Poetry (1900–1920): The Decline and Fall of the Naturalistic Tradition* (Allahabad: Kitab Mahal, 1962) 112–24.

KAVANAGH, PETER, *The Irish Theatre: Being a History of the Drama in Ireland from the Earliest Period up to the Present Day* (Tralee: The Kerryman, 1946) 436–40 (a chronology of the Abbey Theatre).

The Story of the Abbey Theatre: From its Origins in 1889 to the Present (New York: Devin-Adair; Toronto: Thomas Allen, 1950) *passim. See* review article by Eric Bentley, 'Irish Theatre: *Splendeurs et Misères*', *Poetry* (Chicago), LXXIX (Jan 1952) 216–32.

KAY, D. L. *See* KELLAHER, D. L.

KAYSER, WOLFGANG, 'W. B. Yeats: Der dichterische Symbolismus', in *Gestaltung Umgestaltung: Festschrift zum 75. Geburtstag von Hermann August Korff*, ed. Joachim Müller (Leipzig: Koehler &

Amelung, 1957) 239–48 ('The Symbolism of Poetry' from *Ideas of Good and Evil*: translation with commentary and notes).

KELLAHER, D. L. (D. L. Kay), 'Harcourt Street: W. B. Yeats', in *The Glamour of Dublin* (Dublin: Talbot Press; London: Unwin, 1918) 72.

KELLEHER, JOHN V., 'Arnold and the Celtic Revival', in *Perspectives of Criticism*, ed. Harry Levin (Cambridge, Massachusetts: Harvard University Press, Harvard Studies in Comparative Literature No. 20, 1950) 202–5.

KELLNER, LEON, *Die Englische Literatur der Neuesten Zeit* (Leipzig: Tauchnitz, 1921) 368–80.

KELLY, BLANCHE MARY, *The Voice of the Irish* (New York: Sheed & Ward, 1952) 208–19, 231–2, 257–62 (views Yeats from a conservative Catholic viewpoint).

KELLY, T. J., 'William Butler Yeats (1865–1939)', in *The Focal Word: An Introduction to Poetry* (Brisbane: Jacaranda Press, 1965) 261–8 (a selection of poems with commentary).

KENNEDY, J. M., *English Literature 1880–1905* (London: Stephen Swift, 1912) 280–9 *et passim*.

KENNER, HUGH, *The Poetry of Ezra Pound* (London: Faber & Faber, 1951) *passim* (on Yeats and Pound).

'The Sacred Book of the Arts', in *Gnomon: Essays on Contemporary Literature* (New York: McDowell, Obolensky, 1958) 9–29 (on Yeats's poetry). *See* Part V. 'At the Hawk's Well', ibid., 198–214 (on Yeats's letters).

'Yeats and *Chamber Music*', in *Dublin's Joyce* (London: Chatto & Windus, 1955; Bloomington: Indiana University Press, 1956) 39–44; 'Yeats as Tragic Hero', ibid., 45–6; 'Yeats, Dedalus and Mr Duffy', ibid., 46–7; ibid., 158–61 (Yeats's *The Tables of the Law* and Joyce); ibid., *passim*.

KENNY, EDWARD. *See* NIC SHIUBHLAIGH, MAIRE.

KENYON, CHARLES F. (Gerald Cumberland), 'People I Would Like to Meet', in *Set Down in Malice* (London: Grant Richards, 1919) 263–5.

'The Amazing Dubliners: W. B. Yeats . . .', in *Written in Friendship: A Book of Reminiscences* (London: Grant Richards, 1923) 15–18.

KERMODE, FRANK, ' "In Memory of Major Robert Gregory" ', in *Romantic Image* (London; Routledge & Kegan Paul; New York: Macmillan, 1957) 30–42; 'The Dancer', ibid., 49–91 (Yeats and the Dancer-image); ibid., 96–103 (Yeats and the Tree-image); ibid., *passim*. An abridgement of Chapter I, 'The Artist in Isolation', is printed in *Yeats: A Collection of Critical Essays*, ed. John Unterecker, 37–42.

'The Dancer', in *W. B. Yeats: Images of a Poet*, ed. D. J. Gordon, 120–3.

'Players and Painted Stage', in *The Integrity of Yeats*, ed. Denis Donoghue, 47–57.

KILGANNON, TADHG, *Sligo and its Surroundings: A Descriptive and Pictorial Guide to its History, Scenery, Antiquities and Places of Interest in and around Sligo* (Sligo: Kilgannon & Sons, 1926) 316 ('Messrs Pollexfen and Co. Ltd'), 177–82 ('Lough Gill').

KILLHAM, JOHN (ed.), *Critical Essays on the Poetry of Tennyson* (London: Routledge & Kegan Paul; New York: Barnes & Noble, 1960) *passim*.

KING, B. A., 'Yeats's Irishry Prose', in *W. B. Yeats, 1865–1965*, ed. D. E. S. Maxwell and S. B. Bushrui, 127–36.

KIRBY, SHEELAH (compiler), *The Yeats Country: A Guide to Places in the West of Ireland Associated with the Life and Writings of William Butler Yeats*, ed. Patrick Gallagher, with Drawings and Maps by Ruth Brandt (Dublin: Dolmen Press; London: Oxford University Press, 1962) pp. 48, maps on end-papers.

Reviewed by Denis Donoghue, *Guardian*, 11 Jan 1963, 5, and *Guardian Weekly*, 24 Jan 1963, 11; A. N. Jeffares, *Modern Language Quarterly*, XXV 2 (June 1964) 218–22; T. R. Henn, *Modern Language Review*, LVIII 4 (Oct 1963) 627; Charles Tomlinson, *Poetry* (Chicago), CII 5 (Aug 1963) 345 (briefly); *TLS*, 3178 (25 Jan 1963) 62; *Virginia Quarterly Review*, XXXIX 3 (summer 1963) cx.

KLEINSTUECK, JOHANNES, 'William Butler Yeats: *At the Hawk's Well*', in *Das Moderne Englische Drama: Interpretationen*, ed. Horst Oppel (Berlin: Erich Schmidt Verlag, 1963) 149–65.

W. B. Yeats oder Der Dichter in der modernen Welt (Hamburg, Leibnitz-Verlag, 1963) pp. 288. Includes translations into German of

'Sailing to Byzantium', 'Byzantium', 'The Second Coming', 'Lapis Lazuli', 'Long-Legged Fly' and 'Cuchulain Comforted'). Reviewed by J. Blondel, *Études Anglaises*, XVIII 3 (July–Sep 1965) 320–1; K. P. Jochum, *Neueren Sprachen*, XIV 3 (1965) 147–8; Ronald Dunlop, *Poetry Australia*, 1 6 (Oct 1965) 36–9.
'Yeats and Shakespeare', in *W. B. Yeats, 1865–1965*, ed. D. E. S. Maxwell and S. B. Bushrui, 1–17.

KLINGOPOULOS, G. D., 'The Literary Scene', in *The Pelican Guide to English Literature*, vol. VI: *From Dickens to Hardy*, ed. Boris Ford (Harmondsworth: Penguin Books, 1958) 59–116 *passim*.

KNIGHT, G. WILSON, *The Starlit Dome: Studies of the Poetry of Vision* (London: Oxford University Press, 1941, reprinted 1943; Methuen, 1959) 310–11 ('Sailing to Byzantium') *et passim*.
The Golden Labyrinth: A Study of British Drama (London: Phoenix House; New York: Norton, 1962) 324–9 *et passim*.

KNIGHTS, L. C., 'Poetry and Social Criticism: The Work of W. B. Yeats', in *Explorations* (London: Chatto & Windus, 1946; New York: Stewart, 1947; Harmondsworth: Penguin Books, 1964) 170–85.

KOCH, VIVIENNE, *W. B. Yeats: The Tragic Phase. A Study of the Last Poems* (London: Routledge & Kegan Paul, 1951; Baltimore: Johns Hopkins University Press, 1952) pp. 151.
Reviewed by Stanley K. Coffmann, Jr, *Books Abroad*, XXVII 3 (summer 1953) 305; Peter Ure, *Cambridge Journal*, V 9 (June 1952) 571–2; W. W. Robson, *Dublin Review*, CCV 453 (July 1951) 83–6; M.-L. Cazamian, *Études Anglaises*, V 1 (Feb 1952) 50–4; *Guardian*, 3 July 1951, 4; Ewart Milne, *Irish Writing*, no. 16 (Sep 1951) 54–8; *Listener*, XLV (17 May 1951) 807; Earl R. Wasserman, *Modern Language Notes*, LXVIII 3 (Mar 1953) 185–90; *Nation*, CLXXV 20 (15 Nov 1952) 454 (briefly); Kimon Friar, *New Republic*, CXXVI (28 Apr 1952) 17; M. C. Bradbrook, *New Statesman*, XLI (9 June 1951) 658–9; Babette Deutsch, *NYHTB*, 24 Aug 1952, 9; William Becker, *Poetry* (Chicago), LXXXI 5 (Feb 1953) 331–4; H. Peschmann, *Poetry Review*, XLII 5 (Sep–Oct 1951) 275 (briefly); Lawrence Ferling, *San Francisco Chronicle*, 7 Sep 1952, 21; Richard Ellmann, *Sewanee Review*, LXI 1 (Jan–Mar 1953) 149; Helen Bevington, *South Atlantic Quarterly*, LII 1 (Jan 1953) 157; Roger MacHugh, *Studies*, XLI 163–4 (Sep–Dec 1952) 333–4; *TLS*, 2574

(1 June 1951) 339; Richard Eberhart, *Virginia Quarterly Review*, XXVIII 4 (autumn 1952) 618–21.

KOSTKA, Sr MARIA, *The Old Woman: One Phase of the Character Poem in Contemporary British Verse* (Philadelphia: University of Pennsylvania Press, 1931) 27–8 ('Cracked Mary'). (University of Pennsylvania doctoral dissertation.)

KRANS, HORATIO SHEAFE, *William Butler Yeats and the Irish Literary Revival* (New York: McClure Phillips, 1904; London: Heinemann, 1905) pp. xi +196. *See* Part V.

Reviewed by *Bookman*, XXVIII 164 (May 1905) 70; *Dial*, XXXVII (1 Oct 1904) 213; *Nation*, LXXVIII (5 May 1904) 351.

KRAUSE, DAVID, *Sean O'Casey: The Man and His Work* (London: MacGibbon & Kee, 1960; New York: Collier Books, 1962) *passim*.

KREUZER, JAMES R., *Elements of Poetry* (New York: Macmillan, 1955; London: Macmillan, 1956) 117–19 (an analysis of 'The Lake Isle of Innisfree').

KRIPALANI, KRISHNA, *Rabindranath Tagore: A Biography* (New York: Grove Press, 1962) *passim* (on Yeats and Tagore).

KUEHNELT, NARRO HEINZ, *Die Bedeutung von Edgar Allan Poe für die Englische Literatur: Eine Studie anlässliche des 100 Todestages des Dichters* (Innsbruck: Wagner, 1949) 301–3.

KUNITZ, STANLEY JASSPON (Dilly Tante) (ed.), 'William Butler Yeats', in *Living Authors: A Book of Biographies* (New York: H. W. Wilson, 1931) 451–4.

LALOU, RENÉ, 'Yeats et la Poésie', *Panorama de la littérature anglaise contemporaine* (Paris: Éditions Kra, 1926) 182–9.

LAMM, MARTIN, 'Irlandskt drama', *Det Moderna dramat* (Stockholm: Albert Bonniers, 1948) 299–309. Translated by Karin Elliot as *Modern Drama* (Oxford: Blackwell; New York: Philosophical Library, 1952) 293–314.

LANGBAUM, ROBERT, *The Poetry of Experience: The Dramatic Monologue in Modern Literary Tradition* (London: Chatto & Windus, 1957) *passim*.

LARMINIE, WILLIAM, 'Legends as Material for Literature', in *Literary Ideals in Ireland* by John Eglinton and others, 57–65.

LAW, HUGH ALEXANDER, *Anglo-Irish Literature*, with a Foreword by AE (Dublin and Cork: Talbot Press; London and New York: Longmans, Green, 1926) 252–4, 272–87 *et passim*.

LEACOCK, STEPHEN B., 'Thinking of Tomorrow', in *Too Much College* (New York: Dodd, Mead, 1939) 200.

LEARY, LEWIS (ed.), *Contemporary Literary Scholarship: A Critical Review* (New York: Appleton-Century-Crofts, 1958) *passim*.

LEAVIS, F. R., *New Bearings in English Poetry: A Study of the Contemporary Situation* (London: Chatto & Windus, 1932; new edition, 1950, reprinted 1959) 27–52 (mainly on the poetry up to *The Green Helmet*). pp. 27–50 reprinted in *The Permanence of Yeats*, ed. James Hall and Martin Steinmann, 163–78 (146–59).

LE GALLIENNE, RICHARD, *Retrospective Reviews: A Literary Log* (London: John Lane; New York: Dodd, Mead, 2 vols, 1896) vol. I, 168–73 (on *The Countess Cathleen*).

LEHMANN, JOHN, 'The Man Who Learned to Walk Naked', in *Orpheus: A Symposium of the Arts*, ed. John Lehmann (London: John Lehmann, 1948) vol. I, 96–102. Also in his *The Open Night* (London: Longmans, 1952) 15–22.

LENNARTZ, FRANZ, *Ausländische Dichter und Schriftsteller unserer Zeit. Einzeldarstellungen zur schöner Literatur in fremdem Sprechen* (Stuttgart: Kröner, 1955) 737–45.

LERNER, LAURENCE, *The Truest Poetry: An Essay on the Question What is Literature?* (London: Hamish Hamilton, 1960) *passim*.

W. B. Yeats: Poet and Crank, from the *Proceedings of the British Academy*, vol. XLIX (London: Oxford University Press, 1963) pp. 22 (Chatterton Lecture on an English Poet, British Academy, 1963).

Reviewed by *TLS*, 3228 (9 Jan 1964) 28.

LEVIN, HARRY, *Contexts of Criticism* (Cambridge, Massachusetts: Harvard University Press, 1957) *passim*.

LEWIS, CECIL ARTHUR (ed.), *Self-Portrait Taken from the Letters and Journals of Charles Ricketts, R. A.*, collected and compiled by

T. Sturge Moore (London: Peter Davies; Toronto: Saunders, 1939) *passim* (includes letters from Yeats). Wade 324.

LEWIS, CECIL DAY, 'A Note on W. B. Yeats and the Aristocratic Tradition', in *Scattering Branches*, ed. Stephen Gwynn, 157–82.
The Poetic Image (London: Jonathan Cape, 1947) *passim*.
'W. B. Yeats and Human Dignity', in *Notable Images of Virtue: Emily Brontë, George Meredith, W. B. Yeats. Being the Sixth Series of Lectures of the Chancellor Dunning Trust Lectures Delivered at the Queen's University, Kingston, Ontario, 1954* (Toronto: Ryerson Press, 1954) 53–77.

LEWIS, WYNDHAM, *Blasting and Bombadiering* (London: Eyre & Spottiswoode, 1937) 10–13 (Yeats and George Moore), 243 (Yeats and T. E. Lawrence).
Letters. See ROSE, W. K.

LEWISOHN, LUDWIG, *The Modern Drama: An Essay in Interpretation* (New York: Huebsch, 1915; Viking Press, 1928) 267–72 (on Yeats's plays).

LHOMBREAUD, ROGER, *Arthur Symons: A Critical Biography* (London: Unicorn Press, 1963) *passim* (on Yeats and Symons).

LILJEGREN, S. B., *Irish Studies (Irish Essays and Studies VI)* (Uppsala: Lundequistska Bokhandeln; Copenhagen: Munksgaard, 1961) 22–4 (on Yeats's plays) *et passim*.

LINATI, CARLO, 'William Butler Yeats: Sua Lirica, Suoi Drammi e la rinascenza celtico-irlandese', *Tragedie Irlandesi di William Butler Yeats: Versione, proemio e note di Carlo Linati* (Milan: Studio Editoriale Lombardo, 1914) ix–xxxix; 'Bibliographia delle Opere di W. B. Yeats', ibid., xli–xlviii (based on Allan Wade's Bibliography in Yeats's *Collected Works* (1908) vol. VIII. Wade pp. 407–8.

LISTER, RAYMOND, *Beulah to Byzantium: A Study of Parallels in the Works of W. B. Yeats, William Blake, Samuel Palmer and Edward Calvert. Being No. II of the Dolmen Press Yeats Centenary Papers MCMLXV* (Dublin: Dolmen Press, 1965) pp. 40 (numbered [29]–68). *See* MILLER, LIAM, (Part III).

LOFTUS, RICHARD J., 'W. B. Yeats: The National Ideals', in *Nationalism in Modern Anglo-Irish Poetry* (Madison and Milwaukee: University of Wisconsin Press, 1964) 38–66; 'W. B. Yeats: "The Holy Land of Ireland"', ibid., 67–96.

LOMBARDO, A., 'La poesia di William Butler Yeats', *La Poesia inglese dall' Estetismo al Simbolismo* (Rome: Edizioni di Storia e Letteratura, 1950) 249–88.

LONGAKER, MARK, *Ernest Dowson* (Philadelphia: University of Pennsylvania Press, 1945) *passim* (on Yeats and Dowson).

LUCAS, F. L., 'Sense and Sensibility', in *Authors Dead and Living* (London: Chatto & Windus; New York: Macmillan, 1923) 241–6 (on *Plays and Controversies*).

'William Butler Yeats', in *The Drama of Chekhov, Synge, Yeats and Pirandello* (London: Cassell, 1963) 239–355.

LUCE, A. A., *Berkeley's Immaterialism* (London: Nelson, 1945) vii–ix (comments on Yeats's 'Introduction' to Hone and Rossi, *Bishop Berkeley*).

Fishing and Thinking (London: Hodder & Stoughton, 1959) 79–84 (on 'The Fisherman').

LUCY, SEÁN, *T. S. Eliot and the Idea of Tradition* (London: Cohen & West, 1960) *passim*.

LUNARI, GIGI, 'William Butler Yeats e l'idea di un teatro', in *Il Movimento Drammatico Irlandese (1899–1922)* (Bologna: Cappelli, 1960) 41–62 *et passim*.

'Panorama del teatro irlandese', in *Teatro Irlandese*, ed. Gigi Lunari (Milan: Nuova Accademia, 1961) 9–36; ibid., 39–43 (comments on *The Hour Glass* and *The Only Jealousy of Emer*).

LYNCH, WILLIAM F., 'The Evocative Symbol', in *Symbols and Society: The Fourteenth Symposium of the Conference of Science, Philosophy and Religion*, ed. Lyman Bryson, Louis Finkelstein, Hudson Hoagland and R. M. MacIver (New York: Harper, 1955) 427–52.

LYND, ROBERT, *Ireland a Nation* (London: Grant Richards, 1919) 171–81 (an account of an interview with Yeats on the future of the Irish theatre). *See* Part V.

'Mr W. B. Yeats', in *Old and New Masters* (New York and London: Scribner's [1919]) 157–70. Reprinted as 'W. B. Yeats, 1919', in *Essays in Life and Literature* (New York: Dutton, 1951) 160–72.

'William Butler Yeats (1939)', in *Books and Writers*, with a Foreword by Richard Church (London: Dent, 1952) 76–84.

MacBride, Maud Gonne, *A Servant of the Queen* (London: Gollancz, 1938) *passim*.

'Yeats and Ireland', in *Scattering Branches*, ed. Stephen Gwynn, 15–34.

MacCallum, T. W., and Taylor, Stephen, 'Nobel Prize Winner for 1923: William Butler Yeats', *The Nobel Prize Winners and the Nobel Foundation, 1901–1937*, with an Introduction by Gilbert Murray (Zürich: Central European Publishing Company, 1938) 298–9.

MacCarthy, Desmond, 'Yeats', in *Criticism* (London: Putnam, 1932) 81–8.

MacDonagh, Thomas, *Literature in Ireland: Studies Irish and Anglo-Irish* (London: Fisher Unwin; Dublin: Talbot Press, 1916) 67–72 (the rhythm of 'Innisfree') *et passim*.

MacGreevy, Thomas, 'Uileachán Dubh Ó', in *The Capuchin Annual 1952*, ed. Fr Senan (Dublin, n.d.) 211–42 (a tour of the Yeats country with reminiscences of the poet and an account of his reburial in Sligo).

McHugh, Roger (ed.), *W. B. Yeats: Letters to Katharine Tynan* (Dublin: Clonmore & Reynolds; London: Burns, Oates & Washbourne; New York: McMullen, 1953) 11–22 ('Introduction'), 150–84 (Notes). Wade 211 H-I. *See* Part II.

MacKenna, Stephen. *See* Dodds, E. R.

MacLeish, Archibald, 'Public Speech and Private Speech in Poetry', in *Time to Speak* (Boston: Houghton Mifflin, 1940) 59–70. *See* Part V.

Yeats and the Belief in Life: An Address at the University of New Hampshire, January 17, 1957 (Durham: University of New Hampshire Press, 1958) pp. 20.

'The Public World: Poems of Yeats', in *Poetry and Experience* (Boston: Houghton Mifflin; London: Bodley Head, 1961) 115–47.

MacLeod, Fiona. *See* Sharp, William.

MacLiammóir, Micheál, 'Problem Plays', in *The Irish Theatre*, ed. Lennox Robinson (London: Macmillan, 1939) 204–5 (*The Countess Cathleen*).

'W. B. Yeats', in *All for Hecuba: An Irish Theatrical Autobiography* (London: Methuen, 1964; revised and enlarged edition, Dublin: Progress House, 1961) 72–5 (revised edition 68–71) *et passim.*

Theatre in Ireland (Dublin: At the Sign of the Three Candles, for the Cultural Relations Committee of Ireland, 1950) 7–16.

MacManus, Francis (ed.), *The Yeats We Knew* (Cork: Mercier Press, 1965) pp. 94 (the Thomas Davis Lectures, 1965). Contributions by Austin Clarke, Padraic Colum, Earnan de Blaghd, Monk Gibbon and Francis Stuart (q.v.).

Reviewed by W. R. Rodgers, *Listener*, LXXIV (25 Nov 1965) 867–8; *Quarterly Review*, CCCIII 646 (Oct 1965) 465; Michael P. Gallagher, *Studies*, LIV 214–15 (summer–autumn 1965) 284–8.

MacManus, L., *White Light and Flame: Memories of the Irish Literary Revival and the Anglo-Irish War* (Dublin and Cork: Talbot Press, 1929) 15–16, 45, 46–7.

MacManus, M. J., *A Jackdaw in Dublin: A Collection of Parodies of Irish Contemporaries* (Dublin and Cork: Talbot Press, [1924]) 9–11 (parodies of 'In a Cafe', 'The Dreamer' and 'A Poet's Lament').

'The Big House at Coole', in *Adventures of an Irish Bookman: A Selection from the Writings of M. J. MacManus*, ed. Francis MacManus (Dublin: Talbot Press, 1952) 127–31; ibid., 119–21 (on the beginnings of the Irish Literary Revival).

MacNamara, Brinsley. *See* Weldon, A. E.

MacNeice, Frederick Louis, *Modern Poetry: A Personal Essay* (London: Oxford University Press, 1938) *passim.*

The Poetry of W. B. Yeats (London: Oxford University Press, 1941) pp. xi + 242.

Reviewed by Winfield Townley Scott, *Accent*, I 4 (summer 1941) 247–50; W. Soutar, *Adelphi*, XVII 12 (Sep 1941) 421–7; E[lizabeth]. D[rew]., *Atlantic Monthly*, CLXVII (May 1941) Bookshelf; Roibeárd Ó Faracháin, *Bell*, II 2 (May 1941) 93–5; *Booklist*, XXXVII (15 May 1941) 435; S. C. C., *Christian Science Monitor*, 3 May 1941, Weekly Magazine, 10; J. Burnham, *Commonweal*, XXXIV (16 May 1941) 88–9; A. C., *Dublin Magazine*, XVI (Apr–June 1941) 75–7; F. T. Prince, *Dublin Review*, CCIX 418 (July 1941)

101–3; E. Meyerstein, *English*, III 17 (summer 1941) 223–5; A. N. Jeffares, *English Studies*, XXVII 1 (Jan 1946) 29–31; James Craig, *Life and Letters*, XXIX 44 (Apr 1941) 83–6; *Listener*, XXVI (11 Sep 1941) 383; Cleanth Brooks, *Modern Language Notes*, LVIII 4 (Apr 1943) 319–20; Edwin Muir, *New Statesman and Nation*, XXI (26 Apr 1941) 440; R. Mortimer, ibid., XXV (13 Feb 1943) 111–21; Babette Deutsch, *NYHTB*, 1 June 1941, 10; *New Yorker*, XVII (26 Apr 1941) 88; *Notes and Queries*, CLXXX (1 Mar 1941) 161–2; Dudley Fitts, *Saturday Review of Literature*, XXIV 2 (3 May 1941) 6; W. H. M[ellers]., *Scrutiny*, IX 4 (Mar 1941) 381–3; Michael Roberts, *Spectator*, CLXVI 5879 (28 Feb 1941) 234; *Springfield Republican*, 8 Apr 1941, 10; *TLS*, 2043 (29 May 1941) 150.

The Strings Are False: An Unfinished Autobiography (London: Faber & Faber, 1965) 147–8 (short anecdote), 214 (W. B. and Jack Yeats compared).

MAGALANGER, MARVIN, *Time of Apprenticeship: The Fiction of Young James Joyce* (New York: Abelard-Schuman, 1960) *passim* (includes unpublished letters by Yeats).

and KAIN, RICHARD M., *Joyce: The Man, the Work, the Reputation* (New York: New York University Press, 1956; London: John Calder, 1957) 68–70 ('The Tables of the Law' and Joyce) *et passim*.

MAGEE, WILLIAM KIRKPATRICK (John Eglinton), 'National Drama and Contemporary Life', in *Literary Ideals in Ireland*, by John Eglinton, W. B. Yeats, AE, W. Larminie (London: Fisher Unwin; Dublin: The Daily Express Office, 1899) 23–7; 'Mr Yeats and Popular Poetry', ibid., 41–6. Wade 297. *See* Part II.

'Yeats and His Story', *Irish Literary Portraits* (London: Macmillan, 1935) 17–35. *See* Part V.

A Memoir of AE, George William Russell (London: Macmillan, 1937) *passim* (includes a letter from AE about Yeats, 110–12).

'Apologia', in *Confidential or Take It Or Leave It* [Poems] (London: Fortune Press, 1951) 5–10 (reminiscences of Yeats and his literary circle).

MAIN, C. F. and SENG, PETER J., *Poems: Wadsworth Handbook and Anthology* (San Francisco: Wadsworth, 1961) 264–6 ('The Folly of Being Comforted').

MALINS, EDWARD, *Yeats and the Easter Rising. Being No. 1 of the Dolmen Press Yeats Centenary Papers MCMLXV* (Dublin: Dolmen Press, 1965) pp. 28. *See* MILLER, LIAM (Part III).

Reviewed by William Empson, *New Statesman*, LXX (23 July 1965) 123–4.

MALONE, ANDREW E., 'The Founders of the Irish Literary Theatre and their Ideals: (*a*) W. B. Yeats', in *The Irish Drama* (London: Constable, 1926; New York: Scribner's, 1929) 42–53; 'The Poet in the Theatre: W. B. Yeats', ibid., 129–46; ibid., *passim*.

'The Early History of the Abbey Theatre', in *The Irish Theatre*, ed. Lennox Robinson, 3–28 *passim*.

MALYE, JEAN, *La Littérature Irlandaise Contemporaine* (Paris: Sansot, 1913) 53–69 *et passim*.

MAN, PAUL DE. *See* DE MAN, PAUL.

MANNIN, ETHEL, *Privileged Spectator: A Sequel to Confessions and Impressions* (London: Jarrolds, 1939) 60–5, 95, 203–4, 213.

MANSERGH, NICHOLAS, 'The Influence of the Romantic Ideal in Irish Politics', in *Ireland in the Age of Reform and Revolution: A Commentary on Anglo–Irish Relations and on Political Forces in Ireland, 1840–1921* (London: Allen & Unwin, 1940) 215–30.

MARBLE, ANNIE RUSSELL, 'W. B. Yeats and His Part in the Celtic Revival', in *The Nobel Prize Winners in Literature* (New York and London: Appleton, 1925; revised edition, 1932) 253–63. (The revised edition adds a paragraph on Yeats's publications after 1925.)

MARRIOTT, JAMES WILLIAM, 'Irish Dramatists', in *Modern Drama* (London: Nelson, [1936]) 190–203 (compares Yeats's plays unfavourably with Synge's).

MARTIN, GRAHAM, 'The Later Poetry of W. B. Yeats', in *The Pelican Guide to English Literature*, vol. VII: *The Modern Age*, ed. Boris Ford (Harmondsworth: Penguin Books, 1961) 170–93.

'*The Wild Swans at Coole*', in *An Honoured Guest*, ed. Denis Donoghue and J. R. Mulryne, 54–72.

MARTZ, LOUIS L., *The Poetry of Meditation: A Study in English Religious Literature of the Seventeenth Century* (New Haven, Connecticut: Yale University Press, Yale Studies in English, vol. 125, 1954) 320–30 *passim*.

MASEFIELD, JOHN, 'On Mr W. B. Yeats', in *Recent Prose* (New York: Macmillan, 1933) 193–9.

   Some Memories of W. B. Yeats (Dublin: Cuala Press; London and New York: Macmillan, 1940) pp. 35.

   Reviewed by Winfield Townley Scott, *Accent*, I 4 (summer 1941) 247–50; W. Soutar, *Adelphi*, XVII 12 (Sep 1941) 425–7; Horace Reynolds, *Christian Science Monitor*, 28 Dec 1940, 10; *Dublin Magazine*, XVI (Apr–June 1941) 90; *NYHTB*, 24 Nov 1940, 19; C. G., *Personalist*, XXII (1941) 310–11; *TLS*, 2036 (8 Feb 1942) 68.

MASON, ELLSWORTH, and ELLMANN, RICHARD (eds), *The Critical Writings of James Joyce* (London: Faber & Faber; New York: Viking Press, 1959) 68–71 ('The Day of Rabblement'), 102–5 ('The Soul of Ireland'); ibid., *passim*.

MASON, EUGENE, 'The Poet as Mystic: William Butler Yeats', in *A Book of Preferences in Literature* (London: Wilson, 1915) 89–113 (adversely criticises Yeats's plays, with the exception of *Cathleen ni Houlihan*).

MATTHIESSEN, F. O., 'Yeats: The Crooked Road', in *The Responsibilities of the Critic: Essays and Reviews*, selected by John Rackliffe (New York: Oxford University Press, 1952) 25–40. *See Part V.*

MAXWELL, D. E. S., 'Swift's Dark Grove: Yeats and the Anglo–Irish Tradition', in *W. B. Yeats, 1865–1965*, ed. D. E. S. Maxwell and S. B. Bushrui, 18–32.

   and BUSHRUI, S. B. (eds), *W. B. Yeats, 1865–1965: Centenary Essays on the Art of W. B. Yeats* (Nigeria: Ibadan University Press; London: Nelson, 1965) pp. xvi +252. Articles by S. B. Bushrui, MacD. Emslie, E. Engelberg, F. F. Farag, I. Fletcher, R. Fréchet, D. Gerstenberger, R. M. Kain, B. A. King, J. Kleinstück, D. E. S. Maxwell, J. R. Moore, George Brandon Saul, M. J. Sidnell, W. H. Stevenson (q.v.). Foreword by A. Norman Jeffares. Poems by Christopher Okigbo, J. D. Lerner and James Simmons. Bibliography. Wade 361.

MAYHEW, JOYCE, *Ad Multos Annos: William Butler Yeats in His Seventieth Year* (Mills College, Oakland, California: Eucalyptus Press, 1935) pp. [8].

MAYNARD, THEODORE, 'W. B. Yeats: Fairies and Fog', in *Our Best Poets English and American* (New York: Holt, 1922; London: Brentano, 1924) 67–83.

MEENAN, JAMES (ed.), *Centenary History of the Literary and Historical Society of University College Dublin, 1855–1955* (Tralee: The Kerryman [1956?]) 57–8 (on the students' protest against *The Countess Cathleen*).

MÉGROZ, R. L., *Modern English Poetry, 1829–1932* (London: Nicholson & Watson, 1933) *passim*.

MELCHIORI, GIORGIO, *The Whole Mystery of Art: Pattern into Poetry in the Work of W. B. Yeats* (London: Routledge & Kegan Paul, 1960) pp. xiv +306. pp. 283–6 reprinted as 'The Moment of Moments', in *Yeats: A Collection of Critical Essays*, ed. John Unterecker, 33–6.

Reviewed by Donald Davie, *Guardian*, 17 Feb 1961, 6; R. F. Rattray, *Hibbert Journal*, LIX (July 1961) 373; Burton A. Robie, *Library Journal*, LXXXVI (1 Mar 1961) 1001; T. R. Henn, *New Statesman*, LXI (13 Jan 1961) 60; Robert Armstrong, *Poetry Review*, LII (Apr–June 1961) 99; A. N. Jeffares, *Review of English Studies*, n.s., XII 48 (Nov 1961) 437–9; Frank Kermode, *Spectator*, CCVI, 6927 (31 Mar 1961) 448–9; J. B. Morton, *Tablet*, CCXV (Apr 1961) 330; *TLS*, 3077 (17 Feb 1961) 97–8.

MENON, V. K. NARAYANA, *The Development of William Butler Yeats*, with a Preface by Sir Herbert Grierson (Edinburgh and London: Oliver & Boyd, 1942; second edition, revised, 1960; Philadelphia: Dufour Editions, 1961) pp. xiv +92.

Reviewed by *American Mercury*, LVI 233 (May 1943) 629 (briefly); M. D., *Dublin Magazine*, XVIII (Oct–Dec 1943) 59–60; E. Meyerstein, *English*, IV 23 (summer 1943) 162–3; René Fréchet, *Études Anglaises*, XIV 1 (Jan–Mar 1961) 41–5; George Orwell, *Horizon*, VIII 37 (Jan 1943) 67–71; Raymond Mortimer, *New Statesman*, XXV (13 Feb 1943) 111–12; Robert Armstrong, *Poetry Review*, LI (Oct–Dec 1960) 234; R. Lienhardt, *Scrutiny*, XL 3 (spring 1943) 220–4; P. Gannon, *Studies*, XXXII 125 (Mar 1943) 127–9; George

Orwell, *Time and Tide*, XXIV (17 Apr 1943) 325–6; *TLS*, 2135 (2 Jan 1943) 9; ibid., 3051 (19 Aug 1960) 305; A. M. C., *University of Edinburgh Journal*, XII (1943) 124–5.

MERCHANT, FRANCIS, *A. E.: An Irish Promethean. A Study of the Contribution of George William Russell to World Culture* (Columbia, South Carolina: Benedict College Press, 1954) *passim* (on Yeats and A.E.).

MERCIER, VIVIAN, *The Irish Comic Tradition* (Oxford: Clarendon Press, 1962) *passim*.

MILES, JOSEPHINE, *Major Adjectives in English Poetry, from Wyatt to Auden* (Berkeley and Los Angeles: University of California Press, University of California Publications in English, vol. XII, no. 3, 1946) 320–1, 387–8.

The Primary Language of Poetry in the 1940s (Berkeley and Los Angeles: University of California Press, University of California Publications in English, vol. XIX, no. 3, 1951) 413–17, 480–3 (including analytic tables of Yeats's poetic vocabulary).

'The Classical Modes of Yeats', in *Eras and Modes in English Poetry* (Berkeley and Los Angeles: University of California Press, 1957) 178–202 ('Her Praise').

MILLER, ANNA IRENE, 'The National Theatre of Ireland', in *The Independent Theatre in Europe, 1887 to the Present* (New York: Long & Smith, 1931) 262–6 *et passim*.

MILLER, LIAM, 'The Dun Emer and the Cuala Press', in *The World of Yeats*, ed. Robin Skelton and Ann Saddlemyer, 141–51 (Yeats and the private presses).

(ed.), *Thoor Ballylee – Home of William Butler Yeats. Edited from a Paper Given by Mary Hanley to the Kiltartan Society in 1961*, with a Foreword by T. R. Henn (Dublin: Dolmen Press, 1965) pp. 32 (presidential lecture at the second meeting of the Society at Thoor Ballylee, 23 July 1961).

(ed.), *The Dolmen Press Yeats Centenary Papers MCMLXV*, nos. I–V.* *See* ALSPACH, RUSSELL K.; FAULKNER, PETER; LISTER, RAYMOND; MALINS, EDWARD; TELFER, GILES W. L.

* Nos. VI–XII, together with *Preliminaries and Index* (Dolmen Press, 1966–8), have since been published to complete the series.

MILLETT, FRED. B., *The Rebirth of Liberal Education* (New York: Harcourt, Brace, 1945) 166–8 ('After Long Silence').

MINER, EARL, ' "An Aristocratic Form": Japan in the Thought and Writing of William Butler Yeats', in *The Japanese Tradition in British and American Literature* (Princeton, New Jersey: Princeton University Press, 1958) 232–65 (on Yeats and the Noh).

MISRA, B. P., *W. B. Yeats* (Allahabad: Kitab Mahal, 1962) pp. 128.

MITCHELL, SUSAN, *Aids to the Immortality of Certain Persons in Ireland, Charitably Administered* (Dublin and London: Maunsel, 1913) *passim*. (Yeats is mentioned in the 'Author's Review' and in several of the poems. The 'Prologue' parodies 'When you are old . . .'.)

    George Moore (Dublin and London: Maunsel, 1916) 100–4 (on Yeats's collaboration with Moore on *Diarmuid and Grania*).

    (ed.), *Secret Springs of Dublin Song* (Dublin: Talbot Press; London: Unwin, 1918). (Contains parodies of Yeats's verse.)

MIX, KATHERINE LYON, *A Study in Yellow: The Yellow Book and its Contributors* (Lawrence: University of Kansas Press; London: Constable, 1960) *passim*.

MONAHAN, MICHAEL, 'Yeats and Synge', in *Nova Hibernia: Irish Poets and Dramatists of Today and Yesterday* (New York and London: Mitchell Kennerly, 1914) 13–37.

MONRO, HAROLD, *Some Contemporary Poets (1920)* (London: Leonard Parsons, 1920) *passim*.

MONROE, HARRIET, *A Poet's Life: Seventy Years in a Changing World* (New York: Macmillan, 1938) *passim*.

MONTAGUE, C. E., 'Good and Bad Subjects for Plays', in *Dramatic Values* (London: Methuen, 1910; revised edition, London: Methuen; New York: Doubleday, 1925) 215–16 (Yeats's views on drama).

MOORE, GEORGE, 'Introduction', in *The Heather Field and Maeve* by Edward Martyn (London: Duckworth, 1899) xx–xxii (attack on William Archer for ignoring *The Countess Cathleen*). *See also* ARCHER, WILLIAM (Part V).

'Literature and the Irish Language', in *Ideals in Ireland*, ed. Lady Gregory, 43–51. *See* Part V.

Hail and Farewell (London: Heinemann; New York: Appleton, 3 vols, 1911–14, 1925; London: Heinemann, 1933; Ebury Edition, 1936–7) vol. I: *Ave, passim*; vol. II: *Salve*, 69–107 *passim*; vol. III: *Vale*, 113–42 *passim*.

MOORE, J. R., 'The Idea of a Yeats Play', in *W. B. Yeats, 1865–1965*, ed. D. E. S. Maxwell and S. B. Bushrui, 154–66.

MOORE, T. STURGE. *See* LEWIS, CECIL ARTHUR; FRENCH, CECIL.

MOORE, VIRGINIA, *The Unicorn: William Butler Yeats' Search for Reality* (New York: Macmillan, 1954) pp. xxi +519. Wade 344.

Reviewed by Charles Walcutt, *Arizona Quarterly*, XI (1955) 170–3; *Booklist*, L (15 June 1954) 399; Stanley K. Koffman, Jr, *Books Abroad*, XXIX 2 (spring 1955) 226; Mary Brody, *Catholic World*, CLXXIX (July 1954) 317–18; René Fréchet, *Études Anglaises*, XII 4 (Oct–Dec 1959) 365–6; Hugh Kenner, *Hudson Review*, VIII 4 (winter 1956) 609–17; *Kirkus*, XXII (1 Mar 1954) 181; Herbert Cahoon, *Library Journal*, LXXIX 9 (1 May 1959) 858 (briefly); *Nation*, CLXXIX (31 July 1954) 96–7; Babette Deutsch, *NYHTB*, 18 July 1954, 5; Horace Gregory, *NYTB*, 30 May 1954, 8; *New Yorker*, XXX (Aug 1954) 84; Louis Johnson, *Numbers*, I 4 (Oct 1955) 38–40; *Personalist*, XXXVI 4 (Oct 1955) 424–5; Irving David Suss, *South Atlantic Quarterly*, LIV 1 (Jan 1955) 151–3; Hazard Adams, *Western Review*, XIX 2 (winter 1955) 233–4; Reuben A. Brower, *Yale Review*, XLIV 2 (Dec 1954) 290.

MORE, PAUL ELMER, 'Two Poets of the Irish Movement', in *Shelburne Essays (First Series)* (London: Putnam's, 1904; New York: Putnam's, 1906) 177–93.

MORGAN, A. E., 'The Irish Pioneers: I. Yeats', in *Tendencies of Modern English Drama* (London: Constable; New York: Scribner's, 1924) 139–47 *et passim*.

MORGAN, CHARLES, *The House of Macmillan* (London: Macmillan, 1943; New York: Macmillan, 1944) 219–24 (on Yeats's dealings with the Macmillan company).

MORGAN, LOUISE, 'W. B. Yeats', in *Writers at Work* (London: Chatto & Windus, 1931) 1–9.

MORRIS, LLOYD R., *The Celtic Dawn: A Survey of the Renascence of Ireland 1889–1916* (New York: Macmillan, 1917) *passim*.

MORTON, DAVIS, *The Renaissance of Irish Poetry: 1880–1930* (New York: Ives Washburn, 1929) *passim*.

MOSES, M. J., 'W. B. Yeats and the Irish School of Playwrights', in *Representative British Dramas Victorian and Modern* (Boston: Heath, 1918; revised edition, 1931) 889–97; 'William Butler Yeats', ibid., 901–5.

MUDDIMAN, BERNARD, *The Men of the Nineties* (London: Danielson, 1920) *passim*.

MUIR, EDWIN, *The Present Age from 1914* (London: Cresset Press; New York: McBride, 1940) 52–61 *et passim*.

'W. B. Yeats', in *Aspects de la Littérature Anglaise 1918–1945*, ed. Kathleen Raine and Max Pol Fouchet (Paris: Fontaine, 1947) 94–105.

'W. B. Yeats', in *The Estate of Poetry*, the Charles Eliot Norton Lectures, 1955–1956 (London: Hogarth Press; Cambridge, Massachusetts: Harvard University Press, 1962) 42–60.

MULLIK, B. R., *Yeats* (Delhi, Jullundur, Lucknow: S. Chand, 1961) pp. 62 (*Studies in Poets*, vol. XIX).

MULRYNE, J. R., 'The *Last Poems*', in *An Honoured Guest*, ed. Denis Donoghue and J. R. Mulryne, 124–42.

See also DONOGHUE, DENIS, and MULRYNE, J. R.

MURPHY, GWENDOLEN, *The Modern Poet* (London: Sidgwick & Jackson, 1938) 'Introduction', *passim*.

MURRY, J. MIDDLETON, 'Mr Yeats' Swan Song', in *Aspects of Literature* (London: Collins, 1920; New York: Knopf, 1921; revised edition, London: Jonathan Cape, 1934) 53–9. *See* Part V.

NAGY, N. CHRISTOPH DE. *See* DE NAGY, N. CHRISTOPH.

NATHAN, LEONARD E., *The Tragic Drama of William Butler Yeats: Figures in a Dance* (New York and London: Columbia University Press, 1965) pp. xii +307.

Reviewed by Robert F. Berolzheimer, *Library Journal*, XC (15 June 1965) 2865; *TLS*, 3326 (25 Nov 1965) 1701.

NETHERCOT, ARTHUR HOBART, *The First Five Lives of Annie Besant* (Chicago: University of Illinois Press, 1960) 300–4.

NEVINSON, HENRY W., 'The Poet of the Sidhe', in *Books and Personalities* (London: Lane, 1905) 318–25 (the early poetry); 'The Latter Oisin', ibid., 226–32 ('The Shadowy Waters').

NEW INTERNATIONAL YEAR BOOK, THE: *A Compendium of the World's Progress for the Year 1939*, ed. Charles Earle Funk (New York and London: Funk & Wagnalls, 1940) 'William Butler Yeats', 813–14 (obituary note).

NEWBOLT, Sir HENRY, *My World as in My Time: Memoirs of Sir Henry Newbolt, 1862–1932* (London: Faber & Faber, 1932) 192–4 (on Yeats and Robert Bridges).

NEWBOLT, MARGARET (ed.), *The Later Life and Letters of Sir Henry Newbolt* (London: Faber & Faber, 1942) *passim* (includes letters from Yeats to Newbolt). Wade 330.

NICHOLSON, NORMAN, *Man and Literature* (London: S. C. M. Press, 1945) 188–92.

NICOLL, ALLARDYCE, *World Drama from Aeschylus to Anouilh* (London: Harrap, 1949–52) 729–31 *et passim*.

British Drama: An Historical Survey from the Beginnings to the Present Time (London: Harrap, 1925; fifth edition, revised, 1962) 313–15, 317.

NIC SHIUBHLAIGH, MAIRE, *The Splendid Years*. Recollections of Maire Nic Shiubhlaigh, as told to Edward Kenny. With Appendices and Lists of Irish Theatre Plays, 1899–1916. Foreword by Padraic Colum (Dublin: James Duffy, 1955) *passim*.

NIMS, JOHN FREDERICK, 'Yeats and the Careless Muse', in *Learners and Discerners: A Newer Criticism. Discussions of Modern Literature*, ed. Robert Scholes (Charlottesville: University of Virginia Press, 1964) 29–60 (on the 'studied nonchalance' of Yeats's poetry).

NOGUCHI, YONE, 'A Japanese Note on Yeats', in *Through the Torii* (London: Elkin Mathews, 1914) 110–17.

NORMAN, CHARLES, *Ezra Pound* (New York: Macmillan, 1960) *passim* (on Yeats's association with Pound).

O'BRIEN, CONOR CRUISE, 'Passion and Cunning: An Essay on the Politics of W. B. Yeats', in *In Excited Reverie*, ed. A. Norman Jeffares and K. G. W. Cross, 207–78. *See* Part V.

O'CASEY, SEAN, *Drums under the Windows* (London: Macmillan, 1945) 145–50 (includes an anecdote on Yeats's standing as a poet). Also in *Autobiographies: I* (London: Macmillan, St Martin's Library, 1963) 516–20.

Inishfallen Fare Thee Well (London: Macmillan, 1949) 141–54 *passim* (Yeats and Lady Gregory), 287–90 (unflattering account of a performance of *At the Hawk's Well* at Merrion Square). Also in *Autobiographies: II* (London: Macmillan, St Martin's Library, 1963) 114–25 *passim*, 231–4.

'The Silver Tassie', in *Rose and Crown* (London: Macmillan, 1952) 27–45; 'The Friggin Frogs', ibid., 46–61; ibid., *passim*. Also in *Autobiographies: II* (London: Macmillan, St Martin's Library, 1963) 268–80, 281–91 *et passim*.

Sunset and Evening Star (London: Macmillan, 1954) 94–6 (Yeats, O'Casey and Denis Johnston). Also in *Autobiographies: II* (London: Macmillan, St Martin's Library, 1963) 521–2.

O'CONNOR, FRANK. *See* O'DONOVAN, MICHAEL.

O'CONNOR, ULICK, *The Times I've Seen: Oliver St John Gogarty: A Biography* (New York: Ivan Obolensky, 1963; as *Oliver St John Gogarty: A Poet and His Time* (London: Jonathan Cape, 1964) *passim*. Wade 354.

O'CONNOR, WILLIAM VAN, *Sense and Sensibility in Modern Poetry* (Chicago: Chicago University Press, 1948) *passim*.

O'CONOR, NORREYS JEPHSON, 'Yeats and His Vision', in *Changing Ireland: Literary Backgrounds of the Irish Free State 1889–1922* (Cambridge, Massachusetts: Harvard University Press, 1924; London: Milford, 1925) 72–82; ibid., *passim*.

'A Note on Yeats', in *Essays in Memory of Barrett Wendell, by His Assistants*, ed. William Richards Castle and Paul Kaufman (Cambridge, Massachusetts: Harvard University Press; London: Oxford University Press, 1926) 283–9.

O'DONNELL, F. HUGH, *Souls for Gold! Pseudo-Celtic Drama* (London: Privately Printed, 1899) pp. 16. Contains two letters to the editor of the *Freeman's Journal*, here printed as 'A Pseudo-Celtic Drama in Dublin. I. Faith for Gold' (q.v., Part V) 3–8; 'II. Blasphemy and Degradation' (refused publication) 9–14 (*The Countess Cathleen*).

The Stage Irishman of the Pseudo-Celtic Drama (London: John Long, 1904) pp. 47 (an attack on the drama of Yeats and on Stephen Gwynn's support of it in the *New Liberal Review*, q.v.).

O'DONNELL, J. P., *Sailing to Byzantium: A Study in the Development of the Later Style and Symbolism in the Poetry of William Butler Yeats*, Harvard Honors Theses in English, No. 11 (Cambridge, Massachusetts: Harvard University Press, 1939) pp. 95.

O'DONOVAN, MICHAEL (Frank O'Connor), *The Art of the Theatre* (Dublin and London: Fridberg, 1947) 24–6.

Leinster, Munster and Connaught (London: Hale, [1950]) 238–43, 256–61 *et passim* (reminiscences).

O'FAOLÁIN, SEÁN, *The Irish* (Harmondsworth: Penguin Books, 1947) 20–1 ('The Unappeasable Host').

Ó FARACHÁIN, ROIBEÁRD. *See* FARREN, ROBERT.

O'HAGAN, THOMAS, 'The Irish Dramatic Movement', in *Essays on Catholic Life* (Baltimore: Murphy, 1916) 57–73.

OLIVERO, FEDERICO, 'William Butler Yeats: Le Liriche', in *Studi sul romanticismo inglese* (Bari: Laterza e Figli, 1914) 105–9; 'William Butler Yeats: I Drammi', ibid., 120–69.

O LOCHLAINN, COLM, 'William Butler Yeats', in *The British Annual of Literature*, vol. II (London: British Authors' Press, 1939) 24–30 (obituary article).

O'NEILL, MICHAEL J., *Lennox Robinson* (New York: Twayne Publishers, 1964) *passim*.

ORAGE, A. R., 'Ireland: Diagnoses', in *Selected Essays and Critical Writings* (London: Nott, 1935) 54–6 (*Reveries over Childhood and Youth*).

ORWELL, GEORGE (Eric Blair), 'W. B. Yeats', in *Critical Essays* (London: Secker & Warburg, 1946, 1954; New York: Reynal & Hitchcock, entitled *Dickens, Dali and Others: Studies in Popular Culture*, 1946) 129–36 (American edition 161–9). *See* Part V.

Osgood, Charles Grosvenor, *The Voice of England: A History* (New York and London: Harper, 1935; second edition with a chapter in postscript on English literature since 1910 by Thomas Riggs, Jr, New York: Harper, 1952) 580–1, 597–9, 622–3.

Oshima, Shotaro, *Ieitsu Kenkyu* (*W. B. Yeats: A Study*) (Tokyo: Taibunsha, 1927) pp. ix +402.

W. B. Yeats (Tokyo: Kenkyusha, English and American Men of Letters Series, No. 81, 1934) pp. viii +156.

Studies in Modern Irish Literature (Tokyo: Hokuseido, 1956; revised edition, with an additional chapter, 1960) 435–516.

'Translator's Note', in *Ieitsu Shishu* (*Collected Poems of Yeats*), translated into Japanese by Shotaro Oshima (Tokyo: Hokuseido, by arrangements with A. R. Watt & Son, London, 1957) xv–xviii; 'An Interview with Yeats', ibid., 297–309; ibid., 310–42 (the poetry). Wade p. 428.

W. B. Yeats and Japan (Tokyo: Hokuseido Press; London: Luzac, 1965) pp. xiv +198 (contains letters of Yeats, copies of four autograph poems sent by Yeats to Oshima, essays on Eastern aspects of Yeats's work, accounts of interviews with Yeats, an account of Japanese books and periodicals about Yeats, and a bibliography of Japanese writings on Yeats). Wade 359. *See* Part I.

O'Sullivan, Donal, *The Irish Free State and Its Senate* (London: Faber & Faber, 1940) *passim*.

O'Sullivan, Seumas. *See* Starkey, James Sullivan.

Paige, D. D. (ed.), *The Letters of Ezra Pound 1907–1941* (New York: Harcourt, Brace, 1950; London: Faber & Faber, 1951; New York: Harcourt, Brace & World paperback edition, 1962) *passim*.

Painter, James Allan, 'Programmer's Preface', in *A Concordance to the Poems of W. B. Yeats*, ed. Stephen M. Parrish, xxix–xxxvii (on the making of the *Concordance*).

Palmer, Herbert, 'The Irish School of Poetry', *Post-Victorian Poetry* (London: Dent, 1938) 96–103; ibid., 7–10 (the Rhymers' Club) *et passim*.

PALMER, VANCE, *Louis Esson and the Australian Theatre* (Melbourne: Meanjin Press, 1948) 199 (letter from Esson describes conversations with Yeats, 1920).

PARKINSON, THOMAS, *W. B. Yeats, Self-Critic: A Study of His Early Verse* (Berkeley and Los Angeles: University of California Press, 1951) pp. viii +202. *See also* Part V.

Reviewed by Horace Reynolds, *Christian Science Monitor*, 12 June 1952, 7; W. P. M., *Dublin Magazine*, XXVII (Oct–Dec 1951) 80; *Listener*, XLVIII (17 July 1952) 111, 113; J. Graddon, *Poetry Review*, XLIII 4 (Oct–Dec 1952) 232 (briefly); Lawrence Ferling, *San Francisco Chronicle*, 6 Jan 1952, 18; Richard Ellmann, *Sewanee Review*, LXI 1 (Jan–Mar 1953) 149; *TLS*, 2640 (5 Sep 1952) 582; *United States Quarterly Book Review*, VIII (1952) 28–9; Richard Eberhart, *Virginia Quarterly Review*, XXVIII 4 (autumn 1952) 618–21; Martin Price, *Yale Review*, XLI 3 (Mar 1952) 459.

'The World of Yeats' "Nineteen Hundred and Nineteen"', in *The Image of the Work: Essays in Criticism*, by B. H. Lehman and others (Berkeley and Los Angeles: University of California Press, 1955) 211–27.

W. B. Yeats: The Later Poetry (Berkeley and Los Angeles: University of California Press; London: Cambridge University Press, 1965) pp. xiv +260. Wade 355.

Reviewed by Peter Faulkner, *Durham University Journal*, LVII, n.s., xxvi 3 (June 1965) 180–1; Thomas R. Whitaker, *English Language Notes*, II 2 (Dec 1964) 150–4; George T. Wright, *Journal of Aesthetics and Art Criticism*, XXIII 3 (spring 1965) 392–3; W. R. Rodgers, *Listener*, LXXIV (25 Nov 1965) 867–8; T. R. Henn, *Modern Language Review*, LX 3 (July 1965) 440–1; James L. Allen, Jr, *Modern Philology*, LXII 4 (May 1965) 369–70; William Empson, *New Statesman*, LXX (23 July 1965) 123–4; *Quarterly Review*, CCCIII 643 (Jan 1965) 115–16; Peter Ure, *Review of English Studies*, XVI 63 (Aug 1965) 328–31; *TLS*, 3304 (24 June 1965) 529–30; James L. Allen, Jr, *Western Humanities Review*, XIX 1 (winter 1965) 90–2.

'The Later Plays of W. B. Yeats', in *Modern Drama: Essays in Criticism*, ed. Travis Bogard and W. I. Oliver (New York: Oxford University Press, 1965) 385–93 (on the plays Yeats wrote from *At the Hawk's Well* onward, and the influence of the Noh).

PARRISH, STEPHEN MAXWELL, 'Editor's Preface', in *A Concordance to the Poems of W. B. Yeats*, ed. Stephen M. Parrish, v–xxvii (on the significance of the *Concordance*). *See* Part I.

PASCAL, ROY, *Design and Truth in Autobiography* (Cambridge, Massachusetts: Harvard University Press, 1960) 136–9 *et passim*.

PEACOCK, RONALD, 'Yeats', in *The Poet in the Theatre* (London: Routledge, 1946; New York: Harcourt, Brace, 1946; Hill & Wang, 1960) 117–28; ibid., 109 (a comparison of Synge's and Yeats's *Deirdre*).

PEARCE, DONALD R., 'Introduction', in *The Senate Speeches of W. B. Yeats*, ed. Donald R. Pearce (Bloomington: Indiana University Press, 1960; London: Faber & Faber, 1961) 11–26 (on Yeats and the Irish Senate, 1922–8). *See* Part II, and article by W. B. Stanford (Part V).

PEARSON, HESKETH, *Bernard Shaw: His Life and Personality* (London: Collins; as *G.B.S.: A Full Length Portrait*, New York: Harper, 1942) *passim* (brief comment on Wilde by Yeats).

The Life of Oscar Wilde (London: Methuen, 1946, 1951) *passim*.

PELLIZZI, CAMILLO, *Il Teatro Inglese* (Milan: Fratelli Treves, 1934) 234–42; translated by Rowan Williams as *English Drama: The Last Great Phase* (London: Macmillan, 1935) 176–83 (*The Countess Cathleen* and *The Hour Glass*).

PERKINS, DAVID, *The Quest for Permanence: The Symbolism of Wordsworth, Shelley and Keats* (Cambridge, Massachusetts: Harvard University Press, 1959) *passim*.

Wordsworth and the Poetry of Sincerity (Cambridge, Massachusetts: Harvard University Press, 1965) 5–8 ('Identity' and the use of masks; 'The Circus Animals' Desertion') *et passim*.

PETRIE, Sir CHARLES, 'Ireland', in *Scenes of Edwardian Life* (London: Eyre & Spottiswoode, 1965) chap. vi, 166–70 *passim* (on Yeats and Lady Gregory).

PHELPS, WILLIAM LYON, 'The Irish Poets', in *The Advance of English Poetry in the Twentieth Century* (New York: Dodd, Mead, 1918; London: Allen & Unwin, 1920) 162–71, 179, 226.

PINTO, VIVIAN DE SOLA, 'Yeats and Synge', in *Crisis in English Poetry 1880–1940* (London: Hutchinson; New York: Longmans, 1951) 85–111 *et passim*.

PLARR, VICTOR GUSTAVE, *Ernest Dowson 1888–97* (London: Elkin Mathews; New York: L. J. Gomme, 1914) *passim*.

POEPPING, HILDE, *James Stephens. Eine Untersuchung über die irische Erneuerensbewegung in der Zeit von 1900 bis 1930* (Schriftenreihe der 'Deutschen Gesellschaft für Keltische Studien', Heft 4, Halle: Max Niemeyer, 1940) *passim*.

POGSON, REX, *Miss Horniman and the Gaiety Theatre, Manchester* (London: Rockliff, 1952) 8–12.

POLLOCK, J. H., *William Butler Yeats* (Dublin: Talbot Press; London: Duckworth; New York: Nelson, 1940) pp. 112.

Reviewed by P. S. O'Hegarty, *Dublin Magazine*, X (July–Sep 1935) 82–3; K. Arns, *Englische Studien*, LXXI 2 (Dec 1936) 276–7; P. C. T., *Irish Book Lover*, XXIII 4 (July–Aug 1935) 97; F. S., *Studies*, XXIV 95 (Sep 1935) 492–3; *TLS*, 1738 (23 May 1935) 332.

POUND, EZRA, 'The Later Yeats', in *Literary Essays of Ezra Pound*, edited with an Introduction by T. S. Eliot (London: Faber & Faber; Norfolk, Connecticut: New Directions, 1954; Faber paperback, 1960) 378–81. *See* Part V. *Ibid., passim*.

— (ed.), *Passages from the Letters of John Butler Yeats* (Dundrum: Cuala Press, 1917) *passim*.

Reviewed by *American Review of Reviews*, LVII (Feb 1918) 217; *Athenaeum*, 4620 (Aug 1917) 413; *Boston Evening Transcript*, 13 June 1917, 6; T. S. Eliot, *Egoist*, V 6 (June–July 1918) 87 (briefly); *North American Review*, CCVI (Sep 1917) 472; *TLS*, 803 (7 June 1917) 271.

Letters. See PAIGE, D. D.

PRATT, JOHN CLARK, 'Leda and the Swan', in *The Meaning of Modern Poetry* (Garden City, New York: Doubleday, 1962) 375–93 (an elementary reading of the poem).

PRESS, JOHN, *The Fire and the Fountain: An Essay on Poetry* (London: Oxford University Press, 1955) *passim*.

— *The Chequer'd Shade: Reflections on Obscurity in Poetry* (London: Oxford University Press, 1958) *passim*.

Rule and Energy: Trends in British Poetry since the Second World War (London: Oxford University Press, 1963) *passim* (on Yeats's influence on later poets).

PRICE, ALAN, 'Yeats and Synge', in *Synge and Anglo-Irish Drama* (London: Methuen, 1961) 51–68 *et passim*.

PRIESTLEY, J. B., *Literature and Western Man* (London: Heinemann; New York: Harpers, 1960) 398–403, 407–9.

PRIOR, MOODY E., *The Language of Tragedy* (New York: Columbia University Press, 1947) 326–40.

'Poetic Drama: An Analysis and a Suggestion', in *English Institute Essays 1949*, ed. Alan S. Downer (New York: Columbia University Press, 1950) 3–32 (Yeats 24–6).

QUINN, Sr M. BERNETTA, 'William Butler Yeats: The Road to Tir-na-n-Og', in *The Metamorphic Tradition in Modern Poetry: Essays on the Work of Ezra Pound, Wallace Stevens, William Carlos Williams, T. S. Eliot, Hart Crane, Randall Jarrell and William Butler Yeats* (New Brunswick, New Jersey: Rutgers University Press, 1955) 207–36; ibid., 260–3 (Bibliography).

RAINE, KATHLEEN, 'Introduction', in *Letters on Poetry from W. B. Yeats to Dorothy Wellesley* (London: Oxford University Press, 1940; Oxford paperback, 1964) ix–xiii. *See* Part II.

RAIZISS, SONA, *The Metaphysical Passion: Seven Modern American Poets and the Seventeenth Century Tradition* (Philadelphia: University of Pennsylvania Press, 1952) *passim*.

RAJAN, B., *W. B. Yeats: A Critical Introduction* (London: Hutchinson; New York: Hillary House, 1965) pp. 207.

Reviewed by W. R. Rodgers, *Listener*, LXXIV (25 Nov 1965) 867–8; Ronald Dunlop, *Poetry Australia*, 16 (Oct 1965) 36–9; Henry T. Moore, *Saturday Review*, XLVIII (16 Dec 1965) 81; *TLS*, 3316 (16 Dec 1965) 802.

RATTRAY, R. F., 'A Day with Yeats', in *Poets in the Flesh: Tagore, Yeats, Dunsany, Stephens, Drinkwater* (Cambridge: Golden Head Press, 1961) 5–8.

READ, HERBERT, 'The Later Yeats', in *A Coat of Many Colours* (London: Routledge, 1945; revised edition, 1956) 208–12 ('The Sorrow of Love', 1895 and 1933 versions).

'Ideas into Action: Ezra Pound', in *The True Voice of Feeling: Studies in English Romantic Poetry* (London: Faber & Faber, 1953) 116–20 (on Pound's debt to Yeats).

'The Image in Modern Poetry', in *The Tenth Muse: Essays in Criticism* (London: Routledge & Kegan Paul, 1957) 117–37.

READE, A. R., 'The Anglo-Irish and W. B. Yeats', in *Main Currents in Modern Literature* (London: Nicholson & Watson, 1935) 41–56.

REEVES, JOHN A. See FREEDLEY, GEORGE.

REID, B. L., *William Butler Yeats: The Lyric of Tragedy* (Norman: Oklahoma University Press; Nottingham: W. S. Hall, 1961) pp. xiv + 282.

Reviewed by Francis Murphy, *Books Abroad*, XXXVI 3 (summer 1962) 319–20; Patrick Crutwell, *Hudson Review*, XV 3 (autumn 1962) 451–4 (Yeats 453); L. W. Griffin, *Library Journal*, LXXXVII (1 Feb 1962) 560; H. R. MacCallum, *University of Toronto Quarterly*, XXXII 3 (Apr 1963) 307–13.

REID, FORREST, *W. B. Yeats: A Critical Study* (London: Secker; New York: Dodd Mead, 1915) pp. 257.

Reviewed by *Athenaeum*, 4590 (16 Oct 1915) 259–60; *Irish Book Lover*, VII 6 (Jan 1916) 113–14; *New Republic*, V (18 Dec 1915) 176; L. Gilman, *North American Review*, CII 719 (Oct 1915) 592–7; *Spectator*, CXV 4555 (16 Oct 1915) 510–11; *TLS*, 715 (30 Sep 1915) 331.

See also *Forrest Reid: A Portrait and a Study*, by Russell Burlingham, 196–202.

REXROTH, KENNETH, 'The Plays of Yeats', in *Bird in the Bush: Obvious Essays* (New York: New Directions, 1959) 235–41.

REYNOLDS, ERNEST, 'Yeats, Synge and the Irish School', in *Modern English Drama: A Survey of the Theatre from 1900*. With a Foreword by Allardyce Nicoll (London: Harrap, 1949; revised edition, 1950) 87–97.

REYNOLDS, HORACE, *A Providence Episode in the Irish Literary Renaissance* (Providence, Rhode Island: The Study Hill Club, 1929) pp. 41 (reprints articles from the *Providence Journal* for 3, 10, 17 and 24 Oct 1928 on Yeats's connection with that journal).

'Introduction', in W. B. Yeats, *Letters to the New Island*, ed. Horace Reynolds (Cambridge, Massachusetts: Harvard University Press, 1934) 3–66. *See* Part II.

RHYS, ERNEST, *Everyman Remembers* (London and Toronto: Dent, 1931) 251–5 (on Yeats and the Rhymers' Club).

Letters from Limbo (London: Dent, 1936) 155–9 (reproduces some Yeats letters with comment). Wade 323.

RICHARDS, I. A., *Science and Poetry* (London: Kegan Paul, 1926; second edition, 1935) 79–82.

Coleridge on the Imagination (London: Kegan Paul, 1934; New York: Harcourt, Brace, 1935) *passim*.

RICKETTS, CHARLES. *See* LEWIS, CECIL ARTHUR.

RIDING, LAURA, and GRAVES, ROBERT, 'The Perfect Modern Lyric', in *A Pamphlet against Anthologies* (London: Cape; Garden City, New York: Doubleday, Doran, 1928) 95–102 (attacks 'The Lake Isle of Innisfree'). Reprinted in Robert Graves's *The Common Asphodel*, 185–95.

RIEWALD, J. G., *Sir Max Beerbohm: Man and Writer. A Critical Analysis, with a Brief Life and a Bibliography* (The Hague: Martinus Nijhoff, 1953) 163–4 *et passim*.

RIVOALLAN, ANATOLE, 'L'Épanouissement du Théâtre. I. – W. B. Yeats', in *Littérature irlandaise contemporaine* (Paris: Librairie Hachette, 1939) 16–20; ibid., 45–55 (on Yeats's poetry before 1916), 89–90 (on the later plays), 104–13 (on the poetry after 1916) *et passim*.

'Le Romantisme de W. B. Yeats', in *Présence des Celtes* (Paris: Nouvelle Librairie Celtique, 1957) 200–3; ibid., *passim*.

ROBINSON, LENNOX, 'The Irish National Theatre', in *Abbey Theatre, Dublin: Dramatic Festival Souvenir* (Dublin: Abbey Theatre, 1938) 7, 9–11 (the Abbey Theatre Dramatic Festival, 1939).

'The Man and the Dramatist', in *Scattering Branches*, ed. Stephen Gwynn, 55–114.

Curtain Up: An Autobiography (London: Michael Joseph, 1942) 21–72 *et passim*.

'W. B. Yeats', in *I Sometimes Think* (Dublin: Talbot Press, 1956) 101–4.

'William Butler Yeats: Personality', in *In Excited Reverie*, ed. A. Norman Jeffares and K. G. W. Cross, 14–23.

(compiler), *Three Homes*, by Lennox Robinson, Tom Robinson and Nora Dorman (London: Michael Joseph, 1938) 218–27 *passim*.

(compiler), *Ireland's Abbey Theatre: A History 1899–1951* (London: Sidgwick & Jackson; New York: Macmillan, 1951) *passim*. *See also* Roger McHugh, 'Yeats, Synge and the Abbey Theatre' (Part V). Wade 338.

(ed.), *Further Letters of John Butler Yeats* (Churchtown, Dundrum: Cuala Press, 1920) *passim*.

Reviewed by Susan Mitchell, *Irish Statesman*, II (May 1920) 519–21.

(ed.), *The Irish Theatre: Lectures Delivered During the Abbey Theatre Festival held in Dublin in August 1938* (London: Macmillan, 1939) *passim*. Contributions on Yeats by F. R. Higgins, Micheál MacLiammóir, Andrew E. Malone and Walter Starkie (q.v.).

(ed.), 'William Butler Yeats' [editor's title], in *Lady Gregory's Journals, 1916–1930* (London: Putnam's, 1946; New York: Macmillan, 1947) 259–66; ibid., *passim*. Wade 333A.

RODGERS, W. R., 'W. B. Yeats: A Dublin Portrait', in *In Excited Reverie*, ed. A. Norman Jeffares and K. G. W. Cross, 1–13 (transcript of the B.B.C. symposium, the contributors to which were Richard Best, Austin Clarke, Maud Gonne, Arthur Hanna, Brinsley Macnamara, Miss Macnie, Frank O'Connor, Seán O'Faoláin, Lennox Robinson, R. M. Smyllie, Iseult Stuart, Dossy Wright, Anne Yeats and Mrs W. B. Yeats).

RODWAY, A. E., 'The Last Phase', in *The Pelican Guide to English Literature*, vol. VI. *From Dickens to Hardy*, ed. Boris Ford (Harmondsworth: Penguin Books, 1958) 385–405 *passim* (on Yeats and the poets of the 1890s).

ROLLESTON, C. H., *Portrait of an Irishman: A Biographical Sketch of T. W. Rolleston*. Foreword by Stephen Gwynn (London: Methuen, 1939) *passim*.

ROOSEVELT, THEODORE and SHAW, GEORGE BERNARD, *A Note on the Irish Theatre*, by Theodore Roosevelt and an 'Interview' on the Irish Players in America by George Bernard Shaw (New York: Mitchell Kennerley, 1912). Bound together in a copy from Lady Gregory's Library in the Berg Collection, New York Public Library.

ROPPEN, GEORG, 'Yeats: To Byzantium', in *Strangers and Pilgrims: An Essay on the Metaphor of Journey*, ed. Georg Roppen and Richard Sommer (Bergen: Norwegian Universities Press, Norwegian Studies in English, No. 11, 1964) 337–52 (the Byzantium poems).

ROSE, W. K. (ed.), *The Letters of Wyndham Lewis* (London: Methuen, 1963) 193–5 (prints a letter from Lewis to Yeats, probably written in Sep 1928).

ROSENBLATT, LOUISE, 'La fin du siècle: Oscar Wilde et ses contemporains', in *L'Idée de l'Art pour l'Art dans la Littérature Anglaise pendant la Période Victorienne* (Paris: Librairie Champion, 1931) 292–3 *et passim*.

ROSENTHAL, M. L., 'Cultural and Rhetorical Symbolism in Contemporary American Poetry', in *Symbols and Values: An Initial Study*, ed. Lyman Bryson and others (New York: Harper, 1954) 315–18 ('Easter 1916').

'Yeats and the Modern Mind', in *The Modern Poets: A Critical Introduction* (New York: Oxford University Press, 1960) 28–48; ibid., *passim*.

'The Poetry of Yeats', in *Selected Poems and Two Plays of William Butler Yeats*, ed. M. L. Rosenthal (New York: Macmillan, 1962) xv–xxix. Wade 211 W.

ROSSI, MARIO M., *Viaggio in Irlanda* (Milan: Doxa, 1933) translated by Joseph M. Hone as *Pilgrimage in the West* (Dublin: Cuala Press, 1933) *passim*.

ROTHENSTEIN, Sir WILLIAM, *Men and Memories* (London: Faber & Faber; New York: Coward-McCann, 2 vols, 1931, 1935) vol. 1:

Recollections 1872–1900, 282–3 *et passim*; vol. II: *Recollections 1900–1922, passim*. Wade 321.

'The Conversation of Yeats', in *Since Fifty: Men and Memories 1922–1938* (London: Faber & Faber, 1939) 243–54 *et passim*. Wade 337.

'Yeats as a Painter Saw Him', in *Scattering Branches*, ed. Stephen Gwynn, 35–54.

ROUTH, HAROLD VICTOR, *English Literature and Ideas in the Twentieth Century: An Enquiry into Present Difficulties and Future Prospects* (London: Methuen, 1946) 64–7.

RUBERTI, GUIDO, 'W. B. Yeats', in *Storia del teatro contemporaneo* (Bologna: Capelli, second edition, 1928) vol. III, 895–6.

RUDD, MARGARET, *Divided Image: A Study of William Blake and W. B. Yeats* (London: Routledge & Kegan Paul, 1953) pp. xv +239.

Reviewed by *New Statesman*, XLV (4 Apr 1953) 407; Edwin Muir, *Observer*, 22 Feb 1953, 9; Rex Warner, *Spectator*, CXC 6510 (3 Apr 1953) 423; *TLS*, 2665 (27 Feb 1953) 138.

RUSSELL, GEORGE WILLIAM (Æ, AE, A. E.), 'Literary Ideals in Ireland', in *Literary Ideals in Ireland*, by John Eglinton and others, 45–54; 'Nationality and Cosmopolitanism in Literature', ibid., 79–88.

'The Poet of Shadows', in *Some Irish Essays* (Dublin: Maunsel; London: Johnson & Ince, 1906) 35–9. Reprinted in *Imagination and Reveries* (Dublin and London: Maunsel, 1915, 1921; New York: Macmillan, 1916, 1921, 1932) 24–8. *See* part V.

Song and Its Fountains (London and New York: Macmillan, 1932) 9–12 (on Yeats's dualism).

Some Passages from the Letters of AE to W. B. Yeats (Dublin: Cuala Press, 1936) pp. 62.

'Yeats' Essays', in *The Living Torch*, ed. Monk Gibbon, with an Introductory Essay (London: Macmillan, 1937; New York: Macmillan, 1938) 90–1; '*The Winding Stair*', ibid., 91–4; 'A Journal of Yeats', ibid., 94; '*Autobiography*', ibid., 95–6; 'Of Yeats' Style', ibid., 96; 'Yeats and William Morris', ibid., 251–2; '*A Vision*, by Yeats', ibid., 252–6; 'Yeats and the Nobel Prize', ibid., 256–9; 'Heavenly Geometry', ibid., 259–62 (on *A Packet for*

Ezra Pound); 'Yeats Rewritten', ibid., 262–4; '*October Blast*', ibid., 264–7; ibid., *passim*.

See also DENSON, ALAN.

RYAN, WILLIAM PATRICK, *The Irish Literary Revival: Its History, Pioneers and Possibilities* (London: Published by the Author, 1894) 29–30, 36 (Yeats and the Southwark Club), 52–60 (The Irish Literary Society), 132–6 (the Literary Revival in Dublin); ibid., *passim*.

SADDLEMYER, ANN, 'The Cult of the Celt: Pan Celticism in the Nineties', in *The World of Yeats*, ed. Robin Skelton and Ann Saddlemyer, 19–21; ' "The Noble and the Beggar-man": Yeats and Literary Nationalism', ibid., 22–39; ' "The Heroic Discipline of the Looking-Glass": W. B. Yeats' Search for Dramatic Design', ibid., 87–103; ' "Worn Out with Dreams"; Dublin's Abbey Theatre', ibid., 104–32; 'Image-Maker for Ireland: Augusta, Lady Gregory', ibid., 195–202; ' "All Art is a Collaboration": George Moore and Edward Martyn', ibid., 203–22 (Yeats, Moore, Martyn and the Irish National Theatre); ' "A Share in the Dignity of the World": J. M. Synge's Aesthetic Theory', ibid., 241–53 (Yeats, Synge and the Irish Theatre).

In Defence of Lady Gregory (London: Oxford University Press, 1965) *passim*.

See also, SKELTON, ROBIN, and SADDLEMYER, ANN.

SALVADORI, CORINNA, *Yeats and Castiglione: Poet and Courtier. A study of some fundamental concepts of the philosophy and poetic creed of W. B. Yeats in the light of IL LIBRO DEL CORTEGIANO by Baldassare Castiglione* (Dublin: Allen Figgis; New York: Barnes & Noble, 1965) pp. 106. *See also* Part VI.

Reviewed by Harry T. Moore, *Saturday Review*, XLVIII (11 Dec 1965) 81; Michael P. Gallagher, *Studies*, LIV 214–15 (summer–autumn 1965) 284–8.

SANGU, MAKOTO, 'Preface', in *Zen-Aku no Kannen* (*Ideas of Good and Evil*), translated into Japanese by Makoto Sangu (Tokyo: Toundo, 1914) xxiii–xxiv. Wade p. 407.

'W. B. Yeats: A Critical Study', in *Ieitsu Shisō* (*Selected Poems of W. B. Yeats*), translated into Japanese by Makoto Sangu (Tokyo: Iwanami, 1946) 115–51; 'An Hour with Yeats', ibid., 153–63. Wade p. 418.

SAUL, GEORGE BRANDON, *Stephens, Yeats and Other Irish Concerns* (New York Public Library, 1954). Reprints from the *Bulletin of the New York Public Library* the following Yeats items: 'An Introductory Bibliography in Anglo-Irish Literature: The Yeatsian Era' (13–18); 'Thread to a Labyrinth: A Selective Bibliography in Yeats' (19–22); 'The Winged Image: A Note on Birds in Yeats's Poems' (23–9). *See* Parts I and V.

'Yeats's Dramatic Accomplishment', in *W. B. Yeats, 1865–1965*, ed. D. E. S. Maxwell and S. B. Bushrui, 137–53.

See also Part I.

SAVAGE, D. S., 'The Aestheticism of W. B. Yeats', in *The Personal Principle: Studies in Modern Poetry* (London: Routledge & Kegan Paul, 1944) 67–91. *See* Part V. *Ibid., passim.*

SCHELLING, FELIX E., *The English Lyric* (Boston and New York: Houghton Mifflin, 1913) *passim.*

†SCHWEISGUT, ELSBETH, *Yeats' Feendichtung* (Darmstadt: K. F. Bender, 1927) pp. 55.

SCOTT-JAMES, R. A., 'The Irish Literary Movement', *Fifty Years of English Literature 1900–1950* (London: Longmans, Green, 1951) 89–98; ibid., *passim.*

SEIDEN, MORTON IRVING, *William Butler Yeats: The Poet as Mythmaker 1865–1939* (East Lansing: Michigan State University Press, 1962) pp. xiv + 397.

Reviewed by A. Norman Jeffares, *Modern Language Quarterly*, XXV 2 (June 1964) 218–22; Austin Clarke, *Poetry* (Chicago), CIII 3 (Dec 1963) 185–97; *TLS*, 3187 (29 Mar 1963) 218; John B. Vickery, *Western Humanities Review*, XVIII 2 (spring 1964) 182–3; John Unterecker, *Yale Review*, LII 4 (June 1963) 585–8.

SENIOR, JOHN, 'The Artifice of Eternity: Yeats', in *The Way Down and Out: The Occult in Symbolist Literature* (Ithaca, New York: Cornell University Press, 1959) 145–69 *et passim* (Yeats and vision).

SERGEANT, HOWARD, *Tradition in the Making of Modern Poetry* (London: Britannicus Liber, 1952) 18–22 *et passim.*

SETTERQUIST, JAN, *Ibsen and the Beginnings of Anglo-Irish Drama: II. Edward Martyn*, Uppsala Irish Studies No. V (Uppsala: Lundequist;

Dublin: Hodges Figgis; Copenhagen: Munksgaard; Cambridge, Massachusetts: Harvard University Press, 1960) 16–20 *passim; ibid., passim.*

SEWARD, BARBARA, 'Yeats and Transition', in *The Symbolic Rose* (New York: Columbia University Press, 1960) 88–117; ibid., 191–201 *et passim.*

SHANKS, EDWARD, 'The Later Poetry of Mr W. B. Yeats', in *First Essays on Literature* (London: Collins, 1923) 238–44 (*Two Plays for Dancers*).

SHAPIRO, KARL, *Essay on Rime* (New York: Reynal & Hitchcock, 1945) 19.

'W. B. Yeats: Trial by Culture', in *In Defence of Ignorance* (New York: Random House, 1960) 87–113.

SHARP, ELIZABETH A., *William Sharp (Fiona Macleod): A Memoir* (London: Heinemann; New York: Duffield, 1910) *passim.*

SHARP, WILLIAM (Fiona Macleod), 'The Shadowy Waters', in *The Winged Destiny: Studies in the Spiritual History of the Gael* (London: Chapman & Hall, 1904) 320–43, and note, 345. *See* Part V.

SHAW, PRISCILLA WASHBURN, 'William Butler Yeats: A Balance of Forces', in *Rilke, Valéry and Yeats: The Domain of the Self* (New Brunswick, New Jersey: Rutgers University Press, 1964) 175–273.

Reviewed by *Modern Language Journal*, XLIX (March 1965) 193; *New York Review of Books*, III (22 Oct 1964) 19; Geoffrey Hartman, *Yale Review*, LIV 2 (Dec 1964) 270–3.

SHIPLEY, JOSEPH TWADELL, *Guide to Great Plays* (Washington: Public Affairs Press, 1956) 837–9 (*Land of Heart's Desire* and *The Hour Glass*).

SIDNELL, M. J., 'Yeats's First Work for the Stage', in *W. B. Yeats, 1865–1965*, ed. D. E. S. Maxwell and S. B. Bushrui, 167–88.

SIMSON, THEODORE SPICER, *Men of Letters of the British Isles: Portrait Medallions from the Life*, with critical essays by Stuart P. Sherman and a preface by G. F. Hill (London: Bumpus; New York: Rudge, 1924) 130–3.

SITWELL, EDITH, 'William Butler Yeats', in *Aspects of Modern Poetry* (London: Duckworth, 1934) 73–89.

'Three Eras of Modern Poetry, I', in *Trio: Dissertations on Some Aspects of National Genius by Osbert, Edith and Sacheverell Sitwell* (London: Macmillan, 1938) 114–21.

SKELTON, ROBIN, 'Introduction', in *J. M. Synge: Collected Works*, vol. I: *Poems*, ed. Robin Skelton (London: Oxford University Press, 1962) xi–xxix (on Yeats and Synge).

The Poetic Pattern (London: Routledge & Kegan Paul, 1956) *passim*.

'A Literary Theatre: A Note on English Poetic Drama in the Time of Yeats', in *The World of Yeats*, ed. Robin Skelton and Ann Saddlemyer, 133–40; 'Division and Unity: AE and W. B. Yeats', ibid., 223–32; 'Aid to Immortality: The Satirical Writings of Susan L. Mitchell', ibid., 233–40; '"Unarrangeable Reality": The Paintings and Writings of Jack B. Yeats', ibid., 254–65.

and CLARK, DAVID R. (eds), *Irish Renaissance: A Gathering of Essays, Memoirs and Letters from The Massachusetts Review* (Dublin: Dolmen Press, 1965) pp. 168. Reprints contributions to the *Massachusetts Review*, v and vi (winter 1964 and winter-spring 1965), by Curtis Bradford, David R. Clark, Austin Clarke, David Krause, G. O'Malley and D. Torchiana, Ann Saddlemyer, Robin Skelton and John Unterecker (q.v.). Wade 357.

and SADDLEMYER, ANN (eds), *The World of W. B. Yeats: Essays in Perspective*. A Symposium and a Catalogue on the Occasion of the W. B. Yeats Centenary Festival held at the University of Victoria, February 14 to March 16, 1965 (Victoria, British Columbia: Adelphi Bookshop, for the University of Victoria; Seattle: University of Washington Press; Dublin: Dolmen Press, 1965) pp. 278. Contributions by David R. Clark, Joan Coldwell, Gwladys Downes, Liam Miller, Ann Saddlemyer and Robin Skelton (q.v.) Wade 356.

Reviewed by *Booklist*, LXII (1 Nov 1965) 258.

SMITH, ARTHUR J. M., *Poet Young and Old: W. B. Yeats* (Toronto, Ontario: University of Toronto Press, 1939) pp. 255.

SMITH, T. GROVER, Jr, *T. S. Eliot's Poetry and Plays: A Study in Sources and Meaning* (Chicago, Illinois: Chicago University Press, 1956; Phoenix Books, 1960) *passim*.

SOUTHWORTH, JAMES G., 'Age and William Butler Yeats', in *Sowing the Spring: Studies in British Poets* (Oxford: Basil Blackwell, 1940) 33–45.

SPARROW, JOHN, *Sense and Poetry* (New Haven, Connecticut: Yale University Press, 1934) *passim*.

SPENDER, STEPHEN, 'Yeats as a Realist', in *The Destructive Element: A Study of Modern Writers and Beliefs* (London: Jonathan Cape, 1935; Boston and New York: Houghton Mifflin, 1936; Philadelphia: A. Saifer, 1953) 115–32. *See* Part V.

The World Within: The Autobiography of Stephen Spender (London: Hamish Hamilton, 1951) 163–6 *et passim*.

'Hammered Gold and Gold Enamelling of Humanity', in *The Creative Element: A Study of Vision, Despair and Orthodoxy among Some Modern Writers* (London: Hamish Hamilton, 1953) 108–24; ibid., *passim*.

SQUIRE, Sir JOHN C., 'Mr W. B. Yeats's Later Verse', in *Essays on Poetry* (London: Hodder & Stoughton; New York: Doubleday, 1924) 160–70 (*Later Poems*, 1922). *See* Part V.

STAGEBERG, NORMAN C., and ANDERSON, WALLACE, *Poetry as Experience* (New York: American Book Company, 1952) 464–5 ('The Wild Swans at Coole'), 466–8 ('Sailing to Byzantium' and 'Leda and the Swan').

STALLMAN, ROBERT WOOSTER, *The Critic's Notebook* (Minneapolis: Minnesota University Press, 1950) 90 ('Sailing to Byzantium'), 250 ('Among School Children').

STALLWORTHY, JON, *Between the Lines: Yeats's Poetry in the Making* (Oxford: Clarendon Press, 1963) pp. xii + 261. Wade 352.

Reviewed by Horace Reynolds, *Christian Science Monitor*, 26 Sep 1963, 13; *Economist*, CCVII (6 Apr 1963) 54; A. N. Jeffares, *Modern Language Quarterly*, XXV 2 (June 1964) 218–22; Robert Conquest, *Spectator*, CCX 7036 (3 May 1963) 577–8; *TLS*, 3187 (29 Mar 1963) 218; *Virginia Quarterly Review*, XL 1 (winter 1964) xx.

†STAMM, RUDOLF, 'Von Theaterkrisen und ihrer Überwindung', in *Jahrbuch der Gesellschaft für Schweizerische Theaterkultur* (1943).

Three Anglo-Irish Plays (Berne: A. Francke, Bibliotheca Anglicana Series, vol. 5, 1943) 3–18 ('Introduction'), 93–4 ('Later Revisions of *Deirdre*'), 109–10 ('Notes').

Geschichte des englischen Theaters (Berne: A. Francke, 1951) 388–94 *passim*, 404–7 *passim*.

'W. B. Yeats und Oscar Wildes "Ballad of Reading Gaol"', in *Studies in English Language and Literature: Presented to Professor Dr Karl Brunner on the Occasion of his Seventieth Birthday*, ed. Friedrich Wild, *Wiener Beiträge zur englischen Philologie*, LXV Band (Vienna: Braumüller, 1957) 210–19.

Englische Literatur (Berne: A. Francke, 1957) 386–8 (survey of scholarship) *et passim*.

'William Butler Yeats: *Deirdre*', in *Das Modern Englische Drama: Interpretationen*, ed. Horst Oppel (Berlin: Erich Schmidt Verlag, 1963) 62–86.

'William Butler Yeats als Theaterdichter', in *Zwischen Vision und Wirklichkeit. Zehn Essays über Shakespeare, Lord Byron, Bernard Shaw, William Butler Yeats, Thomas Stearns Eliot, Eugene O'Neill und Christopher Fry* (Berne: A. Francke, 1964) 140–62 (particularly *Land of Heart's Desire*, *Deirdre* and *Purgatory*).

STANZEL, FRANZ, 'G. M. Hopkins, W. B. Yeats, D. H. Lawrence, und die Spontaneität der Dichtung', in *Studies in English Language and Literature: Presented to Professor Friedrich Wild on the Occasion of his Seventieth Birthday*, ed. Karl Brunner and others, *Wiener Beiträge zur englischen Philologie*, LXVI Band (Vienna: Braumüller, 1958) 179–93.

STARKEY, JAMES SULLIVAN (Seumas O'Sullivan), 'The Irish National Theatre: A Note', in *The Rose and the Bottle and Other Essays* (Dublin: Talbot Press, 1964) 116–26 *passim*. Reprinted in condensed form as 'How Our Irish Theatre Began', in *Irish Digest*, XXVII (June 1947) 5–7.

STARKIE, ENID, *From Gautier to Eliot: The Influence of France on English Literature, 1851–1939* (London: Hutchinson; New York: Humanities Press, 1960) 52–3, 117–28, 154–5 *et passim*.

STARKIE, WALTER, 'Sean O'Casey', in *The Irish Theatre*, ed. Lennox Robinson, 168–74 (Yeats and *The Silver Tassie*).

'Introduction', in *The Celtic Twilight and a Selection of Early Poems by W. B. Yeats*, ed. Walter Starkie (New York: Signet Classics, 1962) ix–xxv; 'Notes on the Poems', ibid., 209–15. Wade 211 V.

STAUFFER, DONALD A., *The Nature of Poetry* (New York: Norton, 1946) 168–75 ('The Lover Mourns for the Change that has come

upon Him and his Beloved and longs for the End of the World'
and 'Byzantium'), 243–6 ('Sailing to Byzantium') *et passim*.

'The Modern Myth of the Modern Myth', in *English Institute Essays
1947*, ed. James L. Clifford and others (New York: Columbia
University Press, 1948) 23–49.

*The Golden Nightingale: Essays on Some Principles of Poetry in the
Lyrics of William Butler Yeats* (New York: Macmillan, 1949)
pp. vi +165.

Reviewed by *Booklist*, XLVI (1 Sep 1949) 11; Leo Kennedy, *Chicago
Sun*, 15 Aug 1949; Horace Reynolds, *Christian Science Monitor*, 17
Aug 1949, 12; H. W. Wells, *College English*, XI 5 (Feb 1950) 294–5;
Kirkus, XVII (1 May 1949) 246; Richard Ellmann, *Modern Language
Notes*, LXVI 5 (May 1951) 335–6; John Farrelly, *New Republic*, CXXI
(8 Aug 1949) 20; G. F. Whicher, *NYHTB*, 26 June 1949, 4;
Robert Hillyer, *NYTB*, 26 June 1949, 7, 16; W. W. Parrish,
Quarterly Journal of Speech, XXXVI 2 (Apr 1950) 263–4; A. Norman
Jeffares, *Review of English Studies*, n.s., II (July 1951) 291–3; *San
Francisco Chronicle*, 18 Sep 1949, 18; Mary Colum, *Saturday
Review of Literature*, XXXIII (28 Jan 1950) 14–16; Ray C. Brown,
Voices, no. 139 (1949) 165–7; George Whalley, *Yale Review*, n.s.,
XXXIX 1 (autumn 1949) 167.

STEAD, C. K., 'W. B. Yeats, 1895–1916: An Illustration of the
Problems', in *The New Poetic* (London: Hutchinson University
Library, 1964) 16–44; ibid., *passim* (on Yeats's place in twentieth-
century poetry).

STEBNER, GERHARD, 'William Butler Yeats: *The Countess Cathleen*',
in *Das Moderne Englische Drama: Interpretationen*, ed. Horst Oppel
(Berlin: Erich Schmidt Verlag, 1963) 28–43.

STEINER, GEORGE, *The Death of Tragedy* (London: Faber & Faber;
New York: Knopf, 1961) 316–22 (*The Countess Cathleen* and
Purgatory) *et passim*.

STEINMANN, MARTIN. *See* HALL, JAMES, and STEINMANN,
MARTIN.

STEPHENS, JAMES, 'Some Irish Books I Like', in *James, Seumas and
Jacques: Unpublished Writings of James Stephens*, ed. Lloyd Frankenberg (London: Macmillan, 1964) 61–6; 'W. B. Yeats (1942)',

ibid., 67–72; 'Yeats as Dramatist (1943)', ibid., 74–6; 'Byzantium (1944)', ibid., 77–86; 'Yeats and Music (1947)', ibid., 87–8; 'Around and About Yeats (1948)', ibid., 89–95; 'Yeats the Poet (1948)', ibid., 96–100; ibid., *passim*.

STERNFIELD, F. W., 'Poetry and Music: Joyce's *Ulysses*', in *English Institute Essays 1956*, ed. Northrop Frye (New York: Columbia University Press, 1957) 21–4 ('The Three Bushes').

STEVENSON, LIONEL. *See* COOKE, JOHN D.

STEVENSON, W. H., 'Yeats and the English Poets: II. Yeats and Blake: The Use of Symbols', in *W. B. Yeats, 1865–1965*, ed. D. E. S. Maxwell and S. B. Bushrui, 219–25.

STEWART, J. I. M., 'Yeats', in *Eight Modern Writers* (Oxford: Clarendon Press; New York: Oxford University Press, 1963) 294–421; 'William Butler Yeats, 1865–1939', ibid., 671–9 (bibliographical notes).

STOCK, A. G., *W. B. Yeats: His Poetry and Thought* (Cambridge: Cambridge University Press, 1961; paperback edition, 1964) pp. xii +256. Chap. lx ('Vision'), pp. 146–64, reprinted in *Yeats: A Collection of Critical Essays*, ed. John Unterecker, 139–54.

Reviewed by Gustav Cross, *AUMLA*, no. 17 (May 1962) 112–14; John Unterecker, *College English*, XXIII 7 (Apr 1962) 605; Peter Ure, *Durham University Journal*, LV, n.s., xxiv 3 (June 1963) 155–6; *Economist*, CC (8 July 1961) 146; Derek Stanford, *English*, XIII 77 (autumn 1961) 237; René Fréchet, *Études Anglaises*, XVIII 3 (July–Sep 1965) 321–2; A. Norman Jeffares, *Modern Language Review*, LVII 2 (Apr 1962) 255–6; A[erol]. A[rnold]., *Personalist*, XLIII 2 (Apr 1962) 278–9; Robert Armstrong, *Poetry Review*, LIII (Jan–Mar 1962) 44; I. Simon, *Revue des Langues Vivantes*, XXXI (1965) 406–10; Brian Inglis, *Spectator*, CCVI 6940 (30 June 1961) 956; *TLS*, 3101 (4 Aug 1961) 480; H. R. MacCallum, *University of Toronto Quarterly*, XXXII 3 (Apr 1963) 307–13.

'Yeats on Spenser', in *In Excited Reverie*, ed. A. Norman Jeffares and K. G. W. Cross, 93–101.

STOLL, ELMER EDGAR, 'Poetry and the Passions: An Aftermath', in *From Shakespeare to Joyce: Authors and Critics; Literature and Life* (New York: Doubleday, 1944; Ungar, 1964) 169–80 (on Yeats's dramatic theory).

STRONG, L. A. G., *A Letter to W. B. Yeats* (London: Hogarth Press, 1932) pp. 31 (an appreciation).

'William Butler Yeats', in *Scattering Branches*, ed. Stephen Gwynn, 183–299.

'W. B. Yeats', in *Personal Remarks* (London: Peter Nevill; New York: Liversight, 1953) 13–33.

'Memories of Yeats from 1919 to 1924', in *Green Memory* (London: Methuen, 1961) 242–63; 'Yeats, Gogarty, Stephens and A. E.', ibid., 303–11.

STUART, FRANCIS, Reminiscences of Yeats in *The Yeats We Knew*, ed. Francis MacManus, 25–40.

STURGEON, MARY C., 'William Butler Yeats', in *Studies of Contemporary Poets* (London: Harrap, 1916; revised and enlarged edition, 1920) 419–32.

SULLIVAN, KEVIN, *Joyce among the Jesuits* (New York: Columbia University Press, 1958) *passim*.

SULTAN, STANLEY, *The Argument of Ulysses* (Columbus, Ohio: Ohio State University Press, 1965) *passim*.

SWEENEY, JOHN L. *See* DREW, ELIZABETH.

SWINNERTON, FRANK, 'William Butler Yeats', in *The Georgian Scene: A Literary Panorama* (New York: Farrer & Rinehart; as *The Georgian Literary Scene*, London: Heinemann, 1935; Dent, Everyman, 1938) 260–3 *et passim*.

SYMONDS, JOHN, *The Great Beast: The Life of Aleister Crowley* (London: Rider & Co., 1951) 32 ff. (Yeats, Crowley and the Golden Dawn).

Madame Blavatsky (London: Odhams, 1959) *passim*.

SYMONS, ARTHUR, 'The Speaking of Verse', in *Plays, Acting and Music* (London: Duckworth, 1903; Jonathan Cape, 1928) 23–6. *See* Part V.

'Mr W. B. Yeats', in *Studies in Prose and Verse* (London: Dent; New York: Dutton, 1904) 230–41. *See* Part V.

TANTE, DILLY. *See* KUNITZ, STANLEY JASSPON.

TATE, ALLEN, *Reactionary Essays on Poetry and Ideas* (New York: Scribner's, 1936) *passim*.

'Yeats' Romanticism: Notes and Suggestions', in *On the Limits of Poetry* (New York: Swallow Press & Morrow, 1948) 214–24. Also in his *The Man of Letters in the Modern World: Selected Essays 1928–1955* (New York: Meridian Books; London: Thames & Hudson, 1955) 227–36; and in his *Collected Essays* (Denver: Alan Swallow, 1959) 214–24. *See* Part V.

TAYLOR, ESTELLA RUTH, *The Modern Irish Writers: Cross Currents of Criticism* (Lawrence: Kansas University Press, 1954) *passim*.

TELFER, GILES, W. L., *Yeats's Idea of the Gael, Being No. IV of the Dolmen Press Yeats Centenary Papers MCMLXV* (Dublin: Dolmen Press, 1965) pp. 24 (numbered 85–108). *See also* MILLER, LIAM.

TEMPLE, RUTH ZABRISKIE, *The Critic's Alchemy: A Study of the Introduction of French Symbolism into England* (New York: Twayne Publishers, 1925) *passim*.

TÉRY, SIMONE, 'W. B. Yeats', in *L'Île des bardes: Notes sur la littérature irlandaise contemporaine* (Paris: Ernest Flammarion, 1925) 57–98.

THOMAS, WRIGHT, and BROWN, STUART GERRY, *Reading Poems: An Introduction to Critical Study* (New York: Oxford University Press, 1941) 713–16 ('Sailing to Byzantium', 'Byzantium', 'The Second Coming').

THOMPSON, E. P., *William Morris: Romantic to Revolutionary* (London: Lawrence & Wishart, 1955) 643–4 *et passim*.

THOMPSON, FRANCIS, 'A Schism in the Celtic Movement', in *Literary Criticisms by Francis Thompson*, ed. Terence L. Connolly, S.J. (New York: Dutton, 1948) 326–32; 'William Butler Yeats', ibid., 370–3; 'Fiona Macleod', ibid., 373–6. *See* Part V.

'W. B. Yeats', in *The Real Robert Louis Stevenson and Other Critical Essays by Francis Thompson*, ed. Terence L. Connolly, S. J. (New York: University Publishers Inc., 1959) 201–3; 'Mr Yeats's Poems', ibid., 203–9; 'The Irish Literary Movement: Mr Yeats as Shepherd', ibid., 210–15. *See* Part V.

THOULESS, PRISCILLA, 'W. B. Yeats', in *Modern Poetic Drama* (Oxford: Blackwell, 1934) 136–62.

THWAITE, ANTHONY, 'W. B. Yeats', in *Contemporary English Poetry: An Introduction* (London: Heinemann, 1959) 28–41 *et passim*. First published in *Essays in Contemporary Poetry: Hopkins to the Present Day* (Tokyo: Kenkyusha, 1957) 30–47.

TIETJENS, EUNICE, *The World at My Shoulder* (New York: Macmillan, 1938) 59–61.

TILLYARD, E. M. W., *Poetry Direct and Oblique* (London: Chatto & Windus, 1945; revised edition, 1948) 62–3 (*Ideas of Good and Evil*), 68 ('Sailing to Byzantium').

TINDALL, WILLIAM YORK, 'Transcendentalism in Contemporary Literature', in *The Asian Legacy and American Life*, ed. Arthur E. Christy (New York: Day, 1945) 175–92.

Forces in Modern British Literature 1885–1946 (New York: Knopf, 1947; revised edition, entitled *Forces in Modern British Literature 1885–1956*, New York: Vintage Books, 1956) 248–63. *See* Part V. Ibid., *passim*.

James Joyce: His Way of Interpreting the Modern World (New York: Scribner's, 1950; Grove Press Paperback, 1960) *passim*.

The Literary Symbol (Bloomington: Indiana University Press, 1955) 247–53 ('Sailing to Byzantium') *et passim*.

'The Literary Symbol', in *Symbols and Society*, ed. Lyman Bryson and others (New York: Harper, 1955) 337–67 *passim;* 363–5 ('Who Goes with Fergus?').

A Reader's Guide to James Joyce (New York: Noonday; London: Thames & Hudson, 1959) *passim* (notes allusions to Yeats and his works in Joyce's writings).

(ed.), *James Joyce: Chamber Music* (Morningside Heights, New York: Columbia University Press, 1954) 3–106 ('Introduction') *passim;* 181–225 ('Notes to the Poems') *passim*.

TOMLINSON, CHARLES, 'Yeats and the Practising Poet' in *An Honoured Guest*, ed. Denis Donoghue and J. R. Mulryne, 1–7.

TORCHIANA, DONALD T., '"Among School Children" and the Education of the Irish Spirit', in *In Excited Reverie*, ed. A. Norman Jeffares and K. G. W. Cross, 123–50.

TOWNSHEND, GEORGE, 'The Genius of Ireland', in *The Genius of Ireland* (Dublin and Cork: Talbot Press, 1930) 24–51 (especially 35 ff.).

TOWNSHEND, J. BENJAMIN, *John Davidson: Poet of Armageddon* (New Haven, Connecticut: Yale University Press, 1961) *passim*.

TREWIN, J. C., 'The Abbey', in *The Theatre since 1900* (London: Dakers, 1951) 46–8; 'Yeats and Synge', ibid., 48–52.

Dramatists of To-day (London: Staples Press, 1953) 60–3.

TSCHUMI, R., 'Yeats's Philosophical Poetry', in *Thought in Twentieth Century English Poetry* (London: Routledge & Kegan Paul, 1951) 29–73.

TUVE, ROSEMOND, *Elizabethan and Metaphysical Imagery* (Chicago: University of Chicago Press, 1947; Phoenix Books, 1961) *passim*. *See also* EMPSON, WILLIAM (Part V).

TUVESON, ERNEST LEE, *The Imagination as a Means of Grace: Locke and the Aesthetics of Romanticism* (Berkeley and Los Angeles: University of California Press, 1960) 192, 194–8 (Yeats and Symbolism).

TYNAN, KATHARINE (Mrs H. A. Hinkson), *Twenty-five Years: Reminiscences* (London: Smith, Elder & Co.; New York: Devin-Adair, 1913) *passim*.

The Middle Years (London: Constable, 1916; Boston: Houghton Mifflin, 1917) *passim*. Wade 311.

'John Butler Yeats', in *Memories* (London: Nash & Grayson, 1924) 275–87 *passim*.

UEDA, MAKOTO, *Zeami, Bashō, Yeats, Pound: A Study in Japanese and English Poetics* (The Hague: Mouton, 1965) pp. 165. *See* Part VI.

UNDERWOOD, V. P., *Verlaine et l'Angleterre* (Paris: Librairie Nizet, 1956) 463–4 (visit to Verlaine by Yeats).

UNGER, LEONARD and O'CONNOR, WILLIAM VAN, *Poems for Study* (New York: Rinehart, 1953) 582–4 ('The Second Coming').

UNTERECKER, JOHN, *A Reader's Guide to William Butler Yeats* (New York: Noonday Press; London: Thames & Hudson, 1959) pp. x +

310. pp. 7–18 ('The Use of Biography' and 'The Doctrine of the Mask') reprinted as 'Faces and False Faces', in *Yeats: A Collection of Critical Essays*, ed. John Unterecker, 23–32.

Reviewed by Sarah Youngblood, *Books Abroad*, XXXIV 3 (summer 1960) 297; Martin Steinmann, Jr, *College English*, XXII 6 (March 1961) 443–4; René Fréchet, *Études Anglaises*, XIV 1 (Jan–Mar 1961) 45–7; Thomas Hogan, *Guardian*, 27 Nov 1959, 15; *History of Ideas Newsletter*, V 4 (Jan 1960) 93; *Irish Independent*, 19 Dec 1959; Paul C. Wermuth, *Library Journal*, LXXXIV (15 Sep 1959) 2643; *NYHTB*, 8 Nov 1959, 15; Charles Poore, *NYTB*, 8 Aug 1959, 15; Stephen Graham, *Poetry Review*, LI 1 (Jan–Mar 1960) 42 (briefly); Wallace A. Bacon, *Quarterly Journal of Speech*, XLVI 1 (Feb 1960) 102 (briefly); Thomas Parkinson, *Sewanee Review*, LXVIII 1 (Jan–Mar 1960) 143–9.

(ed.), *Yeats: A Collection of Critical Essays* (Englewood Cliffs, New Jersey: Prentice-Hall, 1963) pp. x + 180. Contributions by W. H. Auden, R. P. Blackmur, Curtis Bradford, T. S. Eliot, Richard Ellmann, D. J. Gordon and Ian Fletcher, Hugh Kenner, Frank Kermode, Giorgio Melchiori, A. G. Stock, Allen Tate, W. Y. Tindall, John Unterecker and Alex Zwerdling (q.v.).

Reviewed by George Brandon Saul, *Arizona Quarterly*, XX 4 (winter 1964) 363–4.

UNTERMEYER, LOUIS, *From Another World* (New York: Harcourt, Brace, 1939) *passim*.

'W. B. Yeats', in *Lives of the Poets: The Story of One Thousand Years of English and American Poetry* (London: W. H. Allen, 1960) 615–22.

URE, PETER, *Towards a Mythology: Studies in the Poetry of W. B. Yeats* (Liverpool: Liverpool University Press; London: Hodder & Stoughton, 1946) pp. 120.

Reviewed by A. N. Jeffares, *English Studies*, XXX 1 (Jan 1949) 23–5; Una Ellis-Fermor, *Modern Language Review*, XLIII 2 (Apr 1948) 267–9; J. B. Leishman, *Review of English Studies*, XXIII 92 (Oct 1947) 372–4; *TLS*, 2345 (11 Jan 1947) 24.

Yeats the Playwright: A Commentary on Character and Design in the Major Plays (London: Routledge & Kegan Paul; New York: Barnes & Noble, 1963) pp. viii + 182. *See* Part V.

Reviewed by V. de Sola Pinto, *Critical Quarterly*, VI 2 (summer 1964) 186–7; René Fréchet, *Études Anglaises*, XVIII 4 (Oct–Dec 1965) 425–6; Denis Donoghue, *Guardian*, 11 Jan 1963, 5; G. S. Fraser, *Listener*, LXIX (16 May 1963) 843; Donna Gerstenberger, *Modern Drama*, VI 4 (Feb 1964) 263–4; K. P. S. Jochum, *Neueren Sprachen*, XIV 6 (1965) 297–9; Jon Stallworthy, *Review of English Studies*, n.s., XV 58 (May 1964) 215–17; Keith Harrison, *Spectator*, CCX 7026 (22 Feb 1963) 237; *TLS*, 3179 (1 Feb 1963) 78.

Yeats (Edinburgh: Oliver & Boyd, Writers and Critics Series, 1963; New York: Grove Press, 1964) pp. viii +129.

Reviewed by V. de Sola Pinto, *Critical Quarterly*, VI 2 (summer 1964) 186–7; *New Statesman*, LXX (20 Aug 1965) 257; *Quarterly Review*, CCCII 639 (Jan 1964) 120 (briefly); Harry T. Moore, *Saturday Review*, XLVIII (11 Dec 1965) 81; Anthony Burgess, *Spectator*, CCXIV 7125 (15 Jan 1965) 73.

'The Plays', in *An Honoured Guest*, ed. Denis Donoghue and J. R. Mulryne, 143–64.

USSHER, ARLAND, 'W. B. Yeats: Man into Bird', in *Three Great Irishmen: Shaw, Yeats, Joyce* (London: Gollancz, 1952, 1955; New York: Devin-Adair, 1952; Mentor Books, 1957) pp. 160.

Reviewed by Lore Metzger, *Books Abroad*, XXVIII 1 (winter 1954) 83–4; Katherine Brégy, *Catholic World*, CLXXVIII (Oct 1953) 74–5; J. M. Flynn, *Chicago Sunday Tribune*, 16 Aug 1953, 4; *Christian Century*, LXXV (26 Aug 1953) 965; Walter Kerr, *Commonweal*, LVIII 18 (7 Aug 1953) 446–7; A. J. L., *Dublin Magazine*, XXVIII (Jan–Mar 1952) 72; Gerard Fay, *Guardian*, 26 Aug 1952, 4; Herbert Cahoon, *Library Journal*, LXXVIII 13 (July 1953) 1230 (briefly); *Listener*, XLVIII (16 Oct 1952) 650; W. R. Rodgers, *New Statesman and Nation*, XLIV (27 Sep 1952) 353; Horace Reynolds, *NYTB*, 26 July 1953, 3; Alfred Kazin, *New Yorker*, XXIX 51 (6 Feb 1954) 90–6; Philip Toynbee, *Observer*, 3 Aug 1952, 7; R[oy]. McF[adden]., *Rann*, no. 17 (autumn 1952) 226; *San Francisco Chronicle*, 26 July 1953, 10; P. Colum, *Saturday Review*, XXXVI (5 Sep 1953) 11–12; Patrick Kavanagh, *Spectator*, CLXXXIX 6477 (15 Aug 1952) 226; Raymond Mortimer, *Sunday Times*, 10 Aug 1952, 3; J. Gassner, *Theatre Arts*, XXVIII 8 (Aug 1954) 12; *TLS* 2639 (29 Aug 1952) 560.

'Introduction', in *Yeats at the Municipal Gallery* (Dublin: Dolmen Press, 1959).

VAN DOREN, CARL, and VAN DOREN, MARK, *American and British Literature since 1890* (New York and London: The Century Company, *c.* 1925; revised and enlarged edition, New York: Appleton-Century, 1939) 311–17, 325–8, 350–1 *et passim*.

VAN DOREN, MARK, *Introduction to Poetry* (New York: Holt, Rinehart & Winston, 1963) 80–5 ('The Second Coming'), 85–9 ('The Cat and the Moon'), 130–3 ('The Ballad of Father Gilligan').

VENDLER, HELEN HENNESSY, *Yeats's VISION and the Later Plays* (Cambridge, Massachusetts: Harvard University Press, 1963) pp. xiv +288.

Reviewed by James Reaney, *Canadian Forum*, XLIII (Oct 1963) 163; V. de Sola Pinto, *Critical Quarterly*, VI 2 (summer 1964) 186–7; Padraic Fallon, *Irish Times*, 24 Aug 1963; L. W. Griffin, *Library Journal*, LXXXVIII (15 Mar 1963) 1167; Bernard Herrigman, *Modern Drama*, VI 4 (Feb 1964) 264–5; A. N. Jeffares, *Modern Language Quarterly*, XXV 2 (June 1964) 218–22; E. L. Mayo, *Saturday Review*, XLVI (15 June 1963) 43; *TLS*, 3221 (21 Nov 1963) 945; correspondence by Peter Ure, ibid., 3223 (5 Dec 1963) 1020; James L. Allen, Jr, *Western Humanities Review*, XIX 1 (winter 1965) 90–2; John Unterecker, *Yale Review*, LII 4 (June 1963) 585–8.

VINES, SHERARD, 'Anglo-Irish Writers', in *One Hundred Years of English Literature* (London: Duckworth, 1950) 206–19 *passim*.

VOIGT, MILTON, *Swift and the Twentieth Century* (Detroit: Wayne State University Press, 1964) 133 (*The Words upon the Window-Pane*).

VON BERGHOLZ, HARRY, 'Irish Literary Theatre', in *Die Neugestaltung des Modernen Englischen Theaters 1870–1930* (Berlin: Bergholz, 1933) 81–7; ibid., *passim*.

VON HEISELER, BERNT, 'William Butler Yeats', in *Ahnung und Aussage: Essays* (Gütersloh: Bertelsmann, 1952) 157–68.

WADE, ALLAN, 'Introduction', in *Some Letters from W. B. Yeats to John O'Leary and His Sister from Originals in the Berg Collection*, ed. Allan Wade (New York: New York Public Library, 1953) 3–5; 'Notes', ibid., 19–25. Wade 211 F. *See also* p. 158 below.

WAGNER, GEOFFREY, *Wyndham Lewis: A Portrait of the Artist as Enemy* (London: Routledge, 1957) *passim*.

WAIN, JOHN, 'W. B. Yeats: "Among School Children"', in *Interpretations*, ed. John Wain (London: Routledge & Kegan Paul, 1955) 194–210 (a reading of the poem).

'The Liberation of Wordsworth', in *Preliminary Essays* (London: Macmillan; New York: St Martin's Press, 1957) 79–81 (a Wordsworth–Yeats analogy).

WALKER, A. R. (ed.), *Letters from Aubrey Beardsley to Leonard Smithers* (London: First Editions Club, 1937) *passim*.

WALKLEY, ARTHUR BINGHAM, 'The Irish National Theatre (May 1903)', in *Drama and Life* (London: Methuen, 1907) 309–15 (on performances of *The Hour-Glass* and *Cathleen ni Houlihan*).

WARD, A. C., *Twentieth Century Literature 1901–1950* (London: Methuen, 1956; New York: Barnes & Noble, 1957) *passim*.

WARNER, OLIVER, *English Literature: A Portrait Gallery* (London: Chatto & Windus, 1964) 180–1 (portrait reproduction and biographical notes).

WARREN, AUSTIN, 'William Butler Yeats: The Religion of a Poet', in *Rage for Order: Essays in Criticism* (Chicago: Chicago University Press, 1948; Ann Arbor: Michigan University Press, 1948, 1959) 66–84. Reprinted in *The Permanence of Yeats*, ed. James Hall and Martin Steinmann, 223–36 (200–12).

See also WELLEK, RENE, and WARREN, AUSTIN.

WATTS, HAROLD, 'W. B. Yeats and Lapsed Mythology', in *Hound and Quarry* (London: Routledge & Kegan Paul, 1953) 174–87; 'W. B. Yeats: Theology Bitter and Gay', ibid., 188–208. *See* Part V.

WELDON, A. E. (Brinsley MacNamara), 'Introduction', in *Abbey Plays 1899–1948: Including the Productions of the Irish Literary Theatre*, planned by Colm O Lochlainn (Dublin: At the Sign of the Three Candles, 1949) 7–24 *passim; ibid., passim* (lists performance dates of Yeats's plays at the Abbey Theatre).

WELLEK, RENE, and WARREN, AUSTIN, *The Theory of Literature* (New York: Harcourt, Brace; London: Jonathan Cape, 1949, 1955) *passim*.

WELLESLEY, DOROTHY (Duchess of Wellington), *Beyond the Grave: Letters on Poetry to W. B. Yeats from Dorothy Wellesley* (Tunbridge Wells: Privately printed by C. Baldwin, n.d.) pp. iv +67. Wade 336A.

WELLS, HENRY W., 'The Heritage of Spirit', in *New Poets from Old: A Study in Literary Genetics* (New York: Columbia University Press, 1940) 252–61 (on Yeats and Donne); ibid., *passim*.

WEYGANDT, CORNELIUS, 'Mr William Butler Yeats', in *Irish Plays and Playwrights* (London: Constable; New York and Boston; Houghton Mifflin, 1913) 37–71 *et passim*.

'With Yeats in the Woods at Coole', in *Tuesdays at Ten* (Philadelphia: Pennsylvania University Press, 1928; London: Oxford University Press, 1929) 176–85. *See* Part V.

'William Butler Yeats and the Irish Literary Renaissance', in *The Time of Yeats: English Poetry of Today against an American Background* (New York: Appleton-Century, 1937) 167–251.

WHALLEY, GEORGE, *Poetic Process* (London: Routledge & Kegan Paul, 1953) *passim*.

'Yeats and Broadcasting', in *A Bibliography of the Writings of W. B. Yeats*, by Allan Wade, Appendix III, 409–18.

WHEELOCK, JOHN HALL, *What is Poetry* (New York: Scribner's, 1963) 81–6 ('Sailing to Byzantium').

WHITAKER, THOMAS R., 'W. B. Yeats: History and the Shaping Joy', in *Edwardians and Late Victorians: English Institute Essays 1959*, ed. Richard Ellmann (New York: Columbia University Press, 1960) 80–105.

Swan and Shadow: Yeats's Dialogue with History (Chapel Hill: University of North Carolina Press, 1964) pp. 352.

Reviewed by Robert Scholes, *American Scholar*, XXXIV 1 (winter 1964–5) 137–40; George P. Mayhew, *Books Abroad*, XXXIX 4 (autumn 1965) 459; B. W. Fuson, *Library Journal*, LXXXIX (1 Nov 1964) 4360; Hayden Carruth, *Poetry* (Chicago), CVII 3 (Dec 1965) 192–5; P. W., *Prairie Schooner*, XXXIX 1 (spring 1965) 87–8; Geoffrey Hartman, *Yale Review*, LIV 2 (Dec 1964) 270–3.

WIECZOREK, HUBERT, *Irische Lebenshaltung im Neuen Irischen Drama* (Breslau: Priebatsch, 1937) *passim*. (Breslau doctoral dissertation, 1937.)

WILD, FRIEDRICH, 'Anglo-irisches Drama', in *Die englische Literatur der Gegenwart seit 1870: Drama und Roman* (Wiesbaden: Dioskuren-Verlag, 1928) 83–106 *et passim*.

Die englische Literatur der Gegenwart seit 1870: Versdichtungen (*unter Ausschluss des Dramas*) (Wiesbaden: Dioskuren-Verlag, 1931) 157–60 *et passim*.

WILDE, OSCAR, 'Some Literary Notes, II' and 'Some Literary Notes, III', in *Collected Works*, vol. VIII (London: Methuen, 1908) 406–11, 437–9 (*Fairy and Folk Tales of the Irish Peasantry* and *The Wanderings of Oisin*); 'Three New Poets', ibid., 524–5 (*The Wanderings of Oisin*). See Part V.

WILDE, PERCIVAL, *The Craftsmanship of the One Act Play* (Boston: Little, Brown, 1923) *passim* (brief reference to various plays).

WILDER, AMOS N., 'W. B. Yeats and the Christian Option', in *The Spiritual Aspects of Poetry* (New York and London: Harper, 1940) 196–204; ibid., 224–6 *et passim*.

Modern Poetry and the Christian Tradition: A Study in the Relation of Christianity to Culture (New York: Scribner's; Toronto: Saunders, 1952) 213–14 ('The Second Coming') *et passim*.

WILDI, MAX, *Arthur Symons als Kritiker der Literatur* (Heidelberg: Winter, 1929) 50–61 (Yeats and Symons).

WILLIAMS, CHARLES, 'W. B. Yeats', in *Poetry at Present* (Oxford: Clarendon Press, 1930) 56–69.

WILLIAMS, HAROLD, 'Irish Poets and Playwrights', in *Modern English Writers: Being a Study of Imaginative Literature 1890–1914* (London: Sidgwick & Jackson, 1918; third edition, revised, 1925) 175–240 (Yeats's poems, 183–93; Yeats's plays, 217–18 *et passim*).

Outlines of Modern English Literature 1890–1914 (London: Sidgwick & Jackson, 1920) 151–7 (Yeats's poems), 171–4 (Yeats's plays). Condensed from the corresponding sections of his *Modern English Writers*.

WILLIAMS, RAYMOND, 'W. B. Yeats', in *Drama: From Ibsen to Eliot* (London: Chatto & Windus, 1952) 205–22; ibid., *passim*.

WILLIAMSON, CLAUDE CHARLES HORACE, 'W. B. Yeats and the Irish School', in *Writers of Three Centuries 1789–1914* (London: Richards, 1920) 444–51.

WILSON, COLIN, *The Strength to Dream: Literature and the Imagination* (Boston: Houghton Mifflin; London: Victor Gollancz, 1962) 10–18 *et passim*.

WILSON, EDMUND, 'W. B. Yeats', in *Axel's Castle: A Study in the Imaginative Literature of 1870–1930* (New York and London: Scribner's, 1931, 1950; London: Collins, Fontana Library 1961) 26–64. Reprinted in *The Permanence of Yeats*, ed. James Hall and Martin Steinmann, 15–41 (14–37).

WILSON, F. A. C., *W. B. Yeats and Tradition* (London: Gollancz; New York: Macmillan, 1958) pp. 288. Wade 348.

Reviewed by George Brandon Saul, *Arizona Quarterly*, XV 2 (summer 1959) 177–8; John Rees Moore, *Baltimore Evening Sun*, 28 Jan 1959; Sarah Youngblood, *Books Abroad*, XXXIV 2 (spring 1960) 179; Paul G. Heaney, *Boston Sunday Globe*, 1 Feb 1959; Thomas P. MacDonnell, *Catholic World*, CLXXXVIII (Mar 1959) 520–2; Padraic Fallon, *Dublin Magazine*, XXXIII (Apr–June 1958) 39–41; Christopher Busby, *Dublin Review*, CCXXXII 476 (summer 1958) 178–81; Frank Kermode, *Encounter*, X 3 (Mar 1958) 77–8; T. R. Henn and F. Kermode, ibid., X 5 (May) 69–71; F. A. C. Wilson, ibid., XI 1 (July) 76; Eleanor M. Sickels, *Explicator*, XVIII 1 (Oct 1959) Review, 1; Hugh l'A. Fausset, *Guardian*, 18 Feb 1958, 6; R. F. Rattray, *Hibbert Journal* LVI (Apr 1958) 311–12; John Unterecker, *History of Ideas Newsletter*, V 4 (Jan 1960) 80; R. P. Blackmur, *Kenyon Review*, XX 1 (winter 1958) 160–8; *Kirkus*, XXVI (1 Sep 1958) 686; *Listener*, LIX (13 Feb 1958) 287; Christine Brooke-Rose, *London Magazine*, V 7 (July 1958) 81, 83; A. N. Jeffares, *Modern Language Review*, LIV 2 (Apr 1959) 271–3; Helen Gardner, *New Statesman*, LV (1 Feb 1958) 141–2; reply by Kathleen Raine, ibid. (8 Feb) 170; Babette Deutsch, *NYHTB*, 17 May 1959, 5; Edwin Muir, *Observer*, 12 Jan 1958, 15; Aerol Arnold, *Personalist*, XLI 1 (Jan 1960) 115–16; Harold Orel, *Prairie Schooner*, XXXIII 3 (autumn 1959) 283–4; Andrew G. Hoover, *Quarterly Journal of Speech*, XLV 1 (Feb 1959) 95–6; William Empson, *Review of English Literature*, I 3 (July 1960) 52–6; Harry M. Meacham, *Richmond News Leader*, 7 Jan 1959; Thomas Parkinson, *Sewanee Review*, LXVI 4 (autumn 1958) 678–85; Hazard Adams, *South Atlantic Quarterly*, LVIII 3 (summer 1959) 479–80; Thomas Hogan, *Spectator*, CC 6780 (17 Jan 1958) 78; *Theatre Arts*, XLII 10 (Oct 1958) 70; *TLS*, 2917 (24 Jan 1958) 48;

G. F. H., *Twentieth Century*, CLXIII 975 (May 1958) 482–3; John Edward Hardy, *Yale Review*, XLVIII 3 (Mar 1959) 412–13.

Yeats's Iconography (London: Gollancz; New York: Macmillan, 1960) pp. 349. Wade 350.

Reviewed by R. F. Rattray, *Hibbert Journal*, LIX (Oct 1960) 102; Austin Clarke, *Irish Times*, 23 July 1960; Burton A. Robie, *Library Journal*, LXXXVI (1 Apr 1961) 1463; David Daiches, *Listener*, LXIV (18 Aug 1960) 269–70; G. S. Fraser, *New Statesman*, LX (15 Aug 1960) 280; *NYHTB*, 20 Aug 1961, 14; A[erol]. A[rnold]., *Personalist*, XLIII 2 (Apr 1962) 278–9; Frank Kermode, *Spectator*, CCV 6893 (5 Aug 1960) 220; Birgit Bramsbäck, *Studia Neophilologica*, XXXIV 1 (1962) 168–70; *TLS*, 3051 (19 Aug 1960) 529, 530.

WIMSATT, WILLIAM K., Jr, and BROOKS, CLEANTH, *Literary Criticism: A Short History* (New York: Knopf, 1958) 597–606 *et passim*.

WINTERS, YVOR, *In Defense of Reason* (Denver: Alan Swallow, third edition, 1947; London: Routledge & Kegan Paul, 1960) 490–2 (reply to Theodore Spencer, q.v., Part V).

The Poetry of William Butler Yeats (Denver: Alan Swallow, The Swallow Pamphlets No. 10, 1960) pp. 24. *See* Part V.

Reviewed by Denis Donoghue, *Sewanee Review*, LXIX 3 (summer 1961) 478–84; Marianne Moore, ibid., LXXI 1 (winter 1963) 123–33; *TLS*, 3286 (18 Feb 1965) 126.

WITT, MARION, 'William Butler Yeats', in *English Institute Essays 1946* (New York: Columbia University Press, 1947) 74–101.

'On Yeats, "In Memory of Major Robert Gregory"', in *Readings for Liberal Education*, ed. L. G. Locke and others (New York: Rinehart, 1948, 1952) vol. II, 183–90.

'Great Art Beaten Down', in *First Freedom: Liberty and Justice in the World of Books and Reading*, ed. R. Downs (New York: American Library Association, 1960) 382–8.

WOLFE, HUMBERT, 'W. B. Yeats: Introductory Note', in *W. B. Yeats: The Augustan Books of English Poetry (Second Series) No. 4*, ed. Humbert Wolfe (London: Benn, 1927) iii. Wade 155.

WRENN, C. L., *W. B. Yeats: A Literary Study* (London: Murby, 1920) pp. 16. *See* Part V.

WRIGHT, GEORGE T., 'Yeats: The Tradition of Myself', in *The Poet in the Poem: The Personae of Eliot, Yeats and Pound* (Berkeley and Los Angeles: University of California Press, 1960) 88–123.

YEATS, GEORGE (Mrs W. B. Yeats), 'A Foreword to the Letters of W. B. Yeats', in *Florence Farr, Bernard Shaw and W. B. Yeats*, ed. Clifford Bax, 42–4. Wade 327–9.

YEATS, JOHN BUTLER. *See* HONE, JOSEPH; POUND, EZRA.

YOUNG, ELLA, *Flowering Dusk: Things Remembered Accurately and Inaccurately* (New York and Toronto: Longmans, Green, 1945) *passim*.

YOUNG, G. M., 'Magic and Mudlarks', in *Daylight and Champaign: Essays* (London: Hart-Davis, 1937, 1948) 169–75 (*Dramatis Personae*); 'Forty Years of Verse', ibid., 176–91 (*The Oxford Book of Modern Verse*).

YOUNG, STARK, 'Old Vic Oedipus', in *Immortal Shadows: A Book of Dramatic Criticism* (New York: Scribner's, 1948) 266–70.

ZWERDLING, ALEX, *Yeats and the Heroic Ideal* (New York: New York University Press, 1965; London: Peter Owen, 1966) pp. 196. Wade 358.

Reviewed by Harry T. Moore, *Saturday Review*, XLVIII (11 Dec 1965) 81.

ADDENDA

ALSPACH, RUSSELL K., and ALSPACH, CATHARINE (eds), *The Variorum Edition of the Plays of W. B. Yeats* (New York and London, 1966) pp. xxv + 1336.

WADE, ALLAN, 'Introduction', in *The Letters of W. B. Yeats*, ed. Allan Wade (London: Hart-Davis, 1954; New York: Macmillan, 1955) 11–19. Ibid., 23–9, 193–7, 271–7, 517–22, 639–42, 753–7, 923. Wade 221 J–K.

Part IV

COMMEMORATIVE AND SPECIAL
ISSUES OF PERIODICALS

THE ARROW: W. B. Yeats Commemoration Number, ed. Lennox Robinson (Dublin: The Abbey Theatre, summer 1939) pp. 24. Foreword by L[ennox]. R[obinson]. Articles by Gordon Bottomley, Austin Clarke, Edmund Dulac, Oliver St John Gogarty, Richard Hayes, F. R. Higgins, John Masefield, Lennox Robinson, Sir William Rothenstein, W. J. Turner (q.v.). Illustrations by J. B. Yeats, Charles Shannon, Sean O'Sullivan, Sir Max Beerbohm and Edmund Dulac. Includes a facsimile reproduction of a letter by Yeats to Lennox Robinson, dated 14 Nov [1912?], concerning the revision of *The King's Threshold*, not printed in *The Letters of W. B. Yeats*.

Reviewed by Stephen Spender, *New Statesman and Nation*, XVIII (11 Nov 1939) 686–7.

THE DUBLIN MAGAZINE (formerly *The Dubliner*): W. B. Yeats Centenary Edition, IV 2 (summer 1965) pp. 77. Articles by Muriel C. Bradbrook, George Mills Harper, T. R. Henn, A. Norman Jeffares (q.v.) Includes a poem by Rivers Carew, and photographs of John Butler Yeats's portraits of his son, himself, his wife, and the pencil sketches of J. M. Synge at a rehearsal.

†EIGO SEINEN (*The Rising Generation*): W. B. Yeats Special Numbers I–III, L 9–11 (1 Feb–1 Mar 1924). Articles by Rintaro Fukuhara, Yone Noguchi, Hojin Yanō, Junzō Satō, Masujirō Honda, Makoto Sangū, Sōfū Takemoto, Gisuke Tomita.

ENGLISH: W. B. Yeats, 1865–1939, XV 89 (summer 1965). Articles by Cleanth Brooks, A. Norman Jeffares, Hermann Peschmann, Peter Ure, M[argaret]. W[illy]. (q.v.). Includes a poem by Jon Stallworthy.

HERMATHENA: Yeats Number, CI (autumn 1965). Articles by P. W. Edwards, Brendan Kennelly, H. E. Shields (q.v.).

IRELAND: WEEKLY BULLETIN OF THE DEPARTMENT OF EXTERNAL AFFAIRS, no. 706 (15 June 1965) pp. 16 (biographical and critical pamphlet. Illustrated).

THE IRISH BOOK: Special Yeats Issue, ed. Liam Miller, II 3–4 (autumn 1963). Articles by Russell K. Alspach, Peter Faulkner, Raymond Lister, Liam Miller, Nora Niland, Micheál Ó hAodha, Ann Saddlemyer, Robin Skelton (q.v.). Includes two letters by W. B. Yeats to John O'Leary (69–71).

THE IRISH LIBRARY BULLETIN, IX (Oct 1948). (Not marked as a special issue.) Articles by Robert Farran, T. R. Henn, Lennox Robinson, Joseph Hone (q.v.). Two poems by Shane Leslie.

THE IRISH TIMES: William Butler Yeats: Aetat 70 (Dublin: The Irish Times, 1935) pp. 16 (reprinted from *The Irish Times*, LXXVII 24,315 (13 June 1935) pp. 6–7). Articles by Aodh de Blacam, Francis Hackett, F. R. Higgins, Denis Johnston, Andrew E. Malone, Seán O Faoláin (q.v.).

THE IRISH TIMES: W. B. Yeats 1865–1965. A Centenary Tribute (10 June 1965) pp. viii. Articles by Eavan Boland, Sean Brooks, Rachel Burrows, V. C. Clinton-Baddeley, Richard Ellmann, T. R. Henn, A. Norman Jeffares, Patrick Kavanagh, Brendan Kennelly, A. J. Leventhal, Norah McGuiness, Conor Cruise O'Brien, Stephen Spender, Terence de Vere White (q.v.). Includes a poem by Padraic Fallon, an interview with May Craig, numerous photographs and drawings of the poet and his associates, the Yeats country, and drawings of Yeats's London houses. Reprints 'The Silver Tassie: An Abbey Controversy', from *The Irish Statesman* (June 1928), being the correspondence of Yeats, Lennox Robinson, Walter Starkie and Sean O'Casey concerning O'Casey's play.

IRISH WRITING: W. B. Yeats. A special Number of Irish Writing, ed. S. J. White, no. 31 (summer 1955) pp. 64. Articles by Peter Allt, Donald Davie, Valentin Iremonger, Hugh Kenner, Peter Ure (q.v.). Includes a section from Yeats's unpublished novel, *The Speckled Bird*, edited and with a note by Curtis Bradford. The Editor's Foreword is a review of Yeats's *Autobiographies*.

Reviewed by John Jordon, *Irish Press*, 17 Sep 1955; Denis Donoghue, *Irish Times*, 24 Sep 1955.

THE MASSACHUSETTS REVIEW: John F. Kennedy Memorial Number, V 2 (winter 1964): 'An Irish Gathering. Letters, Memoirs, Poems, Articles of Twentieth-Century Ireland', edited by Robin Skelton and David R. Clark, 249–386. Articles wholly or partly about Yeats by Curtis Bradford, Austin Clarke, G. O'Malley and D. T. Torchiana, Ann Saddlemyer, Robin Skelton, John Unterecker (q.v.). See also *Irish Renaissance: A Gathering of Essays, Memoirs and Letters from the Massachusetts Review*, ed. Robin Skelton and David R. Clark (Part III).

MODERN DRAMA: Yeats Issue, VII 3 (Dec 1964). Articles by David R. Clark, Gabriel Fallon, Marjorie J. Lightfoot, John R. Moore, Daniel J. Murphy, Marilyn Gaddis Rose, Sister Aloyse Scanlon, John Unterecker, Peter Ure, Helen Henessy Vendler, Sidney Warschausky (q.v.). Includes a review of David R. Clark, *The Theatre of Desolate Reality*, by Vivian Mercier.

†NIPPON SIZIN (*Japanese Poets*): Yeats Special Number, IV 1 (Jan 1924). Articles by Yone Noguchi and others; translations by Yaso Saijō.

PHOENIX: Yeats Centenary Number (Seoul: The English Literature Society of Korea University) no. 10 (summer 1965) pp. 122. Articles by William Empson, G. S. Fraser, A. Norman Jeffares, Kim Jong-gil, Kim U-chang, E. W. F. Tomlin (q.v.).

A REVIEW OF ENGLISH LITERATURE: W. B. Yeats, IV 3 (July 1963). Articles by S. B. Bushrui, A. Norman Jeffares, Jon Stallworthy, W. B. Stanford, Donald T. Torchiana and Glenn O'Malley (q.v.). Includes twenty-three letters by W. B. Yeats to Lady Gregory, facsimile reproductions of a letter to Eva Gore-Booth, a MS. version of 'The Statues', and a poem by Jon Stallworthy.

A REVIEW OF ENGLISH LITERATURE: VI 3 (July 1965). Articles by Jean Alexander, Pronoti Baksi, Lennox Robinson (q.v.).

REVUE DES LANGUES VIVANTES, XXI 4 (July 1965). Articles by T. R. Henn, A. Norman Jeffares, I. Simon (q.v.).

†SEI HAI (*The Holy Grail*): William Butler Yeats Special Number, II 6 (1913). Translations by Yaso Saijō, Kōnosuke Hinatsu, Ryōshiro Matsuda. Articles by Kōnosuke Hinatsu, Rintaro Fukuhara.

SHENANDOAH: Yeats and Ireland, XVI 4 (summer 1965). Articles by Austin Clarke, John Montague, Daniel Murphy, Sister M. Bernadette Quinn, John Unterecker (q.v.). Includes a poem on Yeats by Daniel Hoffmann.

†SHIN BUNGEI (*New Literature*): Yeats Number I 5 (1921). Translations by Takeshi Satō. Articles by Kiyoshi Satō, Yū Funabashi.

THE SOUTHERN REVIEW: William Butler Yeats Memorial Issue, VII 3 (winter 1941) pp. 260. Articles by Howard Baker, R. P. Blackmur, Kenneth Burke, Donald Davidson, T. S. Eliot, Horace

Gregory, Randall Jarrell, L. C. Knights, F. O. Matthiessen, Arthur Mizener, John Crowe Ransom, Delmore Schwartz, Allen Tate, Austin Warren, Morton Dauwen Zabel (q.v.).

Reviewed by *College English*, III (1942) 601–2; M. D., *Dublin Magazine*, XVII 3 (July–Sep 1942) 54–5; S. P. C., *Modern Philology*, XL 4 (May 1943) 351.

THRESHOLD: The Theatre of W. B. Yeats Centenary 1965, no. 19 (autumn 1965). Articles by Ronald Ayling, Pronoti Baksi, Austin Clarke, Ruby Cohn, John Jay, Frederick Kalister, Roger McHugh, Mary O'Malley, Shotaro Oshima, Raymond Warren (q.v.).

TRI-QUARTERLY: W. B. Yeats Centenary, I 4 (fall 1965) ed. Colton Johnson, pp. 65–144. Articles by Padraic Colum, Richard Ellmann, William P. Fay, Patrick Kavanagh, John V. Kelleher, Thomas Kinsella, Conor Cruise O'Brien, Moody E. Prior, B. Rajan, W. D. Snodgrass, Stephen Spender, D. T. Torchiana (q.v.). Includes numerous photographs of Yeats.

UNIVERSITY REVIEW (Dublin): Special Yeats Edition, XIII 8 [Aug 1965?]. Articles by Brian Coffey, Thomas Dillon, Denis Donoghue, Thomas MacGreevy, Robert O'Driscoll, John O'Meara (q.v.). Poems by James Liddy, Brian Lynch, Lorna Reynolds.

Part V

ARTICLES WHOLLY
OR PARTLY ABOUT
W. B. YEATS

AAS, L., 'William Butler Yeats og hans Verker Lyrik, prosodiktning og kritik', *Ord och Bild*, XXXVI 3 (Mar 1927) 145–52.

'William Butler Yeats og hans Verker Dramatikeren. Yeats og det irske teater', *Ord och Bild*, XXXVI 8 (Aug 1927) 461–8.

ADAMS, HAZARD, 'Where All Ladders Start', *Western Review*, XIX 2 (winter 1955) 229–34 (*W. B. Yeats and T. Sturge Moore; The Autobiography;* Virginia Moore, *The Unicorn*).

'Yeats the Stylist and Yeats the Irishman', *Accent*, XV 4 (autumn 1955) 234–7 (Richard Ellman, *The Identity of Yeats; The Letters of W. B. Yeats*, ed. Allan Wade).

'Yeats's Country of the Young', *PMLA*, LXXII 3 (June 1957) 510–19 (*The Country of the Young*, Yeats's unpublished variation upon Lady Gregory's play, *The Travelling Man*).

'Yeatsian Art and Mathematical Form', *Centennial Review of Arts and Science*, IV 1 (winter 1960) 70–88 (*A Vision*).

'Symbolism and Yeats's *A Vision*', *Journal of Aesthetics and Art Criticism*, XXII 4 (summer 1964) 425–36.

ADAMS, J. DONALD, 'The Irish Dramatic Movement', *Harvard Monthly*, LIII 2 (Nov 1911) 44–88.

ADAMS, JOHN F., '"Leda and the Swan": The Aesthetics of Rape', *Bucknell Review*, XII 3 (Dec 1964) 47–58.

ADAMS, ROBERT MARTIN, 'Now That My Ladder's Gone–Yeats Without Myth', *Accent*, XIII 3 (summer 1953) 140–52 (the function of myth in Yeats's poetry: 'Byzantium' as an example).

Æ, AE, A. E. *See* RUSSELL, GEORGE WILLIAM.

AGOSTINO. *See* D'AGOSTINO.

ALEXANDER, IAN W., 'Valéry and Yeats: The Rehabilitation of Time', *Scottish Periodical*, I 1 (summer 1947) 77–106.

ALEXANDER, JEAN, 'Yeats and the Rhetoric of Defilement', *Review of English Literature*, VI 3 (July 1965) 44–57.

ALLEN, JAMES LOVIC, Jr, 'Yeats' "Her Vision in the Wood"', *Explicator*, XVIII 8 (May 1960) item 45 (offers an alternative reading to that given by Ellmann in *The Identity of Yeats*, 172–3).

'Yeats's Bird–Soul Symbolism', *Twentieth Century Literature*, VI 3 (Oct 1960) 117–22.

'Yeats's Use of the Serious Pun', *Southern Quarterly*, I 2 (Jan 1963) 153–66.

'Yeats' "Long-Legged Fly" ', *Explicator*, XXI 6 (Feb 1963) item 51.

'The Golden Bird on "The Golden Bough": An Archetypal Image in Yeats' Byzantium Poems', *Diliman Review*, XI 2 (Apr 1963) 168–221 (Yeats and Sir James Frazer. *See also* VICKERY, JOHN B.; SPANOS, WILLIAM V.).

'William Butler Yeats's One Myth', *Personalist*, XLV 4 (autumn 1964) 524–32 (on Yeats's central motif, 'man and god in union').

ALLT, G. D. P., 'W. B. Yeats', *Theology*, XLII (1941) 81–91.

'Yeats and the Revision of His Early Verse', *Hermathena*, LXIV (Nov 1944) 90–101; LXV (May 1945) 40–57.

'Yeats, Religion, and History', *Sewanee Review*, LX 4 (autumn 1952) 624–58.

'Lady Gregory and Yeats's Cult of Aristocracy', *Irish Writing*, W. B. Yeats Special Number, no. 31 (summer 1955) 19–23.

ALSPACH, RUSSELL K., 'Some Sources of Yeats's *The Wanderings of Oisin*', *PMLA*, LVIII 3 (Sep 1943) 849–66.

'Yeats's First Two Published Poems', *Modern Language Notes*, LVIII 7 (Nov 1943) 555–7 ('Song of the Fairies' and 'Voices', published in *Dublin University Magazine*, Mar 1885).

'Two Songs of Yeats's', *Modern Language Notes*, LXI 6 (June 1946) 395–400 (notes three early versions of 'Red Hanrahan's Song about Ireland', and a Greek source for 'The Song of Wandering Aengus').

'The Use by Yeats and Other Irish Writers of the Folklore of Patrick Kennedy', *Journal of American Folk-Lore*, LIX 234 (Oct–Dec 1946) 404–12.

'Yeats's "Maid Quiet" ', *Modern Language Notes*, LXV 4 (Apr 1950) 252–3.

'Yeats's "The Grey Rock" ', *Journal of American Folk-Lore*, LXIII 247 (Mar 1950) 57–71.

'Some Textual Problems in Yeats', *Studies in Bibliography: Papers of the Bibliographical Society of the University of Virginia*. IX (1957) 51–67.

'Irish Legends in Irish Literature', *Folk-Lore in Action*, [3] (1964) 12–20.

ALVAREZ, A., 'Eliot and Yeats: Orthodoxy and Tradition', *Twentieth Century*, CLXII 8 (Aug 1957) 149–63; 9 (Sep 1957) 225–34 (a comparative study). Reprinted in his *The Shaping Spirit*, 11–47.

ANDREWS, IRENE D., 'The Irish Literary Theatre', *Poet Lore*, XXXIX 1 (spring 1928) 94–100.

'A Glimpse of Yeats', *Reading and Collecting*, II 3 (Feb–Mar 1938) 8–9.

ANON.*, 'Dramatic Notes', *Academy and Literature*, LXVI 1665 (2 Apr 1904) 383–4 (*Plays for an Irish Theatre* and comment on performances by the Irish National Theatre Society).

'The Irish Players', *Academy*, LXXX 2041 (17 June 1911) 746–7 (performances at the Court Theatre, including Yeats's *Deirdre*).

'The Irish Players and Playwrights', *America*, V 25 (30 Sep 1911) 581–2.

'Irish Opinion on the Irish Players', *America*, V 26 (7 Oct 1911) 614–15.

'Further Opinion of the Irish Players', *America*, VI 1 (14 Oct 1911) 11–12.

'Plays that may not be Patronized', *America*, VI 7 (25 Nov 1911) 159–60.

'The Latest Nobel Prize for Literature: William Butler Yeats', *American Review of Reviews*, LXIX (Feb 1924) 205–6 (consists largely of quotations from Jeanne Lichnerowicz's article in *Revue Bleue*).

'Two Irish Plays', *Athenaeum*, 4174 (5 Oct 1907) 415–16 (Yeats's *Deirdre* and Synge's *Playboy of the Western World* compared).

'The Close of the Irish Season', *Athenaeum*, 4421 (20 July 1912) 71 (first London performance of *The Countess Cathleen*, Court Theatre, 11 July 1912).

'The Irish Literary Renaissance', *Athenaeum*, 4505 (28 Feb 1914) 303–4 (on Yeats and other leading figures).

From 'The Open Window', *Bell*, V 4 (Jan 1943) 324–5 (Ferguson's translation of the Gaelic poem *Uileachan Dubh O!* – a possible source for 'Innisfree').

---

* Excludes reviews of single books by Yeats listed in Part II.

'Recent Celtic Experiments in English Literature', *Blackwood's Magazine*, CLIX 967 (May 1896) 716–29 (*Poems* (1895), 719–20).

'The Celtic Renaissance', *Bon Accord*, XLI 5 (31 Jan 1907) 20 (report of Yeats's lecture to the Aberdeen Franco–Scottish Society, 'Heroic Poetry of Ireland').

'The Work of Yeats', *Bookman*, XVIII (Dec 1903) 360–3.

'Mr W. B. Yeats', *Bookman* (New York), II (Dec 1895) 258–60.

Catholic Bulletin, XIII (Dec 1923) 817–19 (on Yeats's support for the Catholic Central Library).

Catholic Bulletin, XIV (Jan 1924) 5–7 (on Gogarty's tribute to Yeats as winner of the Nobel Prize).

Catholic Bulletin, XIV (Sep 1924) 745–50; ibid. (Oct) 836–8; ibid. (Nov) 929–37 (on the Aonach Tailteann Literary Awards, 1924). *See* reply by W. F. Trench in the *Irish Statesman*.

Catholic Bulletin, XV (Apr 1925) 290–4; ibid. (July) 641–4 (on Yeats's speech on divorce in the Irish Senate).

Catholic Bulletin, XVI (Mar 1926) 242–52 *passim* (on Yeats and O'Casey's *The Plough and the Stars*; on A. E.'s review of Yeats's *A Vision*).

Catholic Bulletin, XVI (May 1926) 456–8 (replies to Yeats's Senate pronouncements on education).

Catholic Bulletin, XVI (June 1926) 572–4 (on Yeats's opening address at the Exhibition of the Painters' Group of the Radical Club).

Catholic Bulletin, XVIII (July 1928) 676–7 (on the Yeats–O'Casey quarrel).

Catholic Bulletin, XVIII (Oct 1928) 988–91 (on Yeats, George Russell, and 'foul literature').

Catholic Bulletin, XVIII (Oct 1928) 991–2 (on Yeats and the Yogi on birth control).

Catholic Bulletin, XXII (May 1932) 328–30 (on Yeats and the establishment of an Irish Academy of Letters).

'The Pollexfen Peacock Parade', *Catholic Bulletin*, XXII (Oct 1932) 773–5.

'Shaw and Yeats and their Tribe', *Catholic Bulletin*, XXIII (Sep 1933) 693–6 (on the Irish Academy of Letters).

'Festive Interlude: On the Posing of Certain Professors', *Catholic Bulletin*, XXIV (Dec 1934) 948–52 (on Yeats, Thomas Bodkin and Walter F. Starkie).

'Poet Yeats and Poet Noyes', *Catholic Bulletin*, XXVII (Mar 1937) 171–2 (on Yeats's poem against Noyes on the Casement question).

'Latest Egg of the Academy Auk', *Catholic Bulletin*, XXVIII (Mar 1938) 185–6 (*The Herne's Egg*).

'Mr W. B. Yeats', *Catholic Mind*, III (Nov 1932) 247; ibid. (Dec) 276–7.

Critic, XXIX (2 Nov 1895) 284 (a note on Yeats on the occasion of the publication of *Poems* (1895)).

'Irish Home Rule in the Drama', *Current Literature*, (Jan 1911) 81–4.

'Visit of Yeats', *Current Opinion*, LIV (Apr 1914) 294–5.

'*The Countess Cathleen*', *Daily Nation*, 6 May 1899, 4 (a leading-article attack on the play).

'A Literary Foundling', *Douglas Library Notes*, XI 3 (summer 1962) 13–16 (prints an eary draft of 'The Sorrow of Love' entitled 'The Sorrow of the World', as published in *The Independent* (New York), 20 Oct 1892).

'A School of Irish Poetry', *Edinburgh Review*, CCIX 427 (Jan 1909) 96–105 (*Poems 1899–1905*, and *Poems* (1908)).

'Yeats and the Irish Theatre', *English Review*, XII (Aug 1912) 146–8.

'New Irish Plays Produced', *The Gael*, XXI (May 1902) 166–7 (*Cathleen ni Houlihan*).

'A Pen Picture of Dr Douglas Hyde and Mr Yeats', *The Gael*, XXI (Dec 1902) 378–9.

'Mr Yeats as Playwright: The Spirit of the Enigmatic Dean', *Glasgow Herald*, 27 Dec 1934 (*Wheels and Butterflies*; *Collected Plays*).

'Mr W. B. Yeats', *Great Thoughts*, XXXVI (Apr 1902) 356–8.

'Theater of Beauty', *Harper's Magazine*, LV (21 June 1913) 16–17.

'*The Countess Cathleen* at the Court', *Illustrated London News*, CXLI (20 July 1912) 88.

'Recent Writings', *Independent*, 12 Nov 1903, 2691–2.

Irish Book Lover, II 9 (Apr 1911) 142 (note on Yeats's civil list pension of £150).

'Yeats, Synge, and "The Playboy"', *Irish Book Lover*, IV 1 (Aug 1912) 7–8.

'Irish Literary Society; Coming of Age Celebration', *Irish Book Lover*, IV 12 (July 1913) 202–3 (Yeats's lecture).

Irish Book Lover, VI 4 (Nov 1914) 63 (brief advance notice of *Reveries over Childhood and Youth* as *Memory Harbour: A Revery over My Childhood and Youth*).

Irish Book Lover, VI 5 (Dec 1914) 77 (note on Yeats's Thomas Davis address).

Irish Book Lover, VII 6 (Jan 1916) 111–12 (discharge of Abbey Theatre debt of £1200).

Irish Book Lover, VII 11–12 (June–July 1916) 184 (a Yeats reading at charity symposium at Byron's house in Piccadilly).

Irish Book Lover, VIII 1–2 (Aug–Sep 1916) 13 (Yeats's transfer to Macmillan).

Irish Book Lover, IX 5–6 (Dec 1917–Jan 1918) 57 (notes Yeats's marriage).

Irish Book Lover, XIV 1 (Jan 1924) 10–11 (on Yeats's Nobel Prize award).

'Mr Yeats' Confessions', *Irish Book Lover*, XV 2 (Apr 1925) 19–21.

Irish Book Lover, XVIII 6 (Nov–Dec 1930) 155 (a Yeats–Masefield anecdote).

'"As a Bee–not as a Wasp": Senator Yeats in his Old Age"', *Irish Independent*, 22 Oct 1928, 6.

'W. B. Yeats Looks Back', *Irish Press*, 14 June 1935, 7 (an interview with Yeats on his seventieth birthday).

'W. B. Yeats Looks Back', *Irish Press*, 14 Oct 1935, 9 (on the early days of the Abbey Theatre – Radio Athlone interview, 13 Oct 1935).

'National Literary Society', *Irish Times*, 10 June 1892, 6 (foundation meeting, 9 June).

'Modern Irish Literature: Four Epochs of Development', *Irish Times*, 18 Feb 1933 (a report of Yeats's lecture).

'Poetry's Return to the Theatre: Three Books by W. B. Yeats', *Irish Times*, 5 Jan 1935 (*Collected Plays*; *Wheels and Butterflies*; *The King of the Great Clock Tower*).

'Frank O'Connor's Friendship with W. B. Yeats', *Irish Times*, 15 Aug 1962 (a report of O'Connor's Summer School Lecture).

'Why Yeats is a Nobel Prize Man', *Literary Digest*, 8 Dec 1923, 26–7.

'The Revised Poetry of Mr Yeats', *Literature*, VIII 188 (25 May 1901) 439–41 (*Poems* (1901), with particular comment on *The Countess Cathleen*).

'Music and Poetry', *Manchester Guardian*, 19 May 1903.

'Abbey Theatre Uproars', *Manchester Guardian*, 13 Feb 1926, 2 (the Abbey Theatre, 11 Feb 1926).

'On the Line', *Monthly Review*, XVII 50 (Nov 1904) 157–60 (a review of *On Baile's Strand* and *The King's Threshold*).

'The Japanese Masque', *Nation* (London), XX 2 (14 Oct 1916) 87 (*Certain Noble Plays of Japan*: Yeats and the Noh).

'Mr Yeats on Himself', *Nation* (London), XX 4 (28 Oct 1916) 150, 152 (*Reveries over Childhood and Youth; Responsibilities and Other Poems*).

'Mr W. B. Yeats', *Nation* (London), XXV (5 Apr 1919) 20–1 (*Two Plays for Dancers; The Wild Swans at Coole*).

'Mr Yeats Explains Himself', *Nation and Athenaeum*, XXXII 4834 (30 Dec 1922) 520–2 (*The Trembling of the Veil; Later Poems; Plays in Prose and Verse*).

'Meeting Yeats', *New Republic*, XXI (24 Nov 1917) 100.

'Mr Yeats at Seventy' (editorial), *New York Times*, 30 June 1935, IV 8.

'Sophocles, Yeats, and Dr Gogarty', *NYTB*, 15 Jan 1933, 1 (on *Oedipus the King*).

NYTB, 9 June 1935, 14 (on Yeats's seventieth birthday).

'The Finest of Modern Poets?', *Newsweek*, XLVII 15 (9 Apr 1956) 120–2 (*Collected Poems; A Vision*).

'The Abbey Theatre', *Oxford and Cambridge Review*, no. 25 (Nov 1912) 12–16.

'W. B. Yeats and Symbolism', *Poetry Review*, XXXIV (1943) 126–8 (J. M. Hone, *W. B. Yeats 1865–1939*, and Bowra's criticism of Yeats in *The Heritage of Symbolism*).

'The Gaelic Revival in Literature', *Quarterly Review*, CXCV 390 (Apr 1902) 423–49 (*Samhain*, Oct 1901; *Poems* (1901); general survey of Yeats's work).

'Poetry Album', *Scholastic*, 8 Dec 1941, 21.

'World in One Small Room', *Scholastic*, 15 Oct 1945, 20.

'Yeats as Dramatist: Plays in Poetry and Prose', *Scotsman*, 17 Dec 1934 (*Collected Plays*; *Wheels and Butterflies*).

'Yeats: Portrait by a Critical Cousin', *Scotsman*, 25 Apr 1959 (*Mythologies*; Monk Gibbon, *The Masterpiece and the Man*).

'A Fine Poet: Mr W. B. Yeats Visits Sheffield', *Sheffield Daily Telegraph*, 23 Nov 1922, 8 (Yeats's lecture to the Playgoers' Association, 22 Nov 1922).

Sinn Fein, 2 and 9 Feb 1907 (an attack on *The Playboy* and on Yeats's support for it).

'Yeats and the Abbey Theatre', *Theatre Arts Monthly*, XXIII 3 (Mar 1939) 160–1.

'A Tribute to Yeats', *Theatre Arts*, XXIII 11 (Nov 1939) 837 (includes quotations from various contributions to *The Arrow* (1939)).

'Cast a Cold Eye', *Time*, LX (6 Oct 1952) 25 (a Yeats memorial).

'The Abbey Theatre, Its Origins and Accomplishments', *The Times*, 17 Mar 1913, 15.

'Mr. W. B. Yeats: Award of Nobel Prize', *The Times*, 15 Nov 1923, 12.

'Mr W. B. Yeats Looks Back', *The Times*, 22 May 1936, 19 (*Dramatis Personae*).

'The Irish National Theatre', *TLS*, 69 (8 May 1903) 146 (*The Hour Glass* and *Cathleen ni Houlihan* at Queen's Gate Hall).

'Mr Yeats on the Irish Theatre', *TLS*, 156 (6 Jan 1905) 5 (*Samhain* (1905); support for the Irish National Theatre Society).

'Mr Yeats in Middle Age', *TLS*, 770 (19 Oct 1916) 499 (*Responsibilities and Other Poems*; *Reveries over Childhood and Youth*).

'Mr Yeats's Dreams', *TLS*, 1093 (28 Dec 1922) 87 (*Plays in Prose and Verse*; *Later Poems*).

'The New Poetic Drama', *TLS*, 1721 (24 Jan 1935) 37–8 (*Collected Plays*; *Wheels and Butterflies*; *The King of the Great Clock Tower*).

'Yeatsian Fantasy', *TLS*, 1877 (22 Jan 1938) 56 (*Essays* (1931–6); *The Herne's Egg*).

'Yeats's Inner Drama: A Poet of Two Reputations', *TLS*, 1931 (4 Feb 1939) 72, 74 (the appeal of the later work).

'W. B. Yeats, the Last Poems', *TLS*, 1955 (22 July 1939) 438 (*Last Poems and Two Plays*).

'Wise and Gay', *TLS*, 1980 (8 Jan 1940) 279 (leading articles based on *Letters on Poetry to Dorothy Wellesley*).

'Forty Years of Irish Drama: Yeats, Synge, and Lady Gregory: From the Visionaries to the Realists', *TLS*, 1993 (13 Apr 1940) 182, 186 (*Last Poems and Plays*, etc.).

'William Butler Yeats: The Dual Anglo-Irish Heritage', *TLS*, 2141 (13 Feb 1943) 78 (special article on J. M. Hone, *W. B. Yeats 1865–1939*).

'Yeats and His Critics', *TLS*, 2534 (25 Aug 1950) 525–6 (*Collected Poems*; *The Permanence of Yeats*, ed. James Hall and Martin Steinmann).

'Yeats as Dramatist', *TLS*, 2651 (21 Nov 1952) 760 (*Collected Plays*).

'Visual Aids', *TLS*, 2884 (7 June 1957) 349 (leading article on the Reading Exhibition).

'Yeats in Youth and Maturity', *TLS*, 2923 (7 Mar 1958) 126 (*Variorum Edition of the Poems*; Allan Wade, *Bibliography*).

'England is Abroad', *TLS*, 2929 (18 Apr 1958) 200–1; correspondence by Vivian Mercier, ibid., 2936 (6 June) 313 (general article on English writing by non-Englishmen, including Yeats).

'Ideas into Drama', *TLS*, 3051 (19 Aug 1960) 529 (Yeats's plays with special reference to F. A. C. Wilson, *Yeats's Iconography*, and Peter Ure, 'Yeats's Christian Mystery Plays').

'The Man and the Mask', *TLS*, 3051 (19 Aug 1960) 530 (F. A. C. Wilson, *Yeats's Iconography*; V. K. N. Menon, *The Development of W. B. Yeats*).

'Tame Swans at Coole', *TLS*, 3077 (17 Feb 1961) 97–8 (Elizabeth Coxhead, *Lady Gregory*; Giorgio Melchiori, *The Whole Mystery of Art*; *Essays and Introductions*).

TLS, 3098 (4 July 1961) 434 (two recordings of Yeats's verse: Argo 182; Caedmon TC 1081).

'Thinking on Paper', *TLS*, 3187 (29 Mar 1963) 218 (Jon Stallworthy, *Between the Lines*; Morton I. Seiden, *William Butler Yeats*).

'Under Ben Bulben'. *TLS*, 3282 (21 Jan 1965) 47; correspondence by R. O'Driscoll, ibid., 3286 (18 Feb 1965) 132.

'Yeats's in Winters's Grip', *TLS*, 3286 (18 Feb 1965) 126 (reply to attack on Yeats by Yvor Winters, q.v., Parts III and V).

'From Sligo to Byzantium', *TLS*, 3304 (24 June 1965) 529–30 (Thomas Parkinson, *W. B. Yeats: The Later Poetry*; A. Norman Jeffares and K. G. W. Cross (eds), *In Excited Reverie*; Edward Engelberg, *The Vast Design*).

'Poet on America', *TP's Weekly*, V 128 (21 Apr 1905) 493. (on Yeats's impression of America in *Metropolitan Magazine*, Apr 1905, Wade p. 368).

'W. B. Yeats at School', *TP's Weekly*, XIX 500 (7 June 1912) 709 (reminiscences by a classmate).

'The New Reading', *United Irishman*, 24 Sep 1932, 5 (on Yeats's lecture, Sep 1932, 'The Creation of Modern Ireland').

ANONYMOUS OBITUARY NOTICES (signed obituary notices are included under authors):
Christian Century, 15 Feb 1939, 205; ibid., 22 Feb, 254;
Deutsche Rundschau, CCLVIII (Mar 1939) 210–11;
Irish Independent, 30 Jan 1939;
Irish Press, 30 Jan 1939;
Life, VII (25 Oct 1942) 146–50 (on Yeats's burial at Drumcliffe);
Listener, XXI (2 Feb 1939) 247 (B.B.C. Regional Broadcast Programme, 29 Jan 1939);
Nation, CXLVIII (4 Feb 1939) 135;
New Republic, XCVIII (8 Feb 1939) 4;
New York Herald Tribune, 30 Jan 1939, 8;
New York Times, 30 Jan 1939, 13; ibid., 31 Jan, 2;
Newsweek, 6 Feb 1939, 597;
Publishers' Weekly, 4 Feb 1939, 597;
Round Table, XIX (1939) 597;
Theatre Arts Monthly, XXIII 4 (Apr 1939) 289–90;
Time, XXXIII (6 Feb 1939) 37;
The Times, 30 Jan 1939, 14; ibid., 31 Jan, 11, 17;
TLS, 'The Success of Yeats', 4 Feb 1939, 73;
Wilson Bulletin, XIII (Mar 1939) 454.

ARCHER, WILLIAM, 'Mr George Moore as a Dramatic Critic', *Daily Chronicle*, 20 Jan 1899, 3 (reply to George Moore's 'Introduction' in Edward Martyn's *The Heather Field and Maeve* (q.v.); comment on *The Countess Cathleen*). Replies by George Moore, ibid., 25

Jan, 3, and W. B. Yeats, 'Mr Moore, Mr Archer, and the Literary Theatre', 30 Jan, 3. Wade p. 356.

ARMENS, SVEN, 'Supernatural Sources for Poetry', *Western Review*, XXI 1 (autumn 1956) 69–76 (Hazard Adams, *Blake and Yeats*, review article).

ARNOLD, SIDNEY, 'The Abbey Theatre', *Arts and Philosophy*, 1 (summer 1950) 25–30.

ARNS, KARL, 'Der Träger des Nobelpreises', *Literatur*, XXVI 5 (Feb 1924) 261–5.

'William Butler Yeats', *Schöne Literatur*, XXX 6 (June 1929) 248–56.

AUDEN, W. H., 'The Public *v.* the Late Mr W. B. Yeats', *Partisan Review*, VI 1 (spring 1939) 46–51. Reprinted in *The Partisan Reader: Ten Years of the Partisan Review, 1934–1944*, ed. William Phillips and Philip Rahv (New York: Dial Press, 1946); in *Literary Opinion in America*, ed. Morton Dauwen Zabel (New York: Harper, revised edition, 1951) 264–9; and in *Criticism: The Foundations of Modern Literary Judgment*, ed. Mark Schorer, Josephine Miles and Gordon Mackenzie (New York: Harcourt, Brace, 1948) 168–72.

'Yeats: Master of Diction', *Saturday Review of Literature*, XXII 7 (8 June 1940) 14 (*Last Poems and Plays*).

'Yeats as an Example', *Kenyon Review*, X 2 (spring 1948) 187–95. Reprinted in *The Kenyon Critics: Studies in Modern Literature*, ed. John Crowe Ransom (New York and Cleveland: World Publishing Company; Toronto: McClelland, 1951), and in *The Permanence of Yeats*, ed. James Hall and Martin Steinmann, 344–51 (308–14).

'I Am of Ireland', *New Yorker*, XXXI 5 (19 Mar 1955) 142–50 (*The Letters of W. B. Yeats*, ed. Allan Wade).

AUTY, R. A., 'Byzantium', *TLS*, 2532 (11 Aug 1950) 501; correspondence by Gwendolen Murphy, ibid., 2534 (25 Aug) 533; Richard Murphy and Maurice Craig, ibid., 2535 (1 Sep) 549; Peter Ure and Dennis Silk, ibid., 2536 (8 Sep) 565; Gwendolen Murphy and John Christopherson, ibid., 2537 (15 Sep) 581; Bonamy Dobrée and Vernon Watkins, ibid., 2538 (22 Sep) 597; Gwendolen Murphy, ibid., 2544 (3 Nov) 693 (on variant readings of 'Byzantium' and other poems).

AYLING, RONALD, 'Seven Letters of W. B. Yeats', *Theoria* XX (1963) 60–70.

'"Theatre Business: Management of Men": Six Letters by W. B. Yeats', *Threshold*, no. 19, The Theatre of W. B. Yeats Centenary, 1965 (autumn 1965) 48–57 (prints with commentary six letters not listed in Allan Wade's *Bibliography* or included in his *Letters*).

AYNARD, JOSEPH, 'W. B. Yeats, Lauréat du prix Nobel', *Revue de Paris*, XXXI 1 (1 Jan 1924) 176–89.

BACKER, FRANZ DE. *See* DE BACKER, FRANZ.

BAGSHAW, WILLIAM, 'W. B. Yeats', *Manchester Quarterly*, XLI 164 (Oct 1922) 227–48.

BAKER, GEORGE PIERCE, 'Rhythm in Recent Dramatic Dialogue', *Yale Review*, XIX 1 (Sep 1929) 116–33 (comments on how Yeats wished dialogue to be spoken).

BAKER, HOWARD, 'Domes of Byzantium', *Southern Review*, VII 3 (winter 1941–2) 639–52 ('Sailing to Byzantium').

BAKSI, PRONOTI, 'The Noh and the Yeatsian Synthesis', *Review of English Literature*, VI 3 (July 1965) 34–43.

'The Japanese Noh: A Survey', *Threshold*, no. 19, The Theatre of W. B. Yeats Centenary, 1965 (autumn 1965) 74–88 (a description of the genre).

BALL, ARTHUR, *Fortnightly Review*, CXXXVII (Apr 1935) 380–1 (*Collected Plays* (1934)).

BANNERJEE, JAYGOPAL, 'W. B. Yeats', *Calcutta Review*, XXVI (Mar 1928) 277–91; XXVII (Apr) 81–102; (May) 141–67; (June) 361–73; XXVIII (July) 109–25; (Aug) 221–39; (Sep) 421–32; XXIX (Oct) 93–122.

BARNES, T. R. 'Yeats, Synge, Ibsen, and Strindberg', *Scrutiny*, V 3 (Dec 1936) 257–62 (Yeats versus Naturalism).

BECK, WARREN, 'The Boundaries of Poetry', *College English*, IV 6 (Mar 1943) 349–50 ('A Prayer for My Daughter').

BECKER, WILLIAM, '"Introductory Note", to *Diarmuid and Grania: A Play in Three Acts* by George Moore and W. B. Yeats', *Dublin Magazine*, XXVI 2 (Apr–June 1951) 2–4. Reprinted in *The Variorum Edition of the Plays of W. B. Yeats*.

'The Mask Mocked; or, Farce and the Dialectic of Self (Notes on Yeats's *The Player Queen*)', *Sewanee Review*, LXI 1 (winter 1953) 82–108.

'On the Margin of Yeats', *Poetry* (Chicago), LXXXI 5 (Feb 1953) 331–4 (Birgit Bjersby, *The Interpretation of the Cuchulain Legends in the Works of W. B. Yeats*; Vivienne Koch, *W. B. Yeats: The Tragic Phase*).

BEERBOHM, Sir MAX (as 'Max'), 'In Dublin', *Saturday Review*, LXXXVII (13 May 1899) 586–8 (the 1899 production of *The Countess Cathleen*).

(as 'Max'), 'Some Irish Plays and Players', *Saturday Review*, XCVII (9 Apr 1904) 455–7. Reprinted in his *Around Theaters*, 314–19 (*The King's Threshold*).

'First Meetings with W. B. Yeats', *Listener*, LIII (6 Jan 1955) 15–16; *Atlantic Monthly*, CC (Sep 1957) 70–2. Reprinted in his *Mainly on the Air*, 95–101.

BELIS, ANDREW, 'Recent Irish Poetry', *Bookman*, LXXXVI (Aug 1934) 235 (general comment).

BELL, A. *See* KELLY, P. J.

BENÉT, WILLIAM ROSE, 'This Virtue', *Saturday Review of Literature*, X (16 Dec 1933) 349–50 (*Collected Poems* and *The Winding Stair*).

B[ENÉT]., W[ILLIAM]. R[OSE]., 'William Butler Yeats, 1865–1939', *Saturday Review of Literature*, XIX (4 Feb 1939) 8.

BENSON, CARL, 'Yeats and Balzac's *Louis Lambert*', *Modern Philology*, XLIX 4 (May 1952) 242–7 (*A Vision* and Balzac).

'Yeats's "The Cat and the Moon"', *Modern Language Notes*, LXVIII 4 (Apr 1953) 220–3.

BENTLEY, ERIC, 'Yeats as a Playwright', *Kenyon Review*, X 2 (spring 1948) 196–208. Reprinted as 'Yeats's Plays' in his *In Search of Theatre*, 315–26. Also in *The Permanence of Yeats*, ed. James Hall and Martin Steinmann, 237–48 (213–23).

'Irish Theatre: Splendeurs et Misères', *Poetry* (Chicago), LXXIX 4 (Jan 1952) 216–32 *passim* (review article on Peter Kavanagh, *The Story of the Abbey Theatre*).

'On Staging Yeats's Plays', *New Republic*, CXXVIII (15 June 1953) 17–18 (on the occasion of the publication of *The Collected Plays of W. B. Yeats*). Reprinted in his *The Dramatic Event*, 132–5.

BERKELMAN, ROBERT, 'The Poet, the Swan, and the Woman', *University of Kansas City Review*, XXVIII 3 (spring 1962) 229–30 ('Leda and the Swan').

BEUM, ROBERT, 'Yeats's Octaves', *Texas Studies in Literature and Language*, III 1 (spring 1962) 89–96 (on Yeats's use of *ottava rima* in his later poems).

'Yeats's Idealized Speech', *Michigan Quarterly Review*, IV 4 (fall 1965) 227–33.

'Yeats the Rhymer', *Papers on English Language and Literature*, I (1965) 338–50.

BEWLEY, CHARLES, 'The Irish National Theatre', *Dublin Review*, CLII (Jan 1913) 132–44 (*Where There is Nothing*; the 'un-Irish' paganism of Yeats and Synge).

BICKLEY, FRANCIS, 'The Development of William Butler Yeats', *Living Age*, CCLXIV (26 Mar 1910) 802–5; also in *The Thrush*, I 2 (Jan 1910) 147–51.

'Deirdre', *Irish Review*, II 17 (July 1912) 252–4.

BIERMAN, ROBERT, 'Yeats' "The Gyres"', *Explicator*, XIX 7 (Apr 1961) item 44.

BINYON, LAURENCE, 'William Butler Yeats', *Bookman*, LXIII 376 (Jan 1923) 196–9 (*Later Poems* (1922); *Plays in Prose and Verse*; *The Trembling of the Veil*).

BIRMINGHAM, GEORGE A. *See* HANNAY, JAMES OWEN.

BLACKBURN, THOMAS, 'The Contemporary Dream', *London Magazine*, VI 1 (Jan 1959) 39–44 (reply, in part, to R. P. Blackmur, 'The Later Poetry of W. B. Yeats'). Reprinted as 'W. B. Yeats and the Contemporary Dream' in his *The Price of an Eye*, 30–49.

BLACKMUR, R. P., 'Under a Major Poet', *American Mercury*, XXXI 122 (Feb 1934) 245–6 (*Collected Poems* (1933)).

'The Later Poetry of W. B. Yeats', *Southern Review*, II 2 (autumn 1936) 339–62. Also in his *The Expense of Greatness*, 74–106, and in

his *Language as Gesture: Essays in Poetry*, 80–104. Reprinted in
Critiques and Essays in Criticism 1920–1948, ed. R. W. Stallman
(New York: Ronald Press, 1949) 358–76, and in *The Permanence
of Yeats*, ed. James Hall and Martin Steinmann, 42–66 (38–59).

'Between Myth and Philosophy: Fragments of W. B. Yeats',
Southern Review, VII 3 (winter 1941–2) 407–25. Also in his *Language
as Gesture: Essays in Poetry*, 105–23. Reprinted in *Yeats: A Collection
of Critical Essays*, ed. John Unterecker, 64–79.

'Lord Tennyson's Scissors: 1912–1950', *Kenyon Review*, XIV 1
(winter 1952) 1–20 (Yeats, Eliot, Pound, and modern prosody).

BLAIR, ERIC. *See* ORWELL, GEORGE.

BLAKE, W. B., 'Irish Plays and Players', *Independent*, LXXIV 3353 (6
Mar 1913) 515–19.

'The Theatre and Beauty', *Independent*, LXXVII 3403 (23 Feb 1914)
271.

BLENNER-HASSETT, ROLAND, 'Yeats's Use of Chaucer', *Anglia*,
LXXII 4 (1954) 455–62.

BLOCK, HASKELL M., 'Flaubert, Yeats, and the National Library',
Modern Language Notes, LXVII 1 (Jan 1952) 55–6 (reprints with
comment Yeats's letter to the *Irish Times*, 8 Oct 1903, Wade p.
366).

'Yeats's *The King's Threshold*: The Poet and Society', *Philological
Quarterly*, XXXIV, 2 (Apr 1955) 206–18.

BLOOM, EDWARD A., 'Yeats's 'Second Coming': An Experiment in
Analysis', *University of Kansas City Review*, XXI 2 (winter 1954)
103–10.

†BOENNINGER, K., 'W. B. Yeats neue Gedichte', *Neue Zürcher Zeitung*, no. 663 (1934) (*The Winding Stair and Other Poems*).

BOGAN, LOUISE, 'William Butler Yeats', *Atlantic Monthly*, CLXI 5
(June 1938) 637–44 (an Atlantic Portrait). Also in her *Selected
Criticism*, 86–104.

'The Cutting of an Agate', *Nation*, CXLVIII 9 (25 Feb 1939) 234–5.
Reprinted as 'On the Death of William Butler Yeats', in her
Selected Criticism, 133–7 (obituary article: on the greatness of the
late poetry).

'Verse', *New Yorker*, XVI (1 June 1940) 81–2 (*Last Poems and Plays*). Reprinted as part of 'The Later Poetry of William Butler Yeats' in her *Selected Criticism*, 202–6.

'Poet and Mage', *New Republic*, CXXV (17 Sep 1951) 19 (*Collected Poems* (1951)). Reprinted as part of 'The Later Poetry of William Butler Yeats' in her *Selected Criticism*, 202–6.

BOLAND, EAVAN, 'A Young Writer's Reaction', *Irish Times*, (Yeats Centenary Supplement, 10 June 1965, iv (an Irish poet looks at Yeats today).

BOSANQUET, THEODORA, 'Men and Books', *Time and Tide*, XVII (13 June 1936) 849 (*Dramatis Personae*: Yeats and Confucius).

BOSE, ABINASH CHANDRA, 'W. B. Yeats: His Poetry and Thought', *Indian Journal of English Studies*, III 1 (1962) 158–67 (A. G. Stock, *W. B. Yeats: His Poetry and Thought*; B. Chatterjee, *The Poetry of W. B. Yeats*; Joseph Hone, *W. B. Yeats*, second edition; *Selected Poems*, ed. A. N. Jeffares).

BOTTOMLEY, GORDON, 'His Legacy to the Theatre', *The Arrow*, W. B. Yeats Commemoration Number (summer 1939) 11–14. Reprinted in his *A Stage for Poetry: My Purposes with My Plays*, 20–4.

BOULGER, JAMES D., 'Personality and Existence in Yeats', *Thought*, XXXIX (1964) 591–612.

BOYD, ERNEST A., 'The Irish National Theatre: A Criticism', *Irish Times*, 27 Dec 1912, 5.

'The Abbey Theatre', *Irish Review*, II 24 (Feb 1913) 628–34.

'Le Théâtre Irlandais', *Revue de Paris*, XXV 17 (1 Sep 1913) 191–205.

'The Irish Renaissance – Renascent', *Dial*, LXVII (26 July 1919) 53–5 (*Two Plays for Dancers*, with comment on Yeats and the Dublin Drama League).

'Romantic Ireland's Dead and Gone', *New Leader*, 6 Mar 1943.

BOYNTON, H. W., 'W. B. Yeats', *Atlantic Monthly*, XCII 552 (Oct 1903) 565–9 (*Ideas of Good and Evil*; *The Celtic Twilight*; *Where There is Nothing*).

'Three Dramatic Studies', *Atlantic Monthly*, XCIII 559 (May 1904) 712–13 (*The Hour Glass and Other Plays*, vol. II of *Plays for an Irish Theatre*).

BRADBROOK, MURIEL C., 'Songs of Experience', *Scrutiny*, II 1 (June 1933) 77–8 (*Words for Music Perhaps*).

'Yeats and Elizabethan Love Poetry', *Dublin Magazine* (formerly *The Dubliner*), W. B. Yeats Centenary Edition, IV 2 (summer 1965) 40–55.

BRADFORD, CURTIS B., 'Journeys to Byzantium', *Virginia Quarterly Review*, XXV 2 (spring 1949) 205–25 ('personal values and personal morality' in the poetry of Yeats and T. S. Eliot).

'*The Speckled Bird*: A Novel by W. B. Yeats. A Selection from the Novel, with a Note', *Irish Writing*, W. B. Yeats: A Special Number, no. 31 (summer 1955) 9–18 (the editor's 'Note' on pp. 9–12).

'*The Variorum Edition of Yeats's Poems*', *Sewanee Review*, LXVI 4 (autumn 1958) 668–78 (review article).

'Yeats's Byzantium Poems: A Study of Their Development', *PMLA*, LXXV 1 (Mar 1960) 110–25 (prints early drafts of 'Sailing to Byzantium' and 'Byzantium'), Reprinted in *Yeats: A Collection of Critical Essays*, ed. John Unterecker, 93–130, and in *Aspects of Poetry*, ed. Mark Linenthal (Boston and Toronto: Little, Brown, 1963) 64–103.

'The Order of Yeats's Last Poems', *Modern Language Notes*, LXXVI 6 (June 1961) 515–16 (a listing from Yeats's manuscripts).

'Yeats and Maud Gonne', *Texas Studies in Language and Literature*, III 4 (winter 1962) 452–74.

'Modern Ireland: An Address to American Audiences, 1932–1933' by W. B. Yeats, transcribed from the MS. and edited by Curtis Bradford, *Massachusetts Review*, V 2 (winter 1964) 256–68. Reprinted in *Irish Renaissance*, ed. Robin Skelton and David R. Clark, 13–25.

'Discoveries: Second Series', by W. B. Yeats, transcribed from the MS. and edited by Curtis Bradford, *Massachusetts Review*, V 2 (winter 1964) 297–306. Reprinted in *Irish Renaissance*, ed. Robin Skelton and David R. Clark, 80–9.

BRADY, GERARD K., 'Yeats's Tower', *Irish Times*, 13 Sep 1960. Correspondence, ibid., by Gabriel Fallon, 20 Sep 1960.

BRASH, W. B., 'W. B. Yeats', *London Quarterly*, CLXIV (July 1939) 320–33.

BRAUN, HANS, 'William Butler Yeats, Irische Schaubühne', *Deutsche Zeitschrift*, XLVII 11–12 (Aug–Sep 1934) 576–8 (Henry von Heiseler (trans.), *Irische Schaubühne*. Wade p. 376).

BRÉGY, KATHERINE, 'Yeats Revisited', *Catholic World*, CLI (Sep 1940) 677–86.

BRENNAN, DIARMUID, 'As Yeats Was Going Down Grafton Street', *Listener*, LXXI (6 Feb 1964) 236–8 (recollections of Yeats at Rathfarnham).

BROMAGE, MARY C., 'The Yeats–O'Casey Quarrel', *Michigan Alumnus Quarterly Review*, LXIV 14 (1 Mar 1958) 135–44.

BRONOWSKI, J., 'W. B. Yeats', *Cambridge Review*, LIV (June 1933) 475–6 (article based on *Collected Poems* (1933)).

BROOKS, CLEANTH, JR, 'A Note on Symbol and Conceit', *American Review*, III (May 1934) 209–11 ('Sailing to Byzantium').

'The Vision of William Butler Yeats', *Southern Review*, IV 1 (summer 1938) 116–42 (the significance of *A Vision* and Yeats's 'system' for an understanding of the poems; includes a reading of the Byzantium poems). Reprinted as 'Yeats: The Poet as Myth-Maker', in his *Modern Poetry and the Tradition*, 171–98. Reprinted in *The Permanence of Yeats*, ed. James Hall and Martin Steinmann, 67–94 (60–84). *See* review of *The Permanence of Yeats* by Robin Mayhead, *Scrutiny*, XIX 1 (Oct 1952) 68–71.

'Yeats: His Poetry and His Prose', *English*, W. B. Yeats, 1865–1939, XV 89 (summer 1965) 177–80 (on 'A Prayer for my Daughter' and its embodiment of Yeats's ideas).

BROOKS, SEAN, 'The Ties with Sligo', *Irish Times*, W. B. Yeats Centenary Supplement, 10 June 1965, vi (Sligo in Yeats's poems).

BROSNAN, GERALD, 'Dublin's Abbey – the Immortal Theatre', *Theatre Arts*, XXXV 10 (Oct 1951) 36–7.

BROWER, REUBEN A., 'The Incarnation of Yeats', *Yale Review*, XLIV 2 (Dec 1954) 290–2 (Virginia Moore, *The Unicorn*; Richard Ellmann, *The Identity of Yeats*).

BROWN, FORMAN G., 'Mr Yeats and the Supernatural', *Sewanee Review*, XXXIII 3 (July 1925) 323–30.

ARTICLES WHOLLY OR PARTLY ABOUT YEATS

BROWN, T. J., 'English Literary Autographs, XLIX: William Butler Yeats, 1865–1939', *Book Collector*, XIII 1 (spring 1964) 53 (reproduces MS. of 'The Rose Tree' (BM., Ashley MS. 2291, f. I)).

BROWN, W. C., 'A Poem Should Not Mean But Be', *University of Kansas City Review*, XV 1 (autumn 1948) 59–60 ('The Choice'), 63 ('After Long Silence').

†BRUNIUS, AUGUST, 'Yeats och Moore', *Engelska Kåserier* (1927).

BUCHANAN, GEORGE, 'Pages from a Journal', *Rann*, no. 15 (spring 1952) 11–13 (Yeats and 'Unity of Being').

BUCKLEY, VINCENT, 'W. B. Yeats and the Dramatic Lyric', *Melbourne Critical Review*, no. 2 (1959) 12–28 (Yeats's dramatic use of 'lyric' forms; includes readings of 'A Prayer for my Daughter' and 'Sailing to Byzantium').

BUDDINGH, CORNELIS, 'Drama's van een dichter', *Critisch Bulletin*, XX 3 (Mar 1953) 135–8 (*Collected Plays*).

BULLOUGH, GEOFFREY, 'Poetry in Modern English Drama', *Cairo Studies in English* (1959) 26–42.

BURGESS, ANTHONY, 'Cast a Cold Eye', *Spectator*, CCXIV 7125 (15 Jan 1965) 73 (Edward Engelberg, *The Vast Design*; Peter Ure, *Yeats*; A. Norman Jeffares (ed.), *W. B. Yeats: Selected Criticism*).

BURKE, KENNETH, 'On Motivation in Yeats', *Southern Review*, VII 3 (winter 1941–2) 547–61 (on Yeats's system, and the 'metaphors for poetry' in *A Vision*). Reprinted in *The Permanence of Yeats*, ed. James Hall and Martin Steinmann, 249–63 (224–37).

BURROWS, RACHEL, 'The Yeats Theatre', *Irish Times*, W. B. Yeats Centenary Supplement, 10 June 1965, vii (on the Abbey Theatre and the staging of Yeats's plays).

BUSHRUI, SULEIL B., 'William Butler Yeats', *Aswat*, no. 8 (1962) 6–27 (in Arabic).

'*The King's Threshold*: A Defence of Poetry', *Review of English Literature*, IV 3 (July 1963) 81–94 (discusses the play as an early expression of Yeats's theory of poetry and the poet's place in society).

BYRNE, JOSEPH, C.S.Sp., *Catholic Bulletin*, XV (July 1925) 685 (comment on Yeats's speech on divorce in the Irish Senate, 1925).

C., 'The Irish Literary Theatre – 1900', *New Ireland Review*, XIII 1 (Mar 1900) 49–53.

C., P. C., 'Oedipus at the Abbey', *Irish Statesman*, VI (Dec 1926) 326 (reviews the first performance of *King Oedipus*).

'Fighting the Waves', *Irish Statesman*, XII (Aug 1929) 275–6 (reviews the first performance at the Abbey, 15 Aug 1929).

C., R. J., 'Yeats' "The Wild Swans at Coole"', *Explicator* II 4 (Jan 1944) item 20.

CAMBON, GLAUCO, 'Yeats e la lotta con Proteo', *Aut-Aut*, XXXVII (Jan 1957) 1–34. Reprinted in his *La lotta con Proteo*, 71–111.

CAMERON, SUSAN ELIZABETH, 'William Butler Yeats', *McGill University Magazine*, IV (1905) 94–105.

CAMPBELL, HARRY MODEAN, 'Yeats's "Sailing to Byzantium"', *Modern Language Notes*, LXX 6 (Dec 1955) 585–9.

CAMPBELL, JOHN, M.P., 'The Rise of the Drama in Ireland', *New Liberal Review*, VII 39 (Apr 1904) 291–307 (concerned particularly with *The Countess Cathleen* controversy in Ireland).

CARNE-ROSS, D. S., 'A Commentary on Yeats' "Coole Park and Ballylee"', *Nine*, no. 1 (autumn 1949) 21–4.

CARY, ELIZABETH LUTHER, 'Apostles of the New Drama', *Lamp*, XXVII 6 (Jan 1904) 593–8 (the views of Yeats and Shaw on the modern theatre).

CATTAUI, G., 'Rencontres avec W. B. Yeats', *Nouvelles Littéraires*, 4 Feb 1939, 1, 9.

CAVANAGH, PATRICK, in 'Diary', *Envoy*, no. 1 (Jan 1950) 83–4; reply by John D. Sheridan, correspondence, ibid., no. 2 (Feb 1950) 91–2 (on the Yeats film).

CAZAMIAN, MADELEINE-L., 'Un poète irlandais: W. B. Yeats', *Revue Germanique*, VII 7 (Mar-Apr 1911) 129–54.

'W. B. Yeats, poète de l'Irlande', *La Vie des Peuples*, XII (Jan 1924) 102–32.

'William Butler Yeats, 1865–1939', *Études Anglaises*, III 2 (Apr–June 1939) 127–31.

L'évolution de W. B. Yeats d'après ses dernières œuvres', *Études Anglaises*, V 1 (Feb 1952) 50–4 (T. R. Henn, *The Lonely Tower*; Vivienne Koch, *W. B. Yeats: The Tragic Phase*).

'La correspondance de W. B. Yeats', *Études Anglaises*, VIII 1 (Jan–Mar 1955) 50–60 (Allan Wade (ed.), *The Letters of W. B. Yeats*).

CHAKRAVARTY, A., 'William Butler Yeats', *Modern Review*, LXV (Mar 1939) 326–9.

CHAMBERS, E. K., 'The Experiments of Mr Yeats', *Academy*, LXIV 1618 (9 May 1903) 465–6 (*The Pot of Broth*; *Cathleen ni Houlihan*).

CHAPMAN, R. W., correspondence, *TLS*, 2926 (28 Mar 1958) 169 (on the 'misnaming' of *The Variorum Edition of the Poems*). *See also* reviews (Part II).

CHAUVIRE, ROGER, 'Yeats: Avec Yeats a disparu un grand poète', *Journal des Débats*, 9 Apr 1939, 4 (obituary article).

CHESTERTON, G. K., 'W. B. Yeats as Orator', *Daily News*, 16 May 1903 (on Yeats's views on the speaking of verse).

'Efficiency in Elfland', *Living Age*, CCLXXIV 3552 (3 Aug 1912) 317–19 (*The Land of Heart's Desire*).

'Mr. Yeats and his Cosmic Moth', *America*, XV 380 (22 July 1916) 357–8.

CHITTICK, V. L. O., 'Yeats the Dancer', *Dalhousie Review*, XXXIX 3 (autumn 1959) 333–48 (Yeats and the dance: the plays and 'Among School Children').

CHRISTOPHERSON, JOHN. *See* AUTY, R. A.

CHRISTY, M. A., 'Yeats's Teacher', correspondence, *TLS*, 3299 (20 May 1965) 397 (John McNeill remembers teaching Yeats at the High School, Dublin).

CHURCH, RICHARD, 'Yeats and the Creative Mask', *Calendar of Modern Letters*, III (Jan 1927) 316–19 (*Autobiographies*).

'The Later Yeats', *Fortnightly Review*, CLIV, n.s., cxlviii (Aug 1940) 193–9. Reprinted in his *Eight for Immortality*, 41–54.

'A Poet's Design for Living', *Fortnightly Review*, CLIX, n.s., cliii (Apr 1943) 258–62 (Joseph Hone, *W. B. Yeats 1865–1939*).

'The Consistency of Genius', *John O'London's Weekly*, IV 72 (16 Feb 1961) 176 (*Essays and Introductions*).

CHUTE, DESMOND, 'Poets in Paradise: Recollections of W. B. Yeats and Ezra Pound in Rapallo', *Listener*, LV (5 Jan 1956) 14–15.

CIARDI, JOHN, 'The Morality of Poetry', *Saturday Review of Literature*, XL (30 Mar 1957) 11–12.

CLARK, DAVID R., 'W. B. Yeats's *Deirdre*: The Rigour of Logic', *Dublin Magazine*, XXXIII I (Jan–Mar 1958) 13–21 ('The neo-classic tragedy of reason is fused with the romantic tragedy of passion' in Yeats's attempt to create a new dramatic form). An expanded version is printed in his *W. B. Yeats and the Theatre of Desolate Reality*.

'Yeats and the Modern Theatre', *Threshold*, IV 2 (autumn–winter 1960) 36–56 (takes *The Words upon the Window-pane* as an example 'both of Yeats's mastery and rejection of circumstantial realism'). A paper read at the First Yeats International Summer School (Aug 1960), and reprinted in his *W. B. Yeats and the Theatre of Desolate Reality*.

'W. B. Yeats and the Drama of Vision', *Arizona Quarterly*, XX 2 (summer 1964) 127–41. Reprinted in his *W. B. Yeats and the Theatre of Desolate Reality*.

'Nishikigi and Yeats's "The Dreaming of the Bones"', *Modern Drama*, VII 2 (Sep 1964) 111–25 (on the influence of the Noh play *Nishikigi* on *The Dreaming of the Bones* and Yeats's other *Plays for Dancers*). Reprinted in his *W. B. Yeats and the Theatre of Desolate Reality*.

'Aubrey Beardsley's Drawing of the "Shadows" in W. B. Yeats's *The Shadowy Waters*', *Modern Drama*, VII 3 (Dec 1964) 267–72 (finds a passage in an unpublished early version of *The Shadowy Waters* in which the 'shadows' are symbolic figures matching the description of Beardsley's lost illustration given in *Letters from Aubrey Beardsley to Leonard Smithers* (London, 1937)).

'Half the Characters Had Eagles' Faces: W. B. Yeats's Unpublished *The Shadowy Waters*', *Massachusetts Review*, VI I (autumn 1964– winter 1965) 151–80 (gives an account of the early versions and prints from a corrected typescript a finished poetic version of the first half of the play). Reprinted in *Irish Renaissance*, ed. Robin Skelton and David R. Clark, 26–55.

CLARK, JAMES M., 'The Irish Literary Movement', *Englische Studien*, XLIX I (July 1915) 50–98.

CLARKE, AUSTIN, 'The Poetic Drama of Mr Yeats', *London Mercury*, XXXI 184 (Feb 1935) 391–2 (*Wheels and Butterflies*; *Collected Plays*).

'Irish Poetry Today', *Dublin Magazine*, X I (Jan–Mar 1935) 26–32.

'W. B. Yeats', *Dublin Magazine*, XIV 2 (Apr–June 1939) 6–10.

'Poet and Artist', *Arrow*, W. B. Yeats Commemoration Number (summer 1939) 8–9.

'Poetry in Ireland Today', *Bell*, XIII 2 (Nov 1946) 155–61 *passim*.

'A Centenary Celebration', *Massachusetts Review*, V 2 (winter 1964) 307–10 (Yeats at the centenary commemoration of Thomas Davis in the Antient Concert Rooms, Dublin, 20 Nov 1914). Reprinted in *Irish Renaissance*, ed. Robin Skelton and David R. Clark, 90–3.

'Glimpses of W. B. Yeats', *Shenandoah* (Yeats Issue), XVI 4 (summer 1965) 25–36 (reminiscences of encounters with Yeats, Ella Young and Maud Gonne).

'W. B. Yeats and Verse Drama', *Threshold*, no. 19, The Theatre of W. B. Yeats Centenary, 1965 (autumn 1965) 14–29.

See also MOONEY, FR CANICE.

CLARKE, EGERTON, 'William Butler Yeats', *Dublin Review*, CCIV 409 (Apr–May–June 1939) 305–21 (obituary tribute).

CLARKE, W. T., 'The Soul's Quest for Ideal Beauty in W. B. Yeats, Walter de la Mare, and John Masefield', *London Quarterly Review*, CXLVII, 5th series, XXXIII (Apr 1927) 165–73.

CLEMENS, CYRIL, 'The Passing of W. B. Yeats', *Canadian Bookman*, XXII 2 (June–July 1939) 21–5.

CLEMENS, KATHERINE, 'Some Recollections of William Butler Yeats', *Mark Twain Quarterly*, VI I (summer–fall 1943) 17–18.

CLEYMAET, R., 'Yeats's "Lake Isle of Innisfree"', *Tijdschrift voor Levende Talen*, IX (1943) 218–23.

CLINTON-BADDELEY, V. C., 'Reading Poetry with W. B. Yeats', *London Magazine*, IV 12 (Dec 1957) 47–53 (Yeats at the B.B.C.).

'Reciting the Poems', *Irish Times*, Yeats Centenary Supplement, 10 June 1965, iv.

COFFEY, BRIAN, 'A Note on Rat Island', *University Review* (Dublin), III 8 (1965?) 25–8 (a reply, in part, to Robert Graves's attack on 'The Lake Isle of Innisfree' in *A Pamphlet against Anthologies*).

COHANE, J. J., 'Cowley and Yeats', *TLS*, 2880 (10 May 1957) 289 (Yeats's use of the stanza form of Cowley's 'On the Death of Mr William Hervey').

COHEN, JOSEPH, 'In Memory of W. B. Yeats–and Wilfrid Owen', *Journal of English and Germanic Philology*, LVIII 4 (Oct 1959) 637–49 (on Yeats's exclusion of the 'Soldier Poets' from his *Oxford Book of Modern Verse*). *See also* correspondence, ibid., LIX 1 (Jan 1960) 171 (errata noted).

COHN, RUBY, 'The Plays of Yeats through Beckett Coloured-Glasses', *Threshold*, no. 19, The Theatre of W. B. Yeats Centenary, 1965 (autumn 1965) 41–7 (a Yeats–Beckett comparison).

COLE, E. R., 'Three Cycle Poems of Yeats and His Mystico–Historical Thought', *Personalist*, XLVI 1 (winter 1965) 73–80 ('Leda and the Swan', 'The Mother of God' and 'The Magi').

†COLLIJN, GUSTAV, 'Yeats et son théâtre', *Gil Blas*, 4 Jan 1912.

COLUM, MARY M., 'The Later Yeats', *Poetry* (Chicago), VII 5 (Feb 1915) 258–60.

'Worker in Dreams', *Forum*, XCIV (Nov 1935) 278–9 (*Collected Plays*).

'Memories of Yeats', *Saturday Review of Literature*, XIX (25 Feb 1939) 3–4, 14. Reprinted in *Saturday Review Gallery*, selected by Jerome Beatty, Jr, and others (New York: Simon & Schuster, 1959) 183–9.

'Heroic Mind', *Forum*, CIII (June 1940) 323–4 (*Last Poems and Plays*).

COLUM, PADRAIC, 'The Irish Literary Movement', *Forum*, LIII (Jan 1915) 133–48.

'Mr Yeats's Selected Poems', *Dial*, LXXI 4 (Oct 1921) 464–8 (*Selected Poems*).

'A New Dramatic Art', *Dial*, LXXII 3 (Mar 1922) 302–4 (*Four Plays for Dancers*).

'Mr Yeats's Plays and Later Poems', *Yale Review*, XIV 2 (Jan 1925) 381–5 (*Plays in Prose and Verse*; *Later Poems* (1924)).

'A Letter from Ireland', *Saturday Review of Literature*, IV (15 Oct 1927) 206 (*October Blast*; performance at Abbey of *Oedipus at Colonus*).

'On Yeats', *Commonweal*, XX 3 (18 May 1934) 70–1.

'Poet's Progress: Yeats in the Theatre', *Theatre Arts Monthly*, XIX 12 (Dec 1935) 936–43. Reprinted in *Theatre Arts Anthology: A Record and a Prophecy*, ed. Rosamund Gilder and others (New York: Theatre Arts Books, 1950) 143–51.

'A Dublin Letter', *Saturday Review of Literature*, XIII (15 Feb 1936) 24 (on Yeats's seventieth birthday).

'A Poet's Progress in the Theatre', *Dublin Magazine*, XI 2 (Apr–June 1936) 10–23. An expanded version of the article printed in *Theatre Arts Monthly* (*see* above).

'The Greatness of W. B. Yeats', *NYTB*, 12 Feb 1939, 1, 17.

'John Butler Yeats', *Atlantic Monthly*, CLXXII (July 1943) 81–5 *passim*.

'Yeats's Lyrical Poems', *Irish Writing*, no. 2 (June 1947) 78–85.

'A Poet is Brought Home', *Commonweal*, XLIX 1 (22 Oct 1948) 33–6. Reprinted in *Commonweal Reader*, ed. Edward S. Skillen, with an introduction by Anne Fremantle (New York: Harper, 1949) 39–45.

'The Early Days of the Irish Theatre', *Dublin Magazine*, XXIV 4 (Oct–Dec 1949) 11–17; ibid., XXV 1 (Jan–Mar 1950) 18–25.

'My Memories of John Butler Yeats', *Dublin Magazine*, XXXII 4 (Oct–Dec 1957) 8–16 *passim*.

'A Passion that Became Poetry', *Saturday Review*, XLII (1 Aug 1959) 16–17 (*Mythologies*, with a memoir on Yeats and the National Theatre Society).

'Reminiscences of Yeats', *Tri-Quarterly*, W. B. Yeats Centenary Issue, no. 4 (fall 1965) 71–6.

COMERFORD, ANTHONY, 'W. B. Yeats', correspondence, *TLS*, 3307 (15 July 1965) 597 (on Yeats's political views).

CONACHER, W. M., 'The Irish Literary Movement', *Queen's Quarterly*, XLV 1 (spring 1938) 56–65.

CONNOLLY, CYRIL, 'Notes Towards an Understanding of Yeats', *Sunday Times*, 13 June 1965, 43.

CORRIGAN, CYRIL F., 'Priceless Paintings May Soon be Going to Ireland', *The People*, 25 Jan 1931 (the Lane Pictures).

COSMAN, MADELEINE PELNER, 'Mannered Passion: W. B. Yeats and the Ossianic Myths', *Western Humanities Review*, XIV 2 (spring 1960) 163–71 (*The Wanderings of Oisin*).

COURTNEY, NEIL, 'Triumphant Life of W. B. Yeats', *The Age Literary Review*, 12 June 1965, 21 (centenary tribute).

COUSTER, P. J., 'Un poète irlandais: W. B. Yeats', *Échanges* (Mar 1939) 296–303.

COWASJEE, SAROS, 'O'Casey Seen through Holloway's Diary', *Review of English Literature*, VI 3 (July 1965) 58–69 *passim*.

COWEN, HEWSON, 'Compulsory Gaelic', correspondence, *Irish Statesman*, II (Aug 1924) 724 (comments on Yeats's 'Compulsory Gaelic: A Dialogue', Wade p. 382).

COWLEY, MALCOLM, 'A Poet's Anthology', *New Republic*, LXXXIX (16 Dec 1936) 221–3 (*The Oxford Book of Modern Verse*).

'Poet in Politics', *New Republic*, XCVI (21 Sep 1938) 191–2 (*The Autobiography*). Correspondence, ibid., by Delmore Schwartz and M[alcolm]. C[owley]. (12 Oct) 272–3, and James P. O'Donnell (7 Dec) 133–4.

'Socialists and Symbolists', *New Republic*, XCVI (28 Sep 1938) 218–19 (on Yeats's style).

'Yeats', *New Republic*, XCVIII (8 Feb 1939) 4.

'Yeats and O'Faoláin', *New Republic*, XCVIII (15 Feb 1939) 49–50.

'The Hosting of the Shee', *New Republic*, CVIII (8 Feb 1943) 185–6 (J. M. Hone, *W. B. Yeats 1865–1939*).

COX, AEDAN, 'A Weaver of Symbols', *Hermes* (Feb 1907) 7–11.

COXHEAD, ELIZABETH, 'Yeats and Lady Gregory: The Lifelong Literary Friendship', *Irish Times*, Yeats Centenary Supplement, 10 June 1865, vi.

CRAIG, MAURICE. *See* AUTY, R. A.

CRONE, JOHN S., 'Sgéala ó Chathair na gCéo', *Irish Book Lover*, XVI 3 (May–June 1928) 67 (on *The Silver Tassie* controversy).

'Willie Yeats and John O'Leary', *Irish Book Lover*, XXVII 5 (Nov 1940) 245–9 (letters from Yeats to O'Leary sent by Mrs O'Leary to J. S. Crone, Wade p. 362).

CRONIN, ANTHONY, 'Some Aspects of Yeats and his Influences', *Bell*, XVI 5 (Feb 1951) 52–8.

'A Question of Modernity', X, *A Quarterly Review*, I 4 (Oct 1960) 283–92 (Yeats, Pound, Eliot, Joyce).

CROSS, K. GUSTAV W., 'Unless Soul Clap Its Hands ...', *Sydney Morning Herald*, 12 June 1965, 17 (a centenary tribute).

'"My Hundredth Year is at an End": Reflections of the Yeats Centenary', *Quadrant*, X 1 (Jan–Feb 1966) 62–9 (on the extent of Yeats's involvement with Fascist movements).

CROWLEY, MARY, 'The Norman Tradition in Anglo-Irish Literature' *Irish Statesman*, XIII (Jan 1930) 354–6 (the 'oral' quality of Anglo-Irish prose).

CUANA (pseudonym), 'Doctors Bodkin and Yeats in their Animal Coinage Book', *Catholic Bulletin*, XXI (1931) 348–51 (an attack on the design of the Irish coinage).

CUMMINS, GERALDINE, 'W. B. Yeats and Psychical Research', *Occult Review*, LXVI 2 (Apr 1939) 132–0 (episodes in Yeats's psychical investigations).

CURTAYNE, A., *Critic*, XXI (Sep 1962) 48–50 (on the Third Yeats Summer School at Sligo).

CURTIS, PENELOPE, 'Yeats: The Tower in Time of Civil War', *Melbourne Critical Review*, no. 6 (1963) 69–82 ('Meditations in Time of Civil War').

D., A., *Academy*, LXXII 1833 (22 June 1907) 610–11 (*On Baile's Strand* performed by the Abbey Players; compared with *The Land of Heart's Desire*).

D'AGOSTINO, NEMI, 'La poesia di William Butler Yeats: il "Periodo del Sole" (1900–1919)', *English Miscellany*, V (1954) 149–202.

DAICHES, DAVID, 'Jane Austen, Karl Marx and the Aristocratic Dance', *American Scholar*, XVII 3 (summer 1948) 289–96 (Yeats–Austen links: the dance and country-house motifs).

'The Practical Visionary', *Encounter*, XIX 3 (Sep 1962) 71–4 (*Essays and Introductions*; A. G. Stock, *W. B. Yeats: His Poetry and Thought*; Joseph Hone, *W. B. Yeats 1865–1939*, second edition, revised).

DALY, J. J., 'The Paganism of Mr Yeats', *Catholic World*, CXV (Aug 1922) 595–605. Reprinted in his *A Cheerful Ascetic, and Other Essays*, 87–102.

DAVENPORT, ARNOLD, 'W. B. Yeats and the Upanishads', *Review of English Studies*, n.s., III 9 (Jan 1952) 55–62 (supplements A. N. Jeffares, 'The Byzantine Poems of W. B. Yeats').

DAVID, PAUL, 'Structure in Some Modern Poets', *New English Weekly*, XXVII 4 (26 July 1945) 131–2.

DAVIDSON, DONALD, 'Yeats and the Centaur', *Southern Review*, VII 3 (winter 1942) 510–16 (on Yeats's use of folk-lore). Reprinted in his *Still Rebels, Still Yankees*, 23–30. Also in *The Permanence of Yeats*, ed. James Hall and Martin Steinmann, 278–85 (250–6).

DAVIE, DONALD, 'Yeats and Pound', *Dublin Magazine*, XXXI 1 (Oct–Dec 1955) 17–21.

'Yeats, Berkeley, and Romanticism', *Irish Writing*, W. B. Yeats: A Special Number, no. 31 (summer 1955) 36–41.

DAVIES, W. ROBERTSON, 'Observations on Yeats' Plays', *Saturday Night*, LXVIII 17 (31 Jan 1953) 220–3.

DAVISON, DENNIS, 'Word and Sound in Yeats's "Byzantium"', *Theoria*, no. 7 (1955) 111–14 (a reply to D. I. Masson, 'The "Musical Form" of Yeats's "Byzantium"', q.v.).

DAVISON, EDWARD L. 'Three Irish Poets: AE, W. B. Yeats, and James Stephens', *English Journal*, XV 5 (May 1926) 327–36. Reprinted in his *Some Modern Poets and Other Critical Essays*, 173–96.

DAVRAY, HENRY D., 'William Butler Yeats', *L'Ermitage*, VII 8 (Aug 1896) 88–96.

DAVY, CHARLES, 'Yeats and the Desert Titan', *TLS*, 3053 (2 Sep 1960) 561 (a source for the image in 'The Second Coming'). Replies by A. Norman Jeffares, and Rupert and Helen Gleadow, ibid., 3055 (16 Sep) 593.

ARTICLES WHOLLY OR PARTLY ABOUT YEATS

DE BACKER, FRANZ, 'William Butler Yeats', *Dietsche Warande en Belfort*, IV (Apr 1939) 249–68 (obituary article).

DE BLACAM, AODH, 'Yeats and the Nation. A Surrender to Subjectivity: Why the Abbey Idea Failed', *Irish Times*, 13 June 1935, 6–7 (an attack on Yeats and the Abbey Theatre).

'Yeats as I Knew Him', *Irish Monthly*, LXVII (Mar 1939) 204–13; condensed under the same title in *Irish Digest*, III 3 (May 1939) 33–6.

'Yeats Reconsidered', *Irish Monthly*, LXXI 839 (May 1943) 209–17 (on J. M. Hone's *W. B. Yeats*).

'Memories of the Mighty', *Irish Bookman*, I 6 (Jan 1947) 15–18.

DE B[LACAM]., A., '*Fighting the Waves:* A Ballet Play by W. B. Yeats', *Spectator*, CXLIII 5278 (24 Aug 1929) 243.

DE LA MARE, WALTER, 'The Works of Mr Yeats', *Bookman*, XXXV 208 (Jan 1909) 191–2 (*Collected Works*).

DE LIPSKI, W., 'Note sur le symbolisme de W. B. Yeats', *Études Anglaises*, IV 1 (Jan–Mar 1940) 31–42.

DESMOND, SHAW, 'Dunsany, Yeats and Shaw: Trinity of Magic', *Bookman* (New York), LVIII 3 (Nov 1923) 260–6.

DE VALOIS, Dame NINETTE, *Trinity News*, 13 Feb 1964, 5 (talks to Colin Smythe about the Abbey Theatre and W. B. Yeats).

DEVANE, JAMES, 'Is an Irish Culture Possible?' *Ireland Today*, I 5 (Oct 1936) 21–31 *passim* (Yeats: Irish or Anglo–Irish?).

DILLON, THOMAS, 'Ireland 1865–1921', *University Review* (Dublin), III 8 (1965?) 73–87 (a historical sketch).

DISHER, M. WILLSON, 'A Yeats Poem?', *TLS*, 2108 (27 June 1942) 322 ('In Church', printed in *The Variorum Edition*, p. 735). Reply by Seumas O'Sullivan, ibid. 2112 (25 July) 36.

DISKIN, PATRICK, 'A Source for Yeats's "The Black Tower"', *Notes and Queries*, CCVI, n.s., viii 3 (Mar 1961) 107–8 (Standish O'Grady's *Finn and His Companions* a possible source for Yeats's last poem).

'Yeats's "The Black Tower"', *Notes and Queries*, CCX, n.s., xii 7 (July 1965) 278–9 (Yeats's use of Standish O'Grady's *Finn and His Companions*).

DOBRÉE, BONAMY, 'Poetic Drama in England Today', *Southern Review*, IV 3 (winter 1939) 581–9 (comments on Yeats's plays).

See also AUTY, R. A.

DONAGHY, LYLE, 'The Staging of a Play', correspondence, *Irish Statesman*, VI (Mar 1926) 70–1. Further correspondence by Geoffrey Phibbs and C. H. Witton, ibid. (Apr) 97, and Lyle Donaghy, ibid., 125–6.

DONALDSON, ALLAN, 'A Note on Yeats's "Sailing to Byzantium"', *Notes and Queries*, CXCIX, n.s., i 1 (Jan 1954) 34–5 (the 'dying animal' image, stanza 3, and Mme Blavatsky's *The Secret Doctrine*).

DONOGHUE, DENIS, 'Notes Towards a Critical Method: Language as Order', *Studies*, XLIV (summer 1955) 186–7 ('Blood and the Moon').

'Yeats and the Clean Outline', *Sewanee Review*, LIV 2 (spring 1957) 202–25 (*The Shadowy Waters* and *A Full Moon in March*). Also in his *The Third Voice*, 32–61.

'The Vigour of its Blood: Yeats's *Words for Music Perhaps*', *Kenyon Review*, XXI 3 (summer 1959) 376–87.

'Dublin Letter', *Hudson Review*, XIII 4 (winter 1960–1) 579–85 (Yeats and the Irish Theatre).

'Tradition, Poetry and W. B. Yeats', *Sewanee Review*, LXIX 3 (summer 1961) 476–84 (comments on 'tradition' in Yeats and T. S. Eliot, and on Yvor Winters, *W. B. Yeats*).

'The Human Image in Yeats', *London Magazine*, n.s., i 9 (Dec 1961) 51–65 ('The Wild Swans at Coole' and the later poems).

'Countries of the Mind', *Guardian*, 11 Jan 1963, 5 (*A Vision*; S. Kirby, *The Yeats Country*; P. Faulkner, *William Morris and W. B. Yeats*; P. Ure, *Yeats the Playwright*).

'The Human Image in Yeats', *University Review* (Dublin), III 8 (1965?) 56–70.

DOORN, WILLEM VAN. *See* VAN DOORN, WILLEM.

DOTTIN, PAUL, 'W. B. Yeats, Poète national de l'Irlande', *Revue de France*, year 3, VI (1 Dec 1923) 665–72.

'La Littérature anglaise en 1938 (II)', *Revue de France*, year 19, IV (15 July 1939) 236–49 (*The Herne's Egg*).

D[OWDEN]., E[DWARD]. M., 'The Writings of Mr W. B. Yeats', *Fortnightly Review*, XCI, n.s. lxxxv 506 (Feb 1909) 253–70 (*The Collected Works in Verse and Prose* (1908)).

DOWNES, ROBERT PERCEVAL, 'William Butler Yeats', *Great Thoughts*, VIII 1140 (30 Jan 1915) 214–16 (noted in *Irish Book Lover*, VI 8 (Mar 1915) 130).

DRAPER, J. W. 'Yeats and Maeterlinck: A Literary Parallel', *Colonnade*, VII 7 (Apr 1914) 240–5.

DRAVAINE, CLAUDE, *Jeux Tréteaux et Personnages*, XV 112 (Nov–Dec 1946) 276–7, 278 n. (on Yeats and *The Pot of Broth*).

DRAWS-TYCHSEN, HELMUT, 'Die Dramen von William Butler Yeats', *Berliner Tageblatt*, LXIII 71 (11 Feb 1934) 1.

DRUMMOND, ANN, 'Florence Farr Emery', *Discourse: A Review of the Liberal Arts*, IV 2 (spring 1961) 97–100 (Florence Farr, Yeats and the Abbey Theatre).

DUBOIS, LOUIS PAUL-. *See* PAUL-DUBOIS, LOUIS.

DUGGAN, E., 'Dedication: The Artist's Discipline', *America*, LXI (10 June 1939) 210–11.

DULAC, EDMUND, 'Without the Twilight', *The Arrow*, W. B. Yeats Commemoration Number (summer 1939) 14–16.

'Yeats as I Knew Him', *Irish Writing*, no. 8 (July 1949) 77–87 (an address delivered to the Irish Literary Society, London, 19 Nov 1948).

DUME, THOMAS L., 'Yeats' Golden Tree and Birds in the Byzantium Poems', *Modern Language Notes*, LXVII 6 (June 1952) 404–7 (sources for the imagery in Gibbon's *Decline and Fall* and the *Cambridge Medieval History*).

DUNCAN, RONALD, 'Yeats', *Townsman*, II 7 (Aug 1939) 19–21.

D[UNLOP]. D. N., 'Interview with Mr W. B. Yeats', *Irish Theosophist*, II 1 (15 Oct 1893).

DUNLOP, RONALD T., 'W. B. Yeats: 1865–1939' *Poetry Australia*, I 6 (Oct 1965) 36–9 (*In Excited Reverie*, ed. A. Norman Jeffares and K. G. W. Cross; T. R. Henn, *The Lonely Tower*, second edition;

C. K. Stead, *The New Poetic*; Johannes Kleinstück, *W. B. Yeats oder Der Dichter in der modernen Welt*; B. Rajan, *W. B. Yeats: A Critical Introduction*).

DUNSANY, Lord EDWARD, 'Irish Writers I Have Known', *Atlantic Monthly*, CXCII 3 (Sep 1953) 66–8.

'Four Poets: A. E., Kipling, Yeats, Stephens', *Atlantic Monthly*, CCI 4 (Apr 1958) 77–80 (Yeats, 80).

DUNSEATH, T. K., 'Yeats and the Genesis of Supernatural Song', *ELH*, XXVIII 4 (Dec 1961) 399–416 ('Ribh at the Tomb of Baile and Aillin'). Also in *Anglia*, LXXIX 4 (1961) 399–415.

DUPEE, F. W., 'The Deeds and Dreams of Yeats', *Partisan Review*, XXIII 1 (winter 1956) 108–11 (*The Letters of W. B. Yeats*, ed. Allan Wade). Reprinted in *Partisan Review Anthology*, ed. William Phillips and Philip Rahv (New York: Holt, Rinehart & Winston, 1962) 460–3.

EBERHART, RICHARD, 'New Looks at Yeats', *Virginia Quarterly Review*, XXVIII 4 (autumn 1952) 618–21 (T. R. Henn, *The Lonely Tower*; Thomas Parkinson, *W. B. Yeats, Self-Critic*; Vivienne Koch, *W. B. Yeats: The Tragic Phase*).

'Memory of Meeting Yeats, AE, Gogarty, and James Stephens', *Literary Review*, I (autumn 1957) 51–6 (recollections of meetings in 1928).

ECKHOFF, LORENTZ, 'Den estetiske bevegelse', *Edda*, XLVII (1947) 81–97 (on the aesthetic movement).

EDEL, LEON, 'No More Opinions ... No More Politics', *New Republic*, CXXXII (14 Mar 1955) 21–3 (*The Letters of W. B. Yeats*, ed. Allan Wade).

EDGAR, PELHAM, 'The Enigma of Yeats', *Queen's Quarterly*, XLVI 4 (Nov 1939) 411–22. Reprinted in *Across My Path*, ed. Northrop Frye (Toronto: Ryerson Press, 1952) 145–53.

EDWARDS, OLIVER, 'W. B. Yeats and Ulster: And a Thought on the Future of the Anglo-Irish Tradition', *Northman*, XIII 2 (winter 1945) 16–21.

'Yeats's "The Fisherman"', *Wales*, VII 25 (spring 1947) 222–3.

'Aspects of Goethe's Poetry: IV. Yeats and Goethe', *Revue des Langues Vivantes*, XV (Aug 1949) 219–21.

'"Death Exultant": A Poem by John B. Yeats', *Rann: An Ulster Quarterly*, no. 13 (1951) 8–10 (prints the letter to W. B. Yeats referred to by J. M. Hone, *J. B. Yeats: Letters to his Son*, p. 251, together with the poem).

[EDWARDS, OLIVER], *Rann: An Ulster Quarterly*, no. 2 (autumn 1948) 1 (a note on 'Reprisals', a poem on Robert Gregory first printed in this issue). Wade p. 394.

EDWARDS, P. W., 'Yeats and the Trinity Chair', *Hermathena*, Yeats Number, CL (autumn 1965) 5–12 (on Yeats and the Chair of English at Trinity College, Dublin).

EGLINTON, JOHN. *See* MAGEE, WILLIAM KIRKPATRICK.

EICHLER, ALBERT, '"Erzählungen u. Essays" von William Butler Yeats', *Beiblatt zur Anglia*, XXVIII 10 (Oct 1917) 298–302 (*Erzählungen und Essays*, trans. Friedrich Eckstein (Leipzig, 1916) Wade pp. 370–1).

ELEANOR, Mother MARY M., 'The Debate of the Body and Soul', *Renascence*, XII 4 (summer 1960) 192–7 (Yeats's use of this traditional debate).

ELIOT, T. S., 'The Poetry of W. B. Yeats', the First Annual Yeats Lecture delivered to the Friends of the Irish Academy at the Abbey Theatre, June 1940, *Purpose*, XII 3–4 (July–Dec 1940) 115–27. Also in *Southern Review*, VII 3 (winter 1941–2) 442–54. Reprinted as 'Yeats', in his *On Poetry and Poets*, 252–62. Also in *The Permanence of Yeats*, ed. James Hall and Martin Steinmann, 331–43 (296–307), and in *Yeats: A Collection of Critical Essays*, ed. John Unterecker, 54–63.

E[LIOT]., T. S., 'A Foreign Mind', *Athenaeum*, 4653 (4 July 1919) 552–3 (*The Cutting of an Agate*).

'A Commentary', *Criterion*, XIV 57 (July 1935) 610–13 (general comment).

ELLEGAUGE, MARTIN, 'Nogle Hovedtyper indenfor det moderne irske Drama', *Edda*, XXIX 4 (1929) 456–64.

ELLIS, STEWART M., 'Current Literature', *Fortnightly Review*, CXIII 676 (1 Apr 1923) 690–5 (*The Trembling of the Veil*). Reprinted as 'W. B. Yeats' in his *Mainly Victorian*, 280–6.

Fortnightly Review, CXIV 679 (2 July 1923) 163 (notes rejection by Mrs D. L. Todhunter of Yeats's claim, quoted in above article, that he had persuaded Dr John Todhunter to produce his *Sicilian Nights*).

ELLIS-FERMOR, UNA, 'Dramatic Notes: The Abbey Theatre Festival (7–20 Aug 1938)', *English*, II 9 (autumn 1938) 174–7 (with special reference to a production of *Purgatory*).

ELLMANN, RICHARD, 'W. B. Yeats: The End of Youth', *Furioso*, III 3 (spring 1948) 25–31.

'Robartes and Aherne: Two Sides of a Penny', *Kenyon Review*, X 2 (spring 1948) 177–86. Reprinted in *The Kenyon Critics: Studies in Modern Literature*, ed. John Crowe Ransom (New York: World Publishers, 1951) 98–107.

'W. B. Yeats Magician', *Western Review*, XII 3 (summer 1948) 232–40 (Yeats and the Order of the Golden Dawn).

'Black Magic against White: Aleister Crowley Versus W. B. Yeats', *Partisan Review*, XV 9 (Sep 1948) 1049–51 (a tussle in the Order of the Golden Dawn).

'Joyce and Yeats', *Kenyon Review*, XII 4 (autumn 1950) 618–38; Italian translation in *Inventario*, IV (Apr 1952) 18–31 (the relationship between Yeats and Joyce from a biographical viewpoint). Wade p. 363.

'The Identity of Yeats', *Kenyon Review*, XIII 3 (summer 1951) 512–19 (*Collected Poems*).

'Three Ways of Looking at a Triton', *Sewanee Review*, LXI 1 (Jan–Mar 1953) 149–54 (T. R. Henn, *The Lonely Tower*; T. Parkinson, *W. B. Yeats: Self-Critic*; V. Koch, *W. B. Yeats: The Tragic Phase*).

'The Art of Yeats: Affirmative Capability', *Kenyon Review*, XV 3 (summer 1953) 357–85.

'Yeats without Panoply', *Sewanee Review*, LXIV 1 (winter 1956) 145–51 (*The Letters of W. B. Yeats*, ed. Allan Wade; *Letters to Katharine Tynan*, ed. Roger McHugh; *Letters on Poetry from W. B. Yeats to Dorothy Wellesley*; *Florence Farr, Bernard Shaw and W. B. Yeats, Letters*, ed. Clifford Bax; *W. B. Yeats and T. Sturge Moore*, ed. Ursula Bridge).

'Heard and Seen', *New Statesman*, LXII (8 Dec 1961) 887–8 (*The Senate Speeches of W. B. Yeats*, ed. D. Donald Pearce; D. J. Gordon,

Images of a Poet). Correspondence by E. McLysaght and Richard Ellmann, ibid., LXIII (19 Jan 1962) 85.

'Yeats Without Analogue', *Kenyon Review*, XXVI 1 (winter 1964) 30–47 (a devaluation of the critical value of 'sources and analogues').

'Gazebos and Gashouses: Yeats and Auden', *Irish Times*, Yeats Centenary Supplement, 10 June 1965, iii.

'Yeats and Eliot', *Encounter*, XXV 1 (July 1965) 53–5.

'Eliot's Conversion', *Tri-Quarterly*, Yeats Centenary Issue, no. 4 (fall 1965) 77–8, 80 (T. S. Eliot's changing attitude towards Yeats).

EMERSON, D., 'Poetry Corner', *Scholastic*, XXXIV (4 Mar 1939) 25 (on the death of Yeats).

EMPSON, WILLIAM, 'Donne and the Rhetorical Tradition', *Kenyon Review*, XI 4 (autumn 1949) 571–87 (on Rosemund Tuve's reading of 'Byzantium' in her *Elizabethan and Metaphysical Imagery*).

'Mr Wilson on the Byzantium Poems', *Review of English Literature*, I 3 (July 1960) 51–6 (a reply to F. A. C. Wilson, *W. B. Yeats and Tradition*).

'A Time of Troubles', *New Statesman*, LXX (23 July 1965) 123–4 (*In Excited Reverie*, ed. A. Norman Jeffares and K. G. W. Cross; Thomas Parkinson, *W. B. Yeats: The Later Poetry*; Edward Malins, *Yeats and the Easter Rising*). Correspondence by Conor Cruise O'Brien, 'Yeats's Politics', ibid. (27 Aug) 284–5; reply by William Empson, ibid. (10 Sep) 354.

'The Variants for the Byzantium Poems', *Phoenix*, Yeats Centenary Number, no. 10 (summer 1965) 1–26.

ENGELBERG, EDWARD, 'Picture and Gesture in the Yeatsian Aesthetic', *Criticism*, III 2 (spring 1961) 101–20. (An expanded version forms part of chap. iii of his *The Vast Design: Patterns in W. B. Yeats's Aesthetic*.)

'Passionate Reverie: W. B. Yeats's Tragic Correlative', *University of Toronto Quarterly*, XXXI 2 (Jan 1962) 201–22. An expanded version forms chap. v of his *The Vast Design: Patterns in W. B. Yeats's Aesthetic*).

ENRIGHT, D. J., 'A Note on Irish Literature and the Irish Tradition', *Scrutiny*, X 3 (Jan 1942) 247–55.

ERVINE, ST JOHN R., 'The Loneliest Poet: W. B. Yeats', *John O'London's Weekly*, I 13 (5 July 1919) 375 (Yeats's isolation from the life of his times).

'Some Impressions of My Elders', *North American Review*, CCXI 771 (Feb 1920) 225–37; 772 (Mar) 402–10. Reprinted as 'William Butler Yeats' in his *Some Impressions of My Elders*, 264–305 (248–86).

'A Portrait of W. B. Yeats', *Listener*, LIV (1 Sep 1955) 331–2. Reply by C. S. Lewis, correspondence, ibid. (15 Sep) 427.

ESSON, LOUIS, 'Irish Memories and Australian Hopes', *Union Recorder*, 24 Nov 1938, 281–2 (some reminiscences of Yeats).

EVANS, B. IFOR (Lord Evans), 'The Poetry of W. B. Yeats', *Fortnightly Review*, CXLV (Mar 1939) 351–3.

EVERY, Fr GEORGE, 'Life. Life. Eternal Life', *Student World*, XXXI (1938) 139–41 (brief comment on Yeats and 'the Search for Modern Paganism').

FADIMAN, CLIFTON, 'The Magician', *New Yorker*, XVIII (6 Feb 1943) 61–3 (J. M. Hone, *W. B. Yeats 1865–1939*).

FALLON, GABRIEL, 'The Future of the Irish Theatre', *Studies*, XLIV 1 (spring 1955) 92–100 (on Yeats and the Irish Theatre).

'Theatre', *Month*, XVII 3 (Mar 1957) 106–8 (on Yeats's contribution to Irish theatre).

'The Abbey Theatre Today', *Iris Hibernia*, no. 3 (1960) 46–54.

'A Forgotten Prologue: When Did Yeats Write It?', *Irish Times*, 13 Sep 1960 (on the Prologue to *The King's Threshold*). Correspondence, ibid., by Micheál Ó hAodha, 14 Sep; Corinna Salvadori, 16 Sep; Austin Clarke, 17 Sep; Gabriel Fallon, 20 Sep.

'Profiles of a Poet', *Modern Drama*, VII 3 (Dec 1964) 329–44 (recollections of Yeats at the Abbey Theatre).

†FARAG, FAHMY FAWZI, 'Anti-Realism in the Theatre of Yeats', *Hiwar*, II 2 (Jan–Feb 1954) (in Arabic).

† 'W. B. Yeats's Daimon', *Cairo Studies in English* (1961–2) 135–44 (on Leo Africanus).

† 'W. B. Yeats's Antithetical Mask', *Annals of the Faculty of Arts* (1963).

† 'The Unpopular Theatre of W. B. Yeats', *Cairo Studies in English* (1963).

FARRELL, MICHAEL, 'Plays for the Country Theatre', *Bell*, II 1 (Apr 1941) 80–1 (brief production note on *The Land of Heart's Desire*).

FARREN, ROBERT (Roibeárd Ó Faracháin), 'Elements for a Credo', *Irish Monthly*, LXIV 761–2 (Nov–Dec 1936) 751–5, 828–35; LXV 763–6 (Jan–Apr 1937) 39–45, 106–10, 197–202, 258–63 (a series of six articles on the conceptual, the image and rhythm in the poetry of Yeats).

'Yeats: An Anniversary Tribute, 1941', *Irish Library Bulletin*, IX (Oct 1948) 161–3.

FAULKNER, PETER, 'W. B. Yeats and William Morris', *Threshold*, IV 1 (spring–summer 1960) 18–27.

'Yeats as Critic', *Criticism*, IV 4 (fall 1962) 328–39.

'Morris and Yeats', *Journal of the William Morris Society*, I 3 (summer 1963) 19–23.

'Yeats as a Reviewer', *Irish Book*, Special Yeats Issue, II 3–4 (autumn 1963) 115–21.

'Yeats, Ireland, and Ezra Pound', *Threshold*, no. 18 (n.d. (1964)) 58–68.

F[AY]., F[RANK]. J., 'The Irish Literary Theatre – And After', *United Irishman*, VI 143 (23 Nov 1901).

FAY, GERARD, 'The Abbey Theatre and the One Act Play', *One Act Play Magazine and Radio Drama Review*, II 4 (Aug–Sep 1938) 323–6.

FAY, W. G., 'Yeats and the Irish Drama', *Listener*, XXI (2 Mar 1939) 484 (passages from an obituary talk broadcast by the B.B.C.).

FAY, WILLIAM P., 'Le Théâtre National Irlandais ou les Débuts de l'Abbey Theatre', *Revue des Deux Mondes*, no. 17 (1 Sep 1959) 93–103.

'Dublin, capitale littéraire', *Revue des Deux Mondes*, no. 23 (1 Dec 1960) 403–16 *passim* (esp. 412–13).

'A Yeats Centenary', *Tri-Quarterly*, Yeats Centenary Issue, no. 4 (fall 1965) 68–70 (Yeats's concern with Ireland).

FEHR, BERNHARD, 'W. B. Yeats, der Träger des Nobelpreises', *Neue Zürcher Zeitung*, XXI (Nov 1923).

FELTON, JOHN, 'Contemporary Caricatures', *Egoist*, I 15 (1 Aug 1914) 296–7.

FIGGIS, DARRELL, 'Mr. W. B. Yeats', *New Age*, VII (1910) 325–8. Reprinted as 'Mr W. B. Yeats's Poetry', in his *Studies and Appreciations*, 119–37.

FIRKINS, O. W., 'Mr. Yeats and Others', *Review*, I 7 (28 June 1919) 151–3 (*The Wild Swans at Coole*).

'*Cathleen ni Houlihan* at the Bramhall Playhouse', *Weekly Review*, III 62 (21 July 1920) 76.

FISHWICK, MARSHALL W., 'Yeats and Cyclical History', *Shenandoah*, I 2 (winter 1949) 52–6.

FITZGERALD, ROGER. *See* WALL, RICHARD J.

FIXLER, MICHAEL, 'The Affinities between J. K. Huysmans and the "Rosicrucian" Stories of W. B. Yeats', *PMLA*, LXXIV 4 (Sep 1935) 9.

FLACCUS, KIMBALL, 'Yeatsiana', *Saturday Review of Literature*, XII (14 Sep 1935) 9.

FLETCHER, IAN, 'Leda and St Anne', *Listener*, LVII (21 Feb 1957) 305–7 (Yeats and Pater on the 'Mona Lisa').

'*The Variorum Edition of the Poems of W. B. Yeats*', *Victorian Studies*, II 1 (Sep 1958) 72–5.

'Symons, Yeats, and the Demonic Dance', *London Magazine*, VII 6 (June 1960) 46–60.

'The Present State of Yeats Criticism', *Literary Half-Yearly*, II 2 (July 1961) 22–6.

FORD, JULIA E., and THOMPSON, KATE V., 'The Neo-Celtic Poet – William Butler Yeats', *Poet Lore*, XV 4 (winter 1904) 83–9 (a brief review of Yeats's prose, plays and lyrics).

FOX, ARTHUR W., 'The Collected Poems of William Butler Yeats', *Papers of the Manchester Literary Club*, LXI (1936) 62–80 (*Collected Poems* (1933)).

FOX, R. M. 'Modern Irish Drama', *Theatre Arts*, XXIV 1 (Jan 1940) 22–5 *passim* (general comment).

'Yeats and His Circle', *Aryan Path*, XX 7 (July 1949) 306–9.

'Yeats and Social Drama', *Irish Writing*, no. 9 (Oct 1949) 62–7.

'Ibsen and Yeats: Pioneers of National Drama', *Aryan Path*, XXVI 4 (Apr 1955) 154–8.

FRASER, G. S. 'Yeats and the New Criticism', *Colonnade*, no. 1 (spring 1952) 6–12; ibid., no. 2 (winter 1952) 14–21. Reprinted in his *Vision and Rhetoric*, 65–83.

'Yeats's "Byzantium"', *Critical Quarterly*, II 3 (autumn 1960) 253–61. Replies by John Wain, ibid., II 4 (winter) 372–3, and Joan Grundy, 'Yeats and Byzantium', ibid., III 2 (summer 1961) 168–9.

'A Yeats Borrowing', *TLS*, 3287 (25 Feb 1965) 156 ('Easter 1916' and M. I. Ebbutt's *Hero-Myths and Legends of the British Race*).

'Yeats as a Philosopher', *Phoenix*, Yeats Centenary Number, no. 10 (summer 1965) 46–59.

FRÉCHET, RENÉ, 'Les écrivains irlandais et la realité: note brève', *Études Anglaises*, XII 4 (Dec 1959) 339–44 (Herbert Howarth, *The Irish Writers*).

'L'étude de Yeats: textes, jugements et éclaircissements', *Études Anglaises*, XIV 1 (Jan–Mar 1961) 36–47 (Monk Gibbon, *The Masterpiece and the Man*; Krishna Menon, *The Development of W. B. Yeats*; J. Unterecker, *A Reader's Guide to William Butler Yeats*).

'Un poète en quête de sa vérité: W. B. Yeats', *Foi-Éducation* (July–Aug 1961) 49–56.

'À Propos d'A. E., l'irlandais libre et fidèle', *Études Anglaises*, XV 4 (Dec 1962) 365–74.

'Le Centenaire de Yeats', *Études Anglaises*, XVIII 3 (July–Sep 1965) 225–7 (a centenary tribute).

FREYER, GRATTAN, correspondence, *TLS*, 2307 (20 Apr 1946) 187 (misprints in *Poems and Plays* (1940)).

'The Politics of W. B. Yeats', *Politics and Letters*, I 1 (summer 1947) 13–20.

FRIAR, D., 'Politics and Some Poets', *New Republic*, CXXVII (7 July 1952) 17–18.

FRIEDMAN, MELVIN J., 'A Revaluation of *Axël*', *Modern Drama*, I 4 (Feb 1959) 236–43 (Villiers de l'Isle-Adam and Yeats).

FROTHINGHAM, EUGENIA BROOKS, 'An Irish Poet and His Work', *Critic* XLIV 1 (Jan 1904) 26–31 (Yeats and the Celtic Revival).

FRYE, NORTHROP, 'Yeats and the Language of Symbolism', *University of Toronto Quarterly*, XVII 1 (Oct 1947) 1–17. Reprinted in his *Fables of Identity*, 218–37.

GAMBERINI, SPARTACO, 'Il Teatro di William Butler Yeats: L'Abbey Theatre, Ezra Pound e i no, le ultime opere', *Rivista di Studi teatrali*, I 11–12 (July–Dec 1954) 47–8.

GANT, ROLAND, 'W. B. Yeats', *Opus*, no. 13 (New Year 1943) 25–8.

GARAB, ARRA M., 'Yeats's "Dark Betwixt the Polecat and the Owl"', *English Language Notes*, II 3 (Mar 1965) 218–20 ('The Gyres').

'Times of Glory: Yeats's "The Municipal Gallery Revisited"', *Arizona Quarterly*, XXI 3 (autumn 1965) 243–54 (a study of the poem).

'Yeats and the Forged Casement Diaries', *English Language Notes*, II 4 (June 1965) 289–92 (comments on Yeats's letter of 28 Nov 1936, and the composition of 'Roger Casement').

'Fabulous Artifice: Yeats's "The Three Bushes" Sequence', *Criticism*, VII 3 (summer 1965) 235–49.

GARNETT, DAVID, 'W. B. Yeats', *New Statesman*, XVII (4 Feb 1939) 174. Reply by Seán O'Faoláin, 'W. B. Yeats', ibid. (11 Feb) 209.

GARNETT, EDWARD, 'The Work of W. B. Yeats', *English Review*, II 1 (Apr 1909) 148–52 (*The Collected Works in Verse and Prose* (1908)).

GARRETT, J., 'Mr Yeats as Playwright', *Criterion*, XIV 56 (Apr 1935) 488–91 (*Wheels and Butterflies*).

GASKELL, RONALD, '*Purgatory*', *Modern Drama*, IV 4 (Feb 1962) 397–401.

GERARD, MARTIN, 'It Means What It Says', *X, A Quarterly Review*, II 2 (Aug 1961) 100–7 (the unpopular views expressed in Yeats's poetry present no obstacle to criticism).

GERSTENBERGER, DONNA, 'The Saint and the Circle: The Dramatic Potential of an Image', *Criticism*, II 4 (fall 1960) 336–41.

See also Part I.

GIBBON, MONK, 'Literary Ideals in Ireland: A Comparison', *Irish Statesman*, V (Dec 1925) 399–400 (cf. John Eglinton, W. B. Yeats, A. E., and W. Larminie, *Literary Ideals in Ireland*).

GIBSON, WILFRID, 'W. B. Yeats', *Bookman*, LXXVII (Jan 1930) 227–8 (*Selected Poems* (1929)).

GILKES, MARTIN, '*Countess Cathleen* by the Avon', *English*, III 16 (summer 1941) 159–64.

GILL, W. W., 'Kathleen ni Houlihan', *Notes and Queries*, CLXXIV (2 Apr 1938) 248 (on the origin of Kathleen ni Houlihan).

'Pollexfen in W. B. Yeats's Ancestry', *Notes and Queries*, CLXXXVII (30 Dec 1944) 294–5.

GILLET, LOUIS, 'W. B. Yeats (1865–1939)', *Revue des Deux Mondes*, year 109, L 2 (1 Mar 1939) 219–23 (obituary article).

GILLETT, ERIC, 'Some Uncommon People', *National and English Review*, CLII 916 (June 1959) 231–5 (*Mythologies*; Monk Gibbon, *The Masterpiece and the Man*).

GILMAN, LAWRENCE, 'The Neo-Celtic Drama in America', *The Lamp*, XXVII (Oct 1903) 231–3 (*The Land of Heart's Desire*).

'The Last of the Poets', *North American Review*, CCII 719 (Oct 1915) 592–7 (Forrest Reid, *W. B. Yeats*).

GILOMEN, WALTHER, 'George Moore and His Friendship with W. B. Yeats', *English Studies*, XIX 3 (June 1937) 116–20.

GLECKNER, ROBERT F., 'Blake and Yeats', *Notes and Queries*, CC, n.s., ii 1 (Jan 1955) 38 ('A Coat' and Blake's 'Public Address').

GLENDENNING, A., 'Commentary', *Nineteenth Century and After*, CXXV 3 (Mar 1939) 352–5 (on the death of Yeats).

GLICK, WENDELL, 'Yeats's Early Reading of *Walden*', *Boston Public Library Quarterly*, V 3 (July 1953) 164–6.

GLICKSBERG, CHARLES I., 'William Butler Yeats and the Hatred of Science', *Prairie Schooner*, XXVII 1 (spring 1953) 29–36.

'William Butler Yeats and the Role of the Poet', *Arizona Quarterly*, IX 3 (winter 1953) 293–307.

GOGARTY, OLIVER ST JOHN, 'Yeats – by Gogarty', *Evening Standard*, 30 Jan 1939, 3 (with three facsimile signatures of Yeats). Condensed as 'Yeats: The Man and the Poet', *Irish Digest*, III 2 (Apr 1939) 15–16.

'Three Impressions. III', *The Arrow*, W. B. Yeats Commemoration Number (summer 1939), 19–20. *See also* ROTHENSTEIN, Sir WILLIAM; and TURNER, W. J.

[GOGARTY, OLIVER ST JOHN], 'Literature and Civilization', *Irish Statesman*, I 11 (23 Nov 1923) 325–6 (on Yeats's Nobel Prize award).

GOLDGAR, HARRY, '*Axël* de Villiers de l'Isle-Adam et *The Shadowy Waters* de W. B. Yeats', *Revue de Littérature Comparée*, XXIV (Dec 1950) 563–74.

'Yeats and the Black Centaur in France', *Western Review*, XV 2 (winter 1951) 111–22.

'Note sur la Poésie de William Butler Yeats', *Bayou*, XXII 72 (1958) 547–52.

GOLFFING, FRANCIS, and GIBBS, BARBARA, 'The Public Voice: Remarks on Poetry Today', *Commentary*, XXVIII (1959) 63–9.

GOODWIN, K. L., 'Some Corrections to Standard Biographies of Yeats', *Notes and Queries*, CCX, n.s., xii 7 (July 1965) 260–2 (dates Yeats's first meeting with Ezra Pound, and the composition of 'The Grey Rock' and 'The Three Hermits').

GORDON, D. J., and FLETCHER I., 'Only a Magnifying Glass', *Review*, no. 4 (Oct 1963) 55–8 (some corrections to Jon Stallworthy, *Between the Lines*).

GORLIER, CLAUDIO, 'Maschera e confessione: da Yeats a Spender', *Paragone*, VII (Apr 1955) 10–24.

GORMAN, HERBERT S., 'The Later Mr Yeats', *Outlook*, CXXX (19 Apr 1922) 655–6.

GOSE, ELLIOTT B., Jr, 'The Lyric and the Philosophic in Yeats' *Calvary*', *Modern Drama*, II 4 (Feb 1960) 370–7.

GOSSE, EDMUND, 'A Poet's Thanks', *Sunday Times*, 26 July 1925, 6 (*The Bounty of Sweden* and Yeats as a Nobel Prize winner).

GOWDA, H. H. ANNIAH, 'Ideas into Drama: Yeats and Tagore as Playwrights', *Literary Half-Yearly*, II 1 (Jan 1961) 63–76.

GRAVES, ROBERT, 'These Be Your Gods, O Israel', *Essays in Criticism*, V 2 (Apr 1955) 129–50 (an attack on Yeats and other modern poets). Reprinted as 'These be Your Gods', in *The Crowning Privilege*, 112–45. Reply by Peter Ure (q.v.).

GRAY, HUGH, 'The Spoken Word: W. B. Yeats', *Listener*, XXI (23 Feb 1939) 439 (on W. G. Fay's broadcast obituary, 'Yeats and the Irish Drama').

GREENE, DAVID 'Recordings of William Butler Yeats', *Evergreen Review*, II 8 (spring 1959) 200–1.

GREENE, D. J., 'Yeats's Byzantium and Johnson's Lichfield', *Philological Quarterly*, XXXIII 4 (Oct 1954) 433–5 (reply to F. L. Gwynn, q.v.).

GREGORY, Lady AUGUSTA, 'The Coming of the Irish Players', *Collier's Weekly*, XLVIII (21 Oct 1911) 15, 24 (on Yeats's share in the Irish Theatre movement).

GREGORY, HORACE, 'After a Half-Century', *Poetry* (Chicago), XXXIII 1 (Oct 1928) 41–4 (*The Tower*).

'Yeats: Envoy of Two Worlds', *New Republic*, LXXVII (13 Dec 1933) 134–5 (*The Collected Poems* (1933); *The Winding Stair*).

'Yeats: Last Spokesman', *New Republic*, LXXXIV (18 Sep 1935) 164–5 (*The Collected Plays* (1935); *Wheels and Butterflies*; *The King of the Great Clock Tower*).

'Poet in the Theatre', *Poetry* (Chicago), LXVIII 4 (July 1936) 221–8 (*Collected Plays*).

'Personae and Masks', *Nation*, CXLVIII (4 Feb 1939) 153–4 (*The Autobiography*).

'W. B. Yeats and the Mask of Jonathan Swift', *Southern Review*, VII 3 (winter 1941–2) 492–509. (Yeats, Swift and *The Words upon the Window-Pane*). Also in his *The Shield of Achilles*, 136–55.

'Yeats Revisited', *Poetry* (Chicago), LXXXIV 3 (June 1954) 153–7.

GRIERSON, Sir HERBERT J. C., 'Fairies – from Shakespeare to Mr Yeats', *Dublin Review*, CXLVIII 297 (Apr 1911) 271–84; also in *Living Age*, CCLXIX (10 June 1911) 655–8 (on Yeats as a poet of fairyland).

GROSS, MARTHA, 'Yeats' "I am of Ireland"', *Explicator*, XVII 2 (Nov 1958) item 15.

GRUBB, H. T. HUNT, 'William Butler Yeats: His Plays, Poems and Sources of Inspiration', *Poetry Review*, XXVI 5 (Sep–Oct 1935) 351–65; ibid., 6 (Nov–Dec) 455–65.

'A Poet's Dream', *Poetry Review*, XIX 2 (Mar–Apr 1938) 123–41 (*A Vision*).

'A Poet Passes', *Poetry Review*, XXX 3 (Mar 1939) 149–51.

'The Curtain Falls', *Poetry Review*, XXXI 6 (May–June 1940) 217–26 (obituary article based on *Last Poems and Plays*).

GUHA, NARESH, 'A New Interpretation of Yeats's *The Herne's Egg*', *Jadavpur Journal of Comparative Literature*, V (1965) 105–16.

GULLANS, CHARLES B., 'Leda and the Swan', *TLS*, 3167 (9 Nov 1962) 864 (Sturge Moore's bookplate, reproduced in *Modern Woodcuts no. 3: T. Sturge Moore*, a visual source for the poem). Reply by Charles Madge, ibid., 3168 (16 Nov) 873. *See* FRENCH, CECIL (Part III); MADGE, CHARLES.

GULLIVER (pseudonym), 'The Open Window', *Bell*, V 4 (Jan 1943) 324–5 (a source for 'Innisfree').

'The Open Window', *Bell*, IX 1 (Oct 1944) 91 (Yeats and the Nobel Prize).

GUNNELL, DORIS, 'Le nouveau théâtre irlandais', *Revue*, XXIII/VI/ XCIV 1 (1 Jan 1912) 91–106 (on Yeats's plays).

GUTHRIE, WILLIAM NORMAN, 'W. B. Yeats', *Sewanee Review*, IX 3 (July 1901) 328–31 (*The Shadowy Waters*).

GWYNN, FREDERICK L., 'Yeats's "Byzantium" and its Sources', *Philological Quarterly*, XXXII 1 (Jan 1953) 9–21 (Lamb on *King Lear*, Gibbon's *Decline and Fall*, Marvell's 'The Garden', and Celtic fairy-tale sources for the poem).

GWYNN, STEPHEN L., 'The Irish Literary Theatre and its Affinities', *Fortnightly Review*, n.s., LXX 420 (1 Dec 1901) 1050–62.

'An Uncommercial Theatre', *Fortnightly Review*, n.s., LXXII 432 (1 Dec 1902) 1044–54 (National Dramatic Company season, 26 Oct–2 Nov; *Samhain* (1902)).

'Poetry and the Stage', *Fortnightly Review*, n.s., LXXXV 506 (1 Feb 1909) 342–6; also in *Living Age*, CCLXI (3 Apr 1909) 7–10 (*On Baile's Strand*, *The King's Threshold* and *Deirdre* on the stage; Yeats and Stephen Phillips compared).

'The Irish Academy of Letters', *Fortnightly Review*, n.s., CXXXII (1 Nov 1932) 653–5.

Fortnightly Review, n.s., CXXXVIII (Aug 1935) 234–5 (on the occasion of Yeats's seventieth birthday: his work and influence).

'The Passing of W. B. Yeats', *Fortnightly Review*. n.s., CXLV (Mar 1939) 347–9.

HABART, MICHEL, 'W. B. Yeats et le théâtre aristocratique', *Critique*, X 88 (Sep 1954) 739–53 (*Collected Plays*).

HACKETT, FRANCIS, 'Place in World Letters: "A Crucible of Art"', *Irish Times*, 13 June 1935, 6–7.

HACKETT, J. P., 'Shaw and Yeats', *Studies*, XXXII 4 (Sep 1943) 369–78 (Joseph Hone, *W. B. Yeats 1865–1939*).

HAERDTER, MICHAEL, 'William Butler Yeats – Irisches Theater zwischen Symbolismus und Expressionismus', *Maske und Kothurn*, XI (spring 1965) 30–42.

HAEUSERMANN, H. W., 'W. B. Yeats's Criticism of Ezra Pound', *English Studies*, XXIX 4 (Aug 1949) 97–109. Also in *Sewanee Review*, LVII 4 (Sep 1949) 419–21.

'W. B. Yeats and W. J. Turner: 1935–37', *English Studies*, XL 4 (Aug 1959) 233–41; ibid., XLI 4 (Aug 1960) 241–55 (Yeats and W. J. Turner, with some unpublished letters).

HAHN, SR, M. NORMA, 'Yeats's "The Wild Swans at Coole": Meaning and Structure', *College English*, XXII 6 (Mar 1961) 419–21.

HALDAR, S., 'The Poetry of William Butler Yeats', *Modern Review*, CL (Feb 1957) 139–47.

HALL, ROBERT, 'Aengus and Leda', *Lit*, no. 2 (1958) 42–6 ('The Song of Wandering Aengus' and 'Leda and the Swan').

HALLSTRÖM, PER, 'William Butler Yeats', *Edda*, I (1916) 22–39.

HAMEL, ANTON GERARD VAN. *See* VAN HAMEL, ANTON GERARD.

HAMILTON, IAIN, 'All Metaphor', *Spectator*, CXCIII 6580 (6 Aug 1954) 176–7 (Richard Ellmann, *The Identity of Yeats*).

HANNAY, JAMES OWEN (George A. Birmingham). 'The Literary Movement in Ireland', *Fortnightly Review*, LXXXII 492 (2 Dec 1907) 947–57 *passim*.

HARPER, GEORGE MILLS, 'Yeats's Intellectual Nationalism', *Dublin Magazine* (formerly *The Dubliner*), W. B. Yeats Centenary Edition, IV 2 (summer 1965) 8–26.

HARRIS, WENDELL, 'Innocent Decadence: The Poetry of *The Savoy*', *PMLA*, LXXVII 5 (Dec 1962) 629–36 (Yeats, Symons, Beardsley and *The Savoy*).

HARVEY, W. J., 'Visions and Revisions', *Essays in Criticism*, IX 3 (July 1959) 287–99 (*The Variorum Edition of the Poems*).

HAYDN, HIRAM, 'The Last of the Romantics: An Introduction to the Symbolism of William Butler Yeats', *Sewanee Review*, LV 2 (Apr– June 1947) 297–323.

H[AYES]., R[ICHARD]., 'An Old Yeats Ballad', *Dublin Magazine*, II 2 (Apr–June 1927) 59–61 ('The Ballad of Earl Paul').

'W. B. Yeats, a Catholic Poet', *Irish Monthly*, LVI 4 (Apr 1928) 179–86.

HAYWARD, JOHN, 'Mr Yeats's Book of Modern Verse', *Spectator*, CLVII 5656 (20 Nov 1936) Supplement, 3 (*The Oxford Book of Modern Verse*); replies by W. J. Turner, ibid., 5657 (27 Nov) 950; W. B. Yeats and I. M. Parsons, ibid., 5658 (4 Dec) 995.

'His Nationalism', *The Arrow*, W. B. Yeats Commemoration Number (summer 1939) 10–11.

HEAD, CLOYD, 'Mr Yeats' Plays', *Poetry* (Chicago), XIX 5 (Feb 1922) 288–92 (*Four Plays for Dancers*).

HEALY, CAHIR, 'Innisfree', correspondence, *Irish Statesman*, V (Oct 1925) 110.

HEALY, J. V., 'Scientific and Intuitable Language', *Southern Review*, VII 2 (autumn 1941) 214–16.

'Ancient Lineaments', *Poetry* (Chicago), LXII 4 (July 1943) 223–8 (Joseph Hone, *W. B. Yeats 1865–1939*).

'Yeats and His Imagination', *Sewanee Review*, LIV 4 (autumn 1946) 650–9.

HEISELER, BERNT VON. *See* VON HEISELER, BERNT.

HELD, GEORGE, '*The Second Book of the Rhymers' Club*', *Journal of the Rutgers University Library*, XXVIII 2 (June 1965) 15–21 (on Yeats's contribution to *The Second Book of the Rhymers' Club*, a copy of which is in the Rutgers University Library).

HENDERSON, HANFORD, 'Yeats' "The Spur", 2', *Explicator*, XV 5 (Mar 1957) item 41.

HENN, T. R., 'A Note on W. B. Yeats', *Cambridge Review*, LX (Feb 1939) 225–7.

'The Return to the Valley', *Irish Library Bulletin*, IX (Oct 1948) 163–5.

'The Wisdom of W. B. Yeats', *Listener*, XLIV (21 Dec 1950) 790–1, 793 (B.B.C. talk on *The Collected Poems*).

'W. B. Yeats and the Irish Background', *Yale Review*, XLII 3 (Mar 1953) 351–64.

'The Accent of Yeats' *Last Poems*', *Essays and Studies*, IX (1956) 56–72.

'The Yeats Summer School', correspondence, *TLS*, 3030 (25 Mar 1960) 193 (first Summer School at Sligo, 13–27 Aug 1960).

'The Unity of Yeats', *New Statesman*, LXI (13 Jan 1961) 60 (Giorgio Melchiori, *The Whole Mystery of Art*).

'Yeats and the Picture Galleries', *Southern Review*, n.s., I 1 (Jan 1965) 57–75 (the influence of painting of Yeats's thought).

'The Poetry: A Stone with many Facets', *Irish Times*, Yeats Centenary Supplement, 10 June 1965, ii.

'Yeats and the Critical Pendulum', *Spectator*, CCXIV 7146 (11 June 1965) 751 (changes in critical attitudes to Yeats).

'Moore and Yeats', *Dublin Magazine* (formerly *The Dubliner*), W. B. Yeats Centenary Edition, IV 2 (summer 1965) 63–77.

'Yeats Revisited', *Revue des Langues Vivantes*, XXI 4 (1965) 404–5 (*Selected Prose, Poetry, Criticism, Plays*, ed. A. Norman Jeffares).

'Yeats and the Poetry of War', *British Academy Proceedings*, LI (1965) 301–19.

HENNECKE, H., 'William Butler Yeats (25. vi. 1865 bis 28. i. 1939) und der europäische Symbolismus', *Europäische Revue*, XVI (1940) 280–4.

HERTS, BENJAMIN RUSSELL, 'Shadowy Mr Yeats', *Forum*, LII 6 (Dec 1914) 911–14. Reprinted in his *Depreciations*, 33–9.

†HESSE, I., 'William Butler Yeats', *Kölnische Volkszeitung*, no. 192 (1935).

HEWITT, JOHN, 'A Matter of Idiom', *Bell*, I 4 (Jan 1941) 88 (a brief note on Yeats's idiom).

'Irish Poets, Learn Your Trade', *Threshold*, II 3 (autumn 1958) 62–71.

HEXTER, GEORGE J., 'The Philosophy of William Butler Yeats', *Texas Review*, I 3 (Jan 1916) 192–200.

HIGGINS, F. R., 'The Poet of a Dream: Where "Beauty is Taut, Passion Precise"', *Irish Times*, 13 June 1935, 6–7.

'As Irish Poet', *The Arrow*, W. B. Yeats Commemoration Number (summer 1939) 6–8.

HILL, DOUGLAS, 'Yeats and the Invisible People of Ireland', *Brigham Young University Studies*, VII (1965) 61–7.

HILLYER, ROBERT, 'A Poet Young and Old', *New Adelphi*, III 1 (Sep–Nov 1929) 78–80 (*The Tower*).

HINKSON, KATHARINE TYNAN. *See* TYNAN, KATHARINE.

HINKSON, PAMELA, 'Letters from W. B. Yeats', *Yale Review*, XXIX (winter 1940) 307–20. Wade p. 393.

'The Friendship of Yeats and Katharine Tynan. I: Early Days of the Irish Literary Revival', *Fortnightly Review*, n.s., CLXXIV (Oct 1953) 253–64; 'II: Later Days of the Irish Literary Movement', ibid. (Nov) 323–36 (prints some Yeats letters).

HODGSON, GERALDINE E., 'Some Irish Poetry', *Contemporary Review* XCVIII (Sep 1910) 332–8 (*Poems* (1904); *The Wind Among the Reeds*).

HOGAN, J. J., 'W. B. Yeats', *Studies*, XXVIII 109 (Mar 1939) 35–48 (obituary article).

HOGAN, THOMAS, 'Old Man's Anger', *Spectator*, CC 6760 (17 Jan 1958) 78 (F. A. C. Wilson, *W. B. Yeats and Tradition*).

HONE, JOSEPH M., 'A Memory of the Playboy', *Saturday Review*, CXIII 2956 (22 June 1912) 776–7 (in praise of Yeats's support for Synge's play). Reprinted in *Irish Book Lover*, IV 1 (Aug 1912) 7–8.

'The Later Writings of Mr Yeats', *New Statesman*, V 107 (24 Apr 1915) 62–4 (Yeats's changing attitude to the Celtic revival in *Synge and the Ireland of his Time*, *Responsibilities* and *The Green Helmet and Other Poems*).

'Yeats as Political Philosopher', *London Mercury*, XXXIX 233 (Mar 1939) 492–6.

Note on 'W. B. Yeats, *The Speckled Bird*', part of a chapter from an unfinished novel by W. B. Yeats with an editorial note by Seán O'Faoláin, *Bell*, 1 6 (Mar 1941) 23–30. Wade p. 394.

'A Scattered Fair', *Wind and the Rain*, III 3 (Autumn 1946) 110 (prints fragments from a diary kept by Elizabeth Yeats: Yeats and Maud Gonne).

'Yeats Set in Place', correspondence, *TLS*, 2745 (10 Sep 1954) 573 (on Yeats's reading of Leibniz).

HORRELL, JOE, 'Some Notes on Conversion in Poetry', *Southern Review*, VII 1 (summer 1942) 123–36 ('The Second Coming' 123–6).

HOUGH, GRAHAM, 'A Study of Yeats', *Cambridge Journal*, II (Feb 1949) 259–78; (Mar) 323–42. Reprinted as 'Yeats' in his *The Last Romantics*, 216–62.

HOUGHTON, WALTER E., 'Yeats and Crazy Jane: The Hero in Old Age', *Modern Philology*, XL 4 (May 1943) 316–29. Also in *The Permanence of Yeats*, ed. James Hall and Martin Steinmann, 365–88 (327–48).

HOWARTH, HERBERT, 'Yeats' "In the Seven Woods", 6', *Explicator*, XVII 2 (Nov 1958) item 14.

'Whitman among the Irish', *London Magazine*, VII 1 (Jan 1960) 48–55 (Whitman's influence on Yeats, AE and Joyce).

'The Week of the Banquet', *London Magazine*, n.s., V 1 (Apr 1965) 36–45 (the 'Hibernian' Banquet, Dublin, 24 June 1935, for Yeats's seventieth birthday).

'Yeats: The Variety of Greatness', *Western Humanities Review*, XIX 4 (autumn 1965) 335–43.

HOWARTH, R. G. 'Yeats and Hopkins', *Notes and Queries*, CLXXXVIII (19 May 1945) 202–4.

'Yeats's "My Own Music"', *Notes and Queries*, CLXXXIX (20 Oct 1945) 167–8.

HUBBELL, LINDLEY WILLIAMS, 'Yeats, Pound, and Nō Drama', *East–West Review*, I 1 (spring 1964) 70–8.

HUEFFER, FORD MADOX (Ford Madox Ford), correspondence in *Daily News*, 20 June 1910, 10 (endorses appeal by Yeats and Lady Gregory for support for the Irish National Theatre).

HURWITZ, HAROLD M., 'Yeats and Tagore', *Comparative Literature*, XVI 1 (winter 1964) 55–64.

HUTCHINS, PATRICIA, 'Yeats and Pound in England', *Texas Quarterly*, IV 3 (autumn 1961) 203–16.

INGLIS, BRIAN, 'The Poet . . .', *Spectator*, CCVI 6940 (30 June 1961) 956 (Richard Ellmann, *Yeats: The Man and the Masks*; A. G. Stock, *W. B. Yeats*).

IREMONGER, VALENTIN, 'The Byzantium Poems of W. B. Yeats', *Bell*, XIX 10 (Nov 1954) 36–44,

'Yeats as a Playwright', *Irish Writing*, W. B. Yeats: A Special Number, no. 31 (summer 1955) 51–6.

JACKSON, SCHUYLER, 'William Butler Yeats', *London Mercury*, XI 64 (Feb 1925) 396–410.

JACOBSON, DAN, 'Liberalism and Literature', *New Statesman*, LXV (1 Mar 1963) 312–14 (on the opposition to liberal or radical ideology by Yeats and other modern writers).

JAECKLE, ERWIN, 'Yeats zum Gedächtnis', *Mass und Wert*, Jahrg. 2 (1939) 658–76.

JALOUX, EDMOND, 'W. B. Yeats', *Le Temps*, 23 Apr 1939, 5 (obituary article).

JAMESON, GRACE, 'Irish Poets of Today and Blake', *PMLA*, LIII 2 (June 1938) 575–92. *See also* Russell Alspach, 'Two Songs of Yeats's', *Modern Language Notes*, LXI 6 (June 1946) 400, n. 15.

JARRELL, RANDALL, 'The Development of Yeats's Sense of Reality', *Southern Review*, VII 3 (winter 1941–2) 653–66.

JAY, JOHN, 'What Stood in the Post Office?', *Threshold*, no. 19, The Theatre of W. B. Yeats Centenary, 1965 (autumn 1965) 30–40 (Jay's production of the Cuchulain cycle).

JEFFARES, A. NORMAN, '"Two Songs of a Fool" and Their Explanation', *English Studies*, XXVI 6 (Dec 1945) 169–71.

'The Byzantine Poems of W. B. Yeats', *Review of English Studies*, XXII 85 (Jan 1946) 44–52.

'W. B. Yeats and His Methods of Writing Verse', *Nineteenth Century and After*, CXXXIX 829 (Mar 1946) 123–8. Reprinted in *The Permanence of Yeats*, ed. James Hall and Martin Steinmann, 301–8 (270–6).

'"Gyres" in the Poetry of W. B. Yeats', *English Studies*, XXVII 3 (June 1946) 65–74.

'"The New Faces": A New Explanation', *Review of English Studies*, XXIII 92 (Oct 1947) 349–53.

'Thoor Ballylee', *English Studies*, XXVIII 6 (Dec 1947) 161–8.

'The Sources of Yeats's "A Meditation in Time of Civil War"', *Notes and Queries*, CXCIII (27 Nov 1948) 522.

'Notes on Yeats's "Fragments"', *Notes and Queries*, CXCIV (25 June 1949) 279–80.

'Yeats's Mask', *English Studies*, XXX 6 (Dec 1949) 289–98.

'A Source for "A Woman Homer Sung"', *Notes and Queries*, CXCV (4 Mar 1950) 104.

'Notes on Yeats's "Lapis Lazuli"', *Modern Language Notes*, LXV 7 (Nov 1950) 488–91.

'Poet's Tower', *Envoy*, V 20 (1951) 45–55.

'Yeats's "The Gyres": Sources and Symbolism', *Huntington Library Quarterly*, XV 1 (Nov 1951) 87–97 (*A Vision* and Shelley's *Hellas*).

'Saul on Jeffares', *Modern Language Notes*, LXVII 7 (Nov 1952) 501–2 (reply to George Brandon Saul, 'Jeffares on Yeats').

'William Butler Yeats: A Mind Michael Angelo Knew', *Meanjin*, XIV 4 (Dec 1955) 565–8 (*Letters of W. B. Yeats*, ed. Allan Wade; *Autobiographies*).

'Yeats as Public Man', *Poetry* (Chicago), XCVIII 4 (July 1961) 253–63 (*The Senate Speeches*, ed. Donald Pearce).

'Yeats's Byzantine Poems and the Critics', *English Studies in Africa*, v 1 (Mar 1962) 11–28 (with bibliographical note).

'Prose Fed by Experience', *Western Mail*, 16 Jan 1965, 5 (on Yeats as a writer of prose: a centenary tribute).

'The Literary Influence', *Irish Times*, Yeats Centenary Supplement, 10 June 1965, iv (the impact of Yeats).

'W. B. Yeats: The Gift of Greatness', *Daily Telegraph*, 12 June 1965 (a centenary tribute).

'John Butler Yeats', *Dublin Magazine* (formerly *The Dubliner*), W. B. Yeats Centenary Edition, IV 2 (summer 1965) 30–7 (reprints part of his contribution to *In Excited Reverie*, ed. A. Norman Jeffares and K. G. W. Cross).

'Yeats as Critic', *English*, W. B. Yeats: 1865–1939, XV 89 (summer 1965) 173–6.

'The Criticism of Yeats', *Phoenix*, Yeats Centenary Number, no. 10 (summer 1965) 27–45 (on Yeats's critical writings).

'Notes on Pattern in the Byzantine Poems of W. B. Yeats', *Revue des Langues Vivantes*, XXXI 4 (1965) 353–9.

JENSEN, EJNER, 'The Antinomical Vision of W. B. Yeats', *Xavier University Studies*, III 3 (Dec 1964) 127–45.

JEROME, JUDSON, 'Six Senses of the Poet', *Colorado Quarterly*, X (winter 1962) 225–40 (on 'The Second Coming').

JOCHUM, K. P. S., 'W. B. Yeats's *At the Hawk's Well* and the Dialectic of Tragedy', *Visva-Bharati Quarterly*, XXXI 1 (1965–6) 21–8.

JOHNSON, LIONEL, *Academy*, XLII 1065 (1 Oct 1892) 278–9 (*The Countess Cathleen*).

'*The Countess Cathleen*', *Beltaine*, no. 1 (May 1899) 10–11.

JOHNSON, LOUIS, 'Yeats Regained', *Numbers*, I 4 (Oct 1955) 38–40 (*Collected Poems*; *Collected Plays*; *Autobiographies*; *The Letters of W. B. Yeats*, ed. Allan Wade; Virginia Moore, *The Unicorn*; G. S. Fraser, *W. B. Yeats*).

JOHNSON, W. R., 'Crazy Jane and Henry More', *Furioso*, III 2 (winter 1947) 50–3 ('Crazy Jane Talks with the Bishop').

JOHNSTON, CHARLES, 'Personal Impressions of W. B. Yeats', *Harper's Weekly*, XLVIII (13 Feb 1904) 291.

'Yeats in the Making', *Poet Lore*, XVII 2 (June 1906) 102–12 (Yeats's childhood and school days).

'The Poems of W. B. Yeats', *North American Review*, CLXXXVII 629 (Apr 1908) 614–18 (*The Poetical Works in Two Volumes*).

JOHNSTON, DENIS, 'Mr Yeats as Dramatist', *Spectator*, CLIII 5553 (30 Nov 1934) 843 (*Wheels and Butterflies*).

'Yeats as Dramatist; Tenacity of Purpose through Thirty Years', *Irish Times*, 13 June 1935, 6.

JONES, DORA M., 'The Celtic Twilight: The Poems of W. B. Yeats', *London Quarterly Review*, XCIV, n.s., iv (July 1900) 61–70 (*Poems* (1899); *The Wind Among the Reeds*; *The Celtic Twilight*).

JONES, E. ACKROYD, 'The Sincerity of Yeats', *Focus* (June 1965) 127–8 (recalls an evening with Yeats at Oxford, autumn 1921).

JONES, JAMES LAND, 'Keats and Yeats: "Artificers of the Great Moment"', *Xavier University Studies*, IV (1965) 125–50.

JONES, LLEWELLYN, 'The Later Poetry of W. B. Yeats', *North American Review*, CCXIX (Apr 1924) 499–506 (*The Wild Swans at Coole*, 'The Magi', 'The Wild Swans at Coole', 'Upon a Dying Lady').

Reprinted as 'The Later Poetry of Mr W. B. Yeats' in his *First Impressions*, 137–48.

JOSELYN, Sr M., 'Twelfth Night Quartet: Four Magi Poems', *Renascence*, XVI 2 (winter 1964) 92–4 (Yeats's 'The Magi' compared with T. S. Eliot's 'The Journey of the Magi', John Peale Bishop's 'Twelfth Night', and Edgar Bowers's 'The Wise Men').

JUMPER, WILL C., 'Form versus Structure in a Poem of W. B. Yeats', *Iowa English Yearbook*, no. 7 (fall 1962) 41–4 ('From the Antigone').

KAHN, DEREK, 'The Morality of W. B. Yeats', *Left Review*, II 6 (Mar 1936) 252–8.

KALISTER, FREDERICK, 'The Rhythm and Music of Noh Drama', *Threshold*, no. 19, The Theatre of W. B. Yeats Centenary, 1965 (autumn 1965) 103–10.

KANTAK, V. Y., 'Yeats's Indian Experience', *Indian Journal of English Studies*, VI (1965) 80–101.

KAVANAGH, PATRICK, 'On a Liberal Education', *X, A Quarterly Review*, II 2 (Aug 1961) 112–19 (Yeats, the Irish Literary Revival, and Liberal Education).

'William Butler Yeats', *Kilkenny Magazine*, II 1 (spring 1962) 25–8.

'George Moore's Yeats', *Irish Times*, Yeats Centenary Supplement, 10 June 1965, ii (on Moore's portraits of Yeats in *Hail and Farewell*).

See also SPENDER, STEPHEN.

KAVANAGH, PETER, 'The History of Gaelic Drama', *Bell*, XIV 1 (Apr 1947) 56–61 *passim*.

KEELING, ELSA D'ESTERRE, 'Four Irish Books', *Academy*, XLVII 1199 (27 Apr 1895) 349–51 (*A Book of Irish Verse*).

KEITH, W. J., 'Yeats's Arthurian Black Tower', *Modern Language Notes*, LXXV 2 (Feb 1960) 119–23.

'Yeats's Double Dream', *Modern Language Notes*, LXXVI 8 (Dec 1961) 710–15 ('Towards Break of Day').

KELLEHER, JOHN V., 'Yeats's Use of Irish Materials', *Tri-quarterly*, Yeats Centenary Issue, no. 4 (fall 1965) 115–25 (on Yeats's use of 'lebeen-lone' and 'Clooth-na-Bare', and his Cuchulain plays).

KELLY, P. J., 'Personal Recollections of Synge, Moore, Martyn, Lady Gregory, Russell, and Yeats in the Irish Theatre Movement', *New York Times*, 1 June 1919, IV 2, 3; correspondence by A. Bell, on Miss Horniman and the Irish National Theatre, ibid., 29 June, IV 2, 5.

KENNELLY, BRENDAN, 'The Gaelic Epic', *Irish Times*, Yeats Centenary Supplement, 10 June 1965, vi–vii (on Yeats's use of Gaelic epic literature).

'The Heroic Ideal in Yeats's Cuchulain Plays', *Hermathena*, Yeats Number, CI (autumn 1965) 13–21.

KENNER, HUGH, 'The Sacred Book of the Arts', *Irish Writing*, W. B. Yeats: A Special Number, no. 31 (summer 1955) 24–35, and in *Sewanee Review*, LXIV 4 (autumn 1956) 574–90. Reprinted in his *Gnomon: Essays on Contemporary Literature*, 9–29, and in *Yeats: A Collection of Critical Essays*, ed. John Unterecker, 10–22.

'Unpurged Images', *Hudson Review*, VIII 4 (winter 1956) 609–17 (*The Letters of W. B. Yeats*, ed. Allan Wade; Richard Ellmann, *The Identity of Yeats*; Virginia Moore, *The Unicorn*).

'Yeats's Essays', *Jubilee*, IX 10 (Feb 1962) 39–43 (*Essays and Introductions*).

KENNY, M., 'The "Irish" Players and Playwrights', *America*, V 25 (30 Sep 1911) 581–2. (This, and the two following items, are representative of hostile Catholic reaction in America to the Irish Players and their repertoire.)

'The Irish Pagans', *America*, VI 2 (21 Oct 1911) 31–2.

'The Plays of the "Irish" Players', *America*, VI 4 (4 Nov 1911) 78–9.

See also anonymous articles in *America*, listed under ANON.

KERMODE, FRANK, 'Adam's Curse', *Encounter*, X 6 (June 1958) 76–8 (*The Variorum Edition of the Poems*).

'The Spider and the Bee', *Spectator*, CCVI 6927 (31 Mar 1961) 448–9 (*Essays and Introductions*; Giorgio Melchiori, *The Whole Mystery of Art*; Elizabeth Coxhead, *Lady Gregory*).

KERSNOWSKI, FRANK L., 'Portrayal of the Hero in Yeats' Poetic Drama', *Renascence*, XVIII 1 (autumn 1965) 9–15.

KEVIN. *See* SIMINGTON, R. C.

KHAN, JALILUDDIN AHMAD, 'The Role of Intellect in Yeats's Imagination', *Venture*, I 1 (Mar 1960) 58–69.

KIERNAN, THOMAS JOSEPH, 'Lady Gregory and W. B. Yeats', *Southerly*, XIV (1953) 239–51; also in *Dalhousie Review*, XXXVIII 3 (autumn 1958) 295–306.

'Fifty Years of the Cuala Press', *Biblionews*, VII 8 (July 1954) 3.

KILLEN, A. M., 'Some French Influences in the Works of W. B. Yeats at the End of the Nineteenth Century', *Comparative Literature Studies*, VIII (1942) 1–8 (Villiers de l'Isle-Adam's *Axël* and *The Secret Rose*; Mallarmé and *The Wind among the Reeds* and *The Shadowy Waters*).

KIM JONG-GIL, 'The Topography of Yeats's Poetry', *Phoenix*, Yeats Centenary Number, no. 10 (summer 1965) 84–95.

KIM U-CHANG, 'The Embittered Sun: Reality in Yeats's Poetry', *Phoenix*, Yeats Centenary Number, no. 10 (summer 1965) 66–83.

KING, RICHARD ASHE, 'Living Poets: VI. Mr W. B. Yeats', *Bookman*, XII (Sep 1897) 142–3.

KING, S. K., 'Eliot, Yeats and Shakespeare', *Theoria*, no. 5 (1953) 113–19.

KINGSMILL, HUGH, 'Meetings with Yeats', *New Statesman*, XXI (4 Jan 1941) 10–11.

KINSELLA, THOMAS. *See* SPENDER, STEPHEN.

KITCHEN, LAURENCE, 'The Ditch and the Tower', *Listener*, LXXIV (14 Oct 1965) 575–7 (on the conflicting tensions in Yeats's poetry).

KLEINSTUECK, JOHANNES, 'W. B. Yeats, "Sailing to Byzantium"', *Neueren Sprachen*, IX 11 (Nov 1960) 527–39.

'W. B. Yeats, "The Second Coming", Eine Studie zur Interpretation und Kritik', *Neueren Sprachen*, X 7 (July 1961) 301–13.

KNIGHTS, L. C., 'W. B. Yeats: The Assertion of Values', *Southern Review*, VII 3 (winter 1941–2) 426–41. Reprinted as 'Poetry and Social Criticism: The Work of W. B. Yeats', in his *Explorations*, 170–85.

KNOWER, E. T., 'A Modern Minstrel', *American Review*, III 4 (July–Aug 1925) 400–5.

KOSTELANETZ, ANNE, 'Irony in Yeats's Byzantium Poems', *Tennessee Studies in Literature*, IX (1964) 129–42.

KRAMER, HILTON 'The Politics of Yeats', *New Leader*, 22 Nov 1965, 22–3.

KRANS, H. S., 'Yeats and the Irish Literary Revival', *Outlook*, LXXVI (2 Jan 1904) 57–61.

KRAUSE, DAVID, 'The Playwright's Not for Burning', *Virginia Quarterly Review*, XXXIV 1 (winter 1958) 60–76 (Yeats's rejection of O'Casey's *The Silver Tassie*).

'Sean O'Casey, 1880–1964', *Massachusetts Review*, VI 2 (winter–spring 1965) 233–51 *passim*, esp. 427–51 (O'Casey's final judgement of Yeats as a poet). Read as a Lecture in the Humanities at Clark University, Worcester, Massachusetts, 12 Feb 1965. Reprinted in *Irish Renaissance*, ed. Robin Skelton and David R. Clark, 139–57.

KROJER, MAXIM, 'Twintig jaar geleden overleed. William Butler Yeats', *Periscoop*, IX 4 (Feb 1959) 11.

KUHN, CHRISTOPH, 'Zu William Butler Yeats', *Du*, XXIII 7 (July 1963) 53.

KUNITZ, S. J., 'Roving Eye', *Wilson Bulletin*, VIII (Feb 1934) 350–1.

LAGAN, PATRICK, 'Was Yeats referring to Donegal or Sligo Rosses?', *Irish Press*, 14 May 1962 ('The Stolen Child').

LAKIN, R. D., 'Unity and Strife in Yeats' Tower Symbol', *Midwest Quarterly*, I (1960) 321–32.

LANG, ANDREW, 'The Celtic Renaissance', *Blackwood's Magazine*, CLXI 976 (Feb 1897) 181–91 *passim* (rejects William Sharp's view of a Celtic renaissance; Yeats briefly mentioned).

LANGBAUM, ROBERT, 'The Symbolic Mode of Thought', *American Scholar*, XXXI 3 (summer 1962) 454–60 (*Essays and Introductions*, review article).

   'The Mysteries of Identity: A Theme in Modern Literature', *American Scholar*, XXXIV 4 (autumn 1965) 569–86 (Yeats, masks and the notion of reality: 'Among School Children'; 'Lapis Lazuli').

LARMINIE, WILLIAM, 'Legends as Materials for Literature', *Daily Express*, 19 Nov 1898, 3. Reprinted in *Literary Ideals in Ireland*, by John Eglinton and others, 57–65.

LAWRENCE, Sir ALEXANDER, correspondence, *The Times*, 3 Feb 1939, 14 (obituary).

LAWRENCE, C. E. , 'Poetry and Verse and Worse', *Quarterly Review*, CCLXII (Apr 1934) 299–314 (*The Collected Poems* (1933)).

LEACH, ELSIE, 'Yeats's "A Friend's Illness" and Herbert's "Vertue"', *Notes and Queries*, CCVII, n.s., IX 6 (June 1962) 215.

LEAVIS, F. R., 'The Latest Yeats', *Scrutiny*, II 3 (Dec 1933) 293–5 (*The Winding Stair*).

   'The Great Yeats, and the Latest', *Scrutiny*, VIII 4 (Mar 1940) 437–40 (*Last Poems and Plays*).

LEES, F. N., 'Yeats's "Byzantium"', Dante, and Shelley', *Notes and Queries*, CCII n.s., iv 7 (July 1957) 312–13.

LE GALLIENNE, RICHARD, 'Yeats's "Autobiography"', *New York Times*, 28 Aug 1921, III, 1 (on the serialisation in *The Dial*).

LEGGE, M. DOMINICA, 'Yeats and J. G. Legge', correspondence, *TLS*, 2810 (6 Jan 1956) 7.

LEHMANN, JOHN, 'Der Mann, der lernte nackt zu wandeln. Über William Butler Yeats', *Thema*, no. 5 (1949) 24–7.

†LESLIE, SHANE, 'William Yeats', *Échanges*, no. 5 (Dec 1931) 86–91 (translated by Georgette Camille).

LEVANTHAL, A. J., 'Dramatic Commentary', *Dublin Magazine*, XXIV 1 (Jan–Mar 1949) 37–41 (*The Only Jealousy of Emer*).

LEVIN, G., 'The Yeats of the *Autobiographies*: A Man of Phase 17', *Texas Studies in Literature and Language*, VI 3 (autumn 1964) 398–405.

LEWIS, CECIL DAY, 'Poetry To-Day', *Left Review*, II 16 (Jan 1937) 899–901.

LICHNEROWICZ, JEANNE, 'Le dernier prix Nobel de littérature, W. B. Yeats', *Revue Politique et Littéraire (Revue Bleue)*, LXI 23 (1 Dec 1923) 793–4.

'William Butler Yeats', *Europe*, V 18 (15 June 1924) 162–74.

LIENHARDT, R. G., 'Hopkins and Yeats', *Scrutiny*, XI 3 (spring 1943) 220–4 (V. K. B. Menon, *The Development of William Butler Yeats*).

LIGHTFOOT, MARJORIE J., '*Purgatory* and *The Family Reunion*: In Pursuit of Prosodic Description', *Modern Drama*, VII 3 (Dec 1964) 256–66 (on Yeats's prosody in *Purgatory*, and its influence on T. S. Eliot's poetic drama).

LIND, L. R., 'Leda and the Swan: Yeats and Rilke', *Chicago Review*, VII 1 (spring 1953) 13–17.

LINEBARGER, JAMES M., 'Yeats's "Among School Children" and Shelley's *Defence of Poetry*'. *Notes and Queries*, CCVIII, n.s., X 10 (Oct 1963) 375–7 (on Yeats's indebtedness to Shelley for ideas and images in the poem).

LINKE, HANSJURGEN, 'Das Los des Menschen in den Cuchulain–Dramen: zum 100. Geburtstag von W. B. Yeats', *Neueren Sprachen*, XIV 6 (June 1965) 252–68 (on the four tragedies of the Cuchulain cycle: *At the Hawk's Well, On Baile's Strand, The Only Jealousy of Emer*, and *The Death of Cuchulain*).

LIPSKI, W. DE. *See* DE LIPSKI, W.

LISTER, RAYMOND, 'W. B. Yeats and Edward Calvert', *Irish Book*, Special Yeats Issue, II 3–4 (autumn 1963) 72–80 (the influence of Calvert's engravings on Yeats).

LITTELL, P., 'Mr Yeats's Visit to the United States', *New Republic*, XXI (18 Feb 1920) 358.

LOFTUS, RICHARD J., 'Yeats and the Easter Rising: A Study in Ritual', *Arizona Quarterly*, XVI 2 (summer 1960) 168–77 (Yeats's attitude towards the 1916 rising).

LUHRS, MARIE, 'Gentle Poet: I', *Poetry* (Chicago), XXX 5 (Aug 1927) 279–83 (*Autobiographies*); 'Gentle Poet: II', ibid., XXX 6 (Sep 1927) 346–9 (*Poetical Works in Two Volumes*).

LUNN, HUGH, 'An Interview with Mr W. B. Yeats', *Hearth and Home*, 28 Nov 1912, 229.

LYND, ROBERT, 'The Irish Theatre: An Interview with Mr W. B. Yeats', *Daily News*, 6 June 1910.

'Letters to Living Authors: Mr W. B. Yeats', *John O'London's Weekly*, XXI 538 (10 Aug 1929) 608–10 (a tribute: Lynd's 'conversion' to Yeats's poetry). Revised and reprinted as 'Mr W. B. Yeats', in his *Old and New Masters*, 156–70. Reprinted as 'W. B. Yeats, 1919', in *Essays in Life and Literature*, 160–72.

LYRIC PLAYERS THEATRE, BELFAST, 'Production List of Plays by William Butler Yeats', *Threshold*, no. 19, The Theatre of W. B. Yeats Centenary, 1965 (autumn 1965) 61–3.

MAANEN, WILLEM VAN. *See* VAN MAANEN, WILLEM.

M., S. L., ' "At the Hawk's Well" – An Impression', *Irish Statesman*, II (Apr 1924) 142 (on a performance in Yeats's home).

MABBOTT, T. O., 'Yeats' "The Wild Swans at Coole"', *Explicator*, III 1 (Oct 1944) item 5.

McALINDON, T., 'Divine Unrest: The Development of W. B. Yeats', *Irish Monthly*, LXXXII (Apr 1954) 152–9.

MACARDLE, DOROTHY, 'Experiment in Ireland', *Theatre Arts*, XVIII 2 (Feb 1934) 124–32.

McAULEY, JAMES, 'A Moment's Memory to that Laurelled Head', *The Australian*, 12 June 1965, 9 (a centenary tribute).

MacCALLUM, H. R., 'W. B. Yeats: The Shape-Changer and His Critics', *University of Toronto Quarterly*, XXXII 3 (Apr 1963) 307–13 (*Essays and Introductions*; *Explorations*; B. Chatterjee, *The Poetry of W. B. Yeats*; J. M. Hone, *W. B. Yeats 1865–1939* (second edition); B. L. Reid, *William Butler Yeats: The Lyric of Tragedy*; A. G. Stock, *W. B. Yeats: His Poetry and Thought*).

McCARTAN, PATRICK, 'W. B. Yeats the Fenian', *The Ireland–American Review*, I (n.d. (1940)) 412–20.

MacCARTHY, DESMOND, 'The Irish National Theatre', *Saturday Review*, CIX (18 June 1910) 782–3.

'A Note on the Poems of Yeats', *Sunday Times*, 4 Feb 1934, 8 (*The Collected Poems* (1933)).

'W. B. Yeats', *Sunday Times*, 5 Feb 1939, 6 (obituary).

'W. B. Yeats on Poetry', *Sunday Times*, 16 June 1940, 4 (*Last Poems and Plays*; *Letters on Poetry to Lady Dorothy Wellesley*).

McCARTHY, WILLIAM, 'The Irish Censorship', correspondence, *Spectator*, CXL 5232 (6 Oct 1928) 435–6 (reply to Yeats, 'The Irish Censorship', ibid., 5231 (29 Sep) 391–2, Wade p. 385). Further correspondence by Padraig Ua Eichthigheárnan, H. Strachey, ibid., 5233 (13 Oct) 488; 'Areopagitica', ibid., 5234 (20 Oct) 528; Ezra Pound, ibid., 5240 (1 Dec) 819.

McCUTCHION, DAVID, 'The Heroic Mind of W. B. Yeats', *Visva-Bharati Quarterly*, XXVII 1 (summer 1961) 42–62 (on Yeats's intellectual development and his pursuit of 'mystic truth').

MacDONALD, QUENTIN, 'William Butler Yeats and the Celtic Movement', *Book News*, XXII (June 1904) 1024–5.

MacDONNELL, A., 'The New Young Islanders', *Bookman*, XXVII 160 (Jan 1905) 159–64 *passim* (Yeats and his Irish contemporaries).

McGILL, ANNA BLANCHE, 'Concerning a Few Anglo-Celtic Poets', *Catholic World*, LXXV (Sep 1902) 777–81.

McGRATH, JOHN, 'W. B. Yeats and Ireland', *Westminster Review*, CLXXVI I (July 1911) 1–11.

MacGREEVY, THOMAS, 'Gaelic and the Anglo-Irish Culture', correspondence, *Irish Statesman*, III (Mar 1925) 816–17.

'Mr W. B. Yeats as a Dramatist', *Revue Anglo–Américaine*, VII I (Oct 1929) 19–36.

'James Joyce', correspondence, *TLS*, 2034 (25 Jan 1941) 43–5 (Joyce–Yeats anecdotes).

'W. B. Yeats – A Generation Later', *University Review* (Dublin), III 8 (1965?) 3–14 (personal recollections).

McHUGH, ROGER, 'Tradition and the Future of Irish Drama', *Studies*, XL 160 (Dec 1951) 469–74 *passim*.

'Yeats, Synge and the Abbey Theatre', *Studies*, XLI 163–4 (Sep–Dec 1952) 333–40 (Vivienne Koch, *W. B. Yeats: The Tragic Phase*; B. Bjersby, *The Interpretation of the Cuchulain Legend in the Works of W. B. Yeats*; Lennox Robinson (comp.), *Ireland's Abbey Theatre*).

'W. B. Yeats: Letters to Matthew Russell, S. J.', *Irish Monthly*, LXXXI 954–6 (Feb–Apr 1953) 60–3, 111–15, 143–52 (Wade p. 396).

'Literary Treatment of the Deirdre Legend', *Threshold*, I 1 (Feb 1957) 36–49.

'Yeats's Plenty', *Kilkenny Magazine*, no. 4 (summer 1961) 24–30 (*Essays and Introductions*).

'Yeats and Irish Politics', *Texas Quarterly*, V 3 (autumn 1962) 90–100. Also in *University Review* (Dublin), II 13 (1965?) 24–36.

'Yeats: A Phoenix among Hawks, Rooks and Sparrows', *Sunday Press*, 17 Nov 1963 (a review of the Yeats issue of *A Review of English Literature*).

'Yeats's Kind of Twilight', *Tri-Quarterly*, Yeats Centenary Issue, no. 4 (fall 1965) 126–9 (*The Celtic Twilight* and *The Secret Rose*).

'The Plays of W. B. Yeats', *Threshold*, no. 19, The Theatre of W. B. Yeats Centenary, 1965 (autumn 1965) 3–13.

MACKEN, MARY M., 'W. B. Yeats, John O'Leary, and the Contemporary Club', *Studies*, XXVIII 109 (Mar 1939) 136–42.

MacKenna, Stephen (O'L., A.), 'Mr W. B. Yeats. An Argument and Appreciation (By an Admirer)', *Freeman's Journal*, cxlii (2 Jan 1909) 5.

Mackenzie, Sir Compton, 'Sidelight', *Spectator*, cxciii 6588 (1 Oct 1954) 395 (*Letters of W. B. Yeats*, ed. Allan Wade; personal reminiscences).

Mackey, William F., 'Yeats's Debt to Ronsard on a *Carpe Diem* Theme', *Comparative Literature Studies*, xix (1946) 4–7 ('When You are Old' and Ronsard's 'Sonnet pour Hélène', ii 1578, compared).

MacLeish, Archibald, 'Public Speech and Private Speech in Poetry', *Yale Review*, xxvii 3 (Mar 1938) 536–47. Reprinted in his *Time to Speak*, 59–70. Comment by Richard Schafer, *Yale Review*, xxvii 4 (June 1938) 862–4.

'The Poet as Playwright', *Atlantic Monthly*, cxcv 2 (Feb 1955) 49–52.

Macleod, Fiona. *See* Sharp, William.

MacLiammóir, Micheál, 'Yeats, Lady Gregory, and Denis Johnston', *Bell*, vi 1 (Apr 1943) 33–6. *See also* his *All For Hecuba*, Part III.

'Merlin at the Market Place', *Spectator*, ccix 7004 (21 Sep 1962) 403–4 (*Explorations*).

MacManus, Francis, 'Signor Alighieri Meets Mr Yeats', *Irish Monthly*, lxvii (July 1939) 492–7.

'The Adventures of a Sonnet', *Irish Monthly*, lxix 812 (Feb 1941) 85–90 ('When You are Old' – Petrarch, Ronsard, Yeats).

MacM[anus]., M. J., 'Yeats, Shaw, and the New Ireland', *Irish Press*, 10 Aug 1939 (Irish attitudes to Yeats and Shaw).

Macmillan and Company Limited, 'Biography of W. B. Yeats', correspondence, *TLS*, 1949 (10 June 1939) 342.

MacNeice, Louis, 'Some Notes on Mr Yeats's Plays', *New Verse*, no. 18 (Dec 1935) 7–9.

'Yeats's Epitaph', *New Republic*, cii (24 June 1940) 862–3 (*Last Poems and Plays*).

'On Yeats and Synge', *London Magazine*, vii 8 (Aug 1960) 70–3.

McPHARLIN, PAUL, 'A Speckled Shin', *Notes and Queries*, CLV (4 Aug 1928) 87 (second song in *At the Hawk's Well*). Reply by William Cock, ibid. (18 Aug 1928) 122.

MacPHERSON, JAY, 'The Air-Born Helena', *Waterloo Review*, I 2 (winter 1959) 48–54 (Helena in literature from Homer to Yeats).

MADDEN, WILLIAM A., 'The Divided Tradition of English Criticism', *PMLA*, LXXIII I (Mar 1958) 69–80 (Yeats's place in the development of modern criticism).

MADGE, CHARLES, 'Leda and the Swan', *TLS*, 3151 (20 July 1962) 532 (a bas-relief in the British Museum as a source for the poem). Correspondence by Giorgio Melchiori, ibid., 3152 (3 Aug) 557, and Hugh Ross Williamson, ibid., 3156 (31 Aug) 657. *See also* GULLANS, CHARLES B.

MAGEE, WILLIAM KIRKPATRICK (John Eglinton), 'What should be the Subject of a National Drama?', *Daily Express*, 10 Sep and 8 Oct 1898; 'Mr Yeats and Popular Poetry', ibid., 5 Nov 1898. Both items reprinted in *Literary Ideals in Ireland*, by John Eglinton and others, 23–7, 41–6.

'Life and Letters', *Irish Statesman*, II (Feb 1920) 181 (Yeats and the Dublin University Chair of English).

'Life and Letters', *Irish Statesman*, II (June 1920) 566 (Yeats, Goethe, and a National Theatre).

'Dublin Letter', *Dial*, LXXII 3 (Mar 1922) 298–301 (on Yeats's 'Four Years 1887–1891', published in *Dial*, LXXI (June–July–Aug 1921). Wade p. 381).

'Yeats and his Story', *Dial*, LXXX 5 (May 1926) 357–66. Reprinted in his *Irish Literary Portraits*, 17–35.

'Mr Yeats's Autobiographies', *Dial*, LXXXII 2 (Aug 1927) 94–7 (*Autobiographies*).

'Mr Yeats's Tower', *Dial*, LXXXVI I (Jan 1929) 62–5 (*The Tower*).

'Yeats at the High School', *Erasmian*, XXX (June 1939) 11–12.

'Early Memories of Yeats', *Dublin Magazine*, XXVIII (wrongly numbered XXIX) 3 (July–Sep 1953) 22–6.

MAIXNER, PAUL R., 'Yeats' "The Folly of being Comforted"', *Explicator*, XIII I (Oct 1954) item I.

MALINS, EDWARD, 'Yeats and the Bell-Branch', *The Consort*, no. 21 (summer 1964) 287–98 (on Yeats, verse-speaking, and Florence Farr).

MALONE, ANDREW E., 'The Decline of the Irish Drama', *Nineteenth Century and After*, XCVII (Apr 1925) 578–88.

'The Coming of Age of the Irish Drama', *Dublin Review*, CLXXXI 362 (July 1927) 101–14 (the Abbey Theatre).

'Yeats and the Abbey: School of Dramatists and School of Acting', *Irish Times*, 13 June 1935, 6–7.

MALONE, G. P., 'William Butler Yeats: A Centenary Tribute', *Contemporary Review*, CCVII (Aug 1965) 96–9.

MALVIL, ANDRÉ, 'William Butler Yeats', *Le Monde Nouveau* (Oct 1928).

MANLEY, SEON, 'The Yeats Letters: Cold Light of the Celtic Twilight', *New Leader*, 16 May 1955, 21–2 (*The Letters of W. B. Yeats*, ed. Allan Wade).

MARGOLIS, JOSEPH, 'Yeats' "Leda and the Swan"', *Explicator*, XIII 6 (Apr 1955) item 34.

MARRIOTT, ERNEST, 'The Shadow of the Wind (After W. B. Yeats)', *Manchester Quarterly*, XXIX (Jan 1910) 87–92 (a parody of *The King's Threshold*).

MARSHALL, JOHN, 'Some Aspects of Mr Yeats's Lyric Poetry', *Queen's Quarterly*, XIII 3 (Jan–Mar 1906) 241–5.

MARTIN, C. G., 'W. B. Yeats: An Unpublished Letter', *Notes and Queries*, CCIII, n.s., v 6 (June 1958) 260–1 (a letter of 20 Mar 1906, to an unnamed admirer of his poetry, with editorial comment).

'A Coleridge Reminiscence in Yeats's "A Prayer for my Daughter"', *Notes and Queries*, CCX, n.s., xii 7 (July 1965) 258–60 (on Yeats's use of Coleridge's 'Ver Perpetuum').

MARTIN, GRAHAM, 'Fine Manners, Liberal Speech: A Note on the Public Poetry of W. B. Yeats', *Essays in Criticism*, XI 1 (Jan 1961) 40–59.

MARTYN, EDWARD, *United Irishman*, VII (19 Apr 1902) 1 (letter on the production of *Deirdre* and *Cathleen ni Houlihan*).

MARTZ, LOUIS L., 'Donne and the Meditative Tradition', *Thought*, XXXIV 133 (summer 1959) 269–78 (Yeats and the 'meditative tradition').

MASEFIELD, JOHN, 'William Butler Yeats', *The Arrow*, W. B. Yeats Commemoration Number (summer 1939) 5–6.

MASON, EUDO, C., 'Die Stellung von W. H. Auden und seiner Gruppe in der neueren englischen Dichtung', *Schweizer Annalen* (Dec 1945) 495–501.

MASON, H. A., 'Yeats and the Irish Movement', *Scrutiny*, V 3 (Dec 1936) 330–2 (*Dramatis Personae*).

'Yeats and the English Tradition', *Scrutiny*, V 4 (Mar 1937) 449–51 (*The Oxford Book of Modern Verse*).

MASSON, DAVID I., 'The "Musical Form" of Yeats's "Byzantium"', *Notes and Queries*, CXCVIII (Sep 1953) 400–1.

'Word and Sound in Yeats's "Byzantium"', *ELH*, XX 2 (June 1953) 136–60.

MASTERMAN, CHARLES F. G., 'After the Reaction', *Living Age*, CCXLIV (28 Jan 1905) 197–9.

MATTHIESSEN, F. O., 'The Crooked Road', *Southern Review*, VII 3 (winter 1941–2) 455–70 ('I am of Ireland' and 'After Long Silence'). Reprinted in *The Responsibilities of the Critic*, 25–40.

'Yeats and Four American Poets', *Yale Review*, XXIII 3 (Mar 1934) 611–17 (*Collected Poems* (1933)).

MAYHEW, GEORGE, 'A Corrected Typescript of Yeats' "Easter 1916"', *Huntington Library Quarterly*, XXVII 1 (Nov 1963) 53–71.

MAYNARD, THEODORE, 'The Metamorphosis of Mr Yeats', *Poetry Review*, X 4 (July–Aug 1919) 169–75.

MAZZARO, JEROME L., 'Apple Imagery in Yeats' "The Song of Wandering Aengus"', *Modern Language Notes*, LXXII 3 (May 1957) 342–3.

'Yeats' "The Second Coming"', *Explicator*, XVI 1 (Oct 1957) item 6.

MEACHAEN, PATRICK, 'Two Irish Dramatists', *Library Assistant*, XX (June 1927) 123–34 (Yeats and O'Casey).

MELCHIORI, GIORGIO, 'Yeats, simbolismo e magia', *Lo Spettatore Italiano*, VIII (Nov 1955) 453–65.

'"Leda and the Swan": The Genesis of Yeats' Poem', *English Miscellany*, VII (1957)147–239.

'Yeats' "Beast" and the Unicorn: A Study in the Development of an Image', *Durham University Journal*, XX 1 (Dec 1959) 10–23.

'La Cupola di Bizanzio', *Paragone*, XI 128 (Aug 1960) 41–70 (on the making of the Byzantium poems and the sources of the imagery).

MELLERS, W. H., 'A Book on Yeats', *Scrutiny*, IX 4 (Mar 1941) 381–3 (Louis MacNeice, *The Poetry of W. B. Yeats*).

MENANDER (pseudonym), 'Poetry and Prejudice', *TLS*, 2142 (20 Feb 1943) 87 (reply to George Orwell's reference to Yeats's fascism in his review of Menon's *W. B. Yeats*); correspondence by G. Orwell and Menander, *TLS*, 2144 (6 Mar) 115.

MENDEL, SIDNEY, 'Yeats' "Lapis Lazuli"', *Explicator*, XIX 8 (June 1961) item 64.

MENNLOCH, WALTER, 'Dramatic Values', *Irish Review*, I 7 (Sep 1911) 325–9 (on Yeats as a dramatist).

MERCIER, VIVIAN, 'Speech after Long Silence', *Irish Writing*, no. 6 (Nov 1948) 76–81 (the Irish Literary Revival).

'Yeats' Lifelong Immersion in the Spirit of Ireland', *Commonweal*, LXI (25 Mar 1955) 660–1 (*The Letters of W. B. Yeats*, ed. Allan Wade).

'Yeats and "The Fisherman"', *TLS*, 2936 (6 June 1958) 313. *See also* Anon., 'England is Abroad'.

'Oliver St John Gogarty', *Poetry* (Chicago), XCIII 1 (Oct 1958) 35–40 (Yeats and Gogarty compared).

'Standish James O'Grady', *Colby Library Quarterly*, series IV, 16 (Nov 1958) 285–90 (sees O'Grady as the 'father' of the Irish Literary Revival).

'To Pierce the Dark Mind', *Nation*, CXCI (10 Dec 1960) 460–1 (*Senate Speeches*, ed. Donald Pearce).

'Douglas Hyde's "Share" in *The Unicorn from the Stars*', *Modern Drama*, VII 4 (Feb 1965) 463–6 (*Where There is Nothing*, the first version of *The Unicorn from the Stars*, was excluded from his *Collected Plays* because much of it was written by Lady Gregory and Douglas Hyde, whose share in it cannot actually be determined).

'In Defence of Yeats as a Dramatist', *Modern Drama*, VIII 2 (Sep 1965) 161–6.

MEREDITH, HUGH OWEN, 'The Plays of W. B. Yeats', *New Statesman*, XX (27 Jan 1923) 481–3 (*Plays in Prose and Verse*).

MEYERSTEIN, E. H. W., 'The Music of Death and of Change', *English*, IV 23 (summer 1943) 161–3 (Joseph Hone, *W. B. Yeats 1865–1939*; V. K. N. Menon, *The Development of W. B. Yeats*).

MICHIE, DONALD M., 'A Man of Genius and a Man of Talent', *Texas Studies in Literature and Language*, VI 1 (spring 1964) 148–54 (on Yeats's collaboration with George Moore in *Diarmuid and Grania*).

MILLER, LIAM, 'The Dun Emer Press', *Irish Book*, Special Yeats Issue, II 3–4 (autumn 1963) 81–90 (a lecture given at the Third Yeats International Summer School, Aug 1962).

MILLS, JOHN GASCOIGNE, 'W. B. Yeats and the Noh', *Japan Quarterly*, II 4 (Oct 1955) 496–500.

'On the Poetry and Politics of W. B. Yeats', *Ochanomizu Joshi Daigaku Jimbun Kagaku Kiyo* (*Studies in Art and Literature, Ochanomizu University*), XIV (1961) 1–16.

MINER, EARL ROY, 'A Poem by Swift and W. B. Yeats's "Words upon the Window-Pane"', *Modern Language Notes*, LXXII 3 (Apr 1957) 273–5 (Yeats and Swift's sixth poem, 'Written upon Windows at Inns, in England').

MINTON, ARTHUR, 'Yeats' "When You Are Old"', *Explicator*, V 7 (May 1947) item 49.

MIZENER, ARTHUR, 'The Romanticism of W. B. Yeats', *Southern Review*, VII 3 (winter 1941–2) 601–23. Also in *The Permanence of Yeats*, ed. James Hall and Martin Steinmann, 140–62 (125–45).

MOLUA (pseudonym), 'Purging the Pride of Pollexfen', *Catholic Bulletin*, XVI (Sep 1926) 937–43 (on Yeats's article, 'Our Need for Religious Sincerity', in *Criterion* (Apr 1926). Wade p. 383).

'Pollexfen Pride and the People: An Anthology (1912–1925) with a Practical Result (1925–1927)', *Catholic Bulletin*, XVII (Aug 1927) 821–5 (on the Irish Coinage Design Committee and Yeats).

MONROE, HARRIETT, 'Mr Yeats and the Poetic Drama', *Poetry* (Chicago), XVI 1 (Apr 1920) 32–9 (a report on Yeats's address at a banquet given in his honour by *Poetry* (Chicago), 3 Mar 1920).

MONTAGUE, JOHN, 'Under Ben Bulben', *Shenandoah*, XVI 4 (summer 1965) 21–4 (Yeats's poetry transcends the purely local).

MONTGOMERY, K. L., 'Some Writers of the Celtic Renaissance', *Fortnightly Review*, XCVI, n.s., XC 307 (1 Sep 1911) 545–61.

MOONEY, FR CANICE, 'Yeats and "The Salley Gardens"', *Irish Book Lover*, XXXI 4 (Apr 1950) 86–7 (Yeats was the 'editor' rather than author of this poem). Replies by P. S. O'H[egarty]., ibid., XXXI 5 (Feb 1951) 105, and A[ustin]. C[larke]., ibid., XXXI 6 (Nov 1951) 133–4.

MOORE, GEORGE, 'The Irish Literary Renaissance and the Irish Language: An Address', *New Ireland Review*, XIII 2 (Apr 1900) 65–7 (delivered at a meeting of the promoters of the Irish Literary Theatre, Feb 1900). Reprinted in *Ideals in Ireland*, ed. Lady Gregory, 43–51.

'Yeats, Lady Gregory, and Synge', *English Review*, XVI 62 (Jan 1942) 167–80; ibid., 63 (Feb) 350–64 (a chapter from his *Vale*).

MOORE, GERALD, 'The "Nō" and the Dance Plays of W. B. Yeats', *Japan Quarterly*, VII 2 (Apr–June 1960) 177–87.

MOORE, HARRY T., *Saturday Review*, XLVIII (11 Dec 1965) 39, 81 (*In Excited Reverie*, ed. A. Norman Jeffares and K. G. W. Cross; T. R. Henn, *The Lonely Tower*, second edition; Corinna Salvadori, *Yeats and Castiglione*; A. Zwerdling, *Yeats and the Heroic Ideal*; B. Rajan, *W. B. Yeats*; Peter Ure, *Yeats*; Curtis Bradford, *Yeats at Work*).

MOORE, ISABEL, 'William Butler Yeats', *Bookman* (New York), XVIII 4 (Dec 1903) 360–3.

MOORE, JOHN REES, 'Yeats as a Last Romantic', *Virginia Quarterly Review*, XXXVII 3 (summer 1961) 432–49.

'Cuchulain, Christ, and the Queen of Love: Aspects of Yeatsian Drama', *Tulane Drama Review*, VI 3 (Mar 1962) 150–9.

'Swan or Goose?', *Sewanee Review*, LXXI 1 (winter 1963) 123–33 (*Selected Poems*, ed. M. L. Rosenthal; Yvor Winters, *The Poetry of W. B. Yeats*).

'An Old Man's Tragedy – Yeats's *Purgatory*', *Modern Drama*, V 4 (Feb 1963) 440–50.

'Cold Passion: A Study of *The Herne's Egg*', *Modern Drama*, VII 3 (Dec 1964) 287–98.

MOORE, MARIANNE, *Poetry* (Chicago), XLII 1 (Apr 1933) 40–4 (*Collected Poems* (1933); *The Winding Stair*).

M[OORE]., M[ARIANNE]., 'Wild Swans', *Poetry* (Chicago), XIII 1 (Oct 1918) 42–4 (*The Wild Swans at Coole*).

MOORE, T. STURGE, 'Yeats', *English*, II 10 (spring 1939) 273–8.

†MORAWSKI, STEFAN, 'Kipling–Yeats–Auden', *Twórczość*, no. 6 (1949) 84–99.

MORISSET, HENRI, 'William Butler Yeats', *Esprit*, VII 84 (1 Sep 1939) 776–80.

MORTENSON, ROBERT, 'Yeats's *Vision* and "The Two Trees"', *Studies in Bibliography*, XVII (1964) 220–2 (*A Vision* as a source for the revision of the poem).

MORTIMER, RAYMOND, 'Books in General', *New Statesman*, XXI (13 Feb 1943) 111–12 (J. M. Hone, *W. B. Yeats 1865–1939*; Louis MacNeice, *The Poetry of W. B. Yeats*; V. K. N. Menon, *The Development of William Butler Yeats*).

MORTON, J. B., and CLIFTON, V., 'W. B. Yeats: Two Appreciations', *Tablet*, CLXXIII (4 Feb 1939) 136–7.

MOSES, M. J., 'W. B. Yeats and the Irish Players', *Metropolitan Magazine*, XXXV 3 (Jan 1912) 23–5, 61–2.

'With William Butler Yeats', *Theatre Arts Monthly*, VII (June 1924) 382–8.

MOULT, THOMAS, 'The Bard of Houlihan', *Apple* (*of Beauty and Discord*), I 4 (fourth quarter 1920) 220–4 (Yeats as the Irish laureate).

MUIR, EDWIN, 'Yeats', *New Statesman*, XXI (26 Apr 1941) 440 (Louis MacNeice, *The Poetry of W. B. Yeats*).

MULHOLLAND, ROSA, 'William Butler Yeats', *Irish Monthly*, XVII (May 1889) 365–71. Reprinted from the *Melbourne Advocate*, 9 Mar 1889 (*The Wanderings of Oisin*).

MUNRO, JOHN M., 'Arthur Symons and W. B. Yeats: The Quest for Compromise', *Dalhousie Review*, XLV 2 (summer 1965) 137–52 (two responses to 'the antinomies of experience').

MURPHY, DANIEL J., 'Yeats and Lady Gregory: A Unique Dramatic Collaboration', *Modern Drama*, VII 3 (Dec 1964) 322–8 (on Lady Gregory's contribution to Yeats's plays).

'Maud Gonne's *Dawn!*', *Shenandoah*, XVI 4 (summer 1965) 63–77 (gives the text of Maud Gonne's play, and comments on the quarrel of Inghnidhe na h-Eireann with Yeats and the Irish National Theatre Society).

MURPHY, GWENDOLEN. *See* AUTY, R. A.

MURPHY, RICHARD. *See* AUTY, R. A.

MURRAY, T. C., 'The Casting Out of Shaw and Yeats', *Bell*, XII 4 (July 1946) 310–17 (early experiences with Macmillan & Co.).

MURRY, J. MIDDLETON, 'Mr Yeats' Swan Song', *Athenaeum*, 4640 (4 Apr 1919) 136–7 (*The Wild Swans at Coole*). Reprinted in *Aspects of Literature*, 53–9, and in *The Permanence of Yeats*, ed. James Hall and Martin Steinmann, 10–14 (9–13).

MURSHID, K. S., 'Yeats, Woman, and God', *Venture*, I 2 (June 1960) 166–77 (*The Herne's Egg* and *The Upanishads*).

MUSGROVE, S., 'Yeats and Arnold: A Common Rhythm', *Southerly*, III 3 (Dec 1942) 25–6. Reply by A. W. V. (q.v.).

NAIRNE, CAMPBELL, 'From Mallarmé to Yeats', *John O'London's Weekly*, XLVIII 1201 (26 Feb 1943) 205 (C. M. Bowra, *The Heritage of Symbolism*).

NATHAN, LEONARD P., 'W. B. Yeats's Experiments with an Influence', *Victorian Studies*, VI 1 (Sep 1962) 66–74 (the influence of Pater on Yeats).

NÉALL (pseudonym), 'The Irish Literary Movement: IV – "Cathleen ni Houlihan"', *Irish Monthly*, XLVIII (Sep 1920) 457–61.

NEVINSON, HENRY W., 'W. B. Yeats, the Poet of Vision', *London Mercury*, XXXIX 233 (Mar 1939) 485–91.

NEWTON, NORMAN, 'Yeats as Dramatist: *The Player Queen*', *Essays in Criticism*, VIII 3 (July 1958) 269–84.

NIELSEN, MARGARET E., 'A Reading of W. B. Yeats's Poem "On a Picture of a Black Centaur by Edmund Dulac"', *Thoth*, IV 2 (spring 1963) 67–73.

NILAND, NORA, 'The Yeats Memorial Museum, Sligo', *Irish Book*, Special Yeats Issue, II 3–4 (autumn 1963) 122–6.

NIST, JOHN, 'In Defence of Yeats', *Arizona Quarterly*, XVIII 1 (spring 1962) 58–65 (a reply to the attack on Yeats by Yvor Winters in his *The Poetry of W. B. Yeats*).

NOGUCHI, YONE, 'Japanese Note on Yeats', *Academy*, LXXXII 2070 (6 Jan 1912) 22–3. Reprinted in his *Through the Torii*, 110–17.
 'A Japanese Poet on W. B. Yeats', *Bookman* (New York), XLIII 4 (June 1916) 431–3.

NOON, WILLIAM, 'Yeats and the Human Body', *Thought*, XXX (summer 1955) 188–9.

NOTOPOULOS, JAMES A., 'Sailing to Byzantium', *Classical Journal*, XLI 2 (Nov 1945) 78–9.
 'Byzantine Platonism in Yeats', *Classical Journal*, LIV 7 (Apr 1959) 315–21 ('Sailing to Byzantium', *A Vision*, and Plotinus).

NOVICE, A (pseudonym), *Catholic Bulletin*, XXI (July 1931) 670–1 (on the degree of D. Litt. conferred by Oxford University on W. B. Yeats).

NOYES, H., 'William Butler Yeats', *Canadian Poetry*, III (Apr 1939) 5–10.

O., Y., 'The Reading of Poetry', *Irish Statesman*, XIII (Nov 1929) 191–2 (*Three Things*; *Selected Poems*).

O'BRIEN, CONOR CRUISE, 'Yeats and Fascism: What Rough Beast', *New Statesman*, LXIX (26 Feb 1965) 319–22 Reprinted in *In Excited Reverie*, ed. A. Norman Jeffares and K. G. W. Cross, 207–78.

'Passion and Cunning', *Irish Times*, Yeats Centenary Supplement, 10 June 1965, iv. Reprinted in *In Excited Reverie*, ed. A. Norman Jeffares and K. G. W. Cross, 207–78.

'Yeats and Irish Politics', *Tri-Quarterly*, Yeats Centenary Issue, no. 4 (fall 1965) 91–8. Reprinted in *In Excited Reverie*, ed. A. Norman Jeffares and K. G. W. Cross, 207–78.

O'BRIEN, KATE, 'Yeats Comes Home', *Spectator*, CLXXXI 6274 (24 Sep 1948) 394; correspondence by St John Ervine, ibid., 6275 (1 Oct) 432; and by Geoffrey Hollsworth, ibid., 6278 (22 Oct) 530.

Writers of Letters', *Essays and Studies*, IX (1956) 7–20 (on Yeats and other poets as letter-writers).

O'CASEY, SEAN, 'The Abbey Directors and Mr Sean O'Casey', correspondence, *Irish Statesman*, X (June 1928) 268–72 (includes O'Casey's letter requesting publication of the full correspondence on the rejection of *The Silver Tassie*, with letters by Lennox Robinson, W. B. Yeats, Sean O'Casey and Walter Starkie). Reprinted in *Irish Times*, Yeats Centenary Supplement, 10 June 1965, vii–viii.

'Laurel Leaves and Silver Trumpets', *American Spectator*, I 2 (Dec 1932) 4.

O'CONNOR, FRANK. *See* O'DONOVAN, MICHAEL.

O'CONNOR, WILLIAM VAN, 'The Poet as Aesthete', *Quarterly Review*, IV (1948) 311–18.

O'DONNELL, DONAT, 'The Great Conger', *Spectator*, CCII 6829 (22 May 1959) 736 (*Mythologies*; Monk Gibbon, *The Masterpiece and the Man*).

O'DONNELL, F. HUGH, 'Celtic Drama in Ireland', *Freeman's Journal*, 1 Apr 1899, 6 (an attack on *The Countess Cathleen*).

O'DONOGHUE, FLORENCE, 'Letters of Yeats', *Dublin Review*, CCXXVIII 463 (Jan 1954) 102–4 (*Letters of W. B. Yeats to Katharine Tynan*; *W. B. Yeats and T. Sturge Moore*).

O'DONOVAN, MICHAEL (Frank O'Connor), 'Two Friends: Yeats and A. E.', *Yale Review*, XXIX 1 (autumn 1939) 60–88.

'The Old Age of a Poet', *Bell* I 5 (Feb 1941) 7–18.

'The Plays and Poetry of W. B. Yeats: An Appreciation', *Listener*, XXV (8 May 1941) 675–6.

'A Classic One-Act Play', *Radio Times*, XCIV 1214 (3 Jan 1947) 4.

'What Made Yeats a Great Poet', *Listener*, XXXVII (15 May 1947) 761–2.

'A Lyric Voice in the Irish Theatre', *NYTB*, 31 May 1953, 1, 16 (*Collected Plays* (1953)). Reprinted in *The Genius of the Irish Theatre*, ed. Sylvan Barnet, Morton Berman and William Burto, 354–8.

'The Side of Innisfree', *Reporter* XXIII (22 Dec 1960) 44–5.

'Quarrelling with Yeats: A Friendly Recollection', *Esquire*, LXII 6 (Dec 1964) 157, 221, 224, 225, 232 (recollections of Yeats on the Board of the Abbey Theatre).

'The Scholar', *Kenyon Review*, XXVII 2 (spring 1965) 336–43 (Yeats, Russell and Osborn Bergin).

'Yeats', *Sunday Independent*, 13 June 1965 (*In Excited Reverie*, ed. A. Norman Jeffares and K. G. W. Cross).

O'DRISCOLL, ROBERT, 'Under Ben Bulben', *TLS*, 3286 (18 Feb 1965), 132 (comments on *TLS* editorial on Yeats, 21 Jan 1965).

'Two Voices: One Beginning', *University Review* (Dublin), III 8 (1965?) 88–100 (the work and influence of Samuel Ferguson).

(ed.), 'Letters and Lectures of W. B. Yeats', *University Review* (Dublin), III 8 (1965?) 29–55.

O'FAOLÁIN, SEÁN, 'Irish and Anglo-Irish Modes in Literature', correspondence, *Irish Statesman*, V (Jan 1926) 558–9. Reply by Editor, ibid., 559.

'Selected Poems, by W. B. Yeats', *Criterion*, IX (Apr 1930) 523–8.

'W. B. Yeats', *English Review*, LX 6 (Jun 1935) 680–8.

'Philosophy of W. B. Yeats: Two Elements at War', *Irish Times*, 13 June 1935, 6–7.

'Ireland's Literature Now Yeats is 70', *NYTB*, 16 June 1935, 2, 14.

'Yeats a Minor Poet?', *Irish Press*, 9 June 1937, 8 (a reply to Aodh de Blacam's review of Dorothy M. Hoare, *The Works of Morris and Yeats in Relation to Early Saga Literature*).

'The Abbey Festival', *New Statesman*, XVIII (20 Aug 1938) 281–2.

'A. E. and W. B.', *Virginia Quarterly Review*, XV 1 (winter 1939) 41–57 (a comparison).

'William Butler Yeats', *Spectator*, CLXII 5771 (3 Feb 1939) 183.

Editorial note on 'W. B. Yeats: *The Speckled Bird*', *Bell*, 16 (Mar 1941) 23–40. Wade p. 394.

'Yeats and the Younger Generation', *Horizon*, V 25 (Jan 1942) 43–54.

'W. B. Yeats Comes Back to Erin', *Sunday Times*, 12 Sep 1948.

'Ireland After Yeats', *Books Abroad*, XXVI (autumn 1952) 325–33; *Bell*, XVIII 2 (summer 1953) 37–48.

'Fifty Years of Irish Writing', *Studies*, LI 201 (spring 1962) 93–105 (the growth and decline of Irish writing since 1900, with particular reference to Yeats). *See* GARNETT, DAVID.

'Fifty Years of Irish Literature', *Bell*, III 5 (Feb 1942) 327–34.

'Romance and Realism', *Bell*, X 5 (Aug 1945) 373–82 *passim*.

Ó FARACHÁIN, ROIBEÁRD. *See* FARREN, ROBERT.

O'FLAHERTY, LIAM, 'The Plough and the Stars', *Irish Statesman*, V (Feb 1926) 739–40 (a protest against Yeats's protest at the Abbey Theatre on 18 Feb 1926).

O GLASAIN, P., 'Yeats: Symbolist and Mystic?', *Ave Maria*, LIV (19 July 1941) 72–4.

[O'GRADY, STANDISH], 'Notes and Comments', *All Ireland Review*, III (12 Apr 1902) 83–4 (*Kathleen ni Houlihan* and the production of Irish plays). Reply by E. Y., ibid. (19 Apr) 101.

Ó hAODHA, MICHEÁL, 'When Was Yeats First Published?', *Irish Times*, 5 June 1965, 10 (attributes to Yeats poems signed 'Y' in *Hibernia* (1882–3)).

O'HEGARTY, P. S., 'W. B. Yeats and the Revolutionary Ireland of His Time', *Dublin Magazine*, XIV 3 (July–Sep 1939) 22–4.

O['HEGARTY]., P. S., 'Hurling at the High School', *Irish Book Lover*, XXX 1 (Oct 1946) 3.

See also MOONEY, FR CANICE.

O'L., A. *See* MacKENNA, STEPHEN.

O LOCHLAINN, COLM, 'William Butler Yeats', *British Annual of Literature*, II (1939) 24–30.

OLSON, ELDER, '"Sailing to Byzantium"; Prolegomena to a Poetics of Lyric', *University Review* (Kansas) VIII 3 (spring 1942) 209–19. Reprinted in part as an appendix to his 'An Outline of Poetic Theory', in *Critiques and Essays in Criticism 1920–1948*, ed. R. W. Stallman (New York: Ronald Press, 1949) 284–8. Also in *The Permanence of Yeats*, ed. James Hall and Martin Steinmann, 286–300 (257–69); and in *Five Approaches to Literary Criticism: An Arrangement of Contemporary Critical Essays*, ed. W. S. Scott (New York: Macmillan, 1962) 215–30.

O'MALLEY, GLENN, and TORCHIANA, DONALD T. (eds), 'John Butler Yeats to Lady Gregory: New Letters', *Massachusetts Review*, V 2 (winter 1964) 260–77 (prints eight letters written between 18 June 1898 and Sep 1907). Reprinted in *Irish Renaissance*, ed. Robin Skelton and David R. Clark, 56–64.

O'MALLEY, MARY, 'Irish Theatre Letter', *Massachusetts Review*, VI 1 (autumn–winter 1964–5) 181–6 (on the Lyric Theatre, Belfast, which specialises in the production of Yeats's plays).

'The Dream Itself', *Threshold*, no. 19, The Theatre of W. B. Yeats Centenary, 1965 (autumn 1965) 58–60 (the Lyric Players Theatre).

O'MEARA, JOHN, 'Yeats, Catullus and The Lake Isle of Innisfree', *University Review* (Dublin), III 8 (1965?) 15–24 (later version of Yeats's poem possibly influenced by Catullus's 'Paene insularum, Sirmio. . . .')

O'NEILL, GEORGE, S. J., 'The Inauguration of the Irish Literary Theatre', *New Ireland Review*, XI 4 (June 1899) 246–52 (*The Countess Cathleen*).

'Some Aspects of Our Anglo-Irish Poets. The Irish Literary Theatre. Foreign Inspiration of Alleged Irish Plays', *Irish Catholic*, XXIV 51 (23 Dec 1911) 55.

'Irish Drama and Irish Views', *American Catholic Quarterly Review*, XXXVII 146 (Apr 1912) 322–32 (expresses strong disapproval of Yeats as leader of the Irish Theatre, supporting Synge and dramatists purporting to show Irish life and character).

O'REILLY, JAMES P., 'A Reply to Mr Yeats', *Irish Statesman*, IV (Mar 1925) 73–4 (reply to Yeats, 'On Divorce', Wade p. 383).

OREL, HAROLD, 'Dramatic Values, Yeats, and *The Countess Cathleen*', *Modern Drama*, II 1 (May 1959) 8–16.

ORWELL, GEORGE (Eric Blair), *Horizon*, VII 37 (Jan 1943) 67–71 (V. K. N. Menon, *The Development of W. B. Yeats*). *See* Part III.

OSHIMA, SHOTARO, 'The Poetry of Symbolic Tradition in the East and the West', *Waseda Daigaku Daigakuin Bungakuka Kiyō (Bulletin of the Graduate Division of Literature of Waseda University)*, no. 10 (1964) 1–29 (in English).

'Yeats and the Japanese Theatre', *Threshold*, no. 19, The Theatre of W. B. Yeats Centenary, 1965 (autumn 1965) 89–102 (the plays and their connection with Zeami, Michio Itoha and Kaoru Osanai).

O'SULLIVAN, SEUMAS. *See* DISHER, M. WILLSON.

P., C., 'Honours for Yeats, Now 70', *New York Times*, 9 June 1935, VII 14.

PANHUYSEN, JOSEPH, 'Het visioen van William Butler Yeats', *Boekenschouw*, XXXI (1937) 315–20.

'Herzien. Herdenken. William Butler Yeats', *Stem*, XIX (1939) 321–4.

PARISH, JOHN E., 'The Tone of Yeats' "After Long Silence"', *Western Humanities Review*, XVI 4 (summer 1962) 377–9 (replies to the reading of the poem given by Cleanth Brooks and Robert Penn Warren in *Understanding Poetry*, 164–6).

PARKINSON, THOMAS, 'W. B. Yeats: A Poet's Stagecraft, 1899–1911', *ELH*, XVII 2 (June 1950) 136–61. A revised version forms part of chaps ii and iii of his *W. B. Yeats: Self-Critic*.

'The Sun and the Moon in Yeats's Early Poetry', *Modern Philology*, L 1 (Aug 1952) 50–8.

'The Individuality of Yeats', *Pacific Spectator*, VI 4 (autumn 1952) 488–99.

'Yeats and Pound: The Illusion of Influence', *Comparative Literature*, VI 3 (summer 1954) 256–64.

'Intimate and Impersonal: An Aspect of Modern Poetics', *Journal of Aesthetics and Art Criticism*, XVI 3 (Mar 1958) 373–83.

'Two Books on Yeats', *Sewanee Review*, LXVI 4 (autumn 1958) 678–85 (Frank Kermode, *Romantic Image*; F. A. C. Wilson, *W. B. Yeats and Tradition*).

'The Respect of Monuments', *Sewanee Review*, LXVIII 1 (Jan–Mar 1960) 143–9 (G. B. Saul, *Prolegomena to the Study of Yeats's Plays* and *Prolegomena to the Study of Yeats's Poems*; John Unterecker, *A Reader's Guide to W. B. Yeats*).

'Vestiges of Creation', *Sewanee Review*, LXIX 1 (winter 1961) 80–111 (a study of Yeats's poetic process).

PARKS, L. C., 'The Hidden Aspect of "Sailing to Byzantium"', *Études Anglaises*, XVI 4 (Oct–Dec 1963) 333–44 (on the importance Yeats attached to his historical Byzantium and Rosicrucianism).

PARTRIDGE, EDWARD B., 'Yeats's "The Three Bushes" – Genesis and Structure', *Accent*, XVII 1 (spring 1957) 67–80.

PATMORE, BRIGIT, 'Some Memories of W. B. Yeats', *Texas Quarterly*, VIII (winter 1965) 152–9.

PAUL, DAVID, 'Yeats and the Irish Mind', *Twentieth Century*, CLVIII (July 1955) 66–75 (article based on *Autobiographies*).

PAUL-DUBOIS, LOUIS, 'M. Yeats et le mouvement poétique en Irlande: I, le poète du rêve', *Revue des Deux Mondes*, LIII 3 (1 Oct 1929) 558–83; 'II, le philosophe et l'influence', ibid., 4 (15 Oct) 824–46.

PAULY, MARIE-HÉLÈNE, 'W. B. Yeats et les symbolistes français', *Revue de Littérature Comparée*, XX 1 (Jan–Mar 1940) 13–33.

PEACOCK, RONALD, 'Public and Private Problems in Modern Drama', *Tulane Drama Review*, III 3 (Mar 1959) 58–72 (Yeats's plays and social reality).

PEARCE, DONALD, 'Yeats' Last Plays: An Interpretation', *ELH*, XVIII 1 (Mar 1951) 67–76 (*The Herne's Egg*; *Purgatory*; *The Death of Cuchulain*).

'Dublin's "National Literary Society", 1892', *Notes and Queries*, CXCVI (12 May 1951) 213–14 (on Yeats's claim to be the founder of the Society).

'Philosophy and Phantasy: Notes on the Growth of Yeats's "System"', *University of Kansas City Review*, XVIII (spring1952) 169–80 (gives references to Yeats's unpublished notebooks).

'Yeats's "The Delphic Oracle upon Plotinus"', *Notes and Queries*, CXCIX, n.s., I 4 (Apr 1954) 175–6. Reply by Peter Ure, ibid., 8 (Aug 1954) 363 (on Yeats's use of Porphyry's *Life of Plotinus*).

'Yeats and the Romantics', *Shenandoah*, VIII 2 (winter 1956) 40–57.

PERRINE, LAURENCE, 'Yeats' "An Acre of Grass"', *Explicator*, XXII 8 (Apr 1964) item 64.

PESCHMANN, HERMANN, 'Yeats and His English Contemporaries', *English*, IX 51 (springs 1952) 88–93.

'Yeats and the Poetry of War', *English*, W. B. Yeats: 1865–1939, XV 89 (summer 1965) 181–4.

PFISTER, KURT, 'Der irische Dichter William Yeats', *Frankfurter Zeitung*, no. 80 (14 Feb 1934) 9.

PHELPS, ROBERT, 'Walking Naked' *Kenyon Review*, XVII 4 (summer 1955) 495–500 (*The Letters of W. B. Yeats*, ed. Allan Wade).

PHELPS, WILLIAM LYON, 'The Advance of English Poetry in the Twentieth Century: Work of the Irish Poets', *Bookman* (New York), XLVII I (Mar 1918) 60–3 (Yeats's contribution).

PHILLIPS, ROBERT S., 'Yeats' "Sailing to Byzantium" 25–32', *Explicator*, XXII 2 (Oct 1963) item 11 (Hans Andersen's tale of the Emperor and the Nightingale as a probable source).

PHILLIPSON, WULSTAN, 'An Irish Occasion', *Month*, XXIV (Dec 1961) 356–62 (Dooras House becomes a Youth Hostel).

PIRKHOFER, ANTON M., 'Zur Bildersprache von Blake und Yeats', *Anglia*, LXXV 2 (1957) 224–33 (on Blake's influence on Yeats).

PITKIN, WILLIAM, 'Stage Designs, Masks and Costumes for Plays by W. B. Yeats', with introductory notes by Sherman Conrad, *Bard Review*, III 2 (Apr 1949) 93–110 (consists mainly of illustrations).

POGGIOLI, RENATO, '"Qualis Artifex Pereo!" or Barbarism and Decadence', *Harvard Library Bulletin*, XIII I (winter 1959) 135–59 (Cafavy, Bryusov, Yeats; 'Byzantium' and 'Sailing to Byzantium').

POPKIN, HENRY, 'Yeats as Dramatist', *Tulane Drama Review*, III 3 (Mar 1959) 73–82.

PORTER, KATHERINE ANNE, 'From the Notebooks of Katherine Anne Porter – Yeats, Joyce, Eliot, Pound', *Southern Review*, n.s., I 3 (summer 1965) 570–3 (on discovering Yeats's poetry).

PORTEUS, HUGH GORDON, 'W. B. Yeats, *The Winding Stair*', *Criterion*, XIII 51 (Jan 1934) 313–15.

POTEZ, HENRI, 'W. B. Yeats et la renaissance poétique en Irlande', *Revue de Paris*, XI iv 3 (1 Aug 1904) 597–618; (15 Aug 1904) 848–66.

P[OTTER]., G. W., 'The Journal in the Celtic Renaissance', *Providence Journal* (Mar 1955).

POUND, EZRA, 'Status Rerum', *Poetry* (Chicago), I 4 (Jan 1913) 123–37 (comments on Yeats's poetry).

'The Later Yeats', *Poetry* (Chicago), IV 2 (May 1914) 64–9 (*Responsibilities*). Reprinted in *Literary Essays of Ezra Pound*, ed. T. S. Eliot, 378–81.

'Le prix Nobel', *Der Querschnitt*, IV 1 (spring 1924) 41–4 (in English, followed by German translation, 'Der Nobel-Preis', 44–6. Comment on the award of the Nobel Prize to Yeats).

'The Irish Censorship', correspondence, *Spectator*, CXLI 5240 (1 Dec 1928) 819 (on Yeats's article on the Irish Censorship Bill, ibid., 5231 (29 Sep) 391–2. Wade p. 385).

'Past History', *English Journal*, XXII 5 (May 1933) 349–58; reprinted in *College English*, XXII 2 (Nov 1960) 81–6 (a study of Joyce, including Yeats's view of him).

'Two Incidents', *Shenandoah*, IV 2–3 (summer–autumn 1953) 112–16 (prints three letters to Yeats, written in 1931 and 1932).

P[OUND]. [EZRA], 'Mr Yeats' New Book', *Poetry* (Chicago), IX 3 (Dec 1916) 150–1 (*Responsibilities and Other Poems*).

POURRAT, HENRI, 'W. B. Yeats', *Nouvelle Revue Française*, XXII 1 (Jan 1924) 124–8.

POWELL, ANTHONY, 'Celtic Mist', *Punch*, CCXXVIII (18 May 1955) 620 (*The Letters of W. B. Yeats*, ed. Allan Wade).

POWER, ARTHUR, 'My Visit to W. B. Yeats', *Irish Digest*, LXXXII 4 (Feb 1965) 54–6 (on Yeats's early poetry and Irish life).

PRESS, JOHN, 'Anthologies', *Review of English Studies*, I 1 (Jan 1960) 62–70 (on Yeats's *Oxford Book of Modern Verse*, 65–6).

PRIOR (pseudonym), '*The Player Queen*', *Irish Statesman*, I (Dec 1919) 608–9; correspondence by 'Conscientious Objector', ibid. (Dec) 658; II (Jan 1920) 45; reply by 'Prior' (Jan 1920) 22.

PRIOR, MOODY E., 'Yeats's Search for a Dramatic Form', *Tri-Quarterly*, Yeats Centenary Issue, no. 4 (fall 1965) 112–14.

PRITCHETT, V. S., 'Encounters with Yeats', *New Statesman*, LXIX (4 June 1965) 879–80 (recollections of meetings with Yeats).

PROKOSCH, FREDERIC, 'Yeats's Testament', *Poetry* (Chicago), LIV 6 (Sep 1939) 338–42 (*Last Poems and Two Plays*).

PYLES, THOMAS, 'Bollicky Naked', *American Speech*, XXIV (Dec 1949) 255 (comments on Yeats's use of the phrase).

QUILLER-COUCH, Sir ARTHUR T., 'Sundry Poets: Mr Yeats', *Daily News*, 19 May 1903.

QUIN, C. C. W., 'W. B. Yeats and Irish Tradition', *Hermathena*, XCVII (spring 1963) 3–19.

QUINN, JOHN, 'Lady Gregory and the Abbey Theatre', *Outlook*, XCIX (16 Dec 1911) 916–19 (Yeats and Douglas Hyde at Lady Gregory's).

QUINN, KERKER, 'Blake and the New Age', *Virginia Quarterly Review*, XIII 2 (spring 1937) 271–85.

'Through Frenzy to Truth', *Yale Review*, XXVII 4 (summer 1938) 834–6 (*A Vision* and *The Herne's Egg and Other Plays*).

QUINN, SR M. BERNETTA, 'Symbolic Landscape in Yeats: County Sligo', *Shenandoah*, XVI 4 (summer 1965) 37–62 (on Yeats's poetic use of the landscape and weather of County Sligo).

'Yeats and Ireland', *English Journal*, LIV 5 (May 1965), 449–50 (on 'Red Hanrahan's Song About Ireland').

QUINN, STEPHEN, 'Further Placings for W. B. Yeats, Based on Surveys of Two Dublin Journals', *Catholic Bulletin*, XXIX (Apr 1939) 241–4 (Aodh de Blacam in *Irish Monthly* (Mar 1939); Mary Macken and J. J. Hogan in *Studies* (Mar 1939)).

QVAMME, BÖRRE, 'William Butler Yeats, 1865–1939', *Edda*, XLIII (1943) 99–107.

†R., 'Synge a Yeats', *Jeviště*, II (1921–2) 638.

R., 'William Butler Yeats', *Il Dramma*, XXII 10 (1 Apr 1946) 46–7.

RAFROIDI, PATRICK, 'The First Yeats International Summer School, Sligo, Eire (13–27 août, 1960)', *Études Anglaises*, XIII 4 (Dec 1960) 502–3.

RAINE, KATHLEEN, 'A Traditional Language of Symbols', *Listener*, LX (9 Oct 1958) 559–60 (on Blake and Yeats).

RAINES, CHARLES A., 'Yeats' Metaphors of Permanence', *Twentieth Century Literature*, V 1 (Apr 1959) 12–30 (metaphor as a unifying element in Yeats's later poems).

RAJAN, BALACHANDRA, 'W. B. Yeats and the Unity of Being', *Nineteenth Century and After*, CXLVI (Sep 1949) 150–61.

'Now Days are Dragon-Ridden', *American Scholar*, XXXII 3 (summer 1963) 407–14 (on the significance of Yeats's poetry and philosophy for modern India).

'Yeats's "Byzantium"', *Osmania Journal of English Studies*, V 1 (1965) 57–61.

'The Reality Within', *Indian Journal of English Studies*, VI (1965) 44–55.

'Yeats and the Absurd', *Tri-Quarterly*, Yeats Centenary Issue, no. 4 (fall 1965) 130–1, 133–7.

RAMAMRUTHAM, J. V., 'Indian Themes in the Poetry of W. B. Yeats', *Literary Half-Yearly*, I 2 (July 1960) 43–8.

RAMSEY, WARREN, 'Some Twentieth Century Ideas of Verse Theatre', *Comparative Literature Studies*, Special Advance Number, 1963 (Proceedings of the First Triennial Meeting of the American Comparative Literature Association) 43–50 (on *The Death of Cuchulain*).

RANSOM, JOHN CROWE, 'Yeats and His Symbols', *Kenyon Review*, I 3 (summer 1939) 309–22. Also in *The Permanence of Yeats*, ed. James Hall and Martin Steinmann, 95–107 (83–96), and in *The Critical Performance: An Anthology of American and British Literary Criticism of Our Century*, ed. S. E. Hyman (New York: Vintage Books, 1956) 190–214.

'The Old Age of a Poet', *Kenyon Review*, II 3 (summer 1940) 345–7 (*Last Poems and Plays*).

'The Irish, the Gaelic, the Byzantine', *Southern Review*, VII 3 (winter 1941–2) 517–46.

R[ANSOM]., J[OHN]. C[ROWE]., 'The Severity of Mr Savage', *Kenyon Review*, VII 1 (winter 1945) 114–17 (reply to D. S. Savage, 'The Aestheticism of W. B. Yeats').

RAO, K. BHASKARA, 'The Impact of Theosophy on the Poetry of W. B. Yeats', *Aryan Path*, XXVI 12 (Dec 1955) 545–52.

RASCOE, BURTON, 'Contemporary Reminiscences', *Arts and Decoration*, XXI (May 1924) 31 (a meeting with Yeats).

RATTRAY, R. F., 'Yeats and Vacher Burch', correspondence, *TLS*, 2795 (23 Sep 1955) 557.

RAYMOND, WILLIAM O., '"The Mind's Internal Heaven" in Poetry', *University of Toronto Quarterly*, XX 3 (Apr 1951) 215–32 ('Sailing to Byzantium', 231–2).

READ, HERBERT, *Criterion*, XIII 52 (Apr 1934) 468–72 (*Collected Poems* – compares two versions of 'The Sorrow of Love').

'Révolte et réaction dans la poésie anglaise moderne', *Présence* (Apr 1946) 56 (Pound's influence on Yeats).

'Poetry in My Time', *Texas Quarterly*, I 1 (Feb 1958) 87–100 (compares poets of his own generation, including Yeats, with those of the 1930s).

REES, LESLIE, 'W. B. Yeats', *Australian English Association Bulletin*, I 10 (Apr 1939).

REEVES, JAMES, 'Yeats and Reeves', correspondence, *New Statesman*, LXVIII (30 Oct 1964) 651 (on Yeats's comment on Reeves's poetry, in a letter to Laura Riding in 1936).

REID, BENJAMIN LAWRENCE, 'Yeats and Tragedy', *Hudson Review*, XI 3 (autumn 1958) 391–410 (opposes the view of Stephen Spender and Walter E. Houghton that Yeats's Poetry has 'no unifying moral subject').

'The House of Yeats', *Hudson Review*, XVIII 3 (autumn 1965) 331–50.

REID, JANE DAVIDSON, 'Leda, Twice Assaulted', *Journal of Aesthetics and Art Criticism*, XI 4 (June 1953) 378–89 ('Leda and the Swan'; Yeats's sonnet compared with Rilke's).

REINERT, OTTO, 'Yeats' "The Hour Glass"', *Explicator*, XV 3 (Dec 1956) item 19.

†REMÉNYI, JÓZSEF, 'Ket Kolto', *Látóhatár*, V 5 (1954) 305–7 (*Collected Poems*).

REYNOLDS, HORACE, 'Supernatural Plays', *Saturday Review of Literature*, XI (9 Mar 1935) 535 (*Wheels and Butterflies*).

'The Dream-Made World of Yeats the Dramatist', *NYTB*, 1 Sep 1935, 2, 8 (*Collected Plays*).

'Three New Plays in Verse by Yeats', *NYTB*, 29 May 1938, 8 (*The Herne's Egg and Other Plays*).

'He Offers His Son the Poets of Life', *NYTB*, 18 June 1944, 25 (*J. B. Yeats: Letters to his Son W. B. Yeats and Others, 1869–1922*, ed. J. M. Hone).

RHYNEHART, J. G., 'Wilde's Comments on Early Works of W. B. Yeats', *Irish Book*, I 4 (spring 1962) 102–4.

RHYS, ERNEST, 'W. B. Yeats: Early Recollections', *Fortnightly Review*, CXXXVIII, o.s., cxliv (July 1935) 52–7 (on Yeats's seventieth birthday).

RICHARDSON, DOROTHY M., 'Yeats of Bloomsbury', *Life and Letters Today*, XXI (Apr 1939) 60–6.

RIND, L. R., 'Leda and the Swan: Yeats and Rilke', *Chicago Review*, VII 2 (spring 1953) 13–17.

RIVOALLAN, A., 'William Butler Yeats, 1865–1939', *Les Langues Modernes*, XXXVII 2 (Mar 1939) 188–93.

ROBERTS, R. ELLIS, 'W. B. Yeats, Dramatist', *New Statesman and Nation*, X (2 Nov 1935) 636–7 (*The Hour Glass*, *The Pot of Broth*, *The Player Queen* at the Little Theatre, London).

ROBINSON, LENNOX, 'As Man of the Theatre', *The Arrow*, W. B. Yeats Commemoration Number (summer 1939) 20–1.

'Journey's End', *Irish Library Bulletin*, IX (Oct 1948) 166.

'Yeats: The Early Poems', *Review of English Literature*, VI 3 (July 1965) 22–3.

ROBINSON, NORMAN L., 'Poems of W. B. Yeats', *Central Literary Magazine*, XXVIII 5 (Jan 1928) 185–94 (a general study).

RODMAN, SELDEN, 'Poetry Between the Wars', *College English*, V 1 (Oct 1943) 1–8 (the place of Yeats).

ROLL-HANSEN, DIDERIK, 'W. B. Yeats som dramatiker', *Edda*, LXV 3 (1965) 153–64 (Yeats's dramatic practice as an emphatic protest against Ibsen and the naturalistic theatre).

†RONAY, GYÓRGY, 'Yeats versei', *Élet és Irodalom*, IV 43 (21 Oct 1960) 6 (review of *Yeats: Versik*, a Hungarian translation of the poems).

ROONEY, PHILIP, 'The Yeats Country', *Irish Press*, 10, 11 and 12 Aug 1961.

ROSE, MARILYN GADDIS, 'A Visit with Anne Yeats', *Modern Drama*, VII 3 (Dec 1964) 229–307 (an interview with Yeats's daughter in Dublin, 27 May 1964).

ROSE, WILLIAM, 'A Letter from W. B. Yeats on Rilke', *German Life and Letters*, n.s., XV 1 (Oct 1961) 68–70 (Yeats acknowledges Rose's book on Rilke, 17 Aug 1938).

ROSE, W. K., 'Wyndham Lewis in his Letters', *Ramparts*, II 1 (May 1963) 85–9 (comments on Lewis's correspondence with Yeats and others).

ROSENBAUM, S. P., 'Yeats' "Among School Children", V', *Explicator*, XXIII 2 (Oct 1964) item 14.

ROSENTHAL, M. L., 'Sources in Myth and Magic', *Nation*, CLXXXII (23 June 1956) 533–5 (*Collected Poems*; *A Vision*).

'Metamorphoses of Yeats', *Nation*, CLXXXVI (5 Apr 1958) 298–9 (*The Variorum Edition of the Poems*).

ARTICLES WHOLLY OR PARTLY ABOUT YEATS

'On Yeats and the Cultural Symbolism of Modern Poetry', *Yale Review*, XLIX 4 (June 1960) 573–83.

ROSSI, MARIO M., 'Yeats and Philosophy', *Cronos*, I 3 (fall 1947) 19–24.

'Two Unpublished Letters of Yeats', *Cronos*, II 3 (fall 1948) 18.

ROTHENSTEIN, Sir WILLIAM, 'Three Impressions. I', *The Arrow*, W. B. Yeats Commemoration Number (summer 1939) 16–17. *See also* GOGARTY, OLIVER ST JOHN; TURNER, W. J.

ROYER, ANDRÉ, 'In Quest of W. B. Yeats: Notes on the French Production of Three Plays', translated by John Boyle, *Threshold*, I 1 (Feb 1957) 22–30 (*The Countess Cathleen*; *The Land of Heart's Desire*; *The Shadowy Waters*).

RUBENSTEIN, JEROME S., 'Three Misprints in Yeats's *Collected Poems*', *Modern Language Notes*, LXX 2 (Mar 1955) 184–7.

RUSSELL, FRANCIS, 'The Archpoet', *Horizon*, III 2 (Nov 1960) 66–9 (on the incantatory quality of Yeats's poetry).

RUSSELL, GEORGE WILLIAM (Æ, AE, A. E.), 'Literary Ideals in Ireland', *Daily Express*, 12 Nov 1898, 3. Reprinted in *Literary Ideals in Ireland*, by John Eglinton and others, 49–54.

'Nationality and Cosmopolitanism in Literature', *Daily Express*, 10 Dec 1898, 3. Reprinted in *Literary Ideals in Ireland*, by John Eglinton and others, 79–88.

'The Poetry of William Butler Yeats', *The Reader*, II 3 (Aug 1903) 249–50. Reprinted as 'The Poet of Shadows', in his *Some Irish Essays*, 35–9, and in his *Imaginations and Reveries*, 24–8.

RUTHERFORD, ANDREW, 'Yeats' "Who Goes with Fergus?"', *Explicator*, XIII 7 (May 1955) item 41.

RUTHERFORD, MALCOLM, 'The Yeats Centenary: Thoor Ballylee', *Spectator*, CCXIV 7148 (25 June 1965) 806 (a centenary tribute).

RYAN, STEPHEN P., 'W. B. Yeats and Thomas MacDonagh', *Modern Language Notes*, LXXVI 6 (Dec 1961) 715–19 (prints a letter from Yeats to MacDonagh, dated 3 Dec 1907).

S., E., 'Dichter der irischen Wiedergeburt. Zum Tode von William Butler Yeats', *Berliner Börsenzeitung*, no. 55 (1941).

SADDLEMYER, ANN, 'Synge to MacKenna: The Mature Years', *Massachusetts Review*, V 2 (winter 1964) 280–95 *passim* (letters with editor's comments and notes). Reprinted in *Irish Renaissance*, ed. Robin Skelton and David R. Clark, 65–79.

SALERNO, NICHOLAS A., 'A Note on Yeats and Leonardo da Vinci', *Twentieth Century Literature*, V 4 (Jan 1960) 197–8 (on 'The Wheel' and a passage in Leonardo's *Notebooks*).

SALVESEN, CHRISTOPHER, 'Ireland and its Dead Yeats', *New Society*, 10 June 1965, 26–8 (a centenary tribute).

SAMPSON, GEORGE, 'Two Ways of Criticism', *Bookman*, LXVI (July 1924) 201–2 (*Essays* (1924)).

SANDBERG, ANNA, 'The Anti-Theatre of W. B. Yeats', *Modern Drama*, IV 2 (Sep 1961) 131–7 (*Four Plays for Dancers*, esp. *At the Hawk's Well*).

SANESI, ROBERTO, 'Scheda al teatro di W. B. Yeats', *Aut-Aut*, no. 26 (Mar 1955) 130–9.

'Lapis Lazuli', *Osservatore Politico Letterario*, VII 10 (1961) 81–91.

'"Lapis Lazuli" di W. B. Yeats', *Poesia e Critica*, I 2 (1961) 5–18.

'William Butler Yeats uomo pubblico', *Aut-Aut*, no. 67 (1962) 69–71.

SARCAR, SUBHAS, 'Modern Poetic Drama', *Bulletin of the Department of English, University of Calcutta*, IV 3–4 (1963) 38–48 (comments on Yeats's contribution to poetic drama).

SARKAR, SUNIL CHANDRA, 'Modern Poetry and Tagore's Paradox', *Visva-Bharati Quarterly*, Tagore Centenary Issue, XXVI 3–4 (1961) 323–40 (on Yeats, Tagore, and 'modernism' in poetry).

SAUL, GEORGE BRANDON, 'Literary Parallels: Yeats and Coppard', *Notes and Queries*, CLXVIII (4 May 1935) 314.

'Yeats's Hare', *TLS*, 2345 (11 Jan 1947) 23 ('The Collar-Bone of a Hare' and 'Two Songs of a Fool'); correspondence by Marion Witt, ibid., 2385 (18 Oct) 535.

'Yeats and His Poems', *TLS*, 2513 (31 Mar 1950) 208. Reply by Allan Wade, ibid., 2514 (7 Apr) 215 ('The Cap and Bells', etc.).

'Yeats, Noyes, and Day Lewis', *Notes and Queries*, CXCV (10 June 1950) 258.

'Jeffares on Yeats', *Modern Language Notes*, LXVI (Apr 1951) 246–9 (comments on A. N. Jeffares, *W. B. Yeats: Man and Poet*). Reply by A. N. Jeffares, 'Saul on Jeffares', q.v.

'The Winged Image: A Note on Birds in Yeats's Poems', *Bulletin of the New York Public Library*, LVIII 6 (June 1954) 267–73.

'Yeatsian Brevities', *Notes and Queries*, CXCIX, n.s., i 12 (Dec 1954) 535–6 (the sources of 'The Wheel' and 'Towards Break of Day').

'Yeats's Verse Before *Responsibilities*', *Arizona Quarterly*, XVI 2 (summer 1960) 158–67.

'Coda: The Verse of Yeats's Last Five Years', *Arizona Quarterly*, XVII 1 (spring 1961) 63–8 (comments adversely on the later poems).

'The Short Stories of W. B. Yeats', *Poet Lore*, LVII (1962) 371–4.

'A Frenzy of Concentration: Yeats's Verse from *Responsibilities* to *The King of the Great Clock Tower*', *Arizona Quarterly*, XX 2 (summer 1964) 101–16 (on Yeats's lyrical poetry from 1914 to 1934).

SAVAGE, DEREK S., 'The Aestheticism of W. B. Yeats', *Kenyon Review*, VII 1 (winter 1945) 118–34. Reprinted in his *The Personal Principle*, 67–91, and in *The Permanence of Yeats*. ed. James Hall and Martin Steinmann, 193–216 (179–94). (Yeats's acceptance of the doctrine of aestheticism results in a hollowness at the centre of his work 'which time is bound increasingly to reveal'. *See* reply by J[ohn]. C[rowe]. R[ansom]., 'The Severity of Mr Savage'.)

'Two Prophetic Poems', *Adelphi*, XXII 1 (Oct–Dec 1945) 25–32 ('The Second Coming'). Also in *Western Review*, XIII 2 (winter 1949) 67–78.

SCANLON, SR ALOYSE, 'The Sustained Metaphor in *The Only Jealousy of Emer*', *Modern Drama*, VII 3 (Dec 1964) 273–7.

SCHANZER, ERNEST, '"Sailing to Byzantium", Keats, and Andersen', *English Studies*, XLI 4 (Dec 1960) 376–80.

SCHNEIDER, ELISABETH, 'Yeats' "When You are Old"', *Explicator*, VI 7 (May 1948) item 50.

SCHRAMM, RICHARD, 'The Line Unit: Studies in the Later Poetry of W. B. Yeats', *Ohio University Review*, III (1961) 32–41 (the structure of Yeats's verse).

SCHRICKX, W., 'William Butler Yeats: Symbolist en visionair Dichter', *De Vlaamse Gids*, XLIX (1965) 380–96.

'On Giordano Bruno, Wilde and Yeats', *English Studies*, XLV (1964) Supplement Presented to R. W. Zandvoort, 257–64 (a translation of Bruno's *Gli Eroici Furori* in 1887 drew attention to the doctrine of *Anima Mundi*).

SCHROETER, JAMES, 'Yeats and the Tragic Tradition', *Southern Review*, n.s., I 4 (Oct 1965) 835–46.

SCHWARTZ, DELMORE, 'The Poet as Poet', *Partisan Review*, VI I (Mar 1939) 52–9.

'An Unwritten Book', *Southern Review*, VII 3 (winter 1941–2) 471–91. Reprinted in *The Permanence of Yeats*, ed. James Hall and Martin Steinmann, 309–30 (277–95). (On aspects of Yeats's work that call for scholarly or critical attention.)

'Speaking of Books', *NYTB*, 13 June 1954, 2 (*The Autobiography of William Butler Yeats*).

SCOTT, WINFIELD TOWNLEY, 'Yeats at 73', *Poetry* (Chicago), LIII 2 (Nov 1938) 84–8 (*New Poems* (1938)).

'The Foolish Passionate Man', *Accent*, I 4 (summer 1941) 247–50 (John Masefield, *Some Memories of W. B. Yeats*; Stephen Gwynn (ed.), *Scattering Branches*; Louis MacNeice, *The Poetry of W. B. Yeats*; *Letters on Poetry from W. B. Yeats to Dorothy Wellesley*).

'Remaking of an Artist', *Saturday Review of Literature*, XI (7 Dec 1957) 47–50 (*The Variorum Edition of the Poems*).

SCOTT-JAMES, R. A., 'The Farewell to Yeats', *London Mercury*, XXXIX 233 (Mar 1939) 477–80.

SEIDEN, MORTON IRVING, 'A Psychoanalytic Essay on William Butler Yeats', *Accent*, VI 3 (spring 1946) 178–90 (*The Wanderings of Oisin*).

'Patterns of Belief – Myth in the Poetry of William Butler Yeats', *American Imago*, V 4 (Dec 1948) 258–300.

'W. B. Yeats as a Playwright', *Western Humanities Review*, XII I (winter 1959) 83–98.

SELIGO, IRENE, 'Ein Dichter des 20. Jahrhunderts. William Butler Yeats, gestorben 28. Januar 1939', *Frankfurter Zeitung*, 5 Feb 1939, 1–2 (comments particularly on *Cathleen ni Houlihan*).

SEN, SRI CHANDRA, 'The Irish Element in the Evolution of the Poetry of W. B. Yeats', *Bulletin of the Department of English, University of Calcutta*, IV 1–2 (1963) 13–25; ibid., 3–4 (1963) 1–13.

'The Love Lyrics of W. B. Yeats', *Bulletin of the Department of English, University of Calcutta*, V 15–16 (1963) 13–38.

'Time-Theme in the Poetry of W. B. Yeats', *Bulletin of the Department of English, University of Calcutta*, V 18–19 (1964) 82–112.

'A Critical Study of Yeatsian Vocabulary', *Visva–Bharati Quarterly*, XXXI 2 (1965–6) 133–69.

SENA, VINOD, 'W. B. Yeats and English Poetic Drama', *An English Miscellany*, no. 2 (1963) 23–36.

SENG, PETER J., 'Yeats' "The Folly of Being Comforted"', *Explicator*, XVII 7 (Apr 1959) item 48.

SERVOTTE, HERMAN, 'Van Innisfree naar Byzantium: W. B. Yeats (1865–1939)', *Dietsche Warande en Belfort*, CX 1 (Jan 1965) 13–27.

SETHNA, K. D., 'W. B. Yeats – Poet of Two Phases', *Mother India*, I (June 1949) 10–12.

'Shaw and Yeats', *Mother India*, II (Nov 1950) 6–7.

SETURAMAN, V. S., 'Yeats and his Modern Critics', *Aryan Path*, XXX (Oct 1959) 457–61.

'Yeats: *The Tower*: Some Questions and Answers', *Mother India*, XVII (Dec 1965) 97–100.

SHAHANI, RANJEE G., 'Some Recent English Poets', *Asiatic Review*, XXXI (1935) 379–81 (general comments on Yeats's poetry).

SHANKS, EDWARD, 'Prince of Our Poets', *John O'London's Weekly*, XXX 774 (10 Feb 1934) 721 (*Collected Poems* places Yeats at the head of contemporary poets).

SHANLEY, J. LYNDON, 'Thoreau's Geese and Yeats's Swans', *American Literature*, XXX 3 (Nov 1958) 361–4 (on *Walden* and 'The Wild Swans at Coole').

SHAPIRO, KARL, 'Prosody as the Meaning', *Poetry* (Chicago), LXXIII 6 (Mar 1949) 340–1 ('The Wild Swans at Coole').

'Modern Poetry as a Religion', *American Scholar*, XXVIII 3 (summer 1959) 297–305 (on Yeats, Pound, Eliot, Stevens).

SHARP, WILLIAM (Fiona Macleod), 'The Later Work of W. B. Yeats', *North American Review*, CLXXV 551 (Sep 1902) 473–85 (*The Shadowy Waters*). Reprinted as 'The Shadowy Waters', in his *The Winged Destiny: Studies in the Spiritual History of the Gael*, 320–43. *See* THOMPSON, FRANCIS.

'A Group of Irish Writers', *Fortnightly Review*, LXXVII, n.s., lxxi 385 1 (Jan 1899) 33–53 *passim*. Advance notice in the *Daily Express*, 31 Dec 1898, 3.

SHARP, WILLIAM, 'W. B. Yeats: A Poet not in the Theatre', *Tulane Drama Review*, IV 2 (Dec 1959) 67–82 (*Four Plays for Dancers*, and in particular *At the Hawk's Well*).

SHAW, Rev. FRANCIS, S. J., 'The Celtic Twilight', *Studies*, XXIII 89 (Mar 1934) 25–41; 'The Celtic Twilight: Part II. The Celtic Element in the Poetry of W. B. Yeats', ibid., XXIII 90 (June 1934) 260–78.

SHIELDS, H. E., 'Yeats and the "Sally Gardens"', *Hermathena*, Yeats Number, CI (autumn 1965) 22–6 ('The Rambling Boys of Pleasure', an Anglo-Irish ballad, the source for Yeats's poem).

SICKELS, ELEANOR M., 'Yeats' "I am of Ireland"', *Explicator*, XV 2 (Nov 1956) item 10.

'Yeats' "The Gyres," 6', *Explicator*, XV 8 (June 1957) item 60.

SIDGWICK, F., 'William Butler Yeats', *English Illustrated Magazine*, XXIX, n.s., 3 (June 1903) 286–8 (with bibliography).

SILK, DENNIS. *See* AUTY, R. A.

SIMINGTON, R. C. (Kevin), 'Unity and Divorce', *Catholic Bulletin*, XV (Apr 1925) 316–17; ibid. (July 1925) 678–85 (on Yeats's Senate speech on Divorce, Wade p. 383).

SIMON, IRÈNE, 'Yeats Revisited', *Revue des Langues Vivantes*, XXI 4 1965) 406–13 (*Letters on Poetry to Dorothy Wellesley*; A. G. Stock, *W. B. Yeats*).

SIMPSON, LOUIS, 'On Being a Poet in America', *Noble Savage*, no. 5 (1962) 24–33.

SINCLAIR, F., 'A Poet's World in Woburn Walk', *St Pancras Journal*, II 7 (Dec 1948) 124–7.

ARTICLES WHOLLY OR PARTLY ABOUT YEATS

SKEFFINGTON, OWEN SHEEHY, 'W. B. Yeats', correspondence, *TLS*, 3306 (8 July 1965) 579, and by Anthony Comerford, ibid., 3307 (15 July) 597 (on Conor Cruise O'Brien, 'Yeats and Politics', in *In Excited Reverie*, ed. A. Norman Jeffares and K. G. W. Cross); reply by reviewer, ibid., 3306 (8 July) 579.

SKELTON, ROBIN, 'The First Printing of W. B. Yeats's "What Then?"', *Irish Book*, Special Yeats Issue, II 3–4 (autumn 1963) 129–30 (lists variant readings in the unnoticed first printing in *The Year's Poetry 1936*, ed. Denys Kilham Roberts and John Lehmann).

'Twentieth Century Irish Literature and the Private Press Tradition: Dun Emer, Cuala, and Dolmen Presses 1902–1963', *Massachusetts Review*, V 2 (winter 1964) 368–77 (includes an account of Yeats's association with the Dun Emer–Cuala Press). Reprinted in *Irish Renaissance*, ed. Robin Skelton and David R. Clark, 158–67.

See also MASSACHUSETTS REVIEW (Part IV).

SMIDT, KRISTIAN, 'T. S. Eliot and W. B. Yeats', *Revue des Langues Vivantes*, XXI 6 (1965) 555–67 (Eliot's debt to Yeats).

SMITH, A. J. M., 'A Poet Young and Old: W. B. Yeats', *University of Toronto Quarterly*, VIII 3 (Apr 1939) 309–22.

SMITH, GROVER, 'Yeats, Minnaloushe and the Moon', *Western Review*, XI 3 (spring 1947) 241–4 ('The Cat and the Moon').

'Yeats's "The Cat and the Moon"', *Notes and Queries*, CXCV 2 (21 Jan 1950) 35.

SNOW, W., 'A Yeats–Longfellow Parallel', *Modern Language Notes*, LXXIV 4 (Apr 1959) 302–3 (Yeats's 'When you are Old' and Longfellow's *Outre-Mer*).

SOUFFRIN-LE-BRETON, Eileen, 'W. B. Yeats to Mallarmé', *TLS*, 2756 (26 Nov 1954) 759 (prints for the first time Yeats's letter to Mallarmé, postmarked 24 Feb 1894).

SOUTHAM, B. C., 'Yeats: Life and the Creator in "The Long-Legged Fly"', *Twentieth Century Literature*, VI 4 (Jan 1961) 175–9.

'Yeats' "Long-Legged Fly"', *Explicator*, XXII 9 (May 1964) item 73.

SPALDING, P. A., 'The Last of the Romantics: An Appreciation of W. B. Yeats', *Congregational Quarterly*, XVII (July 1939) 332–45.

SPANOS, WILLIAM V., 'Sacramental Imagery in the Middle and Late Poetry of W. B. Yeats', *Texas Studies in Literature and Language*, IV 3 (summer 1963) 214–27. *See also* ALLEN, J. L.; VICKERY, J. B.

†SPARROW, JOHN, 'Extracts from a Lecture on Tradition and Revolt in English Poetry', *Bulletin of the British Institute in Paris* (Apr–May 1939).

SPEAIGHT, ROBERT, 'William Butler Yeats', *Commonweal*, XXIX 23 (31 Mar 1939) 623–4.

'Salute to Yeats', *Colosseum*, V (Apr 1939) 131–8.

'W. B. Yeats and Some Later Friendships', *Greyfriar*, VIII (1965) 14–32.

SPENCER, THEODORE, '*The Tower*', *New Republic*, LVI (10 Oct 1928) 219–20.

'William Butler Yeats', *Hound and Horn*, VII 1 (Oct–Dec 1933) 164–75 (*Words for Music Perhaps*); in part, a reply to Yvor Winters, 'The Poems of T. Sturge Moore', (q.v.). *See also* Winters's rejoinder in his *Defence of Reason*, 490–2. Reprinted as 'The Later Poetry of W. B. Yeats', in *Literary Opinion in America*, ed. Morton Dauwen Zabel (New York: Harper, 1938; revised edition, 1951) 263–77.

'Mr Yeats', *Nation and Athenaeum*, XLIII 3 (21 Apr 1928) 81 (*The Tower*).

SPENDER, STEPHEN, 'Yeats as a Realist', *Criterion*, XIV 54 (Oct 1934) 17–26. Reprinted in his *The Destructive Element*, 115–32, and in *The Permanence of Yeats*, ed. James Hall and Martin Steinmann, 179–92 (160–72).

'The "Egotistical Sublime" in W. B. Yeats', *Listener*, XXI (16 Feb 1939) 377–8.

'Honey Bubblings of the Boilers', *New Statesman and Nation*, XVIII (11 Nov 1939) 686–7 (*On the Boiler*; *The Arrow*, W. B. Yeats Commemoration Number).

'La crise des symboles', *France Libre*, VII 39 (15 Jan 1944) 206–10 ('The Second Coming').

'Movements and Influences in English Literature, 1927–1952', *Books Abroad*, XXVII 1 (winter 1953) 16–17 (Yeats's place; includes comment on Yeats and E. M. Forster).

'A Double Debt to Yeats', *Listener*, LVI (4 Oct 1956) 513, 515 (on Yeats's poetry).

'The Poet and the Legend: An Evaluation', *Irish Times*, Yeats Centenary Supplement, 10 June 1965, i–ii.

'The Influence of Yeats on Later English Poetry', *Tri-Quarterly*, Yeats Centenary Issue, no. 4 (fall 1965) 82–9.

KAVANAGH, PATRICK, KINSELLA, THOMAS, and SNODGRASS, W. D., 'Poetry Since Yeats: An Exchange of Views', *Tri-Quarterly*, Yeats Centenary Issue, no. 4 (fall 1965) 100–6, 108–11.

SPITZER, LEO, 'On Yeats's Poem "Leda and the Swan"', *Modern Philology*, LI 4 (May 1954) 271–6 (takes issue with the interpretation by Hoyt Trowbridge, q.v.). Reprinted in *Essays on English and American Literature*, ed. Anna Hatcher (Princeton, New Jersey: Princeton University Press, 1962) 3–13.

S[QUIRE]., Sir J. C., 'Mr W. B. Yeats's Later Verse', *London Mercury*, VII 40 (Feb 1923) 431–40 (*Later Poems* (1922)). Also in his *Essays on Poetry*, 160–70.

SRIGLEY, M. B., 'The Mathematical Muse', *Dublin Magazine*, XXXI 3 (July–Sep 1956) 13–21 (on the influence of mathematical form on Yeats's poetry).

STACE, W. T., 'The Faery Poetry of Mr W. B. Yeats', *British Review*, I I (Jan 1913) 117–30; also in *Living Age*, CCLXXVI (22 Feb 1913) 483–90.

STAGEBERG, NORMAN C., 'Yeats' "Sailing to Byzantium"', *Explicator*, VI 2 (Nov 1947) item 14.

STALLWORTHY, JON, 'Two of Yeats's Last Poems', *Review of English Literature*, IV 3 (July 1963) 48–69 (on early versions of 'The Long-Legged Fly' and 'The Statues').

'W. B. Yeats and the Dynastic Theme', *Critical Quarterly*, VII 3 (autumn 1965) 247–65 (on Yeats's concern with ancestors and family relationships).

STAMM, RUDOLF, 'Die neuirische Theaterbewegung und wir', *Schweizer Annalen*, I 3 (1944) 156–66 (on the example of Yeats and the Irish theatre).

'"The Sorrow of Love": A Poem by William Butler Yeats Revised by Himself', *English Studies*, XXIX 3 (June 1948) 79–87.

STANFORD, W. B., 'Yeats in the Irish Senate', *Review of English Literature*, IV 3 (July 1963) 71–80 (*The Senate Speeches of W. B. Yeats*, ed. Donald R. Pearce).

STARKIE, WALTER, 'W. B. Yeats, premio Nobel, 1924', *Nuova Antologia*, series 6, CCXXXIV (1 Apr 1924) 238–45.

'"Oedipus at Colonus" at the Abbey Theatre', *Irish Statesman*, IX (17 Sep 1927) 40–1. Reply by T. G. Keller and Arcos (pseudonym), correspondence, ibid., 60.

'Ireland Today', *Quarterly Review*, CCLXXI 538 (Oct 1938) 343–60 *passim* (on recent productions at the Abbey Theatre).

'Yeats and Company', *NYTB*, 14 Nov 1965, 90–2 (reminiscences of the Abbey Theatre).

STAUB, AUGUST W., 'The "Unpopular Theatre" of W. B. Yeats', *Quarterly Journal of Speech*, XLVII 4 (Dec 1961) 363–71 (on Yeats's failure to establish a new dramatic tradition).

STAUFFER, DONALD A., 'W. B. Yeats and the Medium of Poetry' *ELH*, XV 3 (Sep 1948) 227–46.

'Artist Shining through His Vehicles', *Kenyon Review*, XI 2 (spring 1949) 330–6 (Richard Ellmann, *Yeats: The Man and the Masks*).

'The Reading of a Lyric Poem', *Kenyon Review*, XI 3 (summer 1949) 426–40 (an analysis of 'The Wild Swans at Coole').

STEIN, ARNOLD, 'Milton and Metaphysical Art: An Exploration', *ELH*, XVI 2 (June 1949) 129–30 ('Leda and the Swan').

'Yeats: A Study in Recklessness', *Sewanee Review*, LVII 4 (autumn 1949) 603–26.

STEMMLER, T., 'Yeats' "Song of the Happy Shepherd" and Shelley's *Defence of Poetry*', *Neophilologus*, XLVII 3 (July 1963) 221–5.

STEPHENS, JAMES, 'Yeats and the Telephone', *Listener*, XXVII (9 Apr 1942) 106 (an excerpt from the B.B.C. broadcast printed in full as 'W. B. Yeats', in *James, Seumas and Jacques*, ed. Lloyd Frankenberg, 67–72.

'He Died Younger than He was Born', *Listener*, XXIX (17 June 1943) 728. Reprinted as 'Yeats as Dramatist', in *James, Seumas and Jacques*, ed. Lloyd Frankenberg, 74–6.

'W. B. Yeats: A Tribute', *Observer*, 19 Sep 1948, 4 (on Yeats's return to Sligo, 17 Sep 1948).

STOCK, A. G., 'W. B. Yeats: The Poet of Loneliness', *Modern Review* (Nov 1949) 404–7.

'Art, Aristocracy and the Poetry of Yeats', *Literary Criterion*, III (summer 1957) 131–40

'*A Vision* (1925 and 1937)', *Indian Journal of English Studies*, I (1960) 38–47.

'Symbolism and Belief in the Poetry of W. B. Yeats', *Visva–Bharati Quarterly*, XXVII 3–4 (winter 1961–2) 181–96 (on Yeats's use of traditional symbols to relate his intuitive perceptions to ancient ways of thought).

'The World of Maud Gonne', *Indian Journal of English Studies*, VI (1965) 56–79.

STOLL, ELMER EDGAR, 'Poetry and the Passion: An Aftermath', *PMLA*, LV 5 (Dec 1940) 979–92.

STORER, EDWARD, 'Dramatists of Today', *Living Age*, CCLXXXI (9 May 1914) 329–32 (on Yeats's plays).

[STRACHEY, GILES LYTTON,] 'Mr Yeats's Poetry', *Spectator*, CI 4190 (17 Oct 1908) 588 (*Collected Works* (1908) vols I–II).

STRONG, L. A. G., 'The Plays of W. B. Yeats', *John O'Londons' Weekly*, XXXII 821 (5 Jan 1935) 550 (*Collected Plays*, especially *At The Hawk's Well*, with comment on Noh drama).

'W. B. Yeats', *Cornhill Magazine*, CLII (July 1937) 14–29.

'W. B. Yeats', *Spectator*, CLXI 5670 (18 Nov 1938) 856–7.

'Ireland's Grand Old Man', *Living Age*, CCLV (Jan 1939) 438–40.

'W. B. Yeats: An Appreciation', *Cornhill Magazine*, CLVI (Jan 1939) 438–40.

'The Eagle Mind', *Time and Tide*, XXI (9 Mar 1940) 251–2 (*Last Poems and Plays*; Lennox Robinson (ed.), *The Irish Theatre*; Yeats and the Irish theatre).

'Reminiscences of W. B. Yeats', *Listener*, LI (22 Apr 1954) 689–90.

'Yeats at His Ease', *London Magazine*, II 3 (Mar 1955) 56–65 (on Yeats at Oxford).

STURTEVANT, DONALD E., 'The Public and Private Minds of William Butler Yeats', *Thoth*, IV 2 (spring 1963) 74–82.

SUSS, IRVING DAVID, 'The "Playboy" Riots', *Irish Writing*, no. 18 (Mar 1952) 39–42 (on Yeats's defence of Synge's play).

'Yeatsian Drama and the Dying Hero', *South Atlantic Quarterly*, LIV (July 1955) 369–80 (on Yeats's plays and the death theme in Irish legend).

SWIFT, G., 'In Memoriam', *America*, LX (25 Feb 1939) 498–9 (an obituary tribute).

SYMONS, ARTHUR, 'Mr Yeats as a Lyric Poet', *Saturday Review*, LXXXVII (6 May 1899) 553–4 (*Poems* (1899); *The Wind Among the Reeds*). Reprinted in his *Studies in Prose and Verse*, 230–41.

'The Speaking of Verse', *Academy*, LXII 1569 (31 May 1902) 559 (on Yeats's essay, 'Speaking to the Psaltery', Wade p. 363; reply by Yeats, ibid., LXII (7 June 1902) 590–1, reprinted in *The Letters of W. B. Yeats*, ed. Allan Wade, 373–4). Reprinted in his *Plays, Acting and Music*, 23–6.

T., E., '"Deirdre"', *Bookman*, XXXII (Oct 1907) 47.

TALBOT, F. X., 'An Irish Academy of Literature', *America*, XLVIII (10 Dec 1932) 240–1.

TALLQVIST, C. E., 'William Butler Yeats. En Studie', *Finsk Tidskrift*, CII 2 (1927) 119–41; 4 (1927) 281–307.

TARDIVEL, F., 'Mort d'un Bard (W. B. Yeats)', *Culture*, II (Mar 1939) 380–1.

TATE, ALLEN, 'Yeats's Last Friendship', *New Republic*, CIII (25 Nov 1940) 730, 732 (*Letters on Poetry to Dorothy Wellesley*).

'Yeats's Romanticism: Notes and Suggestions', *Southern Review*, VII 3 (winter 1942) 591–600. Also in his *On the Limits of Poetry*, 214–24; *The Man of Letters in the Modern World*, 227–36; and *Collected Essays*, 214–24. Reprinted in *The Permanence of Yeats*, ed. James Hall and Martin Steinmann, 108–17 (97–105), and in *Yeats: A Collection of Critical Essays*, ed. J. Unterecker, 155–62.

TAYLOR, GEOFFREY, 'W. B. Yeats', *Bell*, VI 1 (Apr 1943) 59–62 (J. M. Hone, *W. B. Yeats*).

T[AYLOR]., G[EOFFREY]., *Bell*, v 5 (Feb 1943) 380–1 (a note on musical settings of Yeats's poems).

TAYLOR, J. R., 'William Butler Yeats and the Revival of Gaelic Literature', *Methodist Review*, LXV (Mar 1905) 189–202.

TENNYSON, CHARLES, 'Irish Plays and Playwrights', *Quarterly Review*, CCXV (July 1911) 219–43 *passim* (*Collected Works* (1908)).
'The Rise of the Irish Theatre', *Contemporary Review*, C 548 (Aug 1911) 240–7 (on the debt of Irish playwrights to Yeats).

T[ENNYSON]., C[HARLES]., 'Mr W. B. Yeats' Plays', *Contemporary Review*, CI 558 (June 1912) 902–3 (*Plays for an Irish Theatre*).

TERWILLIGER, PATRICIA J., 'A Re-Interpretation of Stanzas VII and VIII of W. B. Yeats's "Among School Children"', *Boston University Studies in English*, v 1 (spring 1961) 29–34.

TÉRY, SIMONE, 'W. B. Yeats, poète irlandais', *Grande Revue*, CXIII 2 (Dec 1923) 259–72.

THOMAS, JOHN O., 'W. B. Yeats Comes Home to Sligo', *Picture Post*, 9 Oct 1948, 10–13.

[THOMPSON, FRANCIS], review of *The Wanderings of Oisin*, *Weekly Register*, LXXXI 2127 (27 Sep 1890) 407–8. Reprinted in *The Real Robert Louis Stevenson*, ed. Rev. Terence J. Connolly, S.J., 201–3.
'William Butler Yeats', *Academy*, LI 1304 (1 May 1897) 467 (*The Secret Rose*). Reprinted in *Literary Criticisms by Francis Thompson*, ed. Rev. Terence L. Connolly, S.J., 370–3.
'Mr Yeats's Poems', *Academy*, LVI 1409 (6 May 1899) 501–2 (*The Wind Among the Reeds*; *Poems* (1899)). Reprinted in *The Real Robert Louis Stevenson*, ed. Rev. Terence L. Connolly, S.J., 203–9.
'A Schism in the Celtic Movement', *Academy*, LVII 1417 (1 July 1899) 8–10 (*Literary Ideals in Ireland* by John Eglinton and others). Reprinted in *Literary Criticisms by Francis Thompson*, ed. Rev. Terence L. Connolly, S.J., 326–32.
'The Irish Literary Movement: Mr Yeats as Shepherd', *Academy*, LVIII 1454 (17 Mar 1900) 235–6 (*A Book of Irish Verse*). Reprinted in *The Real Robert Louis Stevenson*, ed. Rev. Terence L. Connolly, S.J., 210–15.
'Fiona Macleod on Mr W. B. Yeats', *Academy*, LXIII 1590 (25 Oct 1902) 444–5 (reply to Fiona Macleod's article in *North American*

Review, q.v.). Reprinted in *Literary Criticisms by Francis Thompson*, ed. Rev. Terence L. Connolly, S.J., 373–6.

THOMPSON, FRANCIS J., 'Poetry and Politics: W. B. Yeats', *Hopkins Review*, III 1 (fall 1949) 3–17.

THOMPSON, KATE. *See* FORD, JULIA.

THWAITE, ANTHONY, 'Yeats and the Noh', *Twentieth Century*, CLXII (Sep 1957) 235–42.

TILLEKERATNE, NIHAL, 'The Lake Isle of Innisfree', *Community*, III 1 (Apr 1958) 57–8.

TINDALL, WILLIAM YORK, 'The Symbolism of W. B. Yeats', *Accent*, V 4 (summer 1945) 203–12. Also in his *Forces in Modern British Literature 1885–1946*, 248–63. Reprinted in *The Permanence of Yeats*, ed. James Hall and Martin Steinmann, 264–77 (238–49); revised version (1962) reprinted in *Yeats: A Collection of Critical Essays*, ed. John Unterecker, 43–53.

TODHUNTER, J., *Academy*, XXXV 882 (30 Mar 1889) 216–17 (*The Wanderings of Oisin*). *See also* ELLIS, S. M.

TOMLIN, E. W. F., 'The Continuity of Yeats', *Phoenix*, Yeats Centenary Number, no. 10 (summer 1965) 60–5 (on the 'continuity of diction' from the early to the later poems).

TOMLINSON, CHARLES, 'Pull Down thy Vanity', *Poetry* (Chicago), XCVIII 4 (July 1961) 263–6 (*Essays and Introductions*).

TORCHIANA, DONALD T., 'Senator Yeats, Burke and Able Men', *Newberry Library Bulletin*, V 8 (July 1961) 267–80.

'W. B. Yeats, Jonathan Swift, and Liberty', *Modern Philology*, LXI 1 (Aug 1963) 26–39.

'Some Dublin Afterthoughts', *Tri-Quarterly*, Yeats Centenary Issue, no. 4 (fall 1965) 138–43 (recollections of the Yeats Festival of the Northwestern University, spring 1965).

and O'MALLEY, GLENN, 'Some New Letters from W. B. Yeats to Lady Gregory', *Review of English Literature*, IV 3 (July 1963) 9–47 (prints twenty-three letters written between Mar 1912 and Oct 1920).

See also O'MALLEY, GLENN.

Townshend, G., 'Yeats's Dramatic Poems', *Drama*, no. 5 (Feb 1912) 192–208.

Trench, W. F., 'Dr Yeats and Mr Joyce', *Irish Statesman*, II (30 Aug 1924) 790 (on the Royal Academy's literary awards at the Tailteann Games, Aug 1924).

Trowbridge, Hoyt, '"Leda and the Swan": A Longinian Analysis', *Modern Philology*, LI 2 (Nov 1953) 118–29. *See* reply by Leo Spitzer, above.

Tucker, W. J., 'The Celt in Contemporary Literature', *Catholic World*, CXLVI (Mar 1938) 650–2.

Turner, W. J., 'Broadside Songs', *New Statesman*, X (7 Dec 1935) 848–50 (on the series of *Broadsides* edited by Yeats and F. R. Higgins, issued monthly during 1935, and published as *Broadsides: A Collection of Old and New Songs*, by Yeats and others with music by Arthur Duff. Wade 249).

'Music and Words', *New Statesman*, XIV (24 July 1937) 146–7.

'Yeats and Song-Writing', *New Statesman*, XVII (22 Apr 1939) 606–7.

'Words and Tones', *New Statesman*, XVIII (22 July 1939) 141–2 (Yeats and music).

'Three Impressions, II', *The Arrow*, W. B. Yeats Commemoration Number (summer 1939) 17–19. *See also* Gogarty, Oliver St John; Rothenstein, Sir William.

Tychsen, H. Draws-. *See* Draws-Tychsen, H.

Tyler, Dorothy, 'Carl Milles, Yeats and the Irish Coinage: A Friendship and a Fiasco', *Michigan Quarterly Review*, II 4 (autumn 1963) 273–80 (on Yeats's friendship with the Swedish sculptor who submitted designs for the new Irish currency).

Tynan, Katharine (Katharine Tynan Hinkson), 'Three Young Poets', *Irish Monthly*, XV 165 (Mar 1887) 166–8 (*Mosada*).

'William Butler Yeats', *Magazine of Poetry*, I 4 (Oct 1889) 454 (introduction to a selection of poems from *The Wanderings of Oisin and Other Poems*; editorial note on 'An Old Song Re-Sung').

'W. B. Yeats', *Bookman*, V (Oct 1893) 13–14; also in *Sketch*, IV 44 (20 Nov 1893) 256.

'Personal Memories of John Butler Yeats', *The Double-Dealer*, IV (July 1922) 8–15 (on Yeats and his father).

UNGER, LEONARD, 'The New Collected Yeats', *Poetry* (Chicago), LXXX 1 (Apr 1952) 43–51 (*Collected Poems*).

'Yeats and Milton', *South Atlantic Quarterly*, LXI 2 (spring 1962) 197–212 (on the influence of the *Areopagitica* on Yeats's prose).

UNTERECKER, JOHN, 'Yeats: Seer and Dramatist', *Yale Review*, LII 4 (June 1963) 585–8 (M. I. Seiden, *William Butler Yeats*; Helen Vendler, *Yeats's VISION and the Later Plays*).

'The Putting Together of William Butler Yeats', *Columbia University Forum*, VI 1 (winter 1963) 41–4 (on Yeats's revision of his poetry).

'The Shaping Force in Yeats's Plays', *Modern Drama*, VII 3 (Dec 1964) 345–56.

'An Interview with Anne Yeats', *Shenandoah*, XVI 4 (summer 1965) 7–20 (Miss Yeats discusses her personal experiences at the Abbey Theatre, and her memories of her father and his friends).

'W. B. Yeats: On his Centennial', *NYTB*, 13 June 1965, 7 (a centenary tribute).

(ed.), 'A Fair Chance of a Disturbed Ireland: W. B. Yeats to Mrs J. Duncan', *Massachusetts Review*, V 2 (winter 1964) 315–22 (letters written in 1918 to Mrs James Duncan, curator of Dublin's Municipal Gallery of Modern Art, now in the Special Collections Library of Columbia University). Reprinted in *Irish Renaissance*, ed. Robin Skelton and David R. Clark, 98–105.

URE, PETER, '"The Statues": A Note on the Meaning of Yeats's Poem', *Review of English Studies*, XXV 3 (July 1949) 254–7 ('The Statues' and *On The Boiler*).

'The Integrity of Yeats', *Cambridge Journal*, III 2 (Nov 1949) 80–93.

'Yeats and the Prophecy of Eunapius', *Notes and Queries*, n.s., 1 8 (Aug 1954) 358–9 (sources for *The Resurrection* in Cumont's *Astrology and Religion among the Greeks and Romans*, and Whitaker's *The Neo-Platonists*).

'Yeats's "Demon and Beast"', *Irish Writing*, W. B. Yeats: A Special Number, no. 31 (summer 1955) 42–50.

'Yeats' Supernatural Songs', *Review of English Studies*, VII 1 (Jan 1956) 38–51 (on the first four supernatural songs in *A Full Moon in March*).

'From Wordsworth to Yeats', *Listener*, LVIII (25 July 1957) 133–5 (John Bayley, *The Romantic Survival*; Frank Kermode, *Romantic Image*).

'A Source for Yeats's "Parnell's Funeral"', *English Studies*, XXXIX 6 (Dec 1958) 257–8 (Ezra Pound's translation of Sordello di Goito's planh for the Lord Blacatz as a source for Yeats's poem).

'Yeats and Mr Graves', *TLS*, 2989 (12 June 1959) 353 (a reply to Robert Graves's attack in *The Crowning Privilege* on Yeats's poetry).

'Yeats's Christian Mystery Plays', *Review of English Studies*, XI 2 (May 1960) 171–82 (*Calvary* and *The Resurrection*). Revised and reprinted as chap. vi of his *Yeats the Playwright*. See also Anon., 'Ideas into Drama',

'Yeats's Hero–Fool in *The Herne's Egg*', *Huntington Library Quarterly*, XXIV 2 (Feb 1961) 125–36. Reprinted with revisions as part of chap. vii of his *Yeats the Playwright*.

'Yeats's *Deirdre*', *English Studies*, XLII 4 (Aug 1961) 218–30. Revised and reprinted as chap. iii of his *Yeats the Playwright*.

'The Evolution of Yeats's *The Countess Cathleen*', *Modern Language Review*, LVII 1 (Jan 1962) 12–24. Reprinted with revisions as part of chapter i of his *Yeats the Playwright*.

'Yeats and the Two Harmonies', *Modern Drama*, VII 3 (Dec 1964) 237–55 (on Yeats's mingling of prose and verse in his plays).

'The Hero on the World Tree: Yeats's Plays', *English, W. B. Yeats: 1865–1939*, XV 89 (summer 1965) 169–72.

See also AUTY, R. A.

USSHER, ARLAND, 'The Magi', *Dublin Magazine*, XX 2 (Apr–June 1945) 18–21 (on Yeats, Shaw and Joyce).

UTLEY, FRANCIS LEE, 'Three Kinds of Honesty', *Journal of American Folk-Lore*, LXVI (1953) 189–99 ('The Scholars' and 'The Leaders of the Crowd', 192–3).

V., A. W., and 'PSYCHOLOGIST', 'Voice and Verse', *Notes and Queries*, CLXXV (3 July 1943) 20–1 (replies to S. Musgrove, q.v.).

VALLETTE, JACQUES, 'Un mot sur Yeats', *Mercure de France*, CCCX (Nov 1950) 566–8 (Richard Ellmann, *Yeats: The Man and the Masks*: A. Norman Jeffares, *W. B. Yeats: Man and Poet*).

VAN DOORN, WILLEM, 'William Butler Yeats: A Lopsided Study', *English Studies*, II 9 (June 1920) 65–77. Reprinted as a pamphlet (Amsterdam: Swets & Zweitlinger, 1920) pp. 16.

'How it Strikes a Contemporary, II; W. B. Yeats', *English Studies*, V 6 (Dec 1923) 202–5 (*Later Poems*; *Plays in Prose and Verse*).

VAN HAMEL, ANTON GERARD, 'On Anglo-Irish Syntax', *Englische Studien*, XLV 2 (Sep 1912) 272–93 (*The Unicorn from the Stars* and *Cathleen ni Houlihan* as examples).

VAN MAANEN, WILLEM, 'Voorwoord. *Deirdre* door William Butler Yeats', *Onze Eeuw*, XXIV iii 3 (Sep 1924) 193–5.

VENDLER, HELEN HENNESSY, 'Yeats's Changing Metaphors for the Otherworld', *Modern Drama*, VIII 3 (Dec 1964) 308–21 (on the imagined 'Otherworlds' presented in Yeats's plays).

VESTDIJK, S., 'Kroniek van de poezie: Nestoriaansche overpeinzingen', *Gids*, CXIX 3 (Mar 1956) 203–9 (on A. Roland Holst's translations of Yeats's works).

VICKERY, JOHN B., 'The Golden Bough and Modern Poetry', *Journal of Aesthetics and Art Criticism*, XV 3 (Mar 1957) 271–88 (on the indebtedness of Yeats and other poets to Sir James Frazer's *The Golden Bough*). *See also* ALLEN, J. L.; SPANOS, W. V.

'Three Modes and a Myth', *Western Humanities Review*, XII 4 (autumn 1958) 371–8 (on the Leda myth as used by Yeats, Aldous Huxley and Robert Graves).

'Golden Bough: Impact and Archetype', *Virginia Quarterly Review*, XXXIX 1 (winter 1963) 37–57.

†VICTOR, P., 'Magie et sociétés secrètes: L'Ordre Hermétique de la Golden Dawn', *Tour Saint-Jacques*, nos. 2–3 (Jan–Apr 1956).

VIERECK, P., 'Technique and Inspiration', *Atlantic Monthly*, CLXXXIX (Jan 1952) 81–3 (*Collected Poems*).

VON HEISELER, BERNT, 'Erzählungen und Lyrik', *Deutsche Zeitschrift* XLVII 11–12 (Aug–Sep 1934) 579–80 (*Collected Poems*).

'William Butler Yeats', *Neue Rundschau*, yr 50, II 8 (Aug 1939) 142–9 (an appreciation).

'William Butler Yeats', *Sammlung*, II (1949) 257–63.

WADE, ALLAN (ed.), 'Some Letters from W. B. Yeats to John O'Leary and His Sister. From the Berg Collection', *Bulletin of the New York Public Library*, LVII 1 (Jan 1953) 11–22; ibid., 2 (Feb 1953) 76–87 (with editorial comment and annotation). Wade p. 395.

WAIN, JOHN, 'The Meaning of Yeats', *Observer*, 13 June 1965, 26 (a centenary tribute).

See also FRASER, G. S., 'Yeats's "Byzantium"'.

WAKEFIELD, DAN, 'Sailing to Byzantium: Yeats and the Young Mind', *Nation*, CLXXXII (24 June 1956) 531–2.

WALCUTT, CHARLES C., 'Yeats' "Among School Children" and "Sailing to Byzantium"', *Explicator*, VIII 6 (Apr 1950) item 42.

W[ALKLEY]., A. B., 'Mr W. B. Yeats and *The Wind Among the Reeds*', *Academy*, LVIII 1446 (20 Jan 1900) 63 (includes announcement that for this book Yeats received the Poetry Award 1899, 25 guineas).

WALL, RICHARD J., and FITZGERALD, ROGER, 'Yeats and Jung: An Ideological Comparison', *Literature and Psychology*, XIII 2 (spring 1963) 44–52.

W[ALSH]., E. R., 'Some Reminiscences of W. B. Yeats', *Irish Times*, 10 Feb 1940.

WALSH, WILLIAM, 'Columbia and Byzantium: The Notion of Character in Education and Literature', *Cambridge Journal*, VII (Nov 1955) 101–13.

WALTON, EDA LOU, 'Cast Out Remorse', *Nation*, CXXXVII (13 Dec 1933) 684–6 (*Collected Poems*; *The Winding Stair*).

'Lend a Myth to God', *Nation*, CLXVII (9 July 1938) 51–2 (*A Vision*; *The Herne's Egg and Other Plays*).

WARNER, FRANCIS, 'Explorations in Poetic Growth', *Western Mail*, 16 Jan 1965, 5 (a centenary tribute).

WARNER, REX, 'Modern English Poetry', *International Literature*. no. 7 (July 1939) 81–2.

'Yeats in his Youth', *Spectator*, CXCI 6526 (24 July 1953) 108 (*Letters to Katharine Tynan*).

WARREN, AUSTIN, 'William Butler Yeats: The Religion of a Poet', *Southern Review*, VII 3 (winter 1941–2) 624–38 (on the significance of Yeats's occult studies). Reprinted in his *Rage for Order*, 66–84, and in *The Permanence of Yeats*, ed. James Hall and Martin Steinmann, 223–36 (200–12).

WARREN, C. HENRY, 'William Butler Yeats', *Bookman*, LXXXII 492 (Sep 1932) 284–6.

WARREN, RAYMOND, 'An Idea of Music', *Threshold*, no. 19, The Theatre of W. B. Yeats Centenary, 1965 (autumn 1965) 64–73 (the place of music in Yeats's plays).

WARSCHAUSKY, SIDNEY, 'Yeats's Purgatorial Plays', *Modern Drama*, VII 3 (Dec 1964) 274–86 (*The Dreaming of the Bones, The Words upon the Window-Pane,* and *Purgatory*).

WATKINS, VERNON, 'W. B. Yeats: The Religious Poet', *Texas Studies in Literature and Language*, III 4 (winter 1962) 475–88 (contrasts the early with the later poems).

See also AUTY, R. A.

WATSON, THOMAS L., 'The French Reputation of W. B. Yeats', *Comparative Literature*, XII 3 (summer 1960) 256–62 (despite recent translations, Yeats's works are still relatively unknown in France).

WATSON-WILLIAMS, HELEN, 'All the Olympians: W. B. Yeats and His Friends', *English*, XIV 83 (summer 1963) 178–84 (on Yeats's friends, and the significance of the references to them in his poetry).

WATTS, HAROLD, 'Yeats: Poetry and "Solutions"', *Poetry* (New York), I (1949) 15–21.

'W. B. Yeats: Theology Bitter and Gay', *South Atlantic Quarterly*, XLIX (July 1950) 359–77 (on Yeats's religious thought). Reprinted as chapter xiv of his *Hound and Quarry*, 188–208.

'Yeats and Lapsed Mythology', *Renascence*, III (1951) 107–12 (on Yeats's use of mythology). Reprinted as chap. xiii of his *Hound and Quarry*, 174–87.

WEBB, W. L., 'Ireland's Tongue', *Guardian*, 12 June 1965, 65, 67 (a centenary tribute).

WEEKS, DONALD, 'Image and Idea in Yeats' "The Second Coming"', *PMLA*, LXIII 1 (Mar 1948) 281–92.

WEYGANDT, CORNELIUS, 'With Mr W. B. Yeats in the Woods at Coole', *Lippincott's Magazine*, LXXIII (Apr 1904) 484–7 (recalls an afternoon's walk with the poet). Reprinted in his *Tuesdays at Ten*, 176–85.

WHALLEY, GEORGE, 'Yeats's Mind', *Yale Review*, XXXIX 1 (Sep 1949) 165–7 (Donald Stauffer, *The Golden Nightingale*; Richard Ellmann, *Yeats: The Man and the Masks*).

'Yeats' Quarrel with Old Age', *Queen's Quarterly*, LVIII 4 (winter 1951–2) 497–507 (on Yeats's last poems).

WHEELER, ETHEL, 'The Fairyland of Heart's Desire', *Great Thoughts*, XXXVI (Oct 1901) 375–6.

WHITAKER, THOMAS R., 'The Dialectic of Yeats's Vision of History', *Modern Philology*, LVII 2 (Nov 1959) 100–12 (on Yeats's changing attitude to history from 1889 to 1919, as reflected in 'The Valley of the Black Pig', 'The Magi' and 'The Double Vision of Michael Robartes'). Revised and reprinted as chap. iv of his *Swan and Shadow*.

'The Early Yeats and the Pattern of History', *PMLA*, LXXV 2 (June 1960) 320–8 (on the development of Yeats's cyclical vision of history). Revised and reprinted as chap. ii of his *Swan and Shadow*.

'Yeats's Alembic', *Sewanee Review*, LXVIII 4 (Dec 1960) 576–94 (on Yeats's occultism and his 'apocalyptic romances' – 'Rosa Alchemica', 'The Tables of the Law' and 'The Adoration of the Magi'). Revised and reprinted as chap. iii of his *Swan and Shadow*.

'Yeats's "Dove or Swan"', *PMLA*, LXXVI 1 (Mar 1961) 121–32 (on Yeats's transmutation and symbolic use of historical 'fact'). Reprinted as part of chap. v of his *Swan and Shadow*).

WHITE, ALISON, 'Yeats' "Byzantium" 20, and "Sailing to Byzantium" 30–32', *Explicator*, XIII 1 (Nov 1954) item 8.

W[HITE]., H. O., 'Mr W. B. Yeats: A Brief Study of his Poetry', *Sheffield Daily Telegraph*, 23 Nov 1922, 3.

WHITE, S. J., 'Foreword', *Irish Writing*, no. 31 (summer 1955) 7–8 (*Autobiographies*).

WHITE, TERENCE DE VERE, 'The Social Mask of the Poet', *Irish Times*, W. B. Yeats Centenary Supplement, 10 June 1965, iii–iv (on Yeats as a public figure).

WHITRIDGE, ARNOLD, 'William Butler Yeats 1865–1939', *Dalhousie Review*, XIX 1 (Apr 1939) 1–8.

WIJNGAARDS, NICOLAAS, 'The Shadowy Waters van W. B. Yeats en A. Roland Holst', *Spiegel der Letteren*, VI 3 (1963) 197–209 (on Yeats's influence on Roland Holst).

WILDE, OSCAR, 'Some Literary Notes, II', *Woman's World* (1889) 221–2; 'Some Literary Notes, III', ibid., 278 (*Fairy and Folk Tales of the Irish Peasantry* and *The Wanderings of Oisin*). Reprinted in his *Collected Works*, vol. VIII, 406–11, 437–9.

'Three New Poets', *Pall Mall Gazette*, 12 July 1899, 3 (*The Wanderings of Oisin*). Reprinted in his *Collected Works*, vol. VIII, 524–5.

WILDI, MAX, 'The Influence and Poetic Development of W. B. Yeats', *English Studies*, XXXVI 5 (Oct 1955) 246–53 (on the influence of Arthur Symons and Ezra Pound on Yeats).

WILKINSON, M., 'Talk with John Butler Yeats about his Son, William Butler Yeats', *Touchstone*, VI (Oct 1919) 10–17.

'Irish Literature Discussed by William Butler Yeats', *Touchstone*, VIII (Nov 1920) 81–5 (an interview with the poet).

WILLCOX, LOUISE COLLIER, 'The Poetic Drama', *North American Review*, CLXXXVI 622 (Sep 1907) 91–7 (*Poetical Works in Two Volumes* and works by other writers).

WILLIAMS, RAYMOND, 'Criticism into Drama, 1888–1950', *Essays in Criticism*, I 2 (Apr 1951) 120–38 (on Shaw and Yeats).

WILLIAMSON, HUGH ROSS, correspondence, *TLS*, 3157 (31 Aug 1962) 657 ('On a Picture of a Black Centaur by Edmund Dulac').

WILLY, MARGARET, 'The Poetry of Donne: His Interest and Influence Today', *Essays and Studies*, VII (1954) 78–104 (on Donne and Yeats, 100–2).

W[ILLY]., M[ARGARET]., 'In Excited Reverie', *English*, W. B. Yeats: 1865–1939, XV 89 (summer 1965) 185–6 (*In Excited Reverie*, ed. A. N. Jeffares and K. G. W. Cross).

WILSON, EDMUND, 'W. B. Yeats', *New Republic*, XLII (15 Apr 1925) 8–10 (*Later Poems*; *Plays in Prose and Verse*; *Plays and Controversies*; *Essays*).

'Yeats's Memoirs', *New Republic*, L (23 Feb 1927) 22–3 (*Autobiographies*).

'Proust and Yeats', *New Republic*, LII (5 Oct 1927) 176–7, 179.

'W. B. Yeats', *New Republic*, LVII (16 Jan 1929) 249–51 (*A Vision*).

'W. B. Yeats', *New Republic*, LX (25 Sep 1929) 141–8.

WILSON, F. A. C., 'Patterns in Yeats's Imagery: *The Herne's Egg*', *Modern Philology*, LV 1 (Aug 1957) 46–52. A revised version forms part of chap. iii of his *W. B. Yeats and Tradition*.

'Symbolic Equations', *New Statesman*, LV (1 Mar 1958) 273 (*The Variorum Edition of the Poems*). Reply by Helen Gardner, ibid. (8 Mar) 305.

'Yeats's Last Poems', *Moderna Språk*, LIV 1 (1960) 10–19.

'Yeats and Gerhart Hauptmann', *Southern Review* (Adelaide), 1 (1963) 69–73 (*Hauptmann's Die Versunkene Glocke* and *The Only Jealousy of Emer*).

WIND, EDGAR, 'Raphael: The Dead Child and Dolphin', *TLS*, 3217 (25 Oct 1963) 874 (on a Yeats query, *Letters of W. B. Yeats and T. Sturge Moore*, p. 165); correspondence by Margaret Whinney, ibid., 3219 (7 Nov) 907, and James Tudor-Craig, ibid., 3221 (21 Nov) 956.

WINTERS, YVOR, '*The Poems of T. Sturge Moore, Volumes I and II*', *Hound and Horn*, VI 3 (Apr–June 1933) 534–45 (Sturge Moore and W. B. Yeats. *See* reply by Theodore Spencer, 'William Butler Yeats').

'The Poetry of W. B. Yeats', *Twentieth Century Literature*, VI 1 (Apr 1960) 3–24. Reprinted as *The Poetry of W. B. Yeats*, and in *Dubliner*, no. 2 (May 1962) 7–33. Replies by Basil Payne, correspondence, *Irish Times*, 31 Mar 1962, 9; 7 Apr, 7, 12; and by James Liddy, ibid., 4 Apr, 7; *TLS* 3286 (18 Feb 1965) 126.

WITT, MARION, 'Yeats' "The Wild Swans at Coole"', *Explicator*, III 2 (Nov 1944) item 17.

'Yeats' "Mohini Chatterjee"', *Explicator*, IV 8 (June 1946) item 60.

'Yeats' "A Dialogue of Self and Soul"', *Explicator*, V 7 (May 1947) item 48.

'Yeats' "When You Are Old"', *Explicator*, VI 1 (Oct 1947) item 6.

'Yeats's Hare', correspondence, *TLS*, 2385 (18 Oct 1947) 535 ('The Collar-Bone of a Hare', 'Two Songs of a Fool'). *See* SAUL, G. B.

'Yeats' "The Moods"', *Explicator*, VI 3 (Dec 1947) item 15.

'Yeats' "The Collar-Bone of a Hare"', *Explicator*, VII 3 (Dec 1948) item 21.

'A Note on Joyce and Yeats', *Modern Language Notes*, LXIII 8 (Dec 1948) 552–3 ('A palpable hit at Yeats in *Ulysses*').

'A Competition for Eternity: Yeats's Revision of His Later Poems', *PMLA*, LXIV 1 (Mar 1949) 40–58.

'The Making of an Elegy: Yeats's "In Memory of Major Robert Gregory"', *Modern Philology*, XLVIII 2 (Nov 1950) 112–21.

'Yeats' "To His Heart, Bidding It Have No Fear"', *Explicator*, IX 5 (Mar 1951) item 32.

'Yeats on the Poet Laureateship', *Modern Language Notes*, LXVI 6 (June 1951) 385–8.

'"Great Art Beaten Down": Yeats on Censorship', *College English*, XIII 5 (Feb 1952) 248–58.

'Yeats's "The Song of the Happy Shepherd"', *Philological Quarterly*, XXXII 1 (Jan 1953) 1–8 (on the holograph in the National Library, Dublin).

'An Unknown Yeats Poem', *Modern Language Notes*, LXX 1 (Jan 1955) 26 (reprints 'The Glove and the Cloak' from *Roma* (1897); *see* Wade 295A and *The Variorum Edition of the Poems*, p. 744).

'A Note on Yeats and Symons', *Notes and Queries*, n.s., VII 12 (Dec 1960) 467–9.

'Yeats: 1865–1965', *PMLA*, LXXX 4 (Sep 1965) 311–20 (a centenary tribute).

See also Part I.

WORSLEY, T. C., 'A Poet's Father', *New Statesman*, XXVII (2 Apr 1944) 229–30 (J. M. Hone (ed.), *J. B. Yeats' Letters*).

WRENN, C. L., 'W. B. Yeats: A Literary Study', *Durham University Journal*, XXII 3 (July 1919) 82–8; ibid., 4 (Nov 1919) 118–25. Reprinted as his *W. B. Yeats: A Literary Study*.

WYATT, E. V., 'The Dail and the Druids', *Commonweal*, XXXVII 26 (16 Apr 1943) 637–40 (general article prompted by J. M. Hone's *W. B. Yeats 1865–1939*).

YEOMANS, EDWARD, 'W. B. Yeats and the "Electric Motor Vision"', *Alphabet*, no. 7 (Dec 1963) 44–8 (Yeats's aesthetic system resembles 'a machine in perpetual oscillation').

YOUNGBLOOD, SARAH, 'A Reading of "The Tower"', *Twentieth Century Literature*, v 2 (July 1959) 74–84.

'The Structure of Yeats's Long Poems', *Criticism*, v 3 (fall 1963) 323–35.

Z., O., 'From a Modern Irish Portrait Gallery, V. – W. B. Yeats', *New Ireland Review*, II 10 (Dec 1894) 647–59 (a general study).

ZABEL, MORTON DAUWEN, 'The Summers of Hesperides', *Poetry* (Chicago), XLIII 5 (Feb 1934) 279–87 (*Collected Poems* (1933); *The Winding Stair*).

'Poetry for the Theatre', *Poetry* (Chicago), XLV 3 (Dec 1934) 152–6 (*Collected Plays*).

'Two Years of Poetry', *Southern Review*, v 3 (winter 1939–40) 605–8 (*New Poems* (1938); *Essays* (1931–6); *Last Poems and Two Plays*; Yeats and Rilke compared).

'The Last of Yeats', *Nation*, CLI (12 Oct 1940) 333–5 (*Last Poems and Plays*; *Letters on Poetry from W. B. Yeats to Dorothy Wellesley*).

'The Thinking of the Body: Yeats in the *Autobiographies*', *Southern Review*, VII 3 (winter 1941–2) 562–90.

'Yeats: The Image and the Book', *Nation*, CLVI (6 Mar 1943) 348–50 (J. M. Hone, *W. B. Yeats 1865–1939*; Louis MacNeice, *The Poetry of W. B. Yeats*). Reprinted with revision in *The Permanence of Yeats*, ed. James Hall and Martin Steinmann, 352–64 (315–26).

Z[ABEL]., M[ORTON]. D[AUWEN]., 'Yeats at Thirty and Seventy', *Poetry* (Chicago), XLVII 5 (Feb 1936) 268–77.

ZWERDLING, ALEX, 'W. B. Yeats: Variations on the Visionary Quest', *University of Toronto Quarterly*, XXX 1 (Oct 1960) 72–85 (on Yeats's esoteric thought). Reprinted in *Yeats: A Collection of Critical Essays*, ed. John Unterecker, 80–92.

ADDENDUM TO PART V

DUNCAN, MARGARET S., 'New England Dawn and Celtic
Twilight: Notes on the Philosophy of Henry Thoreau and
the Poems of W. B. Yeats', *Theosophical Review*, XVII 157 (15
Sep 1900) 63–72.

Part VI

DISSERTATIONS
AND
THESES

I. DOCTORAL DISSERTATIONS

ABOOD, EDWARD F., 'The Reception of the Abbey Theatre in America', Chicago, 1962.

ADAMS, HAZARD S., 'Structure of Myth in the Poetry of William Blake and William Butler Yeats', Washington, 1953.

ALLEN, JAMES LOVIC, JR, 'Bird Symbolism in the Work of William Butler Yeats', Florida, 1959. *Dissertation Abstracts*, XX 8 (Feb 1960) 3288.

ALLT, GEORGE D. P., 'The Anglo-Irish Movement in Relation to its Antecedents', St Catharine's, Cambridge, 1953.

ALSPACH, RUSSELL KING, 'A Consideration of the Poets of the Literary Revival in Ireland, 1889–1929', Pennsylvania, 1932 (published in part as *Irish Poetry of the Celtic Renaissance*).

BACHCHAN, HARBANS RAI, 'William Butler Yeats and Occultism: A Study of his Works in Relation to Indian Lore, the Cabbala, Swedenborg, Boehme and Theosophy', St Catharine's, Cambridge, 1954.

BAGG, ROBERT ELY, 'The Sword Upstairs: Essays on the Theory and Historical Development of Autobiographical Poetry', Connecticut, 1965. *Dissertation Abstracts*, XXVI 9 (Mar 1966) 5408.

BARLEY, JOSEPH WAYNE. *See* Part III.

BECKER, A. W. J., 'Yeats as Playwright' (title given as 'The Work of William Butler Yeats in the Field of Drama' in *Index to Theses*, III (1952–3)), Wadham, Oxford, 1953.

BECKSON, KARL E., 'The Rhymers' Club', Columbia, 1959. *Dissertation Abstracts*, XX 3 (Sep 1959) 1021–2.

BENSON, CARL F., 'A Study of Yeats's *A Vision*', Illinois, 1949.

BENSTON, ALICE NAOMI, 'Theatricality in Contemporary Drama', Emory, 1962. *Dissertation Abstracts*, XXIV 5 (Nov 1963) 2026–7.

BERRYMAN, CHARLES BEECHER, 'W. B. Yeats: Design of Opposites', Yale, 1965. *Dissertation Abstracts*, XXVI 8 (Feb 1966) 4624.

BIENS, FRIEDRICH. *See* Part III.

BLAU, HERBERT, 'W. B. Yeats and T. S. Eliot: Poetic Drama and Modern Poetry', Stanford, 1954. *Dissertation Abstracts*, XIV 3 (Mar 1954) 523–4.

BOSE, ABINASH, 'Mysticism in Poetry: A Study of A. E., W. B. Yeats and Rabindranath Tagore', Trinity College, Dublin, 1937.

BRENNAN, SR MARY JEANNETTE, 'Irish Folk History in Drama', Niagara, 1946.

BRUEGGEMANN, THEODOR, 'Das christliche Element in W. B. Yeats dichterischer Symbolik', Münster, 1954.

BRUGSMA, REBECCA P. C., 'The Beginnings of the Irish Revival', Amsterdam, 1933.

BURKHART, CHARLES JOSEPH, 'The Letters of George Moore to Edmund Gosse, W. B. Yeats, R. I. Best, Miss Nancy Cunard and Mrs Mary Hutchinson', Maryland, 1958. *Dissertation Abstracts*, XIX 1 (July 1958) 131.

BUSHRUI, SUHAIL BADI, 'Adam's Curse: A Study of Yeats's Revisions of his Verse Plays, 1900–1910', Southampton, 1962.

BYARS, JOHN ARTHUR, 'The Heroic Type in the Irish Legendary Dramas of W. B. Yeats, Lady Gregory and J. M Synge, 1903–1910', North Carolina, 1963. *Dissertation Abstracts*, XXIV 8 (Feb 1964) 3333.

CASWELL, ROBERT W., 'Sean O'Casey as a Poetic Dramatist', Trinity College, Dublin, 1960 (includes unpublished letters from Yeats).

CLARK, DAVID R., 'W. B. Yeats as a Dramatist', Yale, 1955.

CLEYMAET, R., 'The Poetry of W. B. Yeats', Ghent, 1936.

COLE, ALAN S., 'Stagecraft in the Modern Dublin Theatre', Trinity College, Dublin, 1952.

CONNER, LESTER IRVIN, 'A Yeats Dictionary: Names of the Persons and Places in the Poetry of W. B. Yeats', Columbia, 1964.

COPELAND, TOM W., 'The Proper Names in William Butler Yeats's Non-Dramatic Poetry: An Annotated Index', Texas Technical College, 1957.

CORNWELL, ETHEL F., 'The "Still Point" in Modern Literature', Tulane, 1955–6.

DAVIS, DOROTHY R., 'Parallelism between Classical Tragedy and the Tragedy of William Butler Yeats', Boston, 1937.

DAVIS, ROBERT BERNARD, 'The Shaping of an Agate: A Study of the Development of the Literary Theory of W. B. Yeats from 1885 to 1910', Chicago, 1956.

DE MAN, PAUL MICHAEL, 'Mallarmé, Yeats and the Post–Romantic Predicament', Harvard, 1961.

DENTON, MARILYN JEWELL, 'The Form of Yeats's Lyric Poetry', Wisconsin, 1957. *Dissertation Abstracts*, XVII 12 (Dec 1957) 3012.

DONOGHUE, DENIS, 'A Study of Modern English Verse Drama', National University of Ireland, 1958.

DUME, THOMAS L., 'William Butler Yeats: A Study of his Reading', Temple, 1950.

DUNCAN, JOSEPH E., 'The Revival of Seventeenth Century Metaphysical Poetry, Chiefly in England, 1800–1912', Columbia, 1951.

EDWARDS, JOHN HAMILTON, 'A Critical Biography of Ezra Pound, 1885–1922', Berkeley, California, 1952.

EGERER, Sr MARY ANNE VERONICA, 'The Rogueries of William Butler Yeats', Radcliffe College, 1962.

ELLMANN, RICHARD D., 'Triton Among the Streams: A Study of the Life and Writings of William Butler Yeats', Yale, 1947.

ENGELBERG, EDWARD, 'The Herald of Art: A Study of W. B. Yeats' Criticism and Aesthetic', Wisconsin, 1958.

FARAG, FAHMY FAWZY, 'Oriental Mysticism in W. B. Yeats', Edinburgh, 1960.

FARMER, ALBERT J., 'Le mouvement esthétique et "décadent" en Angleterre (1873–1900)', Paris, 1931.

FAULK, CAROLYN SUE, 'The Apollonian and Dionysian Modes in Lyric Poetry and their Development in the Poetry of W. B. Yeats and Dylan Thomas', Illinois, 1963. *Dissertation Abstracts*, XXIV 10 (Apr 1964) 4173–4.

FEICHTNER, WALTER, 'Das Wiederaufleben des englisches Versdramas im zwanzigsten Jahrhundert', Vienna, 1951.

FRANKLIN, LAURA MABEL, 'The Development of Yeats' Poetic Diction', Northwestern, 1956. *Dissertation Abstracts*, XVI 12 (Dec 1956) 2456.

GARAB, ARRA M., 'Beyond Byzantium: Studies in the Later Poetry of W. B. Yeats', Columbia, 1962.

GARBATY, THOMAS J., '*The Savoy*, 1896: A Re-edition of Representative Prose and Verse, with Critical Introduction, and Biographical and Critical Notes', Pennsylvania, 1957. *Dissertation Abstracts*, XVII 12 (Dec 1957) 3014–15.

GERSTENBERGER, DONNA LORINE, 'The Formal Experiments in Modern Verse Drama', Oklahoma, 1958. *Dissertation Abstracts*, XIX 7 (Jan 1959) 1757–8.

GLASSER, MARVIN, 'The Early Poetry of Tennyson and Yeats: A Comparative Study', New York, 1962. *Dissertation Abstracts*, XXIV 10 (Apr 1964) 4174.

GOLDGAR, HARRY, 'Deux dramaturges symbolistes: Villiers de l'Isle-Adam et William Butler Yeats', Paris, 1948.

GOLDMAN, MICHAEL PAUL, 'The Point of Drama: The Concept of Reverie in the Plays of William Butler Yeats', Princeton, 1962. *Dissertation Abstracts*, XXIII 9 (Mar 1963) 3373–4.

GOODMAN, HENRY, 'The Plays of William Butler Yeats as Myth and Ritual', Minnesota, 1953. *Dissertation Abstracts*, XIII 6 (Dec 1953) 1193–4.

GRAB, FREDERIC DANIEL, 'William Butler Yeats and Greek Literature', Berkeley, California, 1965. *Dissertation Abstracts*, XXVI 2 (Aug 1956) 1040–1.

GREEN, HOWARD L., 'The Poetry of W. B. Yeats: A Critical Evaluation', Stanford, 1952.

GRILL, RICHARD, 'Der junge Yeats und der französische Symbolismus', Fribourg, 1952.

GROSS, HARVEY S., 'The Contrived Corridor: A Study in Modern Poetry and the Meaning of History', Michigan, 1955.

GROSSMAN, ALLEN R., 'The Last Judgment of the Imagination: A Study of Yeats' *The Wind Among the Reeds*', Brandeis, 1960.

GUHA, NARESH, 'W. B. Yeats: An Indian Approach', Northwestern, 1962. *Dissertation Abstracts*, XXIII 12 (June 1963) 4684.

GURD, PATTY. *See* Part III.

HAHN, Sr M. NORMA, 'Yeats' Search for Reality: A Study of the Imagery of his Later Poetry', Fordham, 1960.

HASSAN, IHAB H., 'French Symbolism and Modern British Poetry, with Yeats, Eliot and Edith Sitwell as Indices', Pennsylvania, 1953. *Dissertation Abstracts*, XIII 2 (1953) 232–3.

HETHMON, ROBERT HENRY, Jr, 'The Theatre's Anti-Self: A Study of the Symbolism of Yeats's Unpopular Plays', Stanford, 1957. *Dissertation Abstracts*, XVII 4 (Apr 1957) 917.

HOARE, AGNES M., 'The Works of Morris and Yeats in Relation to Early Saga Literature', Cambridge, 1930.

HOLTON, ROSEMARY T., 'A Study of Romanticism in the Lyric Poetry of William Butler Yeats', Ottawa, 1952.

HUBERT, CLAIRE MARCOM, 'The Still Point of the Turning World: A Comparison of the Myths of Gerard de Nerval and W. B. Yeats', Emory, 1965. *Dissertation Abstracts*, XXVI 2 (Aug 1965) 1042.

HUETTEMANN, GERTA. *See* Part III.

HURWITZ, HAROLD MARVIN, 'Rabindranath Tagore and England', Illinois, 1959. *Dissertation Abstracts*, XX 8 (Feb 1960) 3294–5.

ISHIBASHI, HIRO, 'W. B. Yeats and the Noh', Keiō (Japan), 1956.

JAMESON, GRACE E., 'Mysticism in AE and Yeats in Relation to Oriental and American Thought', Ohio State, 1932. *Ohio State University Abstracts of Doctors' Dissertations*, no. 9 (1932) 144–51.

JEFFARES, ALEXANDER NORMAN, 'The Sources and Symbolism of the Later Poems of William Butler Yeats', Trinity College, Dublin, 1945.

JOHNSON, JOHN CURTIS, '*The Academy*, 1869–1896: Centre of Informed Critical Opinion', Northwestern, 1958. *Dissertation Abstracts*, XIX 6 (Dec 1958) 1382–3.

KALDECK, WILHELM, 'Die Deirdre-Sage und ihre Bearbeitungen', Vienna, 1924.

KEEP, WILLIAM CORBIN, 'Yeats and the Public', Washington, 1965.

KELSON, JOHN HOFSTAD, 'Nationalism in the Theatre: The Ole Bull Theatre in Norway and the Abbey Theatre in Ireland: A Comparative Study', Kansas, 1963. *Dissertation Abstracts*, XXIV 12 (June 1964) 5387.

KERSNOWSKI, FRANK LOUIS, Jr, 'The Irish Scene in Yeats's Drama', Kansas, 1963. *Dissertation Abstracts*, XXIV 12 (June 1964) 5409.

KHAN, S. W., 'Indian Elements in the Work of Yeats, Eliot and Huxley', Nottingham, 1956.

KOSTKA, Sr MARIA. *See* Part III.

KRIEGER, HANS, 'John Millington Synge, ein Dichter der "keltischen Renaissance"', Marburg, 1914 (includes a comparison of AE's, Yeats's and Synge's *Deirdre*).

LEVINE, BERNARD, 'The Dissolving Image: A Concentrative Analysis of Yeats's Poetry', Brown, 1965. *Dissertation Abstracts*, XXVI 6 (Dec 1965) 3341–2.

LINEBARGER, JAMES MORRIS, 'Yeats' Symbolist Method and the Play *Purgatory*', Emory, 1963. *Dissertation Abstracts*, XXIV 9 (Mar 1964) 3750–1.

LINEHAN, MARY C., 'Mysticism and Some Irish Writers: An Examination of the Works of George Russell (AE), William Butler
Yeats, and John Eglinton', Pennsylvania State, 1928.

LYMAN, KENNETH COX, 'Critical Reaction to Irish Drama on the
New York Stage: 1900–1958', Wisconsin, 1960. *Dissertation
Abstracts*, XXI 3 (Sep 1960) 699.

MACHAC, LEOPOLD, 'William Butler Yeats als Mystiker und
Symbolist', Vienna, 1953.

McHENRY, MARGARET, 'The Ulster Theatre in Ireland', Pennsylvania, 1931.

McLEOD, STUART R., 'Problems of Poetry and Dramaturgy in
Modern Verse Drama', Florida, Gainsville, 1961.

MADDEN, REGINA D., 'The Literary Criticism of the Irish Renaissance', Boston, 1938.

MANDL, OTTO W., 'Rational Elements in the Poetry of William
Butler Yeats', Vienna, 1953.

MANVELL, ARNOLD ROGER, 'A Study of W. B. Yeats' Poetic Career
with Special Reference to his Lyrical Poems', London, 1938.

MENON, V. K. NARAYANA, 'The Development of the Poetry of
W. B. Yeats', Edinburgh, 1940.

MERCHANT, FRANCIS JOHN, 'The Place of AE in Irish Culture',
New York, 1951. *Dissertation Abstracts*, XII 2 (1952) 188–9.

MERRITT, ROBERT GRAY, 'Euripides and Yeats: The Parallel Pro-
gression of their Plays', Tulane, 1963. *Dissertation Abstracts*, XXIV
8 (Feb 1964) 3463.

MILLER, MARCIA SCHUYLER KELLEY, 'The Deirdre Legend in
English Literature', Pennsylvania, 1950. *Dissertation Abstracts*, XIII
5 (Oct 1953) 798.

MINER, EARL ROY, 'The Japanese Influence on English and American
Literature, 1850 to 1950', Minnesota, 1955. *Dissertation Abstracts*,
XV 6 (June 1955) 1075.

MOHR, MARTIN ALFRED, 'The Political and Social Thought of
William Butler Yeats', Iowa, 1964. *Dissertation Abstracts*, XXV
4 (Oct 1964) 2497–8.

MOKASHI, S. R., 'The Later Phase in the Development of W. B.
Yeats', Karnatak, Dharwar, 1963 (includes unpublished letters
from Yeats to Shri Purohit Swami).

MOLONEY, Sr M. FRANCIS INÉS, 'Katharine Tynan Hinkson: A
Study of Her Poetry', Pennsylvania, 1952.

MOORE, JOHN REES, 'Evolution of Myth in the Plays of W. B. Yeats', Columbia, 1957. *Dissertation Abstracts*, XVII 7 (July 1957) 1556–7.

MOORE, VIRGINIA, 'Religion and William Butler Yeats', Columbia, 1952. *Dissertation Abstracts*, XII 4 (1952) 427.

MURPHY, DANIEL JOSEPH, 'The Letters of Lady Gregory to John Quinn', Columbia, 1961. *Dissertation Abstracts*, XXII 9 (Mar 1962) 3204.

NARDIN, F. L., 'A Study of Tragic Situation and Character in English Drama, 1900–1912', Missouri, 1914.

NATHAN, EDWARD LEONARD P., 'W. B. Yeats's Development as a Tragic Dramatist, 1884–1939', Berkeley, California, 1961.

O'BRIEN, JAMES HOWARD, 'Theosophy and the Poetry of George Russell (AE), William Butler Yeats, and James Stephens', Washington, 1956. *Dissertation Abstracts*, XVI 11 (Nov 1956) 2167–8.

O'DONNELL, JAMES PRESTON. *See* Part III.

O'NEILL, M. J., 'The Diaries of a Dublin Playgoer as a Mirror of the Irish Literary Revival', National University of Ireland, 1953 (Holloway's diaries).

O'SULLIVAN, FRANCIS E., 'The Forerunners of the Irish Literary Revival', Freiburg, 1924.

PARKINSON, THOMAS F., 'Yeats as a Critic of His Early Verse', Berkeley, California, 1949.

PARKS, LLOYD C., 'The Influence of Villiers de l'Isle-Adam on W. B. Yeats', Washington, 1959. *Dissertation Abstracts*, XX 7 (Jan 1960) 2784–5.

PEARCE, DONALD R., 'The Significance of Ireland in the Work of W. B. Yeats', Michigan, 1949. *Dissertation Abstracts*, IX 1 (1949) 133–4.

PERLOFF, MARJORIE GABRIELLE, 'Rhyme and Meaning in the Poetry of Yeats', Catholic University of America, 1965. *Dissertation Abstracts*, XXVI 11 (May 1966) 6721–2.

PETELER, PATRICIA MARJORIE, 'The Social and Symbolic Drama of the English-Language Theatre, 1929–1949', Utah, 1961. *Dissertation Abstracts*, XXII 12 (June 1961) 4441–2.

PETERS, ROBERT LOUIS, 'The Poetry of the 1890's: Its Relation to Several Arts', Wisconsin, 1953.

POLLETA, GREGORE THOMAS, 'The Progress in W. B. Yeats's Theories of Poetry', Princeton, 1961. *Dissertation Abstracts*, XXII 7 (Jan 1962) 2399–400.

RASMUSSEN, AUDREY L., 'The Drama of William Butler Yeats', Wisconsin, 1953.

REANEY, JAMES, 'The Influence of Spenser on Yeats', Toronto, 1958.

REID, BENJAMIN LAWRENCE, 'William Butler Yeats and Generic Tragedy', Virginia, 1957. *Dissertation Abstracts*, XVII 11 (Nov 1957) 2615.

REISCHLE, HELMUT, 'Die sieben Fassungen des Dramas The Countess Cathleen von W. B. Yeats. Ein Vergleich', Tübingen, 1961.

ROSE, PHYLLIS HOGE, 'Yeats and the Dramatic Lyric', Wisconsin, 1958. *Dissertation Abstracts*, XVIII 6 (June 1958) 2130.

ROSELIEP, RAYMOND, 'Some Letters of Lionel Johnson', Notre Dame, 1954. *Dissertation Abstracts*, XV 3 (Mar 1955) 418. (Some of the letters refer to the Irish Literary Societies of Dublin and London, and to Yeats.)

RUDD, MARGARET E., 'William Blake and William Butler Yeats, a Study of Poetry and Mystical Vision', Reading, 1951.

RYAN, Sr M. ROSALIE, 'Symbolic Elements in the Plays of William Butler Yeats, 1892–1921', Catholic University of America, 1952.

SADDLEMYER, E. ANN, 'A Study of the Dramatic Theory Developed by the Founders of the Irish Literary Theatre and the Attempt to apply this Theory in the Abbey Theatre, with Particular Reference to the Achievement of the Major Figures during the First Two Decades of the Movement', Bedford College, London, 1962.

SANBORN, C. EARLE, 'W. B. Yeats and the Winds of Doctrine: The Literary Environments of his Early Life and their Contribution to his Theory of Poetry', Toronto, 1959.

SCHILLER, Sr MARY BEATRICE, 'Trends in Modern Poetic Drama in English, 1900–1938', Illinois, 1939. *University of Illinois Abstracts of Theses* (1939).

SCHMALENBECK, HILDEGARD, 'The Early Career of W. B. Yeats', Texas, 1957. *Dissertation Abstracts*, XVIII 2 (Feb 1958) 593.

SCHMIEFSKY, MARVEL, 'English Poetic Theory, 1864–1900', New York, 1964. *Dissertation Abstracts*, XXVII 5 (Nov 1966) 1345A–6A.

SCHOCH, OLGA, 'Macpherson, Fiona Macleod, Yeats (Ein Stilvergleich)', Vienna, 1931.

SCHWEISGUT, ELSBETH, 'Yeats Feendichtung', Giessen, 1927.

SEIDEN, MORTON I., 'William Butler Yeats: His Poetry and His Vision, 1914–1939', Columbia, 1952. *Dissertation Abstracts*, XII 4 (1952) 429.

SENGUPTA, S. K., 'The Poetical Development of William Butler Yeats', Leeds, 1936.

SENIOR, JOHN, 'The Occult in Nineteenth-Century Symbolist Literature', Columbia, 1957. *Dissertation Abstracts*, XVII 8 (Aug 1957) 1769–70.

SEWARD, BARBARA, 'The Symbolic Rose', Columbia, 1953. *Dissertation Abstracts*, XIV 1 (1954) 132–3.

SHAW, PRISCILLA WASHBURN, 'The Conception of Self in Rilke, Valéry, and Yeats', Yale, 1960.

SMALL, RAY, 'A Critical Edition of *Diarmuid and Grania* by William Butler Yeats and George Moore', Texas, 1958. *Dissertation Abstracts*, XIX 5 (Nov 1958) 1073–4.

STEAD, C. K., 'The New Poetic: An Investigation into Certain Common Problems Evident in the Work of English-Speaking Poets of the Twentieth Century, the Study Confined Mainly to the Literary Scene in England from 1900 to 1930, and Paying Special Attention to the Work of W. B. Yeats and T. S. Eliot', Bristol, 1962.

STRABEL, AUDREY L. E., 'Yeats's Development of a Symbolic Drama', Wisconsin, 1953. *Wisconsin Dissertation Abstracts*, XIV (1954) 450–1.

STREHLER, MARGUERITE, 'Der Dekadenzgedanke im *Yellow Book* und *Savoy*', Zürich, 1932.

SUSS, IRVING DAVID, 'The Decline and Fall of Irish Drama', Columbia, 1951.

TAYLOR, ESTELLA, 'Mutual Criticism in the Modern Irish School of Literature', Northwestern, 1946.

THEALL, DONALD F., 'Communication Theories in Modern Poetry: Yeats, Pound, Eliot, Joyce', Toronto, 1955.

TORCHIANA, DONALD T., 'W. B. Yeats's Literary Use of Certain Anglo-Irish Augustans', Iowa, 1953. *Dissertation Abstracts*, XIII 5 (Oct–Dec 1953) 815–16.

UEDA, MAKOTO, 'Zeami, Bashō, Yeats, Pound: A Study in Japanese and English Poetics', Washington, 1961. *Dissertation Abstracts*, XXII 11 (May 1962) 4007–8.

UNTERECKER, JOHN EUGENE, 'A Study of the Function of Bird and Tree Imagery in the Work of W. B. Yeats', Columbia, 1956. *Dissertation Abstracts*, XVII 3 (Mar 1957) 637–8.

VENDLER, HELEN M. H., 'A Study of Yeats's *Vision* and the Plays Related to it', Radcliffe College, 1960.

VIGL, HARALD, 'Studien zur Syntax der dramatischen Werke von Lady Gregory, W. B. Yeats, und J. M. Synge', Innsbruck, 1955.

WAGNER, ROBERT DEAN, 'The Last Illusion: Examples of the Spiritual Life in Modern Literature', Columbia, 1952.

WARSCHAUSKY, SIDNEY, 'W. B. Yeats as Literary Critic', Columbia, 1957. *Dissertation Abstracts*, XVII 7 (July 1957) 1559–60.

WATSON, THOMAS LEE, 'A Critical Edition of Selected Lyrics of William Butler Yeats', Texas, 1958. *Dissertation Abstracts*, XIX 5 (Nov 1958) 1080.

WEST, WILLIAM CHANNING, 'Concepts of Reality in the Poetic Drama of W. B. Yeats, W. H. Auden, and T. S. Eliot', Stanford, 1964. *Dissertation Abstracts*, XXV 10 (Apr 1965) 6120–1.

WHITAKER, THOMAS R., 'William Butler Yeats and his Concept of History', Yale, 1953.

WIECZOREK, HUBERT. *See* Part III.

WIEDNER, ELSIE MARGARET, 'The Use of the Theatre for Presentation of Metaphysical Ideas: A Comparative Study of William Butler Yeats and Paul Claudel', Radcliffe College, 1961.

WILSON, F. A. C., 'W. B. Yeats: The Last Plays', St Catharine's, Cambridge, 1959.

WITTIG, KURT, 'Die nationale Literatur Irlands in englischer Sprache von 1889–1939: Motive–Probleme–Charaktere', Halle, 1945.

WOODWARD, CHARLES R., 'Browning and Three Modern Poets: Pound, Yeats and Eliot', Tennessee, 1953.

WORTH, K. J., 'Symbolism in Modern English Drama', Bedford College, London, 1952–3.

YOUNGBLOOD, SARAH, 'William Butler Yeats: The Mature Style', Oklahoma, 1958. *Dissertation Abstracts*, XIX 7 (Jan 1959) 1764.

ZWERDLING, ALEX, 'Yeats and the Heroic Ideal', Princeton, 1960. *Dissertation Abstracts*, XXI 8 (Feb 1961) 2301.

2. OTHER THESES

BANKES, A. G. L., 'W. B. Yeats and his Significance in the Development of Contemporary Poetry', M.A., Bristol, 1955.

COLDWELL, G., 'Experiments of Form in Modern Symbolist Drama', M.A., Bedford College, London, 1960.

COOPER, MABEL, 'The Irish Theatre, its History and its Dramatists', M.A., Manitoba, 1931.

CROSSAN, M. E., 'The Transitional Period (1909–1919) in the Development of W. B. Yeats as a Poet', M.A., Manchester, 1964.

DAVIS, E., 'A Study of Affinities between W. B. Yeats and French Symbolists', B.Litt., St Catherine's, Oxford, 1954.

DONALDSON, A. R., 'The Influence of Irish Nationalism upon the Early Development of W. B. Yeats', M.A., Queen Mary College, London, 1954.

DONOVAN, D. C., 'Lady Gregory and the Abbey Theatre', M.A., National University of Ireland, 1951.

FAULKNER, P., 'The Sources of the Literary Criticism of W. B. Yeats', M.A., Birmingham, 1960.

GOWDA, H. H. A., 'English Verse Drama from 1890–1935', M.Litt., Durham, 1959.

HARRISON, J. R., 'The Social and Political Ideas of W. B. Yeats, Wyndham Lewis, Ezra Pound, T. S. Eliot and D. H. Lawrence', M.A., Sheffield, 1962.

HEARD, G. T., 'A Study of the Influence of Occultism in Modern Poetry, with Particular Reference to the Works of W. B. Yeats, Charles Williams and Edith Sitwell', M.A., Leeds, 1955.

HUBANK, R. W. L., 'Unity of Being in the Poetry of W. B. Yeats', M.A., Nottingham, 1964.

JOHN, B., 'The Philosophic Ideas of W. B. Yeats', M.A., Wales, 1959.

LOUGHLIN, MARIE-THÉRÈSE, 'Poetic Drama', M.A., Western Ontario, 1926.

MCBAIN, MARY NORMILE, 'The Myths and Legends of the Heroic Cycle and their Use in Anglo-Irish Literature', M.A., McGill, 1921.

MCCABE, ELSIE, 'The Deirdre Story', M.A., Acadia, 1928.

MACDERMOTT, DOUGLAS, 'Poetry of the Theatre', M.A., North Carolina, 1960.

MCILHONE, JOHN T., 'The Anglo-Irish Renaissance in Literature and its Influence on the National Character of Ireland', M.A., Montreal, 1939.

MATSUBARA, HISAKO, 'W. B. Yeats and the Japanese Noh Theater', M.A., Pennsylvania State, 1960.

MERRILL, BRO. BERNARDBEHAN, 'Anglo-Irish Literature', M.A., Montreal, 1939.

MORGAN, J. M., 'W. B. Yeats: A Study of the Symbolic Pattern Found in his Later Poems and Plays', B.Litt., St Hugh's, Oxford, 1953.

POTTS, NORMAN, 'A Critical Analysis of the Character Treatment of Judas Iscariot as Portrayed in Five 20th Century Plays', M.A., Denver, 1958.

RANDALL, ETHEL CLAIRE, 'The Celtic Movement: The Awakening of the Fires', M.A., Chicago, 1906.

RHYTHIAN, B. A., 'T. S. Eliot and the Contemporary Revival of Poetic Drama in England', M.A., Manchester, 1955.

ROBINSON, M. E., 'Verse and Prose in Modern British Drama: A Study of the Literary Forms Developed by Four Representative Playwrights – Shaw, Synge, Yeats and T. S. Eliot', M.A., Manchester, 1958.

SALVADORI, C., 'Poet and Courtier: A Study of the Poetic Creed of W. B. Yeats in the Light of *Il Libro del Cortegiano* by Baldassare Castiglione', M.A., National University of Ireland, 1961.

SIDNELL, MICHAEL JOHN, 'A Critical Study of the Evolution of W. B. Yeats's Play, *The Countess Cathleen*, from its Sources to the Version of 1899', M.A., King's College, London, 1961.

SMITH, JEAN C., 'An Investigation of the Dramatic Theory of William Butler Yeats with an Analysis of Typical Examples of his Plays', M.A., Catholic University of America, 1951.

SMITH, Sr ROSE JOSEPHINE, 'A Study of the Mythological and Legendary Material in the Plays of William Butler Yeats, Lady Augusta Gregory, and George William Russell (A. E.)', M.A., Catholic University of America, 1952.

SMYTH, DOROTHY PEARL, 'The Playwrights of the Irish Literary Renaissance', M.A., Acadia, 1936.

SNIDER, PEARL LULU, 'The Contributions of John Millington Synge and William Butler Yeats to the Irish Drama', M.A., Manitoba, 1923.

STALLWORTHY, JON C., 'W. B. Yeats's Poetry in the Making', B.Litt., Magdalen College, Oxford, 1961.

SWIFT, TERESA M., 'The Significance of the Romantic Hero in the Work of W. B. Yeats', M.A., Manchester, 1951.

SZABO, A., 'The Poet and Society: Problems of Communication, with Special Reference to the Work of W. B. Yeats', M.A., Bristol, 1964.

TAYLOR, R. D. P., 'The Doctrine of the Daimon in the Works of AE (George Russell) and W. B. Yeats', M.A., Manchester, 1963.

THORNTON, R. K. R., 'The Poets of the Rhymers' Club', M.A., Manchester, 1962.

WHITE, H., 'A Study of W. B. Yeats as a Dramatist, with Special Reference to his Treatment of Ideas Formulated in *A Vision*', M.A., Leeds, 1957.

WHITEHEAD, J. V., 'Twentieth Century Poetic Drama in English', M.A., McGill, 1941.

LIST OF NEWSPAPERS AND
PERIODICALS CITED

(ABBREVIATIONS USED IN THE BIBLIOGRAPHY ARE SHOWN IN
SQUARE BRACKETS)

(*See also* 'Bibliographies and Abstracts', Part I)

Abstracts of English Studies (National Council of Teachers of English, Boulder, Colorado)

Academy (London; occasionally entitled *Academy and Literature*)

Accent (Urbana, Illinois)

Adelphi (London; third series entitled *New Adelphi*)

Age Literary Review (Melbourne, Australia: *The Age*)

All Ireland Review (Kilkenny, Ireland)

Alphabet (London, Ontario)

America (New York)

American Catholic Quarterly Review (Philadelphia, Pennsylvania)

American Imago (Boston, Massachusetts)

American Literature (Durham, North Carolina)

American Mercury (New York)

American Poetry Magazine (Milwaukee, American Literary Association)

American Review (Bloomington, Illinois)

American Review of Reviews (New York)

American Scholar: A Quarterly for the Independent Thinker (Washington, Phi Beta Kappa) [*American Scholar*]

American Spectator (New York)

American Speech (Baltimore, Maryland)

Anglia: Zeitschrift für Englische Philologie (Halle and Tübingen; see also *Beiblatt zur Anglia*) [*Anglia*]

Anglia Beiblatt; see *Beiblatt zur Anglia*

†*Anglistiches Seminar*

Anglo-Welsh Review (Pembroke Dock, Wales)

Annals of the Faculty of Arts (Cairo)

Annual Register (London)

Apple (of Beauty and Discord) (London)

Arizona Quarterly (Tucson, Arizona)

Arrow (Dublin, Abbey Theatre)

Arts and Decoration (New York)

Arts and Philosophy (London)

Aryan Path (Bombay)

Asiatic Review (London)

Assembly (U.S. Military Academy, West Point)

Aswat (London: University of London Press; in Arabic)

Atalanta (London)

Athenaeum (London; from 11 Feb 1921, *National and Athenaeum*)

Atlantic Monthly (Boston, Massachusetts)

Auckland Weekly News (New Zealand)

AUMLA (Christchurch, New Zealand: Journal of the Australasian Universities Language and Literature Association)

Australian (Sydney, Australia)

Australian English Association Bulletin (Sydney, Australia)

Aut-Aut (Milan)

Ava Maria (Indiana, University of Notre Dame)

Baltimore Evening Sun (Baltimore, Maryland)

Bard Review (Venice, Florida)

Bayou (Houston, Texas)

Beiblatt zur Anglia (Halle and Tübingen; supplement to *Anglia*)

Belfast News-Letter (Belfast)

Belfast Telegraph (Belfast)

Bell (Dublin)

Beltaine (Dublin)

Berliner Börsenzeitung (Berlin)

Berliner Tageblatt (Berlin)

Biblionews (Sydney, Australia: Book Collectors' Society of Australia)

Birmingham Post (Birmingham, England)

Blackwood's Magazine (Edinburgh and London)

†*Boekenschouw* (Netherlands)

Bon Accord (Aberdeen, Scotland)

Book Collector (London)

Book News (Philadelphia, Pennsylvania)

Book of the Month Club News (New York)

Book Society News (London)

Book Week (*Chicago Sun*)

Booklist (Chicago, Illinois: American Library Association)

Bookman (London; discontinued Oct 1934) [*Bookman*]

Bookman (New York) [*Bookman* (after Oct 1934)]

Bookmark (London)

Books Abroad (Norman: University of Oklahoma)

Books of the Month (London)

Boston Evening Transcript (Boston, Massachusetts)

Boston Public Library Quarterly (Boston, Massachusetts)

Boston Sunday Globe (Boston, Massachusetts)

Boston Sunday Herald (Boston, Massachusetts)

Boston University Studies in English (Boston, Massachusetts)

Brigham Young University Studies (Utah)

British Academy Proceedings (London)

British Annual of Literature (London)

British Review (London; incorporates *Oxford and Cambridge Review*)

British Weekly (London)

Bucknell Review (Lewisburg, Virginia)

Buffalo Courier Express (Buffalo, New York)

Buffalo Evening News (Buffalo, New York)

Bulletin (Sydney, Australia)

Bulletin from Virginia Kirkus' Bookshop Service (New York) [Kirkus]

Bulletin of Bibliography and Dramatic Index (Boston, Massachusetts) [Bulletin of Bibliography]

†*Bulletin of the British Institute in Paris*

Bulletin of the Department of English (University of Calcutta)

Bulletin of the Friends of Wellesley College Library (Wellesley, Massachusetts)

Bulletin of the New York Public Library (New York)

Cairo Studies in English (Cairo University, Department of English)

Calcutta Review (Calcutta University Press)

Calendar of Modern Letters (London)

Cambridge Journal (Cambridge, England)

Cambridge Review (Cambridge, England)

Canadian Bookman (Toronto, Ontario)

Canadian Forum (Toronto, Ontario)

Canadian Poetry Magazine (Toronto, Ontario)

Cape Times (Cape Town, South Africa)

Catholic Bulletin (Dublin)

Catholic Herald (London)

Catholic Mind (New York)

Catholic World (New York: Missionary Society of St Paul)

Centennial Review of Arts and Science (Michigan)

Central Literary Magazine (Oxford University Press: for the Birmingham Central Literary Association, England)

Cherwell (Oxford, England)

Chicago Review (Chicago, Illinois)

Chicago Sun (Chicago, Illinois)

Chicago Sunday Tribune (Chicago, Illinois)

Chicago Tribune (Chicago, Illinois)

Christian Century (Chicago, Illinois)

Christian Science Monitor (Boston, Massachusetts)

Church of England Newspaper (London)

Church of Ireland Gazette (Dublin)

Church Times (London)

Churchman (New York)

Cincannati Daily Enquirer (Cincinnati, Ohio)

Classical Journal (London)

Cleveland Plain Dealer (Cleveland, Ohio)

Colby Library Quarterly (Colby College, Waterville, Maine)

College English (Chicago, Illinois: National Council of Teachers of English, U.S.A.)

Collier's Weekly (Springfield, Ohio)

Colonnade (New York, 1907–22)

Colonnade (London, 1952)

Colorado Quarterly (Boulder, Colorado)

Colosseum (London)

Columbia University Forum (New York)

Commentary (New York)

Commonweal (New York)

Community (Colombo, Ceylon)

Comparative Literature (University of Oregon)

Comparative Literature Studies: Études de Littérature Comparée (Cardiff, Wales) [*Comparative Literature Studies*]

Congregational Quarterly (London)

Connoisseur (London)

Consort (London: Journal of the Dolmetsch Foundation)

Contemporary Review (London)

Cork Examiner (Cork, Ireland)

Cornhill Magazine (London: John Murray)

Criterion (London)

Critic (London)

Critic (New York; afterwards *Putnam's Monthly*)

Critic (Chicago, Illinois)

Critical Quarterly (University of Hull, England)

Criticism (Detroit, Michigan: Wayne State University)

Critique (Paris)

Critisch Bulletin (The Hague)

Cronos (Columbus, Ohio)

Culture (Quebec, Canada)

Current History (Philadelphia, Pennsylvania)

Current Literature (London)

Current Literature Literature (New York; after 1912 *Current Opinion*)

Daily Chronicle (London)

Daily Courant (Hartford, Connecticut)

Daily Despatch (Manchester, England)

Daily Express (Dublin)

Daily Nation (Dublin)

Daily News (London)

Daily Oklahoman (Oklahoma City, Oklahoma)

Daily Post; see *Liverpool Daily Post*

Daily Recorder and Mail (Glasgow)

Daily Sketch (London)

Daily Telegraph (London)

Dalhousie Review (Halifax, Nova Scotia)

Dallas Morning News (Dallas, Texas)

Dallas Times Herald (Dallas, Texas)

Detroit News (Detroit, Michigan)

Deutsche Rundschau (Berlin)

Deutsche Zeitschrift (Berlin)

Dial (Boston, Massachusetts)

Dietsche Warande en Belfort (Antwerp)

Diliman Review (University of the Philippines, Manila)

Discourse: A Review of the Liberal Arts (Moorhead, Minnesota: Concordia College)

Dispatch (Columbus, Ohio)

Dissertation Abstracts (Ann Arbor, Michigan)

Double Dealer (New Orleans, Louisiana)

Douglas Library Notes (Queen's University, Kingston, Ontario)

Drana (Chicago, Illinois)

Drama (London: British Drama League)

Drama, Il (Turin)

Du: Kulturelle Monatsschrift (Zürich) [*Du*]

Dublin Evening Mail (Dublin)

Dublin Magazine (Dublin)

Dublin Magazine (Dublin; previously *The Dubliner*)

Dublin Review (London: Oates & Washbourne)

Dubliner; see *Dublin Magazine*

Durham Morning Herald (Durham, North Carolina)

Durham University Journal (University of Durham, England)

East–West Review (Doshisha University, Kyoto)

Échanges (Paris)

Economist (London)

Edda (Oslo)

Edinburgh Review (London and Edinburgh)

Educational Theatre Journal (Ann Arbor, Michigan: American Educational Theatre Association)

Egoist (London)

Egyptian Gazette (Cairo)

Eigo Seinen (Tokyo)

Élet és Irodalom (Hungary)

ELH: A Journal of English Literary History (Baltimore: Johns Hopkins University) [*ELH*]

Encounter (London)

Engelska Kåserier (Stockholm)

Englische Studien (Leipzig)

English (London: The English Association)

English Illustrated Magazine (London and New York)

English Journal (Chicago, Illinois: National Council of Teachers of English)

English Language Notes (University of Colorado, Boulder, Colorado)

English Miscellany (Rome)

English Miscellany, An (St Stephen's College, Delhi)

English Review (London)

English Studies (Amsterdam)

English Studies in Africa (University of Witwatersrand, Johannesburg, South Africa)

Envoy (Dublin)

Erasmian (Dublin)

Ermitage, L' (Paris)

Esprit (Paris)

Esquire (Chicago, Illinois)

Essays and Studies by Members of the English Association (London) [*Essays and Studies*]

Essays in Criticism (Oxford, England)

Études Anglaises (Paris)

Études de Littérature Comparée; see *Comparative Literature Studies*

Europäische Revue (Berlin)

Europe (Paris)

Evening Herald (Dublin)

Evening Standard (London)

Evergreen Review (New York)

Explicator (University of South Carolina, Columbia)

Finsk Tidskrift (Helsinki)

Focus (London)

Foi–Éducation (Paris)

†*Folk-lore in Action*

Fortnightly Review (London)

Forum (New York)

France Libre (London)

Frankfurter Zeitung (Frankfurt-am-Main, Germany)

Freeman (New York)

Freeman's Journal (London)

Furioso (New Haven, Connecticut)

Gael (New York)

German Life and Letters (Oxford, England)

Gids (Amsterdam; later *De Nieuwe Gids*)

Gil Blas (Paris)

Glasgow Herald (Glasgow)

Globe and Mail (Toronto, Ontario)

Grande Revue (Paris)

Granta (London)

Great Thoughts (London)

Greyfriar (Charterhouse School, Godalming, Surrey, England)

Guardian; see *Manchester Guardian*

Guardian Weekly; see *Manchester Guardian*

Harper's Magazine (New York)

Harper's Weekly (New York; later incorporated with *Independent*)

Harvard Library Bulletin (Cambridge, Massachusetts)

Harvard Monthly (Cambridge, Massachusetts)

Hearth and Home (London)

Herald of Wales (Swansea)

Hermathena: A Series of Papers on Literature, Science and Philosophy by Members of Trinity College, Dublin (Dublin and London) [*Hermathena*]

Hermes (Dublin)

Hibbert Journal (London: Allen & Unwin; Boston: Leray Phillips)

Highway (London: Workers' Educational Association)

History of Ideas Newsletter (New York)

Hiwar (Beirut)

Hopkins Review (Johns Hopkins University, Baltimore, Maryland)

Horizon (London)

Hound and Horn (Harvard, Massachusetts)

Houston Post (Houston, Texas)

Hudson Review (New York)

Huntington Library Quarterly (California)

Illustrated London News (London)

Independent (New York; after 1928 *Outlook and Independent*)

Indian Journal of English Studies (Calcutta: Indian Association of English Studies)

Indianapolis News (Indiana)

International Literature (Moscow)

Iowa English Yearbook (Iowa City: Iowa Council of Teachers of English)

Ireland: Weekly Bulletin of the Department of External Affairs (Dublin)

Ireland-American Review (New York)

Ireland Today (Dublin)

Iris Hibernia (University of Fribourg, Switzerland)

Irish Book (Dublin)

Irish Book Lover (Dublin)

Irish Bookman (Dublin)

Irish Catholic (Dublin)

Irish Digest (Dublin)

Irish Independent (Dublin)

Irish Library Bulletin (Dublin)

Irish Monthly (Dublin)

Irish News (Belfast)

Irish Press (Dublin)

Irish Review (Dublin)

Irish Statesman (Dublin)

Irish Theosophist (Dublin)

Irish Times (Dublin)

Irish Writing (Dublin)

Isis (Oxford, England)

Jadavpur Journal of Comparative Literature (Calcutta)

Japan Quarterly (Tokyo)

Jeux Tréteaux et Personnages (Paris)

Jeviště (Czechoslovakia)

Johannesburg Sunday Times (South Africa)

John O'London's Weekly (London)

Journal des Débats (Paris)

Journal of Aesthetics and Art Criticism (New York)

Journal of American Folk-Lore (Boston, Massachusetts: American Folk-Lore Society)

Journal of English and Germanic Philology (Urbana, Illinois)

Journal of the Rutgers University Library (New Jersey)

Journal of the William Morris Society (Kew, England)

Jubilee (New York)

Kansas City Post (Kansas City, Missouri)

Kansas City Star (Kansas City, Missouri)

Kenyon Review (Gambier, Ohio)

Kilkenny Magazine (Kilkenny, Ireland)

Kirkus; see *Bulletin from Virginia Kirkus' Bookshop Service*

Kölnische Volkszeitung (Cologne, Germany)

Lady (London)

Lamp (London)

Langues Modernes (Paris)

Látóhatár (Munich)

Left Review (London: Writer's International)

Letterature Moderne (Turin)

Levende Talen (Groningen)

Library (London: Transactions of the Bibliographical Society)

Library Assistant (London)

Library Chronicle of the University of Texas (Austin, Texas)

Library Journal (New York)

Library Review (Glasgow)

Life and Letters (*Today*) (London)

Life International (Chicago) [*Life*]

Lippincott's Magazine (Philadelphia, Pennsylvania)

Listener (London)

Lit (U.S.A.: Lamda Iota Tau)

Literary Criterion (Mysore, India)

Literary Digest (New York)

Literary Half-Yearly (University of Mysore, India)

Literary Review (Teaneck, New Jersey: Fairleigh Dickinson University)

Literatur (*Berlin*)

Literature (London; merged with *Academy* to become *Academy and Literature*, 1902)

Literature and Psychology (New York)

Littell's Living Age (Boston) [*Living Age*]

Liverpool Daily Post (Liverpool, England)

Living Age; see *Littell's Living Age*

London Magazine (London)

London Mercury (London; merged with *Life and Letters*)

London Quarterly and Holborn Review (London) [*London Quarterly*]

Los Angeles Times (Los Angeles, California)

Louisville Times (Louisville, Kentucky)

Lucifer (London; later *The Theosophical Review*)

McGill University Magazine (Montreal, Canada)

Magazine of Poetry: A Quarterly Review (Buffalo, New York)

Manchester Guardian (Manchester and London) [*Guardian*]

Manchester Quarterly (published with *Papers of the Manchester Literary Club*, Manchester, England)

Mark Twain Quarterly (Kirkwood, Missouri: International Mark Twain Society)

Maske und Kothurn (University of Vienna)

Mass und Wert (Zürich)

Massachusetts Review (Amherst, Massachusetts)

Meanjin (Melbourne, Australia)

Medium Aevum (Munich, Germany)

Melbourne Advocate (Melbourne, Australia)

Melbourne Critical Review (Melbourne, Australia)

Mercure de France (Paris)

Methodist Review (New York)

Methodist Times and Leader (London)

Metropolitan Magazine (New York)

Michigan Alumnus Quarterly (Ann Arbor: University of Michigan)

Michigan Quarterly Review (Ann Arbor: University of Michigan)

Midwest Quarterly (Pittsburg, Kansas: State College of Pittsburg)

Modern Drama (Lawrence, Kansas)

Modern Language Journal (St Louis, Missouri: Modern Language Teachers' Association)

Modern Language Notes (Baltimore, Maryland)

Modern Language Quarterly (London)

Modern Language Review (London)

Modern Philology (University of Chicago)

Modern Review (Calcutta)

Moderna Språk (Malmö, Sweden)

Monde Nouveau (Paris)

Month (London)

Monthly Review (Plainfield, New Jersey)

Montreal Gazette (Montreal, Canada)

Morning Post (London)

Mother India (Bombay)

Nashville Banner (Nashville, Tennessee)

Nashville Tennessean (Nashville, Tennessee)

Nation (London, Mar 1907–Feb 1921, then *Nation and Athenaeum*)

Nation (New York)

Nation (Sydney, Australia)

Nation and Athenaeum (London, Feb 1921–Feb 1931, then *New Statesman and Nation*)

National Review (London; later *National and English Review*)

Nazione (Florence)

Neophilologus (Groningen)

Neue Rundschau (Berlin)

Neue Zürcher Zeitung (Zürich)

Neueren Sprachen (Frankfurt am Main)

New Adelphi (continues *Adelphi*, q.v.)

New Age (London)

New Britain (London)

New Criterion (continues *Criterion*, q.v.)

New English Review (London)

New English Weekly (London)

New Ireland Review (Dublin)

New Leader (New York)

New Liberal Review (London)

New Quarterly of Poetry (New York)

New Republic (New York)

New Society (London)

New Statesman (1913–31, then *New Statesman and Nation*)

New Statesman and Nation (1931–57, then *New Statesman*)

New Verse (London)

New York Drama (New York)

New York Herald Tribune (New York)

New York Herald Tribune Book Review [*NYHTB*]

New York Post (New York)

New York Review of Books (New York)

New York Sun (New York)

New York Times (New York)

New York Times Book Review [*NYTB*]

New York World Telegram (New York)

New Yorker (New York)

Newberry Library Bulletin (Newberry Library, Chicago, Illinois)

News Chronicle (London)

News Leader (Richmond, Virginia)

News Sentinel (Fort Wayne, Indiana)

Newsweek (New York)

Nine (London)

Nineteenth Century (London; Jan 1901– Jan 1951, *Nineteenth Century and After*; then *Twentieth Century*)

Nippon Sizin (Tokyo)

Noble Savage (New York)

North American Review (New York)

Northern Whig (Belfast)

Northman (Belfast: Queen's University)

Notes and Queries (London)

Nouvelle Revue Française (Paris)

Nouvelles Littéraires (Paris)

Numbers (New Zealand)

Nuova Antologica (Rome)

NYHTB; see *New York Herald Tribune Book Review*

NYTB; see *New York Times Book Review*

Observer (London)

Occult Review (London)

Ochanomizu Joshi Daigaku Jimbun Kagaku Kiyo (*Studies in Art and Literature, Ochanomizu University*) (Tokyo)

Ohio University Review (Athens, Ohio)

Old Castle Garden (New York: Mission of Our Lady of the Rosary)

One Act Play Magazine and Radio Drama Review (New York)

Onze Eeuw (Haarlem, Netherlands)

Opus (Tring, Hertfordshire)

Ord och Bild (Stockholm)

Osmania Journal of English Studies (Hyderabad, India)

Osservatore Politico Letterario (Rome)

Outlook (London)

Outlook (New York; after 1928 *Outlook and Independent*) [*Outlook* (New York)]

Oxford and Cambridge Review (London)

Oxford Magazine (Oxford)

Pacific Spectator (Stanford, California)

Pacific Weekly (Carmel, California)

Pall Mall Gazette (London)

Papers of the Bibliographical Society of America (New York)

Papers of the Manchester Literary Club (Manchester, England)

Papers on English Language and Literature (Carbondale: Southern Illinois University)

Paragone (Florence)

Partisan Review (New York; after 1964, Rutgers University, New Brunswick, New Jersey)

Pasadena Star News (Texas)

People (London)

†*Periscoop* (Netherlands)

Personalist (Los Angeles: University of Southern California)

Philogical Quarterly (University of Iowa)

Philosophical Review (Boston, Massachusetts)

Phoenix (Seoul, South Korea: English Literature Society)

Picture Post (London)

Pilot (Boston, Massachusetts)

PMLA; see *Publications of the Modern Languages Association of America*

Poesia e Critica (Milan)

Poet-Lore (Boston, Massachusetts)

Poetry (*Chicago, Illinois*)

Poetry (New York)

Poetry and Drama (London)

Poetry Australia (Sydney)

Poetry Quarterly (Dawlish, Devon)

Poetry Review (London: Poetry Society)

Politics and Letters (London)

Prairie Schooner (University of Nebraska)

Presence (Geneva)

Press (Christchurch, New Zealand)

Princeton University Library Chronicle (Princeton, New Jersey)

Providence Journal (Rhode Island)

Providence Sunday Illustrated Journal (Rhode Island)

Publications of the Modern Languages Association of America (Menasha, Wisconsin) [*PMLA*]

Publishers' Weekly (New York)

Punch (London)

Purpose (London)

Putnam's Monthly (New York; absorbed *The Critic*)

Quadrant (Sydney, Australia)

Quarterly Journal of Speech (New York: Speech Association of America)

Quarterly Review (London)

Queen's Quarterly (Queen's University, Kingston, Ontario)

Querschnitt, Der (Berlin)

Radio Times (London)

Ramparts (Menlo Park, California)

Rand Daily Mail (Johannesburg, South Africa)

Rann: An Ulster Quarterly (Belfast)

Reader (New York)

Reading and Collecting (Chicago)

Renascence (Milwaukee: Catholic Renascence Society)

Reporter (New York)

Review (New York; after June 1920 *Weekly Review*)

Review (Bloomington, Indiana: Indiana University College of Arts and Science)

Review of English Literature (London: Longmans, Green)

Review of English Studies (Oxford: Clarendon Press)

Review of Reviews; see *American Review of Reviews*

Revue (Paris)
Revue Anglo-Américaine (Paris)
Revue Bleue; see *Revue Politique*
Revue des Deux Mondes (Paris)
Revue de France (Paris)
Revue Germanique (Paris)
Revue des Langues Vivantes: Tijdschrift voor Levende Talen (Brussels) [*Revue des Langues Vivantes*]
Revue de Littérature Comparée (Paris)
Revue de Paris (Paris)
Revue Politique et Littéraire: Revue Bleue (Paris)
Richmond News Leader (Richmond, Virginia)
Rivista di Studi Teatrali (Milan)
Round Table (London)

St James Budget (London)
St Louis Post-Dispatch (St Louis, Missouri)
St Martin's Review (London)
St Pancras Journal (London)
Samhain (Dublin)
Sammlung, Die (Göttingen)
San Francisco Chronicle (San Francisco, California)
Saturday Night (Toronto, Ontario)
Saturday Review (London)
Saturday Review of Literature (New York; after 12 Jan 1952 *Saturday Review*)
Savannah Morning News (Savannah, Georgia)
Schoene Literatur (Leipzig)
Scholastic (Pittsburgh, Pennsylvania)
Schweizer Annalen (Zürich)
Scots Observer (Edinburgh)
Scotsman (Edinburgh)
Scottish Periodical (Edinburgh)
Scrutiny (Cambridge, England)
Seattle Post Intelligencer (Seattle, Washington)
Sei Hai (Tokyo)
Sewanee Review (University of the South, Sewanee, Tennessee)
Sheffield Daily Telegraph (Sheffield, England)

Shenandoah: The Washington and Lee University Review (Lexington, Virginia) [*Shenandoah*]
Shin Bungei (Tokyo)
Sign (London)
Sinn Fein (Dublin)
Sketch (London)
South Atlantic Quarterly (Durham, North Carolina)
Southerly (Sydney, Australia)
Southern Quarterly (University of Southern Mississippi, Hattiesburg, Mississippi)
Southern Review (Louisiana State University, Baton Rouge, Louisiana)
Southern Review: An Australian Journal of Literary Studies (Adelaide, Australia) [*Southern Review* (Adelaide)]
Southwest Review (Dallas, Texas; originally *The Texas Review*)
Speaker (London; became *The Nation* in March 1907)
Spectator (London)
Spettatore Italiano (Rome)
Sphere (London)
Spiegel der Letteren (The Hague)
Spirit (New York: Catholic Poetry Society of America)
Springfield Republican (Springfield, Massachusetts)
Stand (London)
Standard (London)
Stem (Arnhem, Netherlands)
Stockholms-Tidningen (Stockholm)
Student (University of Edinburgh)
Student World (Geneva)
Studia Neophilologica (Uppsala)
Studies (Dublin)
Studies in Bibliography: Papers of the Bibliographical Society of the University of Virginia (Charlottesville, Virginia)
Sunday Independent (Dublin)
Sunday Press (Dublin)
Sunday Telegraph (London)
Sunday Times (London)

Sydney Morning Herald (Sydney, Australia)

Tablet (London)

Tatler and Bystander (London)

TCD: A College Miscellany (Trinity College, Dublin)

Temps, Le (Paris)

Tennessee Studies in Literature (Knoxville: Tennessee University)

Texas Quarterly (Austin, Texas: University of Texas)

Texas Review; see *Southwest Review*

Texas Studies in Literature and Language (Austin: Texas University Press)

Theatre Arts Monthly (New York; from 1939 *Theatre Arts*)

Thema (Hamburg)

Theology (London)

Theoria (Durban, South Africa)

Theosophical Review (London)

Thoth (New York: Syracuse University, Department of English)

Thought (New York: Fordham University)

Threshold (Belfast: Lyric Players)

Tijdschrift voor Levende Talen; see *Revue des Langues Vivantes*

Time (New York)

Time and Tide (London)

Times, The (London)

Times Literary Supplement (London) [*TLS*]

Times of India (Bombay)

TLS; see *Times Literary Supplement*

Touchstone (New York)

Tour Saint-Jacques (Paris)

Townsman (London)

TP's Weekly (London)

Trinity News (Dublin)

Tri-Quarterly (Evanston, Illinois: Northwestern University)

Tulane Drama Review (New Orleans: Tulane University)

Twentieth Century; see *Nineteenth Century*

Twentieth Century Literature (Denver, Colorado: Swallow Press)

Twórczość (Warsaw, Poland)

Union Recorder (University of Sydney, Australia)

United Irishman (Dublin)

United States Quarterly Book Review (Library of Congress)

University of California Chronicle (Berkeley and Los Angeles, California)

University of Edinburgh Journal (Edinburgh)

University of Kansas City Review (Kansas City, Missouri)

University of Toronto Quarterly (University of Toronto Press)

University Review; see *University of Kansas City Review*

University Review (University College, Dublin)

Venture (Karachi University English Teachers' Association)

Victorian Studies (Bloomington, Indiana: Indiana University)

Vie des Peuples, La (Paris)

Virginia Quarterly Review (Charlottesville: University of Virginia)

Virginian Pilot (Norfolk, Virginia)

Visva-Bharati Quarterly (West Bengal)

Vlaamse Gids, De (Brussels)

Voices (Boston)

Wales (London)

Waseda Daigaku Daigakuin Bungakuka Kiyo (Bulletin of the Graduate Division of Literature of Waseda University) (Tokyo)

Washington Post (Washington, D.C.)

Waterloo Review (Ontario: Waterloo College and McMaster University; absorbed by *Alphabet*)

Weekend Review (London; incorporated with *New Statesman*, 1934)

Weekly Register (London)

Weekly Review (New York; merged with *Independent*)

Weekly Survey

Western Humanities Review (Salt Lake City: Utah University)

Western Mail (Cardiff; later *Western Mail and South Wales News*)

Western Review (Iowa City, Iowa)

Westminster Review (London)

Wilson Bulletin (New York: H. W. Wilson; later *Wilson Library Bulletin*)

Wind and the Rain (London)

Wings (New York)

Wisconsin Library Bulletin (Madison, Wisconsin)

Woman's World (London)

Worcester Sunday Telegram (New Orleans, Louisiana)

World (London)

X: A Quarterly Review (London: Barrie & Rockliffe)

Xavier University Studies (New Orleans, Louisiana)

Yale Literary Magazine (New Haven, Connecticut)

Yale Review (New Haven, Connecticut)

Yale University Library Gazette (New Haven, Connecticut)

Yorkshire Post (London)

Index

INDEX

INDEX

INDEX

INDEX

311

INDEX

INDEX

INDEX

INDEX

INDEX

INDEX

INDEX

INDEX

INDEX

INDEX

INDEX

INDEX

INDEX

White, Terence de Vere, 162, 272
White, T., 54, 55
Whitehead, J. V., 291
Whitman, Walt, 102, 215
Whitridge, Arnold, 272
Whittaker, Thomas, 266
Widdemer, Margaret, 41
Wieczorek, Herbert, 154, 288
Wiedner, Elsie Margaret, 288
Wijngaards, Nicolaas, 272
Wild, Friedrich, 143, 155
Wilde, Oscar, xxiii, 29, 52, 130, 136, 143, 155, 249, 254, 272
Wilde, Percival, 155
Wilder, Amos N., 34, 155
Wildi, Max, 155, 272
Wilkinson, M., 272
Willcox, Louise Collier, 40, 272
Williams, Charles, 51, 155, 289
Williams, Harold, 155
Williams, Michael, 51
Williams, Raymond, 135, 272
Williams, Rowan, 130
Williamson, Hugh Ross, 229, 272
Willis, K. T., 101
Willy, Margaret, 83, 106, 161, 272
Wilson, Colin, 156
Wilson, Edmund, 15, 26, 27, 30, 31, 36, 42, 50, 51, 83, 95, 273
Wilson, F. A. C., 50, 72, 156-7, 175, 201, 214, 243, 273, 288
Wilson, R. N. D., 30
Wimsatt, William K., Jr, 157
Wind, Edgar, 273
Wing, Donald G., 12
Winterich, John T., 73
Winters, Yvor, 157, 176, 196, 235, 237, 258, 273
Witt, Marion, 12, 50, 157, 252, 273-4
Wittig, Kurt, 288
Witton, C. H., 196
Woburn, 64, 91, 256
Wolfe, Ann F., 21, 36
Wolfe, Humbert, 25, 49, 53, 57, 157
Woman, 236
Wood, Frederick T., 21, 26, 40
Woodcuts. See Paintings, etc.
Woodward, Charles R., 288
Worcester, M. P., 20
Wordsworth, William, 79, 130, 153, 267
Worsley, T. C., 101, 274
Worth, K. J., 288
Wrenn, C. L., 158, 274
Wright, Dossy, 135
Wright, George T., 85, 129, 275
Wyatt, E. V., 31, 99, 275
Wylie, Elinor, 15

Y., E., 240
Y., G., 18, 33
Yale. See Exhibitions; Roth, William
Yale University Library, 3, 9
Yano, Hojin, 161
Year's Poetry, 1936, The, 257
Yeats, Anne, 135, 250, 266
Yeats, Elizabeth, 215
Yeats, George (Mrs W. B. Yeats), 135, 158

Yeats, Jack B., 117, 141
Yeats, John Butler, xxiii, 92, 105, 131, 135, 149, 158, 161, 191, 199, 218, 241, 249, 266, 272, 274
Yeats, Lily, 7
Yeats, William Butler:
  (a) Articles about 'W. B. Yeats', 'Yeats', etc., 168, 170, 171, 177, 178, 179, 180, 181, 182, 183, 184, 185, 186, 187, 189, 191, 192, 194, 196, 197, 198, 200, 202, 204, 205, 206, 207, 208, 211, 214, 215, 216, 220, 222, 223, 224, 225, 228, 229, 230, 231, 234, 235, 236, 237, 239, 240, 242, 244, 245, 246, 247, 248, 249, 252, 255, 256, 257, 258, 260, 261, 262, 263, 265, 268, 271, 272, 274, 275, 282, 287
  (b) Articles, general, 168, 170, 171, 173, 174, 175, 177, 182, 184, 185, 186, 192, 193, 197, 198, 199, 200, 202, 204, 206, 208, 209, 210, 211, 213, 214, 220, 222, 223, 224, 226, 231, 235, 237, 238, 239, 241, 242, 247, 252, 257, 258, 262, 265, 274, 275, 281, 284, 286
  (c) Books about. See Books
  (d) Books wholly or partly by
      Aphorisms of Yoga by Bhagwan Shree Patanjali, xxv
      Arrow, The, xxi
      Autobiographies, xxiv, xxvi (1955), 15 (1926), 15-16 (1955), 61, 78, 87, 130, 137, 162, 172, 187, 217, 218, 224, 225, 229, 243, 271, 273, 275
      Autobiography, The, xxv, 16-17, 61, 167, 192, 224, 254
      Axël, by Villiers de l'Isle-Adam, xxiii
      Beltaine, xx
      Bishop Berkeley, xxiv, 114
      Book of Images, A, by E. T. Horton, xx
      Book of Irish Verse, A, xx, 17, 220
      Book of the Rhymers' Club, The, xix, 17
      Bounty of Sweden, The, xxiii, 17, 208
      Broadsides, 17, 265
      Cat and the Moon and Certain Plays, The, xxiii
      Cathleen ni Houlihan, xx, 17, 254
      Celtic Twilight, The, xix (1893), xx (1902), 17, 143, 182, 219, 227
      Celtic Twilight and a Selction of Early Poems, The, 143
      Certain Noble Plays of Japan, xxii, 18, 172
      Coinage of Saorstát Éireann, xxiv
      Collected Edition (1922-1926), 18. See also Later Poems, Plays in Prose and Verse, Plays and Controversies, Essays, Early Poems and Stories, below
      Collected Plays (1934), xxv, 18-19, 171, 172, 174, 178, 189, 190, 197, 209, 231, 249, 261, 275

INDEX

INDEX